DOWN
TO THE
WIRE:
THE LIVES
OF THE TRIPLE CROWN
CHAMPIONS

Robert L. Shoop

RUSSELL DEAN AND COMPANY, PUBLISHERS
Everson, Washington, USA
Chilliwack, British Columbia, Canada

DOWN to the WIRE:
The Lives of the Triple Crown Champions

By Robert L. Shoop

First Printing: January, 2004

Library of Congress Control Number: **2003095009 (paperback)**
Library of Congress Control Number: **2003109604 (hardbound)**

Shoop, Robert L. (1954-   )
Down to the Wire: *The Lives of the Triple Crown Champions*   p. cm

(Russell Dean and Company – non-fiction)

I. 1. Sports History 2. Thoroughbred Racing   II. 1. Title.   2. Author

ISBN: 1-891954-55-5   Trade Paperback

ISBN: 1-891954-56-3   Casebound

Cover design by Liselotte Bjorck-Posson, Betula Productions, Atascadero, California.
Cover photo of Affirmed and Alydar, 1978 Belmont Stakes, courtesy Steve Cauthen.

Printed and manufactured in the United States of America.

10   09   08   07   06   05   04   06   05   04   03   02   01

Russell Dean and Company
Everson, Washington, USA / Chilliwack, British Columbia, Canada

DOWN TO THE WIRE:
THE LIVES
OF THE
TRIPLE CROWN CHAMPIONS

Robert L. Shoop

CONTENTS

ACKNOWLEDGMENTS   i

FOREWARD **by Ron Turcotte**   v

INTRODUCTION **by Jean Cruguet**   vii

I. THE RACES

1.	The Kentucky Derby	1
2.	The Preakness	6
3.	The Belmont Stakes	10
4.	The Origin: "The Triple Crown"	13
5.	The Demigod: Man o'War	15

II. THE TRIPLE CROWN CHAMPIONS

1.	The Unknown: Sir Barton	33
2.	The Trailblazer: Gallant Fox	55
3.	Victorious Progeny: Omaha & War Admiral	79
4.	The Iron Horse: Whirlaway	115
5.	The Unvanquished: Count Fleet	147
6.	The Obscurity Triumphant: Assault	163
7.	The Icon: Citation	187
8.	The National Hero: Secretariat	215
9.	The Thinking Man's Horse: Seattle Slew	239
10.	The Duelists: Affirmed & Alydar	261

CONTENTS

POSTSCRIPT   295

AFTERWORD: *SEABISCUIT*, FUNNY CIDE,
AND THE TRIPLE CROWN   297

ABOUT THE AUTHOR   299

APPENDICES   301

    I.   THE TRIPLE CROWN CHAMPIONS   301

    II.   WINNING TIMES of the TRIPLE CROWN WINNERS   301

    III.   WINNING LENGTHS of the TRIPLE CROWN WINNERS302

    IV.   THE TRIPLE CROWN RACETRACKS   303

    V.   RACEHORSES, JOCKEYS and TRAINERS
         ELECTED to the NATIONAL MUSEUM of RACING
         and HALL of FAME   304

    VI.   TABULATED RACING RECORDS of the
         TRIPLE CROWN HORSES   306

    VII. TRIPLE CROWN RACE WINNERS
         SIRED by TRIPLE CROWN CHAMPIONS   310

    VIII. RANKINGS of the TRIPLE CROWN WINNERS   311

    IX.   The *BLOOD HORSE* RANKINGS   312

BIBLIOGRAPHY & CHAPTER NOTES   313

INDEX   329

PHOTOGRAPHS

PAGE

12 Aristides, winner of the first Kentucky Derby in 1875. Statue stands at Churchill Downs. Photo by Brenda Cubbage. Used by permission.

32 Man o'War with groom Will Harbut. © Collection of L.S. Sutcliffe, C. Ken Grayson, owner. Used by permission.

39 Sir Barton, 1919 Kentucky Derby. John Loftus up, Guy Bedwell at bridle. © Collection of L.S. Sutcliffe, C. Ken Grayson, owner. Used by permission.

42 Sir Barton, the first Triple Crown winner, 1919. © Collection of L.S. Sutcliffe, C. Ken Grayson, owner. Used by permission.

48 Man o'War. © Collection of L.S. Sutcliffe, C. Ken Grayson, owner. Used by permission.

53 Sir Barton's grave in Douglas, Wyoming. Photo by Sandra Matthews. Used by permission.

58 "Sunny Jim" Fitzsimmons (1874-1966). Trainer, Gallant Fox and Omaha. © Collection of L.S. Sutcliffe, C. Ken Grayson, owner. Used by permission.

59 Gallant Fox, second winner of the Triple Crown, 1930. © Collection of L.S. Sutcliffe, C. Ken Grayson, owner. Used by permission.

65 Earl Sande, Gallant Fox's jockey in 1930. Later photo as trainer. © Collection of L.S. Sutcliffe, C. Ken Grayson, owner. Used by permission.

78 Sunny Jim Fitzsimmons, trainer of Gallant Fox an Omaha, at his last public appearance. © Collection of L.S. Sutcliffe, C. Ken Grayson, owner. Used by permission.

84 Omaha, third winner of the Triple Crown, 1935. Willie Saunders up. © Collection of L.S. Sutcliffe, C. Ken Grayson, owner. Used by permission.

86 Omaha, Willie Saunders up. © Collection of L.S. Sutcliffe, C. Ken Grayson, owner. Used by permission.

96 War Admiral, fourth Triple Crown winner, 1937 Kentucky Derby. Jockey, Charles Kurtsinger. © Collection of L.S. Sutcliffe, C. Ken Grayson, owner. Used by permission.

97   War Admiral. Winner, Triple Crown, 1937. © Collection of L.S. Sutcliffe, C. Ken Grayson, owner. Used by permission.

110   Seabiscuit beats War Admiral at Pimlico, November 1, 1938. © Collection of L.S. Sutcliffe, C. Ken Grayson, owner. Used by permission.

116   Whirlaway as a yearling, 1939. © Collection of L.S. Sutcliffe, C. Ken Grayson, owner. Used by permission.

119   Whirlaway during a workout. © Collection of C. Ken Grayson. Used by permission.

121   Ben Jones and Eddie Arcaro, Whirlaway's trainer and jockey. Photograph taken at the 1952 Kentucky Derby. © Collection of C. Ken Grayson. Used by permission.

128   Whirlaway wins the Kentucky Derby, May 3, 1941. Arcaro up. Original photograph autographed by Eddie Arcaro. © Collection of L.S. Sutcliffe, C. Ken Grayson, owner. Used by permission.

129   Whirlaway under the roses, 1941 Kentucky Derby, Arcaro up. Ben Jones, trainer, holding. . © Collection of L.S. Sutcliffe, C. Ken Grayson, owner. Used by permission.

137   John Longden shakes hands with Eddie Arcaro at Belmont Park, May 4, 1955. © Collection of C. Ken Grayson. Used by permission.

145   Whirlaway. Portrait taken 1948. © Collection of C. Ken Grayson. Used by permission.

149   John Longden (1907-2003). © Collection of C. Ken Grayson. Used by permission.

151   John Longden in Hertz yellow silks speaks with Mrs. John Hertz, Count Fleet's owner. © Collection of C. Ken Grayson. Used by permission.

160   Count Fleet, Longden up. © Collection of C. Ken Grayson. Used by permission.

164   Assault: Triple Crown winner, 1946.King Ranch: Max Hirsch, trainer. © King Ranch, Inc., Kingsville, Texas. Used by permission.

165   Assault's right front hoof. © King Ranch, Inc., Kingsville, Texas. Used by permission.

170   Assault wins the Kentucky Derby by eight lengths, May 4, 1946. Max Hirsch, trainer, Warren Mehrtens up. Spy Song 2nd, Hampden 3rd. © King Ranch, Inc., Kingsville, Texas. Used by permission.

171 Assault is lead to the winner's circle at the Kentucky Derby, May 4, 1946. Max Hirsch, trainer, Warren Mehrtens up. Photo by Bert Morgan, N.Y. © King Ranch, Inc., Kingsville, Texas. Used by permission.

172 Assault: Preakness at Pimlico, May 11, 1946. Max Hirsch, trainer, Warren Mehrtens up. Lord Boswell running 2nd, Hampden 3rd. © King Ranch, Inc., Kingsville, Texas. Used by permission.

196 Jimmy Jones (left) and Ben Jones (right, in white hat) lead Citation into the winner's circle at the 1948 Kentucky Derby. Arcaro up. © Collection of C. Ken Grayson. Used by permission.

197 Jimmy Jones holds Citation with Arcaro up after winning the 1948 Preakness Stakes. © Collection of C. Ken Grayson. Used by permission.

211 Triple Crown Trainers: (left to right) Ben Jones (Whirlaway, Sunny Jim Fitzsimmons (Gallant Fox, Omaha), and Jimmy Jones (Citation). Photographed at Hialeah, Florida, 1958. © Collection of C. Ken Grayson. Used by permission.

213 Eddie Arcaro weighing in. Photo taken in 1955. © Collection of C. Ken Grayson. Used by permission.

229 Secretariat with Ron Turcotte up. © Collection of L.S. Sutcliffe, C. Ken Grayson, owner. Used by permission.

248 Seattle Slew with Jean Cruguet up. 1977 Kentucky Derby. © Collection of L.S. Sutcliffe, C. Ken Grayson, owner. Used by permission.

249 Seattle Slew with Jean Cruguet up, in the winner's circle. 1977 Kentucky Derby. © Collection of L.S. Sutcliffe, C. Ken Grayson, owner. Used by permission.

259 Seattle Slew in retirement at Three Chimneys Farm, Kentucky, 1995. Photo by author Robert L. Shoop.

261 Affirmed at Jonabell Farm, Kentucky, 1995. Photo by author Robert L. Shoop.

268 Young Steve Cauthen in red-and-white silks. Photo courtesy Steve Cauthen. Used by permission.

271 Affirmed. Photo courtesy Steve Cauthen. Used by permission.

277 Affirmed winning the 1978 Kentucky Derby, Steve Cauthen up. In the pink-and-black silks of Harbor View Farm. Photo courtesy Steve Cauthen. Used by permission.

279   Affirmed with Steve Cauthen up wins the 1978 Preakness Stakes over Alydar with Jorge Velasquez up. Photo courtesy Steve Cauthen. Used by permission.

282   Affirmed/Cauthen inside, Alydar/Velasquez outside, 1978 Belmont Stakes. Note whip in Cauthen's *left* hand. Photo courtesy Steve Cauthen. Used by permission.

287   Jockeys Bill Shoemaker, Steve Cauthen, and John Longden. Photo courtesy Steve Cauthen. Used by permission.

293   Steve Cauthen and Eddie Arcaro with their Triple Crown silks. Photo courtesy Steve Cauthen. Used by permission.

299   Author Robert L. Shoop.

The publishers wish to thank in particular Mr. C. Ken Grayson for providing photographs from the L.S. Sutcliffe collection and from his personal archives, King Ranch for their photographs and permissions, and Mr. Steve Cauthen for photographs from his personal collection. These visual images of the real people and events associated with the Triple Crown Champions and the sport of Thoroughbred racing help bring this work alive.

ACKNOWLEDGMENTS

As a voracious reader myself, I was always amazed at the acknowledgments to books: How could there be so many 'thank-yous' owed?, I wondered. Now, years after I began this book, I realize just how many people are involved in a project of this magnitude. Therefore, my thanks go to the following individuals:

Tom Gilcoyne at the National Museum of Racing and Hall of Fame was of constant and invaluable assistance to me;

Cathy Schenck, Phyllis Rogers, and Doris Waren (now retired) at the Keeneland Racetrack Library were always more than gracious to me in my many requests;

Jamene Toelkes and Bruce Cheeseman at the King Ranch archives (Bruce has since left the employ of King Ranch) provided much information on Assault;

Candice Perry at the Kentucky Derby Museum, Churchill Downs, Louisville, Kentucky, graciously permitted me access to the museum's files, including the scrapbook of Charles Kurtsinger;

Ken Grayson of Lexington, Kentucky, provided valuable input;

Ron Turcotte, Secretariat's Triple Crown jockey, wrote the Foreword to this book;

Jean Cruguet, Seattle Slew's Triple Crown jockey, for the Introduction, and other contributions to the work;

Ann Roads, Jeanette DeChristofano, Mary Grant Barnes, Kathy Perez, Linda Munson and others at the Pikes Peak Library District in Colorado Springs, put up with my numerous requests for interlibrary loan materials and aided and witnessed my many hours spent in front of the library's microfilm readers;

Janice Marie and her staff at the Library of Regis University, Colorado Springs, likewise endured other requests for interlibrary loan materials;

Vicki Sharer of Franklin, Kentucky, contributed several helpful articles and books;

Arlene Ekland-Earnst, Curator of the Pioneer Museum of Douglas, Wyoming, sent me much useful material on Sir Barton. Thomas Bueckner, Curator of the Fort Robinson Museum in Crawford, Nebraska, also sent me helpful information on Sir Barton's time in the Army Remount Program;

AK-Sar-Ben racetrack in Omaha, Nebraska, sent me some material from their files on Omaha (the horse), the third Triple Crown winner;

The late Jim Bolus contributed items re. Assault and Gallant Fox;

Brenda Goodwin at *Western Horseman* magazine in Colorado Springs facilitated my research in their back issue files. These yielded helpful items, especially regarding the Army Remount Program;

Karen Bittner, Lola Fennell, and Katie Lucas, Colorado's best court reporters, faithfully (and in some cases, arduously) transcribed the telephone interviews with many of the individuals that appear within;

Ryan Kelly of the Maryland Jockey Club contributed information about the Jockey's Hall of Fame;

Andre K. Silvola ably assisted in the research of this work;

My deep thanks go to the following Triple Crown Jockeys, Owners, and Trainers for their telephone interviews, all of which contributed immeasurably to this book:

Steve Cauthen (Affirmed's Jockey);
Penny Chenery (Secretariat's Owner);
Jean Cruguet (Seattle Slew's Jockey);
H.A. "Jimmy" Jones (Citation's Trainer, also Whirlaway's);
John Longden (Count Fleet's Jockey, also Whirlaway's);
Warren Mehrtens (Assault's Jockey);
Ron Turcotte (Secretariat's Jockey);
Billy Turner (Seattle Slew's Trainer);

(I spoke with Eddie Arcaro, but illness prevented him from granting me a telephone interview. Arcaro died a few months after our contact. As well, H.A. "Jimmy" Jones, Warren Mehrtens, and John Longden have passed away since I interviewed them.

Also, great thanks go to the following for their telephone interviews:
Bill Boland (jockey on Assault);
Tom Gilcoyne (recollections of most Triple Crown winners);
Margaret Glass (recollections of Calumet Farm, including Whirlaway, Citation and Alydar);
Monte Moncrief, D.V.M. (veterinarian at King Ranch);
Anne Scardino, (pony rider for Seattle Slew in the 1977 Swaps Stakes);
Paula Turner (first person to ride Seattle Slew).

Also, thanks are due to CBS Sports, for permission to use the race call of the 1973 Kentucky Derby; ABC Sports, for permission to quote from the videotape, "Jewels of the Triple Crown;" and WHAS Radio, Louisville, Kentucky, for permission to use the race call of the 1948 Kentucky Derby.

Then, my thanks to the crew at 305 South Cascade Avenue in Colorado Springs: Al, Joe, Fred, Jeff, Ann, Tricia, Debbie, Dan, Luise, and Tommie. They heard so much about the Triple Crown winners for so long; during 1993-1995, and again from 1996-2000.

Thanks, too, go to the group at 326 East Colorado Avenue in Colorado Springs with whom I worked during a brief interlude in 1995-1996: Ed, Leone, Brenda, and Shannon. They saw this book in its intermediate stages.

Thanks also go to the numerous friends and acquaintances who urged me to persevere with this effort. I would not trade one minute of the time I spent working on this book for anything else.

Finally, to some special people: my late father, Thomas W. Shoop; my stepmother, Mary Crook Shoop, and to my wife Toni, who came into my life and gave me joy. Their love and encouragement has been beyond measure.

Special thanks to my editor and publisher, Bradd Hopkins of Russell Dean and Company. His guidance made this a better book; his unflagging interest made it a reality.

But no matter how many people were involved, the conclusions and interpretations are my own. Any errors are my responsibility. In the process of writing this book, each Triple Crown winner came alive to me. I hope the same happens for each and every reader of this book.

Robert L. Shoop
Colorado Springs, Colorado
September, 1993-February, 2003

FOREWORD

By Ron Turcotte

In the winter of 1972, I was riding for Meadow Stable. I had gone home to visit my family in New Brunswick, Canada, for Christmas. After a visit with them, I went to Florida to ride in the winter. I couldn't wait to see my Derby mount, Riva Ridge, the champion two-year-old horse the year before and the horse that was favored to win the 1972 Kentucky Derby. I spotted this big, good-looking, red horse two stalls before getting to Riva Ridge's stall. I stopped and asked Lucien Laurin, Meadow Stable's trainer, "Who is this pretty boy?" Mr. Laurin replied that it was a colt by Bold Ruler out of Somethingroyal. I didn't know the colt's real name just then, but the "pretty boy" turned out to be Secretariat.

As they say, "the rest is history." And it's a history that you'll read in Robert L. Shoop's book, *Down to the Wire: The Lives of the Triple Crown Champions*. It's all here, the story of Secretariat and our Triple Crown. But it's more than that; it's the story of the eleven horses, ten jockeys, and ten trainers that have faced and passed horse racing's ultimate challenge: victories in the Kentucky Derby, Preakness, and Belmont Stakes. Robert Shoop has written the complete stories of the Triple Crown winners, using contemporary newspaper and magazine accounts, memoirs, and personal interviews with the key players — jockeys, trainers, owners, and others involved with the Triple Crown. He talked with all my Triple Crown-winning jockey colleagues (and me, too), and the excerpts he's used from those interviews make reading the stories of the Triple Crown winners seem as if you're in the saddle at Churchill Downs, Pimlico, and Belmont Park.

It was a massive task to write about all of the Triple Crown winners, but Robert Shoop has done it admirably: Sir Barton, the horse that had never won a race before the Kentucky Derby; Gallant Fox, the horse that dominated racing in 1930; Omaha and War Admiral, the sons of great racehorses; all of them through Secretariat, Seattle Slew, and the battles between Affirmed and Alydar, are wonderfully related in this book.

At a time when racing's future seems uncertain, it may help to look back to see what made racing successful in past years. The answer: great horses, great jockeys, great trainers, all of which combined to make for magnificent success stories. I'm fortunate to have been a part of the Triple Crown story and to share the story of my success on Secretariat with the readers of *Down to the Wire*. You'll love reading this book. Secretariat (and, I'm sure, all the other Triple Crown horses, jockeys, and trainers) would be proud that his story and theirs are told so well and lovingly. *Down to the Wire* is 1 to 10 with me…which just happens to be Secretariat's final odds in the Belmont Stakes.

Ron Turcotte
Grand Falls, New Brunswick, Canada

INTRODUCTION
by Jean Cruguet

One day at the 1976 summer meet in Saratoga Springs, New York, jockey Eddie Maple was scheduled to ride a big, dark brown, two-year-old colt trained by Billy Turner. But on that morning, Maple had a schedule conflict and sent his agent to say he was unavailable. So Billy Turner, wanting to work this big two-year-old horse, knew I was nearby, and said, "Go get Jean, go get Jean." The big two-year-old horse? Seattle Slew.

Needless to say, that morning changed my life. The next year on Seattle Slew, I became the ninth member of an exclusive fraternity: the Triple Crown jockeys. I joined John Loftus, Earl Sande, Willie Saunders, Charles Kurtsinger, Eddie Arcaro, John Longden, Warren Mehrtens, and Ron Turcotte. All were fine jockeys; many of them are in horse racing's Hall of Fame. (Steve Cauthen joined us in 1978 when he rode Affirmed to the Triple Crown.) Seattle Slew became only the tenth horse to win racing's Triple Crown. To win the Kentucky Derby, Preakness, and Belmont Stakes is horse racing's greatest challenge and there's nothing else like it in the world. Seattle Slew is one of the kings of the sport of kings and I am proud to have ridden him.

In recent years, horse racing has made a comeback. Several fine new tracks have opened, there is increased interest in horse racing, and cable television airs horse racing regularly. After a number of years of uncertainty, horse racing's future looks bright. Yet, it is good to look back and remember the giants of the sport. And the truly great horses, the ones that won the Triple Crown, should be specially remembered.

Robert L. Shoop has written a fine account of Seattle Slew's career and mine. His story of all the Triple Crown horses, jockeys, and trainers is complete and accurate. I am very glad I was able to help him with this book. I recommend it to all racing fans, horse lovers, and sports fans everywhere.

Jean Cruguet
Versailles, Kentucky

DOWN TO THE WIRE:
THE LIVES
OF THE
TRIPLE CROWN CHAMPIONS

By
Robert L. Shoop

"...Spencer was sure a wonder
And Miller was worth his hire,
Seldom he made a blunder
As he rode 'em down to the wire... "
— Damon Runyon, "A Handy Guy Like Sande"

"There's not a more beautiful animal than a Thoroughbred.
That's it."
— Anne Scardino, 1999.

I. THE RACES

THE KENTUCKY DERBY

"I think the Derby has come to be a kind of a religious thing in this country, like church for people that don't have no Confession."
— Hall of Fame Jockey Conn McCreary

More than any other horse race, the Kentucky Derby is the story of two men: Meriwether Clark and Matt Winn. Clark founded the Derby and got it going; Winn raised the Derby to the stature of a national event. But it didn't happen overnight.

The Commonwealth of Kentucky did not secede from the Union in 1861-1865, but neither did it stay unabashedly with the North. It was a "neutral" state, sending troops to both sides of the conflict. Its neutrality didn't guarantee safety from battle; a fair amount of fighting took place in Kentucky, and the Commonwealth suffered — not as much as Virginia or South Carolina, but Kentucky was hurt nonetheless.

Even for some time after Lee surrendered at Appomattox, guerilla bands raided farms and seized horses. As a result, racing was not all rosy in Kentucky. Lexington had a track, but Louisville's latest racecourse, Woodlawn, was an unsuccessful venture and went bankrupt in 1870.

Enter the Louisville city fathers, and particularly, one Meriwether Lewis Clark, Jr. Let's get it out of the way right now: Yes, he was a grandson of William Clark of Lewis and Clark Expedition fame. In 1872, some local breeders approached Clark, then prominent in Louisville society. They asked what, if anything, he could do to revive Thoroughbred racing in Louisville. Their entreaty worked: Clark agreed to lend a hand.

Others would have started immediately to build a racecourse, not knowing what to do after the last nail in the grandstand was driven home. Not Clark; he shelved plans for a racetrack. Then, conscious of his abysmal

1

knowledge of the racing business, Clark went off to Europe for two years to study racing management. He enjoyed the stakes races in England — particularly, the Epsom Derby, and also the Epsom Oaks, the St. Leger Stakes, and the Ascot Gold Cup. He went to France and learned the French method of "Paris-Mutuel" wagering, where the odds on a horse are set by the pool of money bet on the horse.

Back in Louisville in 1874, he called the local horse breeders together and outlined his plan. He envisioned a series of races modeled after the English classics. One race would be called the Kentucky Derby, after the Epsom Derby in England. Clark, with remarkable prescience but poor calendar sense, predicted that within ten years the winning horse of the Kentucky Derby would be worth more than the farm the horse came from. He formed a corporation that year, the Louisville Jockey Club and Driving Park Association, for the promotion of racing. He selected a track site slightly south of the center of the city, raised $32,000 in working capital, and leased the land from his uncles. Construction started on the one-mile track and after it was graded, the money ran out. A Louisville merchant, W.H. Thomas, loaned enough money to construct a small grandstand.

Bad winter weather combined with labor and material shortages to delay completion of the grandstand until just before Opening Day, May 17, 1875, the first running of the Kentucky Derby. Fifteen horses ran the race, which at that time was one-and-a-half miles in length. A chestnut colt called Aristides won the race. An African-American jockey named Oliver Lewis rode Aristides and went down in history as the first jockey to win the Kentucky Derby. The purse was $2850, and the attendance was a nice ten thousand spectators. Sitting in the infield that day in his father's flat-bed grocery wagon was a thirteen-year boy named Matt Winn.

It was a good start. One press account called the first Kentucky Derby a race "...which has created deep interest throughout the country." It was a fortunate time for the fledgling racetrack: America was coming out of the Reconstruction era and becoming an industrial nation. Moreover, the new track had little competition: only three tracks of any importance existed in the north and east (Monmouth, Jerome, and Saratoga), and only three tracks of any importance in the south (New Orleans, Nashville, and Lexington). In the 1980s, Business Schools taught the concept of "market niches" to their MBA candidates. Churchill Downs is an early example of filling a market niche.

Over the years, the Derby grew in importance. One of racing's greatest jockeys, Isaac Murphy, an African-American, set an early record, winning three Derbies in 1884, 1890, and 1891. Meriwether Clark ran the track cleanly, fairly, and imaginatively. He encouraged women to attend, on the theory that if the women liked horse racing, they would in turn encourage their husbands' attendance at races. Still, the track ran at a loss for several years. Finally, Churchill Downs was sold in 1894, although Clark stayed on as presiding judge.

The existing grandstand was torn down in 1894 and a new grandstand replaced it in 1894-1895. It was then that the twin spires on the grandstand, Churchill Downs' most prominent feature, were built. By 1899, Clark was in ill health. Despondent at the loss of old friends, badly overweight, suffering from liver trouble, Meriwether Lewis Clark committed suicide on April 22, 1899.

Derby history has been categorized into three periods. From 1875 to 1886, the Derby was established with good horses running. The next period, from 1886 to 1913, marked a decline in the Derby's status. During that period, the Kentucky Derby was little more than a local race of some slight note outside of Kentucky. The era of the modern Derby began in 1913 when it became the nation's premier horserace.

But Derby history can be divided in another manner: pre-1902, and post-1902. In that year, Matt Winn, a Louisville tailor, was asked by Charles Price, a former official at Churchill Downs, to buy the track. He was the track's last chance. Winn was under pressure. Without him, Price told him, the track and the Kentucky Derby would die out.

In its first decade, the Kentucky Derby attracted national attention. In 1886, however, a situation arose that put the Derby into a decline for over twenty-five years. James Ben Ali Haggin was an influential horse breeder, and in 1886 his horse Ben Ali won the Derby. That was great, but Haggin brought New York bettors with him to Churchill Downs on May 14, 1886, and that caused a problem. Louisville's bookmakers went on strike on Derby Day, and Haggin and his guests could not wager as they hoped. Haggin complained, but was rebuffed by Churchill Downs' management. That ruffled Haggin's feathers even more, so he spread the word: ignore Churchill Downs and that stinking little race called the Kentucky Derby.

Haggin's strategy worked. The East Coast racing community immediately turned away from Kentucky and back to tracks like Belmont, Gravesend, Sheepshead Bay, Saratoga, and Pimlico. That loss of attention, coupled with the decline in Meriwether Clark's health and the inevitable problems created by the construction of the new grandstand, put the Derby into a position of a local race — interesting, yes; a national race, no. By 1902, the Kentucky Derby was in severe trouble. Charlie Price's exact words to Matt Winn were: "If you don't buy it, the track will have to close and there won't be any more Kentucky Derbies."

Matt Winn watched every Kentucky Derby: He saw Aristides win the first one in 1875. Winn was thirteen then, and watched the race from the back of his father's wagon. By 1902, Winn was a force in Louisville: he knew the Mayor, City Councilmen, and the leaders of the city's business community. So when Churchill Downs' future came into question, the Louisville leaders thought of Winn, the tailor who had seen every Kentucky Derby. He wasn't thrilled about taking over management of the track at age forty-two, but on the other hand, the Kentucky Derby was the Kentucky Derby...

Churchill Downs had suffered in the last years of Clark's era, and during the three years after his death, matters became even worse. After the 1902 Derby, it looked as if Churchill Downs would close for good. So Matt Winn may have been literally the last chance for the track and not just the object of an impassioned plea. Winn went to work, built a new clubhouse, and reconditioned the grandstands. More than a devoted racing fan, Winn was one of the great promoters of all time. He was a master of publicity and arrived just at the right time to give the faltering horserace a shot in the arm. He courted the eastern stables to race at Churchill Downs, and wooed the newsmen, too: Damon Runyon, Grantland Rice, Frank Graham, Dan Parker, Bob Considine, Bill Corum, and Red Smith all received his attention over the years. When radio came onto the scene, Winn courted the broadcasters: Ted Husing, Bryan Field, and Clem McCarthy all went to Louisville for the Derby. For the press, nothing was too good. Often, Derby week was on the house, courtesy of Matt Winn.

But the real salvation of the Kentucky Derby came on the track. Ironically, a shutdown in New York racing helped: in 1911, the New York legislature passed anti-gambling laws that failed to exempt horse racing. That legislation effectively closed all the race tracks in New York State. By necessity, New York racing went elsewhere; inevitably, attention focused on Kentucky, and its Derby. New York's anti-gambling laws only lasted two years, until 1913, but that brief window shifted the focus from the East to Kentucky. Because of the shutdown, New York horses began to race in Kentucky, and one New York horse, Worth, won the 1912 Derby.

At the same time, the Derby itself had good races: Donerail won the 1913 Derby at odds of 91 to 1[1], and that attracted attention. Old Rosebud's eight-length victory in 1914 marked another increase in the attention given to the Kentucky Derby. The next year, Regret became the first filly to win the Derby[2]. Those victories opened the floodgate: Exterminator in 1918, Sir Barton in 1919, and the other winners who followed. From that time on, the Kentucky Derby became an event to attract national acclaim.

It took a few years, but by the end of the "Great War", the Derby had become a national sporting event. It rivaled baseball's World Series or a championship heavyweight prizefight in national attention.

In many ways, Winn is the "father" of pari-mutuel betting. In 1908, the Louisville city council outlawed bookmaking. Winn read the new law carefully and found it contained a significant exception: the "Pari-mutuel" betting system was exempt from the new law. So Winn rummaged around in Churchill Downs'

---

[1] Donerail's victory remains the record for the longest odds of any Kentucky Derby winner.

[2] Fans of old movies may remember Francis, the Talking Mule, uttering, "By the hair of my Great-Aunt Regret, who won the Derby!"

storerooms, found some of the old "Paris-Mutuel" machines from Meriwether Clark's days, and stayed in business. Winn remained as manager of Churchill Downs for forty-seven years. He died on October 6, 1949, having seen every one of the first seventy-five Kentucky Derby races.

The most renowned feature of the Derby is the blanket of roses draped over the withers of the winning horse. Every Kentucky Derby winner since the 1890's received some floral tribute — whether a wreath, a garland, or a floral blanket. This tradition started in obscurity; it's been said that ladies attending a post-Derby party in 1883 were each given roses. This was so impressive that Meriwether Clark adopted the rose as the official Derby flower.

This ritual, however, was not followed strictly every year. It wasn't until the early part of the Twentieth Century that roses were given to honor the winning horse. The rose tradition stuck, and in 1925, sportswriter Bill Corum coined the phrase, "Run for the Roses," to describe the Derby. In 1931 Churchill Downs asked a Louisville florist to design and produce a rose blanket for the Derby winner. The 1932 Derby victor, Burgoo King, was the first to receive the blanket of five hundred red roses. The tradition and the nickname continue to this day.

Today, in the first week of May, Louisville is a center of national attention. Movie and television stars fly in; elegant balls are held throughout the week. It is no accident that the Run for the Roses is America's greatest horse race. Meriwether Clark and Matt Winn literally devoted their lives to the Kentucky Derby.

THE PREAKNESS STAKES

It is axiomatic that to win the Triple Crown, a horse must win all three races. The Kentucky Derby has the prestige; the Belmont Stakes has the distance and New York media attention. But the Preakness, lacking the attributes of the other two races, has a certain charm and compelling history of its own.

Through 2003, forty-seven horses won two of the three Triple Crown races. Of those forty-seven, almost one-quarter of them — eleven horses — won the Kentucky Derby and the Belmont Stakes, but lost the Preakness. Moreover, the horses written about in this book sired only five Preakness-winning horses (as opposed to seven Kentucky Derby winners and eleven Belmont Stakes winners). As will be seen, four Triple Crown winners (Gallant Fox, War Admiral, Assault, and Affirmed) squeaked by in the Preakness. On the positive side, two of the most incredible performances in racing history — Whirlaway in 1941 and Secretariat in 1973 — occurred in the Preakness. So, despite its lack of a Kentucky cachet or New York media hype, the Preakness cannot be taken for granted.

The Maryland Jockey Club (MJC) formed at Annapolis in 1743. A horse named Duncannon won the first trophy, the Annapolis Subscription Plate on May 4, 1743. The MJC regularly held races, but beginning in 1755, the MJC's races were held irregularly due to interruptions caused by the French and Indian War. During this early period, a Virginia planter named George Washington attended MJC races as a spectator. By 1775, the fires of the Revolutionary War caused the suspension of MJC races, and races in Annapolis were not held again until 1782. The Maryland Jockey Club was resurrected on March 1, 1783, with two signers of the Declaration of Independence part of the membership. In 1830 Congress got into the act, and issued the MJC a new charter, which remains in archive in the Library of Congress. The city of Baltimore was growing well at this time, and the MJC moved from Annapolis to Baltimore. Even Andrew Jackson was a member of the MJC. His stable raced under the name of his secretary, A.J. Donelson.

But war again interrupted racing. Maryland racing was put "on hold for the duration" in 1861 and did not start again there for seven years. In 1868

Maryland's Governor Oden Bowie and a few others attended a race at Saratoga. They devised a race, the Dinner Party Stakes, for a track laid out in northwest Baltimore the year before: Pimlico[3]. The track opened on October 25, 1870, for the Dinner Party Stakes. A horse named Preakness won the race.

The name Preakness derives from the American Indian word "Pra-qua-les," meaning "quail woods" in the language of the Minisi, a northern New Jersey tribe. Eventually, the spelling of "Pra-qua-les" evolved into "Preakness."

In the 19th century, a horse owner named Milton H. Sanford called his New Jersey and Kentucky farms "Preakness." Sanford bought a Kentucky yearling and named the colt after his farms. At age three, Preakness the colt started in the 1870 Dinner Plate Stakes at the then-new Pimlico racetrack. Preakness was called a "cart horse" due to his less-than-sleek appearance, but he won. His jockey was Billy Hayward, whom history and urban planning immortalized in the name of one of the streets, Hayward Avenue, that adjoins Pimlico. Preakness made only one start at Pimlico, but it was enough. Three years later, Oden Bowie, by then a private citizen, sponsored a new race and decided to name it after Pimlico's first stakes winner. So, the Preakness Stakes the new race became.[4]

The first running of the Preakness was on Tuesday, May 27, 1873, and the track was slow. Seven horses ran in it. The race was then 1 1/2 miles. The crowd was estimated at twelve thousand. The winner was a bay colt named Survivor, who won by ten lengths,[5] and the purse was $1,850.

Like the Derby two years later, the Preakness was off to a good start. Over the next seventeen years, the Preakness grew in both attendance and stature.[6] In 1877, Congress adjourned for the day so its members could sojourn

---

[3] The name Pimlico comes from the Pimlico district in London. The landowner who sold the site for the track came from that part of London. One of Pimlico's older nicknames is "Old Hilltop," because early on, there was a mound in the infield. Thus the Hilltop sobriquet. The mound obscured the backstretch and was leveled long ago, but the link to the past remains.

[4] Preakness (the horse himself) came to a bad end. He raced through his eight-year-old season, and in his career he won several important races. But in 1875 Preakness was sold for brood stock to the Duke of Hamilton and taken to England. Preakness grew bad-tempered in his older years and became difficult to handle. In a temper tantrum, the equally irascible Duke of Hamilton shot and killed the animal. Preakness' death spurred English reform laws governing the handling of animals.

[5] Survivor's ten-length margin remains the all-time Preakness record, though the race has changed length over the years, settling on its present 1 3/16 miles in 1925. Count Fleet (1943) had the record (eight lengths) for the post-1925 Preakness until Funny Cide won it by 9 1/4 lengths in 2003.

[6] According to one source, an 1876 Baltimore *Sun* article included the Preakness

7

to Pimlico to attend the Preakness, certainly the greatest service any race track anywhere on the planet has rendered to its native land. From 1878 to 1882, horses owned by George P. Lorillard, of the tobacco Lorillard family, won the Preakness each year. Those five consecutive victories by one owner are still a Preakness record.

In 1889 the MJC ran into trouble: New York and New Jersey expanded horse racing in those states, while the growth of the railroads opened up other states. As a result of these developments, Maryland racing, and Pimlico in particular, got squeezed. The MJC ran into financial trouble and abandoned racing at Pimlico for fifteen years, although some steeplechases and other events occurred there during this period. In 1890 a fire destroyed Pimlico's grandstand.

For many years, it was thought that there were NO Preaknesses run between 1890 and 1909. But in the 1940s, research revealed that a race entitled "The Preakness Stakes" took place at Gravesend Park in Brooklyn, N.Y. from 1894 through 1908. Somehow, the newspapers never connected the Gravesend Park Preaknesses with the Pimlico Preaknesses. Moreover, the great Baltimore fire of 1904 destroyed the records of the MJC, so no record remains of an official transfer of the Preakness to Gravesend. Despite this, the "Lost Preaknesses of Gravesend Park" were officially incorporated into the Preakness record.

That still left a gap in the records from 1890 through 1893. In the 1960's, the hole was partially filled: another researcher found that the 1890 Preakness ran at Morris Park in New York. That race, too, was incorporated into the official Preakness history. This particular Preakness is an oddity: it was open to three-year-old horses "and upward." This is the ONLY Triple Crown race that was open to horses other than three-year-olds, and indeed, was won by a five-year-old horse named Montague. To date, research has unearthed no records of a Preakness in 1891, 1892, or 1893. But who knows? Perhaps somewhere in an attic or basement a trunk filled with old racing programs will turn up, and the three "lost" Preakness races will no longer be mysteries.

After the 1904 Baltimore fire, the MJC regained some strength although the Preakness didn't return to Maryland for another five years. Effendi won the 1909 Preakness, the first horse to win the race after it returned to Pimlico.

From that point it was onward for both the Preakness and Pimlico. Pari-mutuel windows opened at 1912, and in 1916 the Preakness ran in two divisions. The purse increased to $15,000. By 1919 the Preakness was an integral part of Thoroughbred racing, and in the thirties, it emerged in prominence as part of the Triple Crown.

---

with the Breckenridge Stakes and the Dixie Handicap as Maryland's "Triple Crown." This was one of the first uses of "Triple Crown" in racing, and is also proof that the Preakness quickly became an important race.

Not much in Maryland works like it does in other states, and that extends to the blanket of flowers that drape the Preakness winner. Maryland's state flower is the black-eyed Susan, a summertime flower. Few, if any, are in bloom in the middle of May. The Preakness winner gets draped with a blanket of black-eyed Susans, and there's the problem. Pimlico long ago solved it by buying enough daisies to make the floral blanket and then dyeing the centers black. So the Preakness winner has to be content with an *ersatz* state flower blanket. There's more, however, for the Preakness winner than that. There's also the Woodlawn Vase, appraised at $1 million in 1983, and probably the most valuable trophy in American sport. It was created by the Tiffany Company in 1860 for the long-gone Woodlawn Racing Association in Louisville. It was won in 1861, and the winner kept it during the Civil War. In fact, it was buried in Louisville during the Civil War to keep it safe. It wasn't assigned to any particular race, and the Woodlawn Vase made its way to New York in 1878. There it stayed until 1917. Thomas Clyde, a horse owner, won it twice. Clyde was an MJC Director. In 1917, Clyde presented the Woodlawn Vase to the MJC. Immediately, it became the trophy for that year's Preakness. There it has stayed. Formerly, the winning owner kept the Woodlawn Vase for one year; nowadays, the winning Preakness owner receives a copy of the Woodlawn Vase to keep. The most immediate tangible sign of the Preakness winner is seen on the weathervane atop the clubhouse in Pimlico's infield. After the Preakness winner is officially confirmed, an attendant carrying paint and brushes climbs a ladder and paints the horse and jockey-shaped weathervane in the colors of the silks of the winning stable.[7]

So there it is: one of sport's most valuable trophies; one of racing's greatest events; and a race with its own unique characteristics and a shorter distance (1 3/16 mile); a short time between the Derby and the Preakness. Never more than two weeks separate the two races, thus testing a horse's stamina and endurance; and a curious bit of geometry: Pimlico's turns are tighter than at other courses, so racing skill and the ability to hang the inside rail on a turn are at a premium. All those factors justly combine to make the Preakness "The Middle Jewel of the Triple Crown."

---

[7] This tradition has been emulated, in a way, for the Kentucky Derby and the Belmont Stakes. In Churchill Downs' courtyard stands a small cement statue of a horse groom. The groom's clothing is painted in the colors of the silks of the Kentucky Derby winner. Near Belmont Park, the slats of the fences surrounding Esposito's Tavern are painted in the colors of the silks of the Belmont Stakes winner.

THE BELMONT STAKES

Between the stables and the track at Belmont Park stands a magnificent white pine tree. Its branches splay in every direction, and it needs wires to support it. Belmont Park celebrated its 90th birthday in 1995; the tree in question is 150 years old. Already a full-grown tree in 1905, the Belmont track was built around it. It has survived, and every horse that has run at Belmont Park since 1905 — Man o'War, Sir Barton, Gallant Fox, Omaha, War Admiral, Whirlaway, Count Fleet, Assault, Citation, Nashua, Kelso, all of them, through Secretariat, Seattle Slew, Affirmed, and down to Cigar, Touch Gold, Victory Gallop, and Point Given — walked by that tree on the way to a race. It is an enduring symbol of racing's continuity, and the longest and oldest of the Triple Crown races.

In 1867, August Belmont, a prominent New York banker and racing fan, decided to establish a new race. It was modeled after the England's Epsom Derby (1 1/2 miles). Belmont's idea was for three races to be held in New York State that would be the equivalent of the English Triple Crown. The result was three races which were among the most important in American racing — the Withers, at 1 mile, the Belmont Stakes, (originally at 1 mile, 5 furlongs, now 1 1/2 miles), and the Lawrence Realization at 1 5/8 miles. The Withers and the Lawrence Realization have been surpassed in importance by other races — the American Triple Crown, and more recently, the Breeders Cup races — but the Belmont Stakes has remained the third jewel in the Triple Crown.

The Belmont is the most punishing of the three races in many respects. Run at 1 1/2 miles, it is now the longest of the Triple Crown races. It occurs in early June, a time in New York when the weather is apt to be hotter and more humid than the May races in Kentucky or Maryland. Finally there is the combination of race length and time. While there is a gap of three weeks between the Preakness and Belmont Stakes, the physical exertion needed to win the Kentucky Derby and Preakness frequently operates as a winnowing factor at Belmont. Twenty-six horses came to Belmont after winning the Derby and Preakness; of those, fifteen lost the Belmont Stakes. The weather, the exertion, and the distance of 1 1/2 miles are often fatal to Triple Crown chances.

First run at the old Jerome Park from 1867 to 1890, it is the oldest Triple

Crown race, possessing its share of oddities. The first horse to win any Triple Crown race was a filly, Ruthless. Belmont was also the race which inaugurated the post parade in 1880, where the horses walk in front of the spectators prior to the race.

Prior to 1921, the Belmont Stakes was run in a *clockwise* direction, not the counter-clockwise direction found in other American races. Also, it moved around over the years: in 1890 the race was moved to Morris Park.[8] Finally, with the construction of Belmont Park on Long Island in 1905, it found a permanent home. That didn't stop the moving, though; in 1963, Belmont Park was found to have structural aging problems, necessitating a five-year rebuild of the track. From 1963 through 1967, the Belmont Stakes was run at Aqueduct. Like the Derby and Preakness, the Belmont's length has varied over the years. It was originally a mile and five furlongs from 1867 to 1889, but from then to 1926, it gradually increased in length. It increased to 1 1/4 miles in 1890, and increased again to 1 3/8 miles in 1906. The Belmont increased in length to its present 1 1/2 miles in 1926.

The Belmont, like the Kentucky Derby and Preakness, has had its shares of triumphs and troubles. The present site was established in 1905, and the first races were held on May 4. The featured race was the Metropolitan Handicap. Running in that raced was the great horse, Sysonby. He finished in a dead heat with Race King. That event alone should have told the world that nothing at Belmont should be taken for granted. Three years later, the New York legislature passed a law banning betting at racetracks. It took two more years for another law to be passed which finally shut down racing in New York altogether.

Belmont Park stood raceless for two years. The Wright brothers held an international aerial tournament there in 1910 to use the park, but not until 1913 did Belmont reopen. Still there was no betting: the stockholders of the Westchester Racing Association, owner of Belmont Park, made up the purse money. (Legal betting did not return to New York until 1934.)

It was good for racing to have the track open again, and the Belmont Stakes has been run continuously since 1913. As with the other Triple Crown races, the winning horse receives a blanket of flowers, in this case woven of white carnations. The winning owner gets temporary possession of a silver Tiffany bowl and permanent possession of a silver tray.

Belmont Park has seen much: the simultaneous victory and injury of Count Fleet in the Belmont Stakes, the triumphs of Man o'War, War Admiral, Citation and Seattle Slew; the tragedy of Ruffian and the disappointing match race between Armed and Assault. The Belmont Stakes is the daunting and

---

[8] The 1890 Belmont and the 1890 Preakness were both run on the same day at Morris Park. It is the *only* time that two Triple Crown races have been run on the same day at the same park. Naturally, that concurrence of races prevented a Triple Crown winner in 1890.

11

fitting conclusion to the spring campaign that is the Triple Crown.

ARISTIDES, first winner of the Kentucky Derby on May 17, 1875. Statue displayed on the grounds of Churchill Downs. *Photograph courtesy of Brenda Cubbage. Used by permission*

ORIGIN OF THE TERM "TRIPLE CROWN"

Out of all the other race combinations possible, how did the Kentucky Derby, Preakness Stakes, and Belmont Stakes come to be known as "The Triple Crown?"

History should clarify matters, but sometimes it does exactly the opposite. What was thought to be a simple answer to a history question in reality is fairly complex.

For years, the short answer was that Charles Hatton of the *Daily Racing Form* came up with the term. That appears not to be the case, however.

The basic term, "Triple Crown," comes from Britain. One source points out that the British crown encompasses three regions: England, Scotland, and Wales. Therefore, the British monarch effectively wears a three-sided — "triple"— crown for those lands. This term was then applied to English racing to denote the winners of three races: the Epsom Derby, the 2,000 Guineas, and the St. Leger Stakes.

That's simple enough, but it becomes less illuminating when viewed across the Atlantic Ocean. This is where Charles Hatton comes into the picture. Hatton was a racing columnist for the *Daily Racing Form* for many years. The *DRF*, in the 1930s, as now, was the chief publication for racing enthusiasts. In those days of manual typewriters, Hatton, like many newspapermen, was not much of a typist. By 1935, so the story is told, Hatton was covering Omaha's victories in the Derby, Preakness, and Belmont, and wearied of laboriously typing out the names of the three races. Those three races had become the premier American races, so a shortcut was definitely needed. According to the story, the idea using the term "Triple Crown" to describe them came to him out of the blue. It was an ideal shorthand term: crisp, noble, and unforgettable. He used the term to denote the winner of the three races and it caught on. Thus was born one of the most durable phrases in American Thoroughbred racing and American sports in general.

That's the story, and it would be nice to leave it there. However, we can't do that. First, it's not clear that Charles Hatton thought of "Triple Crown" with Omaha in 1935; both the *1995 Kentucky Derby Media Guide* and the 2002 *Information Please Sports Almanac* state that Hatton coined "Triple Crown" while covering Gallant Fox in 1930, not while covering Omaha five years later.

But 1930 is the year when "Triple Crown" was coined by *someone*. In its June 14, 1930 issue, *The Blood-Horse* magazine referred to Sir Barton and Gallant Fox, the first horses to win all three races, as "Triple Event winners." On June 8, 1930, *The New York Times* led off the Bryan Field article on Gallant Fox with the phrase, "Woodward's Preakness, Derby Winner Ties Sir Barton as Triple Crown Hero." An unattributed article in that same issue stated, "In America the idea of the Triple Crown being duplicated came when the Preakness, the Kentucky Derby, and the Belmont Stakes reached such prominence as to overshadow all other spring three-year-old events in this country." William Woodward, in his 1930 privately published book, *Gallant Fox: A Memoir,* refers to the three races as the "triple crown." Even before 1930, there is evidence indicating that "Triple Crown" was used in the nineteenth century, in one instance to denote horses winning three Maryland races, and another time to denote the winner of the Brooklyn, Metropolitan, and Suburban Handicap races in New York in 1894.

We will probably never know exactly who first said it, or how, or when "Triple Crown" came into regular American usage, although Charles Hatton became identified with the term in the 1930s. "Triple Crown" has been applied to sporting achievements outside horse racing; for example, in baseball, a player hitting the most home runs, having the highest batting average and having the most runs-batted-in has won the "Triple Crown."

The Kentucky Derby, Preakness, and Belmont Stakes have been run continuously since 1913. In the years since, only eleven horses have won all three races, and one other horse placed second in all three. But before we look at the lives of the Triple Crown champion horses, jockeys, and trainers, we must examine one horse, the greatest horse *never* to win the Triple Crown. As M. A. Stoneridge said so well, "How can one possibly write of great horses without considering Man o'War?"

THE DEMIGOD: MAN O'WAR

Preakness & Belmont Stakes, 1920: Jockey, Clarence Kummer

The tribute to him that endures to this day was from his groom, Will Harbut. In the rich tone of a southern black man in the 1930s and 1940s, Harbut said Man o'War was "De mostest hoss." Indeed, Man o'War was the most horse. In public impact, Man o'War has only one serious competitor, Secretariat, and two far-behind challengers, Whirlaway and Citation. In some ways, Man o'War's influence is still felt, and his contemporary public image must have been huge. Secretariat benefited from modern sports media; but only the printed pages of 1919-1920 sang Man o'War's praises. He was the first great sports figure of the "Golden Age of Sports." Ruth, Dempsey, Tilden, Grange, Budge; all of the great human sports champions of the 1920s follow on the fiery red horse of Faraway Farm. Whatever Man o'War was, Thoroughbred racehorse, mythical beast, or what he became, racing's demigod, he was something. He ran twenty-one races, won twenty of them and placed second once.

His owner, Sam Riddle, was asked to sell Man o'War for $1 million in 1920. Riddle's response was immediate and clear: "You go to France and bring back the sepulcher of Napoleon from *Les Invalides*. Then you go to England and buy the jewels from the crown. Then to India and buy the Taj Mahal. Then I'll put a price on Man o'War."

Man o'War was foaled on March 29, 1917, at the Nursery Stud of the Belmont family near Lexington, Kentucky. It was the same Belmont family for whom Belmont Park and the Belmont Stakes were named. Perhaps the first American casualty of World War I was the Belmont family's ownership of Man o'War: Congress declared war on Imperial Germany one week after Man o'War's birth, and August Belmont, scion of Nursery Farm, volunteered for the U.S. Army. Even though August Belmont was sixty-five at the time, he was commissioned a major and sent to France. Before his departure, Belmont decided to auction off his entire 1917 yearling crop, with one exception: the colt named Man o'War. But later, from France, Belmont cabled Kentucky with

15

instructions to include Man o'War in the sale.

A few days before the auction on August 17, 1918, Sam Riddle, owner of Glen Riddle Farm in Maryland, was inspecting the Belmont colts. One caught his eye, and Riddle asked a groom to lead Man o'War outside to get a better look at him. Riddle remembered later that as "Soon as I saw him in the daylight he simply bowled me over...I couldn't think of anything but that colt after that...." Riddle purchased Man o'War and ten other Belmont yearlings for a total of $25,000. Man o'War's auction price was a fifth of that, $5000.

Man o'War was taken to Glen Riddle Farm and broken to saddle. Predictably, he wasn't easy to train, but with effort he became accustomed to racing. He had some fairly impressive bloodlines: one grandsire won the English Triple Crown in 1903; another grandsire, Hastings, possessed a fierce temperament. Man o'War's sire, Fair Play, was the product of those two horses, and was able to carry high weight over distance, albeit with a fair amount of Hastings' ferocity. Man o'War's dam, Mahubah, inherited a more equable disposition from her sire, Rock Sand, an English Thoroughbred. The Fair Play-Mahubah combination produced a distance runner under heavy weight with the speed of a sprinter, and a personality with the fire of Fair Play tempered by the intelligence and gentility of Mahubah.[9] That was Man o'War, who debuted in the spring of 1919.

Louis Feustel trained Man o'War. He was born on January 2, 1884 in Lindenhurst, Long Island, and began working at August Belmont's nearby farm in 1895. By 1908, Feustel had the job of breaking yearlings at Belmont's farm; one of those yearlings was Hastings, and Feustel somehow survived breaking Hastings. By 1910 Feustel was Belmont's chief trainer. But August Belmont had other ideas. He wanted Sam Hildreth to train his horses, and Hildreth became available in 1917. So, about the time August Belmont lost Man o'War to Sam Riddle, Belmont lost Feustel to Riddle's stable, too. Feustel, having trained his grandsire and sire, now did the same for Man o'War.

The two jockeys most identified with Man o'War are John Loftus and Clarence Kummer. Loftus rode Man o'War in all of the horse's two-year-old races in 1919; Kummer rode Man o'War in most of his races in 1920, including the Preakness, Belmont, and Dwyer Stakes. Their careers are intertwined with each other, Man o'War, and Sir Barton, the first Triple Crown winner.

John Loftus was born in Chicago in 1895. He became a jockey in 1910 at Latonia Park in Kentucky. At first it seemed that Loftus would not get too far on the turf; he was left-handed and looked as if he would grow beyond jockey limits. His first employer, George Moreland, said that Loftus would never ride

---

[9] In addition, Fair Play and Mahubah produced a filly named Masda, who was a great-grand-dam of Assault. Assault won the Triple Crown in 1946 and will be discussed in Chapter 6 of the next section.

in races; he had "calves like a wrestler." Moreland refused to let Loftus ride, and later, apparently traded Loftus' contract to trainer John M. Goode in exchange for a mare. It was the beginning for Loftus; he rode his first victors for Goode at Latonia Park. Over time, he moved into the major leagues, and won the 1916 Kentucky Derby on George Smith and the 1918 Preakness on War Cloud. He also won other important races such as the Travers, Withers, the Suburban Handicap, the Hopeful and the Kentucky Oaks.

More important was what happened in 1919: J.K.L. Ross hired Loftus to ride Sir Barton. With Loftus up, Sir Barton became the first horse to win the Triple Crown.[10] In the midst of a string of victories (Loftus on Sir Barton won the Kentucky Derby, the Preakness, and the Withers) Loftus rode the two-year old Man o'War in his first race at Belmont Park on June 6, 1919.

John Loftus is remembered in racing history as the first jockey to win the Triple Crown, Man o'War's first jockey, and the only jockey ever to lose a race on Man o'War. He was more than that; he was the best jockey of his day. Loftus knew when to keep a horse back and when to let him go. He was an excellent horse handler and a powerful finisher. It is unlikely that Sam Riddle and Louis Feustel could have found a better jockey for Man o'War in 1919 than John Loftus.

On June 6, 1919, Man o'War made his debut in the sixth race at Belmont Park. Seven horses were entered, but Man o'War was the favorite, at odds of 3 to 5, based solely on his workouts. It was a short race; 5/8 of a mile, straight with no turns. Man o'War was seventh from the pole position, and the start was delayed for two minutes while the horses, two-year-old maidens all, settled down. Loftus' instructions were to keep Man o'War back for the first furlong and then go after the pack.

Loftus tried to follow the instructions, but "Big Red" did not cooperate. They were first at the start, and then slipped back into second by the 1/4 mile mark. But they were second only by a neck to the leader, Retrieve. There they stayed for another quarter mile, and Retrieve never got more than a half-length in front of Man o'War. After the half-mile, Loftus let him go, and Man o'War pulled away easily from Retrieve and the other horses. By the finish, Man o'War was six lengths in front of Retrieve. The *Daily Racing Form* notes to the race reported that Man o'War "Won cantering." *The New York Times* article on the race said "The colt [Man o'War] proved to be all that he was claimed to be..." Much more was to come.

Three days later Man o'War raced again at Belmont. The race was the 5 1/2-furlong Keene Memorial Stakes, another straight race with no turns. Man o'War was once again the 7 to 10 favorite of the bettors. He was third from the post, broke well, and stayed with the pack for most of the race. At the start he was second and stayed there through the 1/2 mile. Then Loftus let him ease

---

[10] Sir Barton's career will be related in the next chapter.

back some, and Man o'War was in third, but only a length separated him from the leader. Loftus sent Man o'War in the stretch and won easily by three lengths. He was spotted for greatness immediately: in his second race, the headlines of *The New York Times* the next day read:

"MAN O"WAR SAILS IN AN EASY WINNER."

The article started with, "The best two-year-old filly and the best colt [Man o'War] seen this year were scheduled to meet yesterday at Belmont Park yesterday in the Keene Memorial Stakes." All that after only two races!

Twelve days later Man o'War raced at the Jamaica track in the 5 1/2-furlong Youthful Stakes. The word was out; only three horses challenged Man o'War, who was the 1 to 2 favorite. He carried a massive weight handicap, 120 pounds; the other horses carried 105 or 108 pounds. That didn't bother Man o'War; he took the lead by the quarter-mile and stayed there. At one point he was four lengths ahead of the second horse, until Loftus asked him to ease up some. Man o'War won by 2 1/2 lengths.

Two days after that the Hudson Stakes at Aqueduct was run on the same day as the Brooklyn Handicap, one of the most important handicap races. Man o'War attracted little attention. Only five horses appeared for the 5/8 mile race, and Man o'War with Loftus up won it handily. He jumped to the lead early, never gave it up, and won by 1 1/2 lengths. But there was something odd in the race: the handicappers already started weighing Man o'War down. As a two-year-old horse with only three races behind him, he carried *130* pounds in the race, an almost unheard-of weight for a two-year-old. It was remarkable that he did not break down immediately.

The Tremont Stakes, held twelve days later at Aqueduct, was a significant race for two-year-olds. It was longer than the Hudson Stakes, 3/4 of a mile, and Man o'War went into it as the favorite at odds of 1 to 10. Again, he carried 130 pounds. Only two horses challenged him, and the outcome was never in doubt. He jumped to an early lead, held on again, and Loftus guided him home one length ahead of his nearest challenger.

He was now five-for-five and had never really been tested; Loftus kept him under restraint during most of his races. But it was time for a rest. The Saratoga meet was a month off, and Feustel thought it unwise to work Man o'War too much. He rested for the balance of July, 1919, then Riddle and Feustel took him north to Saratoga for August racing.

On August 3 he and Loftus ran in the United States Hotel Stakes, a major race for two-year-olds. The race, named for a hotel in Saratoga, was 3/4 of a mile. Again, Man o'War and his jockey made it look easy: they took the lead immediately, never let go, and won by two lengths. *The New York Times* prophesied: "After the race, it was quite generally imagined that Man o'War was the best two-year-old that had been seen this season, and therefore, the most likely to be crowned champion of his age."

Now he was six for six, and there was no doubt about his greatness. But few great athletes escape without tasting defeat once, and defeat was waiting for him, eleven days later, in the Sanford Stakes at Saratoga.

Man o'War, again carrying 130 pounds, was the 11 to 20 favorite in the race. But also entered was a horse named Upset. Upset was a horse to be reckoned with: He was owned by Harry Payne Whitney and ridden by Willie Knapp. If Loftus was the number one jockey at that time, Knapp was a very close second. Also entered was Golden Broom, owned by Mrs. Walter Jeffords. Golden Broom was the number two two-year-old at that time, and he and Man o'War rode against each other in private match races. Each horse won once. (There were four other horses entered but they were of negligible impact in this race.)

Golden Broom was the bettors' second choice, and Upset was third. Riddle tried to withdraw Man o'War from the Sanford, in order to give Golden Broom the win. But Whitney, Upset's owner, wouldn't hear of it; he wanted a legitimate, by-god, face-to-face meeting between his horse and Man o'War.

As tough as the race would have been for Man o'War anyway, a sudden turn of events made it impossible for him to win. The post parade went all right and the horses lined up at the starting barrier (in those days, a web barrier raised at the start of a race.) Then disaster struck.

While the horses were at the barrier, the starter, Mars Cassidy, took ill. Immediately, C.J. Pettingill, a retired starter who was the placing judge that day, took over the starter's job.

There could not have been a worse development. Pettingill went down in history as having been responsible for the fiasco of the 1893 American Derby, when it took him an *hour and a half* to start that race. Pettingill might have been at other times a competent starter, but he was in way over his head on August 13, 1919.[11]

Man o'War was sixth in the lineup, while Golden Broom was third from the post and Upset was fifth. Man o'War hated the starting barrier, any starting barrier. When he went out on a track, he wanted to race with no delays. On this day, he was his usual impatient self. The delay while Pettingill was put in the starter's job just made things worse.

Man o'War reared and broke through the barrier. Loftus brought him back, but he had his hands full handling the horse. Man o'War's misbehavior agitated Golden Broom, and *he* broke through the web barrier. Finally, Pettingill sent the barrier up and started the race, *but only when he saw that the horses nearest the rail were ready*. Golden Broom took off into the lead, and Upset

---

[11] Pettingill had a very bad day as a substitute starter: only two of his starts were good ones.

was right behind him. Man o'War, far out from the rail, had his head still turned sideways when the barrier went up. For the first and perhaps only time in his career, he was left at the post.

Now Loftus and Man o'War had their work cut out. Eddie Ambrose, Golden Broom's jockey, won the Withers with Golden Broom just the week before by taking an early lead. Perhaps the same tactic would work with Man o'War. Loftus and Man o'War went right after the pack, but Upset was still close on Golden Broom. By the clubhouse turn, Man o'War started his move. Then, Golden Broom increased his lead over Upset by two lengths. Down the backstretch, Man o'War took over third and was closing on Upset and Golden Broom. Then Man o'War was challenged by Captain Alcock, one of the nonentities in the race, and Loftus let Man o'War run even faster.

That put them squarely up against Golden Broom, who was running just a length ahead of Upset. The two leaders formed an impassible obstacle; Loftus tried to squeeze Man o'War between them, but there was no "give" from either horse. Loftus was forced to pull up Man o'War, costing time and distance, and take his horse to the outside.

Loftus thought that Golden Broom would eventually fade, but it hadn't happened so far. He was still slightly ahead of Upset. Man o'War ran close, never more than a length behind Upset. Then Upset passed Golden Broom and that gave Loftus and Man o'War the opportunity they needed. Down the stretch it was one of the greatest battles in racing history. With one hundred feet to go, Man o'War drew within three-quarters of a length of Upset. At fifty feet, Man o'War ran at Upset's shoulder. But Man o'War ran out of race; no matter how hard he charged, no matter how hard Loftus whipped him, the finish line was coming up too fast. At the wire, Upset was a neck in front of Man o'War. Had the race been just twenty feet longer, Man o'War would have won.

The 1919 Sanford Stakes was the only race Man o'War ever lost. Some muttered that the race was fixed. That wasn't the case, but what caused the loss? The bad start, certainly, was a major factor. Loftus took much of the blame for his alleged bad handling of Man o'War. His critics say he shouldn't have run into the wall formed by Golden Broom and Upset. (Considering Loftus won six races on Man o'War before the Sanford, and won another three races on Man o'War after the Sanford, that statement just doesn't seem to hold up.) And William H.P. Robertson, author of *The History of Thoroughbred Racing in America*, called the Sanford "merely another race in which a high-flying two-year-old had been trapped and had his wings clipped — a commonplace occurrence."

Willie Knapp absolved Loftus from blame: "He, Loftus, rode a good race. When you consider the poor start and the way Ambrose and me wouldn't let him through down the stretch, Loftus can't be blamed for the loss. He was a very good boy, one of the very best," Knapp remembered later. Man o'War's defeat was due most likely to a combination of factors: the bad start, the tactics used by the other jockeys. Loftus may have made an error (what jockey does *not* make an error in a race?), and perhaps it was just Man o'War's time to be defeated. The controversy over Man o'War's only loss has raged since 1919.

If anything, Man o'War's stature grew due to the Sanford Stakes loss. Ten days later, he won the Grand Union Hotel Stakes at Saratoga. He was promptly crowned by *The New York Times,* "KING OF TWO-YEAR-OLDS." Man o'War got even in this race: he beat Upset by one length.

One week later, he ran in the Hopeful Stakes at Saratoga, then one of the most important events for two-year-olds. Eight horses entered, but weather intervened. It drizzled for most of the day. As the horses passed in the post parade for the Hopeful, the drizzle changed to rain. As they were being lined up for the start, the rain became a downpour.

Starter Mars Cassidy (recovered from his previous ailment) had the very devil of a time. Man o'War lunged through the barrier several times and even kicked another horse. It seemed there was a conspiracy to shut off Man o'War early. Every time Man o'War got back in line, another jockey pulled his horse out of line. With the heavy rain, the other jockeys, and Man o'War's natural antipathy to the starting gate, it took Cassidy twelve minutes to start the race.

Cassidy finally raised the barrier, and they were off. A filly, Constancy, took the early lead followed by another horse, Dr. Clark. Man o'War broke well, and he cruised nicely. Constancy lead going around the turn, but Man o'War closed on her. At the top of the stretch, Loftus let him go, and Man o'War thundered by the filly. The charge was so great that it looked as if "he was running all alone." He splashed through the muddy track four lengths ahead of Constancy. As they neared the finish line, Loftus, mindful of the track conditions, pulled his horse up and looked around for challengers. No one was close.

Max Hirsch, a veteran horseman, watched the race. His take on Man o'War: "He is a marvelous horse. I have never known his equal in my time."[12]

Man o'War's last race of 1919 was the 3/4-mile Belmont Futurity at Belmont Park on September 14. He had established himself absolutely as the best two-year-old around, and there seemed not much purpose in running him in many more races and risking an injury. Nine horses challenged him, including Upset, but no one really felt that Man o'War would be beaten. For this race, Loftus let him stay in third for the first quarter-mile. Then he made his move. Man o'War passed the lead horses easily and eventually won by 2 1/2 lengths.

The season closed with ten Man o'War races; nine victories, and the oh-so-close second place in the Sanford Stakes. He won $82,725 for the year. *The*

---

[12] Twenty-five years later, Hirsch had the chance to train a pretty good horse himself: Assault, winner of the 1946 Triple Crown. Assault's story will be covered in chapter 6 of the next section.

New York Times summed it up: Man o'War had "the most brilliant season enjoyed by a two-year-old since the days of Colin."[13] Wisely, Riddle and Feustel decided that it was time for a rest. They didn't need to risk Man o'War in any more two-year-old races when the rich prizes of a three-year-old season lay ahead. In 1920 he would be a year older, a year stronger, a year more experienced. What would happen then?

Riddle and Feustel returned Man o'War to Glen Riddle Farm on Maryland's shore for the winter. He spent those good days playing and running. He filled out, grew stronger and taller, and gave everyone the impression that he was the horse to beat in 1920.

This most fiery of racers was generally pretty tranquil in the stall. He was curious about all the goings-on around him. He had one bad habit: he seemed to worry between races and took to chewing on his hooves, much like humans chew on fingernails. To calm him, Riddle and Feustel put a retired fox hunting horse named Major Treat in the stall next to him. The two horses became devoted to each other, to the point that, after a race, if Man o'War didn't see his horse friend, the champion would snort and kick the walls of his stall until Major Treat came back into view. Major Treat would accompany Man o'War to the post and then draw away. That may have been one reason Man o'War was so fractious at the post: he may have been upset because Major Treat was no longer near and he wanted to get the race over with.

He was a big eater; so much so that Feustel put a bit in his mouth to slow him down. Otherwise Man o'War was apt to develop colic.

Security became a problem. Glen Riddle Farm regularly heard rumors that something was going to happen to the champion. Ominously, the rumors usually ended with the admonition, "Be prepared." George Conway, Feustel's assistant, or Frank Loftus, Man o'War's groom (no relation to John Loftus,) now slept in a stall next to Man o'War.[14] The concerns grew to such an extent that Riddle even worried about Feustel. Riddle had Feustel followed by a private detective.

Nothing came of these threats. With the rest, growth, care, and security, Man o'War made his 1920 debut on May 18, in the Preakness Stakes at Pimlico. He was hale, hearty, and ready to race.

The 1920 Kentucky Derby is remembered as the race that Man o'War

---

[13] Colin raced in 1907-08 and was unbeaten in twelve races as a two-year-old and three races as a three-year-old. He was one of the great horses of all time.

[14] George Conway also trained a great race horse: he trained War Admiral, Man o'War's best son and winner of the 1937 Triple Crown. Conway's life and career will be discussed in the section on War Admiral.

didn't run in. Why didn't he run in it? The popular explanations were that a) Riddle didn't like "western" racing (the west being defined as anything west of Baltimore), and b) he believed that a 1 1/4-mile race at 126 pounds in early May was too far, too much, and too soon for the young horse. Riddle's concerns about the distance, weight and timing of the Derby are still valid. In 1920, the Derby had only just returned to national prominence (recall the earlier discussion on the Derby's history.) As will be seen, Riddle broke his rule about *not* entering his horses in the Derby only once, with War Admiral in 1937.

There is another explanation, far more prosaic than Riddle's beliefs, for why Man o'War didn't run in the 1920 Kentucky Derby. In all likelihood, he would have won it. Two of his sons, Clyde Van Dusen in 1929, and War Admiral in 1937, won the Kentucky Derby and there's virtually no reason to think that Man o'War wouldn't have done the same. In the 1950s Louis Feustel was a publican in southern California. A bar patron befriended him, and one day asked Feustel about the 1920 Derby. There were three reasons, the old trainer said: they didn't want to risk the long train trip to Kentucky with Man o'War; the horse was off his feed and not doing well; and they wanted to save him for the summer races ahead and not tire him out with an early spring campaign.[15]

Whatever the explanation, Man o'War was denied the opportunity to be the second Triple Crown winner. (The first was Sir Barton in 1919, who is the subject of the next chapter.) Riddle and Feustel pointed him in the direction of Pimlico and the Preakness on May 18, 1920. And here a new problem emerged: For reasons that are still unknown, John Loftus, clearly the number one jockey of the day, had his Jockey's license suspended in 1919. Riddle forgave Loftus for Man o'War's defeat in the Sanford Stakes, and even went before the Jockey Club to have Loftus reinstated, to no avail. So Riddle and Feustel engaged Clarence Kummer, a jockey that exercised Man o'War at Saratoga in 1919. The combination of Kummer and Man o'War made a great team — as great as Loftus and Man o'War in 1919.

> *"Marylanders have seen some of the greatest Thoroughbred of American history perform at Pimlico and other State tracks, but it was the consensus of expert opinion, after watching Man o'War win the Preakness yesterday at Old Hilltop, that nothing like him ever has been seen in action."*
> — C. Edward Sparrow,
> *Baltimore Evening Sun,* May 19, 1920.

---

[15] Paul Jones, the horse that won the 1920 Kentucky Derby, occupies a unique and sad position in racing history. Many horses have been overshadowed by the horse that beat them. Some horses, like Affirmed, are compared to the horse they beat [e.g. Alydar.] But Paul Jones is the *only* Kentucky Derby winner that is overshadowed by a horse that wasn't even entered in the race: Man o'War.

On May 18, 1920, Man o'War was the bettors' choice at odds of 4 to 5. Those were low odds for him, but handicappers knew he had been away from the track for almost eight months. Layoff or no, Man o'War took up where he left off in the Belmont Futurity, silencing any doubts as to his fitness in the first few strides after the barrier was raised. Upset, his old adversary, took an immediate lead, but by the clubhouse turn, Man o'War took over the lead. Kummer kept him under restraint for most of the race. Only at the end did Upset challenge the champion. It wasn't enough, and never would be; Man o'War won by 1 1/2 lengths. The closeness at the end was due to Kummer's restraining him for most of the race; Man o'War could have won by twenty lengths.[16]

"At the conclusion of the Preakness some experienced horsemen expressed the opinion that Man o'War is undoubtedly the greatest colt that this county has produced in a score of years."
— *The New York Times,* May 19, 1920

Eleven days later Man o'War won the Withers Stakes at Belmont Park. The Withers was an important race then, and Man o'War virtually *had* to run in it. Only two horses challenged him, and he was the 1 to 7 favorite. Once again, he made it look easy: Kummer took him to the lead immediately, and he never gave it up. He won by two lengths and set a new American record for a one-mile race: 1:35 4/5.

In Belmont Stakes history, only two races can be fairly said to have been hopelessly one-sided: Count Fleet's victory in 1943 was the second; the 1920 Belmont was the first. Really, it should have been a walkover for Man o'War, but the Belmont Stakes was the Belmont Stakes, and that was just not permitted. Only two horses, Donnacona and David Harum, were entered, but David Harum was scratched before the race. Sir Barton had set the previous Belmont Stakes time record in his quest for the Triple Crown the year before; everyone expected Man o'War to break it. The real question was by how much.

It was the functional equivalent of a walkover: Man o'War was favored at odds of 1 to 25, and he proved that the odds were right. Kummer took him straight to the lead. The Belmont that year was 1-3/8 miles, and by the quarter-mile, he led by two lengths. He kept that margin through the half-mile, and then he decided to run. At the three-quarter, he led by seven. At the head of the stretch, it was twelve lengths; at the finish, it was twenty lengths. That length margin record lasted twenty-three years, and even today is good enough to hold third place. His time of 2:14 1/5 was a new track record.

---

[16] The author is in possession of a poem, "A Pimlico Dream," in the meter and style of "The Night Before Christmas." The poem relates a ghostly procession of Preakness winners from 1873 through 1994. Man o'War, naturally, is the leader.

Ten days later he won the 1-mile Stuyvesant Handicap at Jamaica. Only one other horse challenged Man o'War and again it was the functional equivalent of a walkover. Kummer took him to the lead immediately. They never gave it up and won by eight lengths. Aside from being one of Man o'War's victories that year, there are two other things notable about the race: first, he carried a massive weight handicap, 135 pounds, while the other horse, Yellow Hand, carried only 103. Carrying *thirty-two* pounds more than his challenger, he still won by eight lengths. Next, even with the weight impost, he went off as the bettors' favorite, at odds of *1 to 100*. *The New York Times* reported: "Having literally smashed world's records and literally scared all the other three-year-olds in the country out of the stakes for horses of that age, Samuel D. Riddle's champion Man o'War had little left except to establish a record for the shortest price ever against a horse in this country..."

Almost scared off, it turned out. Man o'War rested for nearly three weeks and returned to the races on July 10 at the 1 1/8-mile Dwyer Stakes at Aqueduct. Again, he had only one other opponent in the race. But this one was different from the hapless Donnacona or Yellow Hand. His challenger in the Dwyer was John P. Grier, owned by H.P. Whitney, trained by Jim Rowe, and ridden by Eddie Ambrose.

Jim Rowe thirsted for revenge on Man o'War. The Riddle horse had beaten Upset and also another horse he trained, Wildair. Man o'War's continual victories over his horses were just too much to take. With the exception of the Sanford, Riddle's horse beat Rowe's horses every time. Riddle knew Rowe had one good horse left in reserve, John P. Grier. They had only met once before, in the 1919 Belmont Futurity.

John P. Grier was good material, as were his trainer and jockey. They set out to hand Man o'War his second defeat and they very nearly did. John P. Grier carried 108 pounds, while Man o'War carried 126 pounds, the same weight as he carried in the Preakness and Belmont Stakes. Rowe conditioned his horse well; it is said that John P. Grier was one of the fastest horses at one mile around. Rowe was confident: "We'll see if Man o'War can beat a horse that can stay with him all the way. I think he's ready to be taken, and Grier is the horse that can do it," Rowe told reporters.

Man o'War was on the rail at the start of the Dwyer, and Grier was on the outside. The barrier lifted, and the horses went off. But this race was different: instead of taking an early lead, or coming from behind, Man o'War fought from the very beginning. Grier stayed with him every step of the way, and the whole race was a great battle. They did the half-mile is 0:46, a track record, the three-quarter mile in 1:09 3/5, another track record. *John P. Grier just would not fade.* Now it was a fight for life, as it were. They hit the mile in 1:36, yet another track record. Sooner or later, one of them had to crack. Which one would it be?

For the first time, Kummer used the whip. Man o'War kept going, but so did John P. Grier. At the eighth pole, John P. Grier got his head in front of the champion.

Kummer again went to the whip, and Man o'War dug in, came back, and drew even with his challenger. Ambrose applied the whip again, but this time, fifty yards away from the line, it was useless. Grier just was used up. Ambrose eased him a bit, and Man o'War finished 1 1/2 lengths ahead of his challenger.

> *"John P. Grier had his head in front for a moment at the eighth pole, but the moment I went after him in earnest the race was over. As to whether Man o'War was all in, well, when horses run like they did from the start something has to crack and while I would not like to say how much Man o'War had left it was enough so that he could have gone on to give another horse a battle had there been a third horse in the race. He ran a hard race, but he was not all in at the end."*
>
> — Clarence Kummer,
> quoted in *The New York Times,* July 20, 1920.

The Dwyer Stakes was the high-point of Man o'War's career. Never again did he face such a challenger as John P. Grier. His time of 1:49 1/5 set yet another American record. It was his greatest race, and he got a well-deserved one-month rest before going back to the track.

Man o'War raced next at Saratoga on August 7, 1920. The occasion was the 1 3/16-mile Miller Stakes. There was not much competition expected for him, but something could always go wrong. During Man o'War's month of rest, Kummer rode other horses. In a race at Jamaica, he took a spill and fractured a shoulder. *That* kept him out of the Saratoga meet. Riddle and Feustel contacted J.K.L. Ross, owner of Sir Barton, the first horse to win what was later called the Triple Crown. Ross's contract jockey was Earl Sande, and Ross agreed to let Sande ride Man o'War in the Miller Stakes.

It was a risk; Man o'War had known only two jockeys, John Loftus and Clarence Kummer. They both did well on him, but who could tell in advance how he would do with a new rider?

Riddle and Feustel needn't have worried. Sande was in the nascent stages of one of the greatest jockey careers of all time. Man o'War was at the peak of his prowess. All the worries about the jockey change were dispelled when the barrier was lifted in the Miller Stakes. Man o'War went straight to the lead. Sande held him in restraint throughout the race, but Man o'War's two other challengers never threatened. Sande and Man o'War cruised home six lengths in front with a time of 1:56 3/5. Even under restraint, Man o'War came within 3/5 of a second of the track record.

After the race, Sande was more tired than his horse; the jockey held him back for the whole race. The press asked the jockey for his opinion of Man o'War: "I never felt anything under me like that colt in my life. Why, he is the greatest horse I've ever ridden." (Sande's candor cost him with his regular employer, J.K.L. Ross. When Sande had an opportunity to ride Sir Barton against Man o'War, we shall see that Ross replaced him at the last minute. Perhaps part of the reason was Sande's earlier praise of Man o'War.)

Man o'War was back, and it was time for the Travers Stakes on August 21, America's oldest continuous race, and one of its most prestigious. Man o'War faced Upset and John P. Grier again, but the Riddle horse was still favored at 2 to 9. There was yet another jockey change: Kummer was still unable to ride, and J.K.L. Ross had sent Sande to race in Canada. Riddle and Feustel hired Andy Schuttinger. Schuttinger was a fine jockey, a good judge of pace. By all accounts, the 1 1/4-mile Travers, with Man o'War facing his two great challengers with yet another new jockey, should have been his toughest race.

But it wasn't. Man o'War jumped off to an immediate lead and never gave it up. Both Upset and John P. Grier tried, but they never seriously challenged the great champion. Perhaps all their other battles with him had taken something out of them. Schuttinger and Man o'War finished 2 1/2 lengths in front with a time of 2:01 4/5 that matched the track record for that distance. It was so easy that Schuttinger was actually standing up in the stirrups as they crossed the finish line, trying to slow his horse down.

With that triumph, Man o'War left Saratoga for good. He ran well there, but it was time to go back to Belmont Park. The Lawrence Realization Stakes, a 1 5/8-mile race, was scheduled for September 4. As in the Belmont Stakes, Man o'War scared off every other horse around. One horse, Sea Mint, was entered and subsequently scratched. Mrs. Walter Jeffords, a prominent horsewoman, came to the rescue. She entered one of her horses, Hoodwink, and prevented a walkover.

But like the Belmont Stakes, it was the functional equivalent of one. No one gave Hoodwink a chance, and Man o'War again went off at odds of 1 to 100. The race was never in doubt. Kummer had recovered and was back on Big Red, while Eddie Ambrose rode the sacrificial entry. We will never know exactly *how* far Man o'War finished ahead of Hoodwink, but the official race chart has it at *100* lengths. It is still the length record for any race. And, Man o'War did it again: he ran the race in time of 2:40 4/5, yet another American record.

The Jockey Club Gold Cup, a 1 1/2-mile race, was next for Man o'War on September 11.[17] Again, only one other horse could be found to run against him. This was Damask, owned by H.P. Whitney, and ridden again by Eddie Ambrose. By now, victory was getting repetitious: Kummer took Man o'War to the lead immediately. Despite Ambrose's best efforts, it was no contest. Man

---

[17] It will be noted in later chapters that the Jockey Club Gold Cup became a two-mile race. Many prominent races have been run at varying distances over the years.

27

o'War finished fifteen lengths ahead of Damask in time of 2:28 4/5 to set yet another American record.[18]

The great Belmont Races were over: the Withers, Belmont Stakes, Lawrence Realization, and Jockey Club Gold Cup. Man o'War won *all* of them. There wasn't much more he could do in New York, so he was taken south to Havre de Grace, Maryland, for the 1 1/16-mile Potomac Handicap on September 18. He carried a staggering weight burden — *138 pounds* — and that drove the odds on him down slightly to 15 to 100. Three other horses challenged him: Wildair, Blazes, and Paul Jones, the Kentucky Derby winner. There was the trip to Maryland, all the previous racing, the weight burden, and none of that made any difference. Kummer and Man o'War made it look easy. Once again, they jumped off to the lead at the start and never gave it up. Man o'War finished 1 1/2 lengths ahead of Wildair, 16 1/2 lengths ahead of Blazes, 18 1/2 lengths ahead of Paul Jones. His time of 1:44-4/5 was a track record.

Man o'War struck himself in the Potomac Handicap and his tendon bowed slightly. It could have been a career-ending injury. Feustel and George Conway looked after him and he came around quickly. But the injury had to give Riddle and Feustel pause: Man o'War carried the massive weight and was only slightly injured. He might not be so lucky a second time. Moreover, it was time to consider a 1921 racing campaign. Riddle inquired of the Jockey Club what the handicap weights for Man o'War would be in 1921. He was told, "More weight than any other horse has ever carried." How much? 145, even 150 pounds. That was begging for trouble. What if Man o'War broke down in a race and had to be destroyed? Riddle wisely decided not to tempt fate. He announced that a match race against Sir Barton, the first Triple Crown winner,[19] would be the final race of Man o'War's career.

That race was run on October 17, 1920, at Kenilworth Park in Windsor, Ontario, Canada. Man o'War went into the race the heavy favorite, and it was no contest. Although Sir Barton took an early lead, Kummer and Man o'War took the lead after the clubhouse turn, stayed there, and eventually won by seven lengths. Man o'War ran the 1 1/4-mile race in 2:03 and set a new track record. Moreover, Man o'War brought home $75,000 for Sam Riddle. That made the great horse the leading American money-winner. The victory was so emotional that Riddle emptied the gold trophy cup holding champagne, filled it with water, and let Man o'War drink from it.

There is one other matter to report: Kummer's stirrup leather had been slashed. Whoever did it obviously hoped that the leather would break, causing

---

[18] Man o'War was again quoted at odds of 1 to 100, and the one-sided nature of the contest had a curious result: It was one of the few times his victory did not make headlines. It was getting to be old stuff.

[19] The match race from Sir Barton's perspective will be related in the next chapter.

Kummer to fall off and thus give the race to Sir Barton. The job was done so cleverly that the slashed stirrup leather was not found until after the race.[20]

It was Man o'War last race. Suggestions were made that he go to England to race, but Riddle turned those down. After a triumphant tour through the east and some time in Maryland, he was returned to Kentucky. For a short time he stayed at Elizabeth Dangerfield's farm in Lexington. In the spring of 1922, Riddle bought Mount Brilliant Farm, which was a bit farther away from Lexington. Riddle and Dangerfield worked together; the barns and paddocks were rebuilt, and they renamed the property Faraway Farm. Man o'War was moved to Faraway Farm in May of 1922, and it was there that Big Red spent the last twenty-five years of his life.

The later careers of John Loftus and Earl Sande will be related in forthcoming chapters. Clarence Kummer lived only ten years after Man o'War retired. Kummer rode Coventry to victory in the 1925 Preakness, but the following year his career disintegrated. He had only one mount in 1926, and less than fifty mounts each year in 1927 and 1928. One of those was impressive: He won the 1928 Belmont Stakes on Vito. But that was it; he did not ride in 1929 and 1930. Overall, Kummer rode in 2,468 races in thirteen seasons, winning 464, placing in 405, and showing in 350. He had a win percentage of 18 and a money percentage of 49.

In the middle of December, 1930, Man o'War's second jockey contracted pneumonia. In those pre-antibiotic days, pneumonia was tantamount to a death sentence. Clarence Kummer died early on December 18, 1930, in Jamaica, New York. He was thirty-one years old. Sam Riddle said, "He rode a great many races for me, and he never gave me a bad ride."

Louis Feustel lived fifty years beyond Big Red's retirement. He continued to train horses, and left Riddle to work for Elizabeth Arden Graham's stable. He worked there for four years, and dabbled in training for some time thereafter. He moved to California and operated a pub near the Santa Anita Track in the late 1950s. Mementos of Man o'War were displayed on the walls of the pub, but few of the patrons made a connection between the elderly bartender and the photos and relics of Man o'War in view. In the late 1960s Feustel moved east to live with a daughter. He died in July, 1970.

Man o'War in retirement was both a folk hero and a great sire. He stayed

---

[20] The Man o'War/Sir Barton match race is historically significant. It was the first horse race on a circular track ever filmed in its entirety by movie cameras. Edward Muybridge, who forty years earlier had been the first photographer to record a running horse on film, was in charge. He used fourteen cameras to record the race. The film of the race survived, and parts of it can be seen in the videotape, "Jewels of the Triple Crown."

frisky into late life, capable of kicking up his heels, and coming out of his stall rearing, flailing his front legs in the air. He sired 386 registered foals. His greatest was War Admiral , who won the Triple Crown in 1937. Man o'War also sired Clyde Van Dusen, who won the 1929 Kentucky Derby, American Flag, who won the 1925 Belmont, and Crusader, winner of the 1926 Belmont. Also, he sired Battleship, the 1938 winner of the English Grand National Steeplechase.

Man o'War's influence is still felt dimly even today. Through War Admiral, he appears in the bloodlines of the last two Triple Crown winners, Seattle Slew and Affirmed. Through American Flag, he appears in the bloodlines of Alydar and his son, Alysheba, who was the all-time leading money winner until displaced by Cigar, a Seattle Slew grandson, in 1996. Many experts believe a horse has little or no influence in a bloodline beyond the grand-sire level. That's probably true, but it is nice to believe that the spirit of Man o'War is still at work, however faintly, in modern racehorses.

To the public Man o'War's siring record wasn't as important. Hundreds of thousands of people came to see him in retirement, and the visitors got a good show. His groom, Will Harbut, became a legend, probably the most famous groom in racing history. Harbut would lead Man o'War (or as Harbut pronounced it, "Mannie Wah") out to a waiting crowd, and in a full deep southern African-American voice, would regale the onlookers with tales of "Mannie Wah's" racing career and life. Harbut was almost as big an attraction as the horse. Once, the British Ambassador, Lord Halifax, came to Faraway Farm to see Man o'War and hear Harbut's spiel. The groom didn't disappoint: Harbut went on for twenty minutes while the British aristocrat-diplomat sat spellbound listening to the African-American horse groom. Afterwards, Lord Halifax said, "It was worth coming halfway around the world to hear that."

The champion had a long and wonderful retirement, but by 1947 it was clear that Man o'War had not much longer to live. He suffered a heart attack in 1943 and was retired from stud. He outlived his contemporaries and many of his own offspring. Man o'War had suffered three previous colic attacks, but recovered from them. But time now ran short; Sam Riddle commissioned a statue of him. Man o'War posed proudly for it, but after the model was finished, Big Red suffered yet another colic attack. This one was more trying for him. Moreover, he may have been lonesome; Will Harbut had a heart attack of his own in the spring of 1947 and was no longer able to come to Man o'War's stall. So, Riddle closed Faraway Farm's gates to visitors. Man o'War had been retired from racing some twenty-six years and had been seen by countless visitors. (A half-million people signed Faraway Farm's guest books in those years, but that number obviously does not hint at the numbers of visitors that did not sign a guest book.)

The next few months were quiet for Man o'War. He stayed in his stall or sunned in the paddock. Will Harbut died on October 3, 1947, and that seemed to signal the end. A few weeks later Man o'War suffered a fifth colic attack. Nothing could be done for him other than administering sedatives to ease the pain. He should have been put down, but Sam Riddle couldn't bring himself to order that done. His instructions were to keep the horse as comfortable as possible to the end. Perhaps Riddle wanted Man o'War to go out as he had raced — *his* way.

Man o'War's long life ended from a heart attack at 12:15 P.M. on November 1, 1947. He was embalmed (the first racer *that* ever happened to) and lay in state at Faraway Farm.[21] Thoroughbred racing fans filed by to see him one last time. The funeral rites were elaborate, and a bugler played "Taps" at the ceremony. Later, Herbert Haseltine finished the statue of him and today it surmounts his grave. Some thirty years later, Man o'War's remains, complete with statue, as well as the remains of War Admiral and War Relic, two of his sons, were moved to the Kentucky Horse Park in Lexington.

In late 1992 *Sports Illustrated* asked a panel of racing experts to name the ten best American Thoroughbreds. The result: Man o'War was *still* in first place, followed by Secretariat and Citation. It will never be clear which one of those three was the best. To choose between those three horses is really a matter of personal preference. But forty-five years after his death, seventy-two years after his retirement, for Man o'War to be named the greatest American racehorse says it all.[22]

The Law of Unintended Consequences is well-illustrated by the semi-deification of Man o'War since 1920. Every year from 1930 to his death, *The New York Times* ran an article commemorating Man o'War's birthday. For the racer's 21st birthday, he was given a cake with icing, but Man o'War was allowed only to sniff and look at it, not to eat it. The hoopla surrounding Man o'War has served only to tarnish him; in this hardened, technological world, the image of Man o'War seems hopelessly artificial. A modern racing fan, looking back to a simpler age when heroes were viewed differently, might ask, "Could all that have been true? Did Man o'War deserve all the tribute? Was he really that good?" Well, it was, he did, and he was. Only two other horses, Citation

---

[21] Man o'War remains the only Thoroughbred racer to be embalmed, thus giving him another record of sorts. Only one other racehorse, a harness horse named Meadow Skipper, was embalmed at his death in 1982. For the reader with morbid curiosity, Man o'War required nearly 23 bottles of embalming fluid.

[22] Man o'War did it again in 1999. In its February 22, 1999 issue, *The Blood-Horse* published a list of the Top 100 Thoroughbreds of the Twentieth Century. Once again, Man o'War led the list, again followed by Secretariat and Citation. See Appendix IX for the rankings as applied to the horses in this book.

and Secretariat, seriously challenge him for the title of the greatest racehorse of all time.

MAN o'WAR with groom Will Harbut. © *Collection of L. S. Sutcliffe, C. Ken Grayson, Owner. Used by permission.*

II. THE TRIPLE CROWN CHAMPIONS

"Opinions die, records live."
— John Madden,
breeder of Sir Barton,
first Triple Crown Champion.

1. THE UNKNOWN: SIR BARTON

Triple Crown, 1919. Jockey, John Loftus

"Horsemen speak of Thoroughbreds with this faraway gaze as 'having the look of the eagle' and they believe that it is invariably the sign of greatness. Sir Barton was an irascible, exasperating creature. But he had the look of the eagle."
—J.K.M. Ross,
Boots and Saddles, 1956.

The first Triple Crown winner was not called a Triple Crown winner. As we have seen, the term was first popularized in the 1930s. Sir Barton was the first horse to win the Kentucky Derby, the Preakness Stakes, and the Belmont Stakes. The honor of being the first Triple Crown winner was bestowed on him retroactively. Of all the horses that won those three races, he had the strangest life.

During the period 1918-1920 three horses dominated Thoroughbred racing: Exterminator, "Old Bones," (the horse that started a hundred races in eight years and won fifty of them) was the star in 1918; Sir Barton dominated the next year; and Man o'War in 1920. It is curious that the least of these, Sir Barton, was the only one of them to win the three most important races.

For the xenophobe, Sir Barton wasn't even a 100 percent red-blooded

American horse. He was the son of Star Shoot (whose sire, Isinglass, won the English Triple Crown in 1893) and the filly Lady Sterling[1]. Sir Barton was foaled in the U.S. on April 26, 1916, at John E. Madden's Hamburg Place in Lexington, Kentucky, (the barn in which he was born still stood in 1993) but was owned during most of his racing career by Commander J.K.L. Ross of Canada. Sir Barton's sire had delicate hooves, and Sir Barton turned out to be even more tender-footed than his sire. Sir Barton's hooves were so soft that he frequently lost one horseshoe in a race. In one race, he lost all four shoes. His farrier had to layer piano felt between each hoof and shoe. One can only speculate as to the task that shoeing Sir Barton must have been.

He was not a friendly horse: Sir Barton was surly. He ignored other horses, and despised humans, (with the apparent exception of his groom, Toots Thompson.) J.K.M. Ross said: "As for other deficiencies, I think I can blanket them as the products of a nasty disposition. Sir Barton was at times downright evil."

Sir Barton kicked powerfully, and if upset, he lashed out and attempted to bite anything or anyone in reach. Many racehorses love animal companionship — another horse, a dog, or a cat — but not Sir Barton. He took little interest in anything that went on around the farm, refused to have any kind of animal friend, and apparently, lived only for racing.[2] He was difficult to train, and had to be tricked into workouts. Other horses had to be present and running on the practice track to simulate racing conditions. Bedwell once remarked of Sir Barton, "To get him fit you have to half kill him, and a lot of other horses as well."[3]

Some of his surliness may have been due to his sore hooves, but one allegation which traces back to the famed sportswriter Red Smith holds that Sir Barton was celebrated as a "Great Hophead"— one stoned on cocaine to run faster.

A most unlikely candidate for immortality? Absolutely. But that, too, is a

---

[1] In strict form, it should be written *Star Shoot. The asterisk in front of the name denotes a horse imported into the USA. This convention would also apply to other horses mentioned in this book such as Sir Gallahad III, Gallant Fox's sire; Blenheim II, Whirlaway's sire; Hydroplane II, Citation's dam; and Noor, a horse that competed against Assault and Citation in 1950. However, I have found in practice that the asterisk before the horse's name is distracting, and I have omitted it for reading ease.

[2] His conduct on the track was nearly the exact opposite of his conduct when not racing: Sir Barton almost never acted up or tried to bite another horse during a race.

[3] These characteristics of Sir Barton have been widely-quoted, although the evidence for them is scanty. J.K.M. Ross, the son of J.K.L. Ross, made these assertions in his 1956 chronicle of the Ross stables, *Boots and Saddles*. He ought to have known what his father's most famous racehorse was like.

part of his legend. In the 1960s Sir Barton would have been an icon of the counter-culture: an anti-hero, a rebel, the loner who came out on top. His image is perversely appealing: the foreign-owned, surly, sore-footed, possibly drugged-up, difficult-to-train, human-hating loner, the antithesis of a public relations man's dream...and still the first to win the three most important American races.

Sir Barton's racing career resembled the plot of a Grade B movie of the 1930s: the unknown who came out of obscurity, briefly dominated his field, sank back into obscurity, and finally died in exile. He is overshadowed by the horse that came before him and also by the horse that came after him. But Sir Barton starts the saga of the Triple Crown winners.

Sir Barton's two-year-old racing season was lackluster. He didn't finish higher than fifth in any of his first four starts. But he immediately attracted attention: in his first start, the Tremont Stakes on July 6, 1918, he finished fifth. The race chart notes say, "Sir Barton, a good looker, rated green and is promising." So there was something about him; maybe it was his large chest and dark chestnut coat, maybe something else.[4] Even as a yearling, he attracted attention. A handler at breeder John Madden's Hamburg Place showed a visitor Madden's newest crop of foals. The handler guided the visitor to a separate stall, where he pointed to the young Sir Barton and said, "Here is the king of them all."

In August, 1918, after Sir Barton's fourth race, J.K.L. Ross entered the picture. J.K.L. Ross was the son of a founder of the Canadian National Railway and the younger Ross apparently inherited $12 million from his father. He commanded a destroyer for the fledgling Royal Canadian Navy in World War I, earning the title "Commander" from his sea-faring days. Ross was, in the spirit of the wealthy of that day, interested in philanthropy, yachts, and Thoroughbred horses. During the period 1918-1922 Ross' stable was at the top among North American stables. Ross employed H. Guy Bedwell as a horse trainer, and Bedwell purchased Sir Barton in 1918 from John E. Madden for about $10,000 (the exact price is unknown.)

H. Guy Bedwell was tough; his nickname was "Hard Guy" Bedwell, and he was one of the best trainers around. He was born in Oregon in 1876 and became a cowboy in his early teens. In that frontier environment, he learned

---

[4] There is a good reason for the mediocrity of Sir Barton's two-year-old record. His first starts were while he was owned by John E. Madden. Madden was primarily a horse breeder, although he kept and raced a *few* horses for himself. Madden didn't want to push two-year-olds, preferring to save his mounts for a three-year-old season. Therefore, Madden did not bring Sir Barton along in his two-year-old season as another stable might have. When Madden sold Sir Barton to J.K.L. Ross, things changed quickly.

about horses quickly. He drifted throughout the west and at one time was the county clerk for Mesa County, Colorado. But horses continued to attract his attention and he opened a livery stable in Grand Junction, Colorado. From there he built a racecourse for the Mesa County fairgrounds, and from that start traveled to one local fair with horse racing after another throughout the west. He was very successful with his own stable of local racehorses, but the purses were small. Bedwell decided to get into the big time, and he moved east.

In his first season, horses that he trained won sixteen races in fourteen days. That caught everyone's attention immediately. He was the leading winning trainer in 1909 and again during the years 1912 through 1917. Bedwell's training methods were unusual for the care and feeding he gave his horses: instead of one heavy horse blanket, he covered his charges with several lighter blankets. The feeding program was fairly simple, but not one used by eastern horsemen: a nightly supply of cooked oats and corn mixed with bran. And Bedwell believed in the curative effects of one of nature's oldest remedies: mud. He opined that the best cure for aching hooves was to make the horses stand in pails filled with mud. (This belief paid off at Churchill Downs on May 10, 1919.)

The western upstart quickly gained a reputation as a trainer who could take a losing horse and make him or her into a winner. J.K.L. Ross heard about him and hired Bedwell in the autumn of 1917. The "Hard Guy" took over training the sore-footed grouch, Sir Barton.

Bedwell was all business. He was, in J.K.M. Ross's words, "…a hard-hitting relentless campaigner who gave himself completely to his job." Ross also said that Bedwell had little apparent sentiment, but he had a soft side, too. When Sir Barton came down with life-threatening blood poisoning, Bedwell nursed Sir Barton night and day and rarely left the stall until the crisis passed. Later, he refused any credit for the medical treatment. He attributed the cure to "Sir Barton's own fighting spirit and inherent robustness which pulled him through the critical illness."

The nadir of Sir Barton's two-year-old season was reached on August 31, 1918, when he finished a miserable sixteenth in the Hopeful Stakes at Saratoga. But from the perspective of history, it was a turning point. It had required a bit of time for Bedwell's training methods to take effect, but in Sir Barton's next race, his last of 1918, he finished second in the Futurity at Belmont Park on September 14. Here he showed what he could do. In the field of fifteen horses in the 3/4-mile straight race, he was fourth after a quarter-mile, third after a half-mile, and by the stretch, moved up to second and stayed there to the finish. The race chart notes said, "SIR BARTON was always racing forwardly and held on resolutely to withstand PURCHASE'S final rush." (The jockey might have made a difference, too. Sir Barton was ridden by Earl Sande, who was just beginning his great jockey career.)

Encouraged, Ross and Bedwell hoped for more from Sir Barton. There were still some races left that autumn, but the horse came down with the blood poisoning mentioned earlier. That brought an end to Sir Barton's two-year-old season.[5] His overall record that year was dismal on its face: six starts; no wins; the second-place finish in the Futurity; no thirds; and five unplaced other finishes. Yet he had showed a bit of talent. There was another year yet to come.

Ross also purchased a horse named Billy Kelly in 1918. Billy Kelly was good material and was teamed with Sir Barton for the 1919 Kentucky Derby. Not much attention was paid to Sir Barton, but one reporter, Sam H. McMeekin of the Louisville *Courier-Journal*, thought Sir Barton might have a chance: "The writer fancies the chances of Sir Barton. This son of Star Shoot has never won a race. But he ran second to Dunboyne in the [Belmont] Futurity and in private trials this spring has demonstrated that he is a high-class colt." One other individual expressed optimism regarding Sir Barton's chances in the Kentucky Derby. Bedwell's assistant, Cal Shilling, worked both Billy Kelly and Sir Barton in morning trials. Therefore, Shilling knew them both and expressed, as J.K.M. Ross put it, "A shadowy and lurking suspicion that the son of Star Shoot might surprise everyone." But McMeekin and Shilling were virtually alone in their opinions.[6]

A "rabbit" is a racing term of art. It refers to a horse that is brought to the race to start out fast and take an early lead. The favorite horse, and most of the pack, for that matter, will presumably take after the rabbit and tire out. Then another horse on the track, from the same stable as the "rabbit", (who has been held back) will have enough energy left in reserve to make a late run, come from behind, and secure a victory. Anyway, that was the quoted strategy of the Ross Stable for the 1919 Derby. The favorites were a pair of horses owned by J.W. McClelland, Eternal and Sailor. J.K.L. Ross's pair came next: Billy Kelly, ridden by Earl Sande, and Sir Barton, ridden by John Loftus.

History has said the Ross-Bedwell plan was for Sir Barton to be the rabbit: to take the early lead, wear out Eternal, Sailor, and the rest of the pack, and allow Sande and Billy Kelly to come on at the end. This is partially true.

---

[5] Even without the blood poisoning, it is doubtful whether Sir Barton would have raced further in the autumn of 1918. That was the time of the great influenza epidemic of 1918. Ross and Bedwell might have curtailed racing for that autumn anyway, for safety's sake.

[6] Carroll "Cal" Shilling is an unsung hero in the Sir Barton story. He was an ex-jockey turned trainer, Bedwell's assistant. Shilling was considered one of the great riders of his day, and won the 1912 Kentucky Derby on Worth. He was elected to membership in the National Museum of Racing and Hall of Fame in 1970. Ross's stable had a substantial depth of talent if such a distinguished horseman as Shilling was only an *assistant* trainer.

Indeed, Ross and Bedwell gave Loftus instructions to set the pace and tire out Eternal, Sailor, and the rest. They, as with most observers, thought that Billy Kelly with Earl Sande up was by far the stronger combination of horse and jockey. But J.K.L. Ross and H. Guy Bedwell were also ready with an alternate scenario; Ross's son wrote years later, "in the unlikely event that Sir Barton did not tire, Loftus was instructed to do his best to win." (Perhaps Shilling's "Shadowy and lurking suspicion" had finally gotten through to Ross and Bedwell.) In short, the plan was for Sir Barton to be the "rabbit," but Ross and Bedwell also thought there was a chance Sir Barton could win.

Moreover, Sir Barton at that point was a "maiden", a horse that had never won a race. That made a difference; as a maiden, Sir Barton received a weight allowance; he only carried 112 1/2 pounds, while Eternal had to carry 122 pounds. (Most of the other horses carried weights of 117 or 119 pounds.)

> *"All that I had to do was sit steady in the boat and let Sir Barton run. I did not even have to cluck at him, as he was running easily at all times and never did he show the least sign of distress. He is a much better 3-year-old than he was given credit for..."*
> — John Loftus,
> *Louisville Courier-Journal*, May 11, 1919

As Robert Burns put it, "The best-laid plans of mice and men..." The plan worked, but not in the primary way that Ross and Bedwell envisioned. On Derby Day, May 10, 1919, the track was heavy from rain. (This, too, might have made a difference. Did the cool mud of the track sooth Sir Barton's sore feet, literally taking the sting out of racing?) Loftus and Sir Barton came out of the pole position and took the lead immediately. By the half-mile, Sir Barton lead by two lengths; by 3/4 of a mile, he led by a half-length. At the mile, he and Loftus led by two lengths; then at the stretch, the lead was a half-length again. Eternal was tiring, and most thought that Sir Barton would tire, too.

But Sir Barton didn't race according to plan. He just kept going and stayed firmly in the lead. Loftus later recalled: "Seeing nothing of Billy Kelly, I gave Sir Barton a cut of the whip, and he jumped off as if it were the start. Then I rode him the rest of the way, figuring to hell with Bedwell, Sande, and Billy Kelly..." Billy Kelly and Sande made a move, but it was too late. Sir Barton pulled away and won by five lengths. Sir Barton and Loftus maintained the lead throughout the race. A J.K.L. Ross horse won all right, but the winning horse was Sir Barton the rabbit, not Billy Kelly. Sir Barton's first start of the year and his very first winning race was the Kentucky Derby.[7]

---

[7] It was the first time that two horses from the same stable finished one-two in the Derby. Sam McMeekin couldn't resist crowing; his story on the 1919 Kentucky Derby began, "I TOLD YOU SO."

*"The orders to Loftus, who was again up on Sir Barton,
were identical to those he had received before the Derby:
'Get to the front as soon as possible and stay there!'"*
— J.K.M. Ross,
Boots and Saddles, on the 1919 Preakness

SIR BARTON, 1919 Kentucky Derby. John Loftus up, Guy Bedwell at bridle. *From the © Collection of L.S. Sutcliffe. C. Ken Grayson, Owner. Used by permission.*

Well, okay, maybe the grouchy horse with the lousy two-year-old record *did* have something. Before the three races were standardized into their modern sequence (two weeks between the Derby and the Preakness, three weeks between the Preakness and the Belmont Stakes) the races were scheduled almost in a random pattern. The Preakness was only four days after the Kentucky Derby that year, but Ross and Bedwell decided to enter Sir Barton.

With only the briefest rest, Loftus and Sir Barton ran in the Preakness against eleven other horses.[8] As in the Derby, Sir Barton and Loftus were paired

---

[8] This fact made the Preakness results even more remarkable. These were the days before interstate highways and air-conditioned horse trailers, or shipment by air. The only real way was to send Sir Barton via rail. The railroads were efficient in 1919, but the trip from Louisville to Baltimore was still a long one. Some horses did not travel well by train, although rail travel didn't appear to bother Sir Barton. Anyway, consider Sir Barton's circumstances; a major race, followed by a long train trip, no real rest, and

with another J.K.L. Ross horse, Milkmaid, ridden by Earl Sande. And, as in the Derby, Sir Barton did it again: he grabbed the lead early in the race and never gave it up. Eternal, also racing with four days' rest, stayed close to Sir Barton, at times coming within one length of him, but Eternal tired after the 3/4-mile mark. Sir Barton was six lengths ahead of Eternal at the beginning of the stretch, and Loftus eased him at the end. He won the Preakness by four lengths. The time for what was then a 1 1/8-mile race was 1:53, only two seconds off the record. Sir Barton became the first horse to win the Kentucky Derby *and* the Preakness. What was going on? Was he a fluke? Or, had he come into his own?

> *"Sir Barton has carved his name into everlasting turf fame. He will be remembered and spoken of as the greatest 3-year old of his time, no matter what others do during the season of 1919."*
> — C. Edward Sparrow,
> *Baltimore Sun*, May 15, 1919

After the Preakness, Sir Barton went to Belmont to run in the Withers. The one mile race was important in its time. In the 1940s, sportswriters spoke of a "V Crown", the Triple Crown races plus the Withers and the Wood Memorial — and Sir Barton won *that as well*. This time Bedwell's instructions to Loftus were different: Let Eternal take a lead, and challenge him when he swung wide on the far turn.

Something else was different. By this time, Sir Barton was the up-and-coming race horse. A large crowd surrounded him in the Belmont Park paddock, and track security formed a cordon around him while he was saddled. Strangely, the horse that was so surly in the barn was calm during this commotion. He stayed so until the bugle for the race sounded; then he pricked up his ears. Bedwell legged up Loftus, and Sir Barton got the scent of the race. The jockey had difficulty controlling him as he went through the crowd: He wanted to canter, not trot. Ultimately Bedwell took hold of Sir Barton's bridle and lead him out onto the track.

He had the respect of the crowd. When Loftus and Bedwell entered onto the track with Sir Barton, the crowd cheered loudly. Loftus touched the peak of his cap repeatedly in acknowledgement of the crowd's tributes. Sir Barton may have known the cheers were directed at him. In J.K.M. Ross's words, "His head bobbled up and down in apparent recognition as he led the small procession postward."

Unlike the Derby, the race went exactly according to plan for Ross, Bedwell, Loftus and Sir Barton. On May 24, 1919, five other horses (including Eternal) challenged Sir Barton and Loftus on a fast Belmont track. Sir Barton took the lead for the first quarter-mile, but was eased back. Eternal took the lead

---

then another major race.

by the half-mile and stayed in first to the head of the stretch. Then, as Bedwell predicted, Eternal swung wide on the far turn. At that very moment, J.K.L. Ross, watching the race through binoculars, muttered, "Now! Come on with him, Johnny!"

As if he had heard Ross's muttered instructions, Loftus immediately used the whip on Sir Barton. The Kentucky Derby and Preakness winner responded; he moved up, easily passed Eternal on the inside and took the lead. Sir Barton and Loftus won by 2 1/2 lengths. The time of 1:38 4/5 was the second fastest time in Withers history. Sir Barton wasn't a fluke any more. *The New York Times* put it very well: Sir Barton "...left no doubt in the minds of the 15,000 spectators that he is far above the average and perhaps one of the best that the American turf has seen."

After the Withers, Sir Barton ran the Belmont Stakes on June 11. The Belmont then was shorter than it is now, a 1 3/8-mile race, not the present 1 1/2 miles. Whatever its length, it was still one of the most important races in America. Twenty-five thousand people came to see the horse that was "Superbly muscled, with quarters that indicate strength, and strong, straight legs that taper to the fine point desirable in a horse bred for speed."

Sir Barton took on just two other horses that day; the track was fast, but the start was poor and slow. Sir Barton was at the post and "...leaped into the lead." By the quarter-mile he trailed another horse, Natural Bridge, by two lengths and stayed in second place through the three-quarter mile mark. Sir Barton was fully five lengths behind Natural Bridge at that point, but then Natural Bridge tired, and Loftus and Sir Barton made their joint move. At the head of the stretch they led by three lengths and increased the winning margin to five lengths. They had set a new American record for the 1 3/8 mile of 2 minutes, 17 2/5 seconds. (The third horse, Sweep On, was never a factor, but caught the tired Natural Bridge for second place.)

They had done it, Sir Barton and Loftus. The magnitude of the achievement was not recognized for ten or more years to come. The term "Triple Crown" was not in usage at that time, as we have seen. Sir Barton was simply the first horse to win the Kentucky Derby, the Preakness, and the Belmont Stakes. Loftus, likewise, was the first jockey to win all three races in the same year. Something else was overlooked with the advent of the "Triple Crown": only one other Triple Crown winner, Count Fleet in 1943, won the Withers in addition to the Triple Crown races. In one month, against most expectations, Sir Barton broke his maiden, won four of the most important American races, set a Belmont track record, and became, though no one then knew it, the first Triple Crown winner.

SIR BARTON, the first Triple Crown winner, 1919. *From the © Collection of L.S. Sutcliffe. C. Ken Grayson, Owner. Used by permission.*

Only ten horses followed Sir Barton into Triple Crown membership. More might have entered the fraternity except for "bounce-back"—a euphemism for fatigue. A horse that has won the Derby and Preakness may simply be too tired to run well enough to win the Belmont Stakes.

Bounce-back didn't affect Sir Barton in his Triple Crown races and the Withers, but now it caught up to him. He had been sore when he went to the post at Belmont but managed to overcome that pain to win. Four weeks later he ran in the Dwyer Stakes at Belmont Park, and went in as the favorite over the other two horses entered, Purchase and Crystal Ford. But, Sir Barton carried nine pounds more than Purchase and eighteen pounds more than Crystal Ford. For most of the race, it looked like a replay of the Triple Crown: Sir Barton took the lead at the start and held it for most of the race. But the 1 1/8 miles in the Dwyer with the weight imbalance, coming so soon after the other races, were too much. He was first at the stretch, but tired. Purchase caught him in the stretch to win by three lengths. Still, the effort was impressive; after all the other racing, and carrying extra weight, Sir Barton ran well.

That was a signal. A tired horse with that much extra weight was just daring a crippling or even fatal injury. It was time to rest Sir Barton. Bedwell didn't run him again for two months. His next start was at Havre de Grace,

Maryland on September 11, 1919. It was the 3/4-mile Hip Hip Hooray Purse. Billy Kelly with Sande up was also entered and both of Ross's horses had to carry fifteen more pounds of weight than their nearest competitor. Once again, Sir Barton took the lead early and stayed there through the 1/2-mile mark. Then he tired, and Earl Sande on Billy Kelly took revenge for the Kentucky Derby. They dashed ahead of Sir Barton and won by a length.

The loss could easily be attributed to the extra weight alone, or in combination with fatigue and the layoff from racing. But Sir Barton needed to win again, and he did, impressively, just two days later. It was the 1 1/16-mile Potomac Handicap at Havre de Grace. It should have been named "The J.K.L. Ross Handicap," for only five horses were entered, and three of them belonged to Ross: Sir Barton, Billy Kelly, and the fine filly racer, Milkmaid. Despite another severe weight handicap (132 pounds versus 125 for Billy Kelly and 117 for Milkmaid) Sir Barton went to the lead quickly and stayed there throughout the race. He finished 1 1/2 lengths ahead of Billy Kelly. Milkmaid finished only a neck behind Billy Kelly. Ross's horses finished 1-2-3 in the race, but there was no doubt as to the best horse. The notes to the race chart said, "SIR BARTON outran the others all the way and was never in trouble."

He rested eleven days and raced again in a 1-mile Allowance Race at Havre de Grace. Something didn't go right this time. He wasn't carrying much weight, 110 pounds, but maybe he had been raced a bit too much. He was in second the entire race, but never seriously threatened the winner, The Porter. Three days later, he raced again in the 1 1/8-mile Havre de Grace Handicap. He showed his usual strategy: go out early and hold on to the lead. That had worked in other races, but not this one: he ran in first through three quarters of a mile, but then he faded. He finished third, behind his stable mate, Cudgel, and behind Exterminator. Still, he didn't give up; the race chart notes stated, "SIR BARTON set a fast early pace and hung on resolutely to the end."

John Loftus rode Sir Barton through the Dwyer Stakes. During that time, Man o'War made his debut, and Loftus spent much of the time riding Man o'War while Sir Barton rested in Maryland. In October, Loftus was available again, and went back on Sir Barton for the Maryland Handicap at the Laurel track. The Triple Crown winner was burdened with an incredible 133 pounds of weight; *fifteen pounds* more than any of the other five horses entered. It was a different race for Sir Barton: He was fifth at the start, fourth at the 1/4-mile mark, and Loftus eased him back into fifth at the 1/2-mile. Loftus waited through the backstretch, but made his move on the far turn. Sir Barton picked up horses, passed them, and moved into the lead in the last 1/8 mile. He turned on the speed and "…won going away." His time was 2:02 2/5, the fastest mile-and-a-quarter race run at Laurel. The record stood into the 1950s. (It is also remarkable that Sir Barton could even run at all. During the race, his soft hooves caused him to throw off two horseshoes.)

After the impressive victory, Sir Barton rested for a month. He returned to the turf on November 5, 1919, in the Pimlico Autumn Handicap. Loftus was on Sir Barton again, and they carried 132 pounds. That was eleven pounds more than Milkmaid (who was also entered) and twenty-one pounds more than another entry, Mad Hatter. Sir Barton tried valiantly, but the weight and a slow track were just too much; he went to the inside, near the rail, where the track had been churned up in the other races. He tired and finished third. Still, it wasn't a bad showing, given all the obstacles he faced.

He was entered two days later in the 1-mile Pimlico Fall Serial Weight-For-Age Race No. 2. (These were a series of races matching up a horse's age with a weight handicap.) As a three-year-old, Sir Barton got a break. He and Billy Kelly each carried 120 pounds in the race. The other two horses, The Porter and Lucullite, were each a year older and accordingly carried 126 pounds. Loftus was unavailable, so Clarence Kummer rode Sir Barton. Most of the race was close; Sir Barton was in first by the 1/4-mile mark, but he was only a neck in front of Billy Kelly. The stable mates dueled through the half-mile mark, but The Porter passed Billy Kelly and Sir Barton at the 3/4-mile mark. Then Sir Barton dug in, came back, passed The Porter, and won by two lengths. As the race chart put it, "SIR BARTON showed a high flight of speed from the start and held the race safe all the way, shook off THE PORTER in the last eighth and won easing up."

Sir Barton's last race of 1919 was at Pimlico on November 11, in the 1 1/8-mile Pimlico Fall Serial Weight-For-Age Race No. 3. Only Billy Kelly and Lucullite challenged Sir Barton in that race. Clarence Kummer rode him, and Kummer allowed the other horses to come up close through the clubhouse turn. On the backstretch, Kummer let him go and Sir Barton took off; he won easily by three lengths. The race chart said that he "…drew away in the stretch to win in a canter."

The year 1919 was, in J.K.M. Ross's phrase, "the zenith" for his stable. Never again did the Ross stable so thoroughly dominate racing. Ross had other good horses (Billy Kelly, Constancy, Cudgel, and Milkmaid), but Sir Barton was his unquestioned star. The horse spent the rest of the autumn and winter resting at Ross's farm in Maryland. Sir Barton had started the year a maiden, and his journey had been immense: 13 races, 8 wins, 3 seconds, 2 thirds. He was never out of the money. Sir Barton won the Kentucky Derby, the Preakness, the Withers, the Belmont Stakes and four other races. His losses, such as they were, could be accurately and easily attributed to fatigue, weight, and/or bad track conditions. Sir Barton won $88,250, making him the leading money winner of 1919. No "Horse of the Year" title existed in 1919, but in 1973, *The Blood-Horse* created a list of the top racehorses by year, starting with 1901 and ending in 1973. Sir Barton was retrospectively named in that list "Champion Three-Year-Old Colt" and "Champion Horse" for 1919. And, in the 1930s, he was recognized as the first Triple Crown winner. Few horses ever came so far in such a short time.

But remember Satchel Paige's rule for living: "Don't look back. Something might be gaining on you." The second-place money winner for 1919 was the two-year-old, Man o'War. Sam Riddle's fiery chestnut won $83,325 that year. Sir Barton was the champion horse of 1919, all right, but Man o'War was not far behind him and was ready to go in 1920.

J.K.L. Ross briefly considered retiring Sir Barton and not letting him run as a four-year-old. His horse would have to run with weight handicaps, and that risked defeat — and a resultant lower stud value. In the end, Ross' sportsmanship and faith in Sir Barton took over: the Triple Crown winner would run in 1920. If Sam Riddle's colt had a year in 1920 to equal 1919, and Sir Barton was still sharp, there was no way around it. Sometime in 1920, J.K.L. Ross, Guy Bedwell, and Sir Barton would have to cross paths with Sam Riddle, Louis Feustel, and Man o'War.

Sir Barton's first race in 1920 was on April 19 at Havre de Grace. He was entered in the 3/4-mile Belair Handicap with five other horses, Billy Kelly included. Billy Kelly was ready to go; Sir Barton wasn't. Ross and Bedwell sent Sir Barton back to the races before he was properly conditioned. He carried 133 pounds, the most weight of the field. Billy Kelly took the lead from the start; Sir Barton was second for much of the race, but with 1/8th of a mile left in the race, he tired and finished fourth.

Ross and Bedwell entered Sir Barton again at Havre de Grace five days later in the 3/4-mile Climax Handicap. Milkmaid, not Billy Kelly, was his chief rival. He looked like the Sir Barton of the Derby, Preakness, and Belmont; his jockey, Clarence Kummer, took him to the lead immediately, and they never gave it up. He won by 1 1/2 lengths.[9] (Milkmaid finished second.)

Encouraged, Ross and Bedwell pushed their luck. They entered Sir Barton in yet another race just three days later: the 1 1/16th mile Marathon Handicap at Havre de Grace. Again Sir Barton carried the most weight, 135 pounds, while the other two horses, Wildair and Bolster, carried 110 and 106 pounds respectively. There was one other problem: a muddy track. Sir Barton broke well and held second for most of the race, but went wide coming into the stretch. The longer distance of the Marathon Handicap, the tremendous weight penalty, the muddy track, and two races in the previous eight days combined to exact their toll. Sir Barton tired and finished third, 4 1/2 lengths behind the winner, Wildair.

Somehow the message didn't get through to Ross and Bedwell. They gave Sir Barton just two days' rest and entered him in the Philadelphia Handicap at

---

[9] Clarence Kummer was the most fortunate jockey in America at that time. He was riding the previous year's best horse, and in just a month, he would ride Man o'War in most of his three-year-old races.

Havre de Grace, another 1 1/16-mile race. Again, Sir Barton carried the most weight in the field: 132 pounds. The track was fast, which probably didn't help Sir Barton's sore feet any. He ran well, but never got above his final spot of fourth place. The race chart paid tribute to him: "SIR BARTON ran well and finished gamely under his big weight."

Ross and Bedwell just couldn't seem to let Sir Barton rest. They entered him in Pimlico's 1-mile Rennert Handicap just four days after the defeat in the Philadelphia Handicap. He carried 132 pounds again, and once again, it was the most weight carried by any horse in the race. He trailed in second through the far turn, but passed the leader to take over first. It was a battle down the stretch. Another horse, Foreground, challenged Sir Barton. Earl Sande, Sir Barton's jockey in this race, used everything he could to win. They crossed the finish line one length ahead of Foreground.

The narrow win signaled that Sir Barton couldn't go on forever. The concentrated racing, five races in fifteen days, all under incredible weight, was just too much for Sir Barton. He came back from the Rennert Handicap so sore that now Bedwell *had* to rest him. The punishment the horse took in that short time forced him to the sidelines for nearly three months. It wasn't until August 2 that he raced again.

The occasion was the 1 1/4-mile Saratoga Handicap in Saratoga. Sir Barton met four of his old challengers (Mad Hatter, The Porter, Wildair, and Exterminator), and this time he beat them all. He carried the most weight again, 134 pounds, and Sande again rode him. The long rest helped; as he done so often before, Sir Barton took the lead early and never gave it up. Sande said later, "Old Bones [Exterminator] comes up with Andy Schuttinger. We're lapped at the quarter pole. I hit Sir Barton twice. Surprise! He pulls away and we coast under the wire three lengths' winner with a little left." Wildair, The Porter, and Mad Hatter finished in that order behind Exterminator. Sir Barton's time was 2:01 4/5, a new track record. J.K.L. Ross and H. Guy Bedwell were exultant: the old champ was back.[10]

Bedwell had learned something; Sir Barton needed rest between races. Unlike his unfortunate spring campaign, he got nine days' rest before racing in the Dominion Handicap at the Fort Erie track in Canada. Earl Sande rode him against three other horses, and it was no contest from the beginning. Once again Sande took Sir Barton to the front and stayed there. Despite carrying ten pounds more than any other horse in the race, the Triple Crown winner finished 1 1/2

---

[10] J.K.M. Ross in *Boots and Saddles* makes a curious statement: both John Loftus and Earl Sande each chose Sir Barton as his favorite horse for a single race. Loftus's choice of Sir Barton was based on the 1919 Maryland Handicap and Sande's choice of Sir Barton was based on the 1920 Saratoga Handicap. It's curious because each rode Man o'War and Sande later rode Gallant Fox. Still, that says just *how* good Sir Barton could be in a race.

lengths ahead of the pack.

This time Sir Barton rested for seventeen days before returning to Saratoga for the 1 3/16-mile Merchants and Citizens' Handicap. Sande rode him again and as always in 1920, Sir Barton carried the most weight: 133 pounds. The other two horses, Gnome and Jack Stuart, carried weights of 115 and 109 pounds. Again, Sande hustled Sir Barton promptly into the lead and set an incredible pace. In spite of a challenge by Gnome at the end, Sande and Sir Barton won by a neck. Sir Barton's time of 1:55 3/5 was a new American record for a 1 3/16-mile race. A few days earlier, Man o'War ran the Miller Stakes, a race of the same distance as the Merchants and Citizens' Handicap, in time of 1:56 3/5. Man o'War carried 131 pounds in the Miller. With two extra pounds, Sir Barton bettered Man o'War's time.

It was the last race Sir Barton ever won. In twenty-six days, he won the three races he ran and set two records. When he was in top form, no horse could beat him — at least, no horse yet entered against him.

Now the pressure, immense and unavoidable, came for a match race between Man o'War and Sir Barton. J.K.L. Ross and Sam Riddle discussed such a race. Several offers came in, including one from Matt Winn at Churchill Downs. Finally Kenilworth Park in Windsor, Ontario, Canada was chosen. It was a good feeling for Ross; the ex-Royal Canadian Navy officer would race his horse on Canadian soil. But even Ross and Bedwell knew they had bitten off too much. They only hoped Sir Barton would give a good account of himself.

Many races have been called "The Race of the Century" The first Twentieth Century race to seriously claim that title was to be held on October 12, 1920, at Kenilworth Park. The 1 1/4 mile match race between Sir Barton and Man o'War was finally "on". Sir Barton rested between the Merchants and Citizens' and the match race, but he didn't look very sharp in workouts.

Things worsened when the Ross crew inspected the Canadian track. First, the track was dry, rock-hard. That didn't sit well with Sir Barton's tender feet. Then there was a jockey problem; Earl Sande was scheduled to ride Sir Barton, but Sande was extremely nervous. A few days earlier, Sande had ridden one of Ross's horses in a race and had not done well. That was attributed to his nervous state. In fact, some accounts state that Sande was even on the edge of a nervous breakdown. That put Ross and Bedwell in a quandary: John Loftus had his jockey license suspended, so he couldn't ride Sir Barton; Clarence Kummer was unavailable: He was to ride *Man o'War* in the match race. At the very last minute, (just one hour before the start of the race) Ross and Bedwell substituted Frank Keogh.[11] Ross said in part, "I have decided to substitute Jockey Frank G.

---

[11] This race is filled with prominent names. Besides the many racing notables gathered, the immortal tenor Enrico Caruso was present in one of Riddle's boxes. Also present was a fourteen-year-old boy named H.A. "Jimmy" Jones. Twenty-five years later, he and his father became Calumet Farm's trainers, and Jimmy Jones trained

Keogh for Earl Sande on Sir Barton in today's race for the reason that my boy is not in good form, as his recent performances show...Keogh is at the top of his form at present, and I want to take advantage of it so there will be no excuse after the race is won or lost."

The track conditions and the last-minute jockey change were bad enough, but on top of it all, Man o'War had a significant weight advantage. He carried 120 pounds, while Sir Barton, the older and presumably more experienced horse, carried 126 pounds. There's a theory that every pound of extra weight a horse carries correlates to one length on the track, meaning in this race that Sir Barton, by carrying six extra pounds, gave Man o'War the equivalent of a six-length lead.

In the race Sir Barton jumped out to an immediate lead, but after the clubhouse turn, Man o'War passed the Triple Crown horse. Sir Barton stayed two lengths behind Man o'War through the backstretch, but Man o'War pulled away thereafter and won by seven lengths.

Sir Barton never gave up. J.K.L. Ross said during the race, "He's not himself. I think his feet are hurting him, but he certainly is game." (The finish tends to bear out the weight theory: six pounds to Man o'War, a seven-length victory.)

Regardless of the outcome, Ross remained gallant. He was first to congratulate Sam Riddle and even stated that Man o'War could beat any horse in the world. That was probably true.

After the match race with Man o'War, Sir Barton ran three other races, all in Maryland. He finished second

MAN 0'WAR. © *Collection of L.S. Sutcliffe, C. Ken Grayson, owner. Used with permission.*

once and third twice. These weren't bad results, but it has been conjectured that

Citation, one of the few horses to challenge Man o'War for the post of greatest horse of all time. Lastly, Frank Keogh normally rode for Dr. Cary Grayson, President Woodrow Wilson's physician.

the loss to Man o'War took the spirit out of Sir Barton. We'll never know. Unlike Francis the Mule or Mister Ed, Sir Barton couldn't talk and left us with no direct testimony. In Sir Barton's defense, he was another "victim" of Man o'War: *The New York Times* noted that "Every horse that has tried to race with the champion has suffered a setback."

Sir Barton's racing time may have been coming to a natural end in any event. Many horses, most of the Triple Crown winners included, don't race past their four-year-old season, or even after their three-year-old season.[12] All the racing and the soreness might have simply taken the ability out of him. There was also a prosaic reason: Bedwell left Ross's employ in 1921, and Bedwell's successor decided he didn't want to deal with all the problems associated with shoeing Sir Barton. The horse was accordingly retired to stud.

No matter how it ended, Sir Barton had an incredible list of career achievements. He was the first horse to win the Kentucky Derby and the Preakness; the first horse to win the Kentucky Derby, Preakness, and the Withers; the first horse to win the Kentucky Derby, Preakness, the Withers, *and* the Belmont Stakes. He set two American records and one track record. He accomplished all of that with the burden of sore, tender hooves, and quite often, an almost-crushing weight handicap. The question is not, why did he not do better; but rather, how did he do so well?

The year of 1920 was the Rubicon for all the principals in Sir Barton's story.

J.K.L. Ross broke up much of his stable in 1922. He hung on for a few more years, but financial difficulties forced him to curtail all remaining racing activities in 1927. Ross retired to Jamaica and maintained a tie to racing as a steward with the Jamaica Jockey Club. He received the first Triple Crown trophy from the Thoroughbred Racing Association in 1950. He died on July 25, 1951. In keeping with his love of the ocean and his ties to the Royal Canadian Navy, he was buried at sea. He outlived Sir Barton by fourteen years.

H. Guy Bedwell's trainer's license was suspended in 1921-1922. After regaining it, he trained for the Maine Chance Farm after leaving the Ross stable. In his later years, he spent time in the politics of racing, fighting for horseman's

---

[12] Of the horses in this book, Man o'War, Gallant Fox, Count Fleet, and Secretariat were retired after their three-year-old seasons. In addition to Sir Barton, Omaha, Seattle Slew, Affirmed, and Alydar were retired after their four-year-old seasons. War Admiral and Whirlaway each made it into their five-year-old seasons, but just barely: War Admiral raced just once that year before he was retired, and Whirlaway raced only twice in his five-year-old season before being retired. Only Assault and Citation raced past their five-year-old seasons. Those abbreviated careers are evidence of how grueling and punishing Thoroughbred racing can be. It's very possible that, even without the loss to Man o'War, Sir Barton would have been retired after the 1920 racing season.

rights. He had his own stable of racers and also helped form the Maryland Horseman's Association. Bedwell died at his farm in Maryland on December 31, 1951, five months and six days after J.K.L. Ross. He was elected to membership in the National Racing Museum and Hall of Fame posthumously in 1971.

Cal Shilling, the great ex-jockey who worked for Bedwell and prophesied that Sir Barton might surprise everyone in the Kentucky Derby, was found dead under a horse van in Belmont Park on the morning of January 12, 1950. *The New York Times* report attributed his death to natural causes.

John Loftus also rode Man o'War during Sir Barton's victory year of 1919. But after losing the Sanford Stakes on Man o'War, Loftus received a good portion of the blame. He lost his jockey's license after the 1919 season and became a trainer. The reason for the loss of his jockey's license is not known; in those days, it was a common practice for a jockey or trainer to be suspended for a year or two for no apparent reason and then be reinstated. Loftus had some success as a trainer, and remained in that line of work for fifty-one years before his retirement in 1971. Loftus kept a low profile, but was occasionally in the public eye; he was a technical advisor in a 1950 movie on Man o'War.

In ten years of racing, Loftus rode 2449 mounts and won 580 times, a very creditable winning record of 23.7%. He was elected to the National Museum of Racing and Hall of Fame in 1959. The next year Loftus was elected to the Jockey's Hall of Fame at Pimlico, but failed to attend the induction ceremony. In his later years, he lived with his daughter in Carlsbad, California. In March, 1976, at the age of eighty, Loftus was admitted to Tri-City Hospital for surgery. He died on March 20, 1976, of a heart attack.

Sir Barton's post-racing life was the oddest of all the Triple Crown champions. Ross auctioned Sir Barton for stud in 1922. He stood for a time at Audley Farm in Virginia, and later stood in Kentucky. Popular history branded him a failure at stud, which is not quite true. Eight of his foals were stakes winners, and one offspring, Easter Stockings, won the 1928 Kentucky Oaks. During 1928-1930, his foals won $100,000 in purses. A recent article states that Sir Barton's offspring won some 848 races. None, however, came close to his brilliance on the racetrack. One source avers that Sir Barton's talent was siring fillies, and they were more successful in racing than the stallions he sired. In any case, the success he achieved in 1919-1920 raised expectations: He was expected to be every bit as successful a sire as he was a racer. That didn't happen. (As we shall see, only two Triple Crown winners, Count Fleet and Seattle Slew, really passed that test with flying colors, although other Triple Crown winners have been good sires.)

In the early portion of the Twentieth Century, the U.S. Army's

Quartermaster Corps operated the Army Remount Service. It was designed to provide an adequate equine supply for the Army in time of war. The Army bought Thoroughbred stallions and mated them with range mares to produce horses that met the Army's various needs. One of the largest Remount stations was at Fort Robinson, Nebraska, and Sir Barton wound up there in 1933. His stud fee was $5 to $10. At first glance, it sounds like a harsh, tragic exile for such a great racehorse; from the green hills of Kentucky and Virginia to the plains of Nebraska. But at that time, much of the U.S. Cavalry was still horse-mounted, not mechanized. Moreover, the Army had a jumping team at Fort Riley, Kansas. Many officers still owned and rode horses, and horsemanship was an admired skill in the U.S. Army of the 1930s. The Army Remount Service was important, and the acquisition of a great racehorse with some proven siring ability made sense. With that in mind, Sir Barton's relocation to Nebraska may not have been harsh at all. In fact, the care given to Sir Barton by the Army may have been as good, or even better, than that he received in Kentucky or Virginia. Sir Barton apparently sired some horses at Fort Robinson, but later that year he was placed at the ranch of Dr. J.R. Hylton, near Douglas, Wyoming. It was there the first horse to win the Kentucky Derby, Preakness, and Belmont Stakes spent the remainder of his life.

First the Madden family, next J.K.L. Ross, followed by Audley Farm, then the U.S. Army, and finally Joseph Roy Hylton, M.D., of Douglas, Wyoming; Sir Barton's life was punctuated by ownership by one portion of the upper class after another. Dr. Hylton was a country doctor, and a local character. He was one of Wyoming's best-known surgeons, and his medical skills even brought him to the attention of the Mayo Clinic. He was the town doctor for Douglas, and his family owned ranches in Wyoming's Converse and Albany Counties. Hylton was also at one time Wyoming's Democratic National Committeeman. Improbably (for a doctor in 1930s rural Wyoming) Dr. Hylton was a member of the Jockey Club and raised Thoroughbreds in addition to quarter horses and more usual ranch stock. He heard about Sir Barton and bought the racer from the Army.

For four years, the sore-footed grouch grazed on Dr. Hylton's ranch. One picture survives, showing Sir Barton grazing in a corral, snow streaking the earth. While in Wyoming, Sir Barton was apparently once again a sire; a recent article states that some of his Wyoming-born offspring may even have raced in California. It would be fascinating to know how many ranch horses in the Rocky Mountains and Midwest have a bit of the first Triple Crown winner's bloodline in them.

On November 13, 1937, *The New York Times* carried the following article on page 16:

"SIR BARTON DEAD ON WYOMING RANCH"
WINDSOR, Ont., Nov. 12 –Sir Barton, one of the highest priced sires on

the continent and outmatched at his peak only by the great Man o'War, is dead on a farm at Douglas, Wyo., where he had lived in retirement for more than seventeen years.

Formerly owned by Commander J.K.L. Ross of Montreal, Sir Barton was recognized as the greatest Thoroughbred ever to carry a Canadian owner's colors on the turf..."

There was more to the article, but even though the statement about Sir Barton's time in Wyoming was incorrect, the essence was in the opening paragraph: the horse eclipsed by Man o'War. Unmentioned was the drama of the unknown horse that came out of nowhere, captured the racing world so briefly, and returned to obscurity. There was another error in the press release: Sir Barton had died of colic thirteen days earlier, on October 30, 1937.

Sir Barton lies today beneath a fiberglass statue of a horse in Washington Park in Douglas, Wyoming. The statue's existence is a charming epilogue to Sir Barton's story. He was first buried in a nice little plot on Dr. Hylton's ranch. But Dr. Hylton died in 1946, the ranch changed hands, and the first Triple Crown winner rested in almost complete obscurity. In 1968, Gordon Turner, a Douglas native who spent time in Kentucky, started a drive to move Sir Barton from the obscure gravesite into town. Turner put a letter in a racing journal, asking for contributions. The response was sparse. Two elderly men who had been Sir Barton's grooms, one from the horse's racing career, the other from Audley Farm, sent small contributions. The Douglas Junior Chamber of Commerce took over and raised enough money to disinter Sir Barton, rebury him in Washington Park, and erect the statue. The Douglas Jaycees wanted an exact bronze replica of Sir Barton, but there was not enough money for anything more than a generic fiberglass horse. Preston Madden, the grandson of Sir Barton's first owner, initially tried to get Sir Barton's remains returned to Kentucky. That idea was rejected, so Madden donated a plaque for the statue.

SIR BARTON'S grave in Douglas, Wyoming. *Photo by Sandra Matthews.*

The plaque reads:

SIR BARTON

1916-1937

STAR
SHOOT

LADY
STERLING

FIRST TRIPLE CROWN WINNER 1919
(KENTUCKY DERBY-PREAKNESS-BELMONT)
BRED BY JOHN E. MADDEN AND RAISED
AT HAMBURG PLACE, LEXINGTON, KENTUCKY

53

II. THE TRAILBLAZER: GALLANT FOX

Triple Crown, 1930. Jockey, Earl Sande.

> *"I guess that would have to be Gallant Fox, son.*
> *He would always battle for you.*
> *There were never any excuses with him.*
> *The other horse just had to be the best horse if he was to beat him."*
> — Trainer "Sunny Jim" Fitzsimmons,
> when asked which of his horses was the greatest.

Gallant Fox set the pattern for future Triple Crown Winners: the powerful horse with a great jockey that swept away all comers. The Fox was the trailblazer; War Admiral, Whirlaway, Count Fleet, Citation, Secretariat, and Seattle Slew all follow in his hoof prints.

Gallant Fox was the result of the convergence of five great streams of racing history: Arthur B. Hancock's Claiborne Farm; the Fox's sire, Sir Gallahad III; William Woodward; James Edward "Sunny Jim" Fitzsimmons, Gallant Fox's trainer; and Earl Sande, Gallant Fox's jockey in 1930.

Claiborne Farm, in Paris, Kentucky, is without doubt the most durable breeding farm in racing history. Others challenged Claiborne — J.K.L. Ross, Calumet Farm, Faraway Farm, Spendthrift Farm, to name a few — but while many of those vanished or went bankrupt, Claiborne Farm survived. To visit its horse cemetery is to visit the graves of horses that made racing history: Bold Ruler, Blenheim II, Buckpasser, Swale, Secretariat, and Gallant Fox, among others. The farm has stayed within the Hancock family for nearly one hundred years. It is a record of racing accomplishment that is unlikely to be surpassed.

Richard Johnson Hancock, a Confederate soldier, was wounded in a Civil War battle and hospitalized near Charlottesville, Virginia. He fell in love with a Virginia lady, married her, and worked on his wife's estate. His hard work paid off; by the late 1880s, Hancock became a success in the horse business. He had successful studs: Knight of Ellerslie, the 1884 Preakness winner, was one of his stallions.

Arthur B. Hancock, Richard's fourth son, graduated from the University of Chicago in 1895 and went home to run the family business. He, too, was successful, and over time his reputation in the horse community grew. In 1907 he was a judge at the Bluegrass Fair in Lexington, Kentucky, met Nancy Clay there, and fell in love. She inherited her family's farm, and her husband decided to raise horses on the property. Over time, Arthur Hancock transferred his energies to the Kentucky property now called Claiborne Farm.

Claiborne prospered, but like all businesses, it had rough periods, too. One of those came in 1925 when Claiborne lost two stallions and badly needed a good sire. Stories about a French-bred horse caught Hancock's attention. Sir Gallahad III was a champion in England and France. The foreign horse interested him, and Hancock checked into Sir Gallahad III's pedigree.

It was impressive; Sir Gallahad III's sire, Teddy, was the outstanding French stallion in 1923 and his dam, Plucky Liege, was an outstanding broodmare. Hancock inquired if Sir Gallahad III was for sale. Sir Gallahad III's owner replied in the affirmative and offered to let Hancock come to France to inspect the horse. Hancock formed a syndicate to finance the purchase, sailed to France, and within seventy-two hours of landing in Cherbourg, he purchased Sir Gallahad III. Hancock promptly shipped his purchase to America, and Sir Gallahad III became one of the most important sires in American racing history.

William Woodward, one of the members of the syndicate that financed Sir Gallahad III's purchase, was president of the Jockey Club and probably the most influential man in American racing at that time. He had a mare, Marguerite, who only raced once before an injury forced her retirement. Woodward sent Marguerite to Claiborne to mate with Sir Gallahad III. Woodward was to keep any resulting foal. On March 23, 1927, Marguerite gave birth to a son of Sir Gallahad III. It was a bay colt with a blaze face and white coronets. They named the colt Gallant Fox.

Woodward had his own racing priorities: he wasn't overly concerned about two-year-old races such as the Hopeful Stakes or the Belmont Futurity. Woodward wanted to win the major three-year-old races; the Kentucky Derby, Preakness, and Belmont Stakes among others. Gallant Fox was weaned at Woodward's Belair Stud in Maryland, and then sent to Aqueduct Race Track in New York City. Woodward's trainer at Aqueduct was the best in the business: James Edward Fitzsimmons.

It seems just too good to be true, but true it is: One of Thoroughbred racing's greatest trainers, perhaps its greatest, grew up literally on a racetrack. James Edward Fitzsimmons, "Mr. Fitz," "Sunny Jim," was born in Brooklyn, N.Y. on July 23, 1874. In 1877 a new race track was being built in the Sheepshead Bay section of Brooklyn. All but one of the houses presently on the site of the proposed track had to go. The odd one out stood in the middle of the proposed infield, and that house could stay until the very end of the construction. The house belonged to the Fitzsimmons family. Starting at three,

James Fitzsimmons watched the leveling of nearby houses, the construction of the grandstand, the building of the track. He saw something else: the working horses of the construction crews. He got hooked on horses.

After the Sheepshead Bay track was built, the Fitzsimmons family moved to other quarters. In those days, children worked alongside their parents and the young Sunny Jim made deliveries, dug potatoes, and went to school. One of his delivery stops was the stable kitchens at the Sheepshead Bay Race Track, and there, at the age of ten, he got a job as a stable boy at the Brannan Brothers Stable. On March 4, 1885, Grover Cleveland's first day as President of the United States, James Fitzsimmons started his career in racing. (Later Sunny Jim remembered his new co-workers as "…probably all Democrats from the way they were cheering Cleveland.")

He worked with racehorses for another seventy-eight years, and although he became a jockey in 1889, his real fame on the track was as a trainer. For sixty-three years, from 1900 to his retirement on June 15, 1963, Sunny Jim Fitzsimmons was a racing fixture. He got the nickname, "Sunny Jim," because of his good-natured spirit. He almost always had time for people on the track, whether a rich owner or a lowly stable boy. He trained two Triple Crown winners, Gallant Fox and Omaha; he trained Johnstown, winner of the 1938 Kentucky Derby. In his eighties, Sunny Jim trained Nashua, winner of the 1955 Preakness and Belmont Stakes; and Bold Ruler, winner of the 1957 Preakness and later the sire of Secretariat. Sunny Jim's horses won at least 2,275 races, but the exact total will never be known: The records are incomplete for the early portion of his career.

Racing was his life. Even in old age, bent nearly double with spinal arthritis and needing crutches or canes for support, he went to work. In fact, on his last day on the job, James E. "Sunny Jim" Fitzsimmons, age 88, showed up at Belmont at 6:00 A.M., put in a full morning's work, and then headed to Aqueduct for his retirement ceremony. He lived another three years in retirement, passing away in Miami on March 11, 1966, at the great age of ninety-one.

In his career, Sunny Jim Fitzsimmons trained three Kentucky Derby winners, four Preakness winners, five Belmont Stakes winners, six Dwyer Stakes winners, eight Lawrence Realization winners, eight Saratoga Cup winners, and two Triple Crown winners. But only one horse he trained won all of those races: Gallant Fox.

"Sunny Jim" Fitzsimmons (1874-1966). Trainer, Gallant Fox and Omaha.© *Collection of L.S. Sutcliffe, C. Ken Grayson, owner. Used with permission.*

Gallant Fox was temperamentally the opposite of Sir Barton. He was calm, friendly, and curious about what went on around him. In one race, the 1929 Tremont Stakes, he was so interested in what was happening around him that he failed to notice the race barrier raised up. The other horses broke, and Gallant Fox just stood there watching the pack run off. Finally, it dawned on him that he was supposed to race. (Another account of the Tremont says that the Fox got interested in a low-flying airplane over the Aqueduct track and didn't notice the barrier had lifted. Whichever version was correct, the incident showed the Fox's tendency to be distracted.) Usually, during the post parade before a race, Gallant Fox scrutinized the crowd. During the 1930 racing season at Saratoga, there was a baseball game about a mile away. The atmospherics were such that the crowd noise wafted to Gallant Fox's stall and he spent the whole day curious as to the source of the cheers.

Instead of ignoring people, Gallant Fox enjoyed company and was easy to handle. Many horses need to be restrained by a lead. Not so the Fox; once William Woodward watched as two grooms took the bandages off Gallant Fox's legs. The horse was unfettered by any lead or chain. He could have run off at any time. Instead, he just stood there and let the grooms do their work. After the Kentucky Derby, a horde of reporters crowded his stall and some even leaned up against him. Sir Barton would have cleared the stall with one kick, but the Fox just stood there and enjoyed the attention.

He possessed the annoying trait of curiosity and to that must be added Jimmy Breslin's charge that Gallant Fox was "about as lazy an animal as anybody ever came across." If other horses were around him, he ran his heart out. But if no other horses were present, then it was hard to get him to exert himself. Yet, we must disagree with Breslin: Perhaps Gallant Fox *knew* he was the best horse of his time, and he knew when to run and when to conserve himself. If there were no other horses around, why work at it? When he raced, he had one noteworthy trait: as he approached the finish line, he pricked his ears up. It was his way of saying, "Don't worry, I've won this one."

GALLANT FOX, second winner of the Triple Crown, 1930. © *Collection of L.S. Sutcliffe, C. Ken Grayson, owner. Used by permission.*

Of all the Triple Crown winners, Gallant Fox was one of the best-looking. Woodward saw him as a yearling and quickly noted the well-shaped legs, deep shoulders, a rich bay coat, and even then, a good frame. Gallant Fox filled out as he grew and became a truly impressive equine figure. He had one physical oddity; his right eye had a little too much white around the iris, and gave the Fox a perpetual wild-eyed look. Some called it an evil eye, while some called Gallant Fox the "Wall-Eyed Wonder."

59

He wore blinkers, not because he was hard to handle, but because Fitzsimmons didn't want to change things. Gallant Fox ran with blinkers in his first victory, so there was no reason to risk a change. The blinkers, however, were highly modified. A pair of normal blinkers with full eye cups would have restricted the Fox's vision to the point he might think there were no other horses around him in a race. Then he would have slowed down, which meant sure defeat. Fitzsimmons solved that problem by cutting back the eye cups until not much of them remained. His solution allowed the Fox to look around while still wearing "lucky" blinkers. It also allowed other horsemen, a superstitious lot, to claim that Gallant Fox put the evil eye on the other horses.

At times he could be stubborn. When Gallant Fox wanted things *his* way, that was that. On the day of the 1930 Kentucky Derby, Sunny Jim sent him around the track to accustom him to the crowd and the track. A stable boy rode him for that walk, and the trip itself was uneventful. But as Gallant Fox came off the track onto the runway, he stopped, insistent on looking at the Churchill Downs crowd. There he stood for ten minutes, unmoving, unbending. The stable boy knew he couldn't mess around with Gallant Fox, and so he sat there, on top of the horse, waiting for the Fox to finish surveying the crowd. Finally, Gallant Fox unbent and moved back to the paddock.[1]

Gallant Fox's two-year-old record was good, but on its face, not great: seven starts, two firsts, two seconds, and two thirds, one unplaced. It is necessary to look beyond the statistics to find out what really went on: the real story is more impressive than the mere numbers might suggest.

His first start was at Aqueduct on June 24, 1929, in a five-furlong, $1,000 purse race for two-year-old horses. Ten horses started, and Gallant Fox was loaded sixth from the post. When the barrier was lifted, Gallant Fox looked around at the people and scenery and didn't break well. His jockey for that race, J.H. Burke, got him back into the race. He was eighth at the 1/4-mile mark, but he improved and passed most of the other horses. He finished third. The notes accompanying the race chart said "GALLANT FOX raced green, but finished with a rush."

The Fox's finishing rush impressed Woodward and Fitzsimmons; in Woodward's words, "This indicated to us that he was going to be all right...he was beaten due to his fast start and greenness." They started him again, five days later in the 3/4-mile, $5,000 Tremont Stakes at Aqueduct. While he was

---

[1] An allegation crops up occasionally that Gallant Fox went to the winner's circle "with his lights blazing" (meaning that he was doped up.) This seems unlikely. Gallant Fox's exercise boy, by then a veteran horseman, stated fifty years later that he never saw any evidence of doping with Gallant Fox. Moreover, doping a horse was out of character for William Woodward and Sunny Jim Fitzsimmons. If there ever was a horse that *didn't* need doping, it was Gallant Fox.

second choice in the betting, once again, he got into trouble at the start. Whether it was curiosity about the scenery, or a low-flying airplane (still a bit rare in 1930), the barrier was raised and Gallant Fox was left literally at the gate. Twelve other horses started, and Gallant Fox was far behind them. He moved up well during the race, but the bad start was too great a handicap: he finished eighth. Woodward and Fitzsimmons realized that Gallant Fox needed practice at the barrier. He sat out a month and missed the two-year-old races at Empire City at Yonkers. The owner and trainer considered him too valuable to run in those races, and they wanted to save him for the Saratoga races.

On July 29, 1929, Woodward was vacationing at Newport, Rhode Island. He received a telegram from a friend who was at Saratoga. The telegram was a marvel of brevity: "You won Flash by about 2 lengths. Came from behind and going easily at finish. By far best horse in race."

Woodward's entry in the Flash Stakes at Saratoga was, of course, Gallant Fox. It was a 5 1/2-furlong race with twelve horses entered. The Fox had improved during the last month and started reasonably well. He was in sixth place for most of the race, but on entering the stretch, he moved out. He steadily passed the other horses and drew away. Gallant Fox won by 1 1/2 lengths. It was his first victory.

Five days later he ran in the 3/4-mile United States Hotel Stakes, another race at Saratoga. Again he started badly, but quickly got into second place. He passed the lead horse, Hi-Jack, in the stretch, but then Gallant Fox slowed. Another horse, Caruso, also passed the Fox and Hi-Jack to win the race.

The Fox came back sore from the race and rested for a month. Woodward and Fitzsimmons didn't know it then, but Gallant Fox's nature lost the race; after he passed the horses, he slowed down, thinking his work was done. That trait permitted Caruso to come on at the end. In the future, it was necessary to work the Fox with relays of other horses, for as Woodward put it later: "He would race a horse until death, but when it disappeared he would, so to speak, look around for another."

His next start was on September 10 at Belmont in the 3/4-mile Futurity Trial Purse, worth $1,200. Gallant Fox's jockey was Dan McAuliffe, and therein lurked a problem. For some reason, McAuliffe and Gallant Fox didn't work well together. Gallant Fox suffered interference at the start and worse came during the race; he swerved in the stretch. All that prevented him from winning, but the Fox gave a great effort: he finished merely a neck behind the winner.

The Futurity at Belmont, a 7/8-mile race worth $105,730, came one week later. It was a massive field of fifteen horses. McAuliffe rode Gallant Fox again, and in this race the two did reasonably well together. The Fox broke well and stayed in the middle of the track. A horse running on the inside, Whichone, took the lead. Hi-Jack passed by Gallant Fox. The result was Whichone, three lengths ahead of Hi-Jack, and Hi-Jack, a mere nose in front of Gallant Fox.

61

Woodward vowed that his horse would start in the Junior Champion Stakes and then, "win or lose," stop for the year after that.

Gallant Fox's 1929 racing ended with his second victory. Gallant Fox and three other horses entered the Junior Champion Stakes at Aqueduct on September 28. John Maiben rode him and the Fox's start was the usual rocky one. The race was one mile, and for the first three-quarters of it, Maiben let him coast in third or fourth position. Then Maiben let him go and Gallant Fox took the lead at the top of the stretch. He won by two lengths and, in the words of the race chart, "…had speed in reserve at the end."

True to his promise, Woodward ended Gallant Fox's racing season with that victory. The Kentucky Jockey Club Stakes at Churchill Downs was scheduled a week after the Junior Champion Stakes, but Woodward and Fitzsimmons didn't want to risk Gallant Fox with a train trip.

Woodward spent the winter 1929-1930 in Arizona, and kept in touch with Fitzsimmons. The trainer's reports were encouraging. Gallant Fox filled out and trained well. Woodward had his heart set on running Gallant Fox in the Belmont Stakes, but there were other races before that one. In fact, the experts picked the Fox as the early favorite for the Kentucky Derby. The Wood Memorial Stakes in late April was chosen for Gallant Fox's first start of 1930. The trainer was great, the horse was doing well. What was still needed was the right jockey. A couple of Gallant Fox's losses in 1929 might have been due to poor jockeying, a problem that needed to be addressed.

Who could be found to ride Gallant Fox? Only the best would do. Woodward read in a newspaper that a great retired jockey might be making a comeback in 1930. It was manna from heaven, a sign from the Almighty, the perfect solution to the problem at hand. Woodward wrote later, "Although many people thought he had lost his nerve and would not ride with his former ability, I felt that I would much rather have a boy of his great ability, even though not at his best, than someone of lesser merit. Furthermore, I felt that [the jockey's] smoothness and great finish were the requirements necessary to bring out the best in Gallant Fox."

Woodward telephoned the jockey's employer, Joseph Widener, asking whether Earl Sande would be interested in riding Gallant Fox in 1930. He answered in the affirmative, and the rest is history.

In one version of Damon Runyon's poem, "*A Handy Guy Like Sande*", Runyon pays tribute to jockey Earl Sande, creating the closest poem Thoroughbred racing has ever had to "*Casey at the Bat*."

"A Handy Guy Like Sande"

Sloan, they tell me, could ride 'em,
Maher, too, was a bird;

Bullman was a guy to guide 'em—
      Never worse than third.
Them was the old-time jockeys;
      Now when I want to win
Gimme a handy
Guy like Sande
  Ridin' them hosses in.

Fuller he was a pippin,
      Loftus one of the best —
Many a time come rippin'
      Down there ahead of the rest.
Shaw was a bear of a rider,
      There with plenty of dome —
But gimme a dandy
Guy like Sande
  Drivin' them hosses home!

Spencer was sure a wonder,
      And Miller was worth his hire.
Seldom he made a blunder
      As he rode 'em down to the wire.
Them was the old-time jockeys;
      Now when I want to win
Gimme a handy
Guy like Sande
  Bootin' them hosses in!

As with any list of great jockeys, like any list of great athletes, there will be agreement on some names and disagreement as to others. But a few modern jockeys will be found on any list of greats: Eddie Arcaro, John Longden, Bill Shoemaker, Bill Hartack, and Steve Cauthen.

Of the early jockeys, among the names from the past, one in particular stands out: Earl Sande. Great jockeys came before him; great jockeys came after him; but Sande's place in racing history remains immovable.

What put him there? First, he had great balance and moved in connection *with* his horse. Second, he had strong hands and a great sense of timing that let him know when to move and when to stay back. Gene Smith said it all in a recent article: "Horses have to run for some riders; for Sande they wanted to."

Earl Sande was born in Groton, South Dakota, on November 13, 1898. Later his family moved to Idaho, and at age thirteen he bought his first horse, a roan mare. Cocky even then, Sande declared he had the fastest horse around. Many challenged him, but Sande even then knew his horse. He said later, "I forget how many times she ran. But I do know that the roan and I were never beaten."

At age fifteen, Sande was leaning against a fence rail at a rural race in Idaho when a horse trainer came down the track hollering that he needed a jockey to ride in a race that day. Sande volunteered and rode the trainer's horse to victory. He received one dollar, a full ten percent of the winner's purse. In 1917, he got a job as a hotwalker and that got his foot in the door.

On January 6, 1918, he rode his first race as an apprentice. Two weeks later, he won his first race; in fact, he won three races that day. He quickly came to the attention of J.K.L. Ross; he rode Sir Barton, Billy Kelly, and Man o'War in 1918-1920. He moved to the Rancocas Stable and won the Kentucky Derby and Belmont Stakes on Zev in 1923. He won the Belmont Stakes the next year on Mad Play and in 1925, he won the Kentucky Derby again with Flying Ebony.

Sande was at the height of his career, but injuries dogged him. He was seriously injured in a race at Saratoga in 1924; so seriously, in fact, that his survival was doubtful. He came back in 1925 and won the Kentucky Derby. Yet even with the good news again came misfortune: his wife died in 1927.

The next year, tired of trying to hold his weight down, Sande retired. He tried training, but the combination of bad horses and the stock market crash in October, 1929 ended that. Sande needed money, and the call from William Woodward and Sunny Jim should have been irresistible. But Sande at first demurred, not sure he wanted to ride Gallant Fox. Even as late as April 4, 1930, just three weeks before the Wood Memorial, Sande was unsure whether he wanted to come back as a jockey at all. Finally, Sande agreed to ride the Fox. Woodward and Sande arranged a different fee structure; in place of a flat fee for Sande for each race, Sande would get a monthly salary plus ten per cent of Gallant Fox's purse. It was a chance at the time; looking back, it was the closest thing to a sure bet Sande ever had.

He was tall for a jockey, nearly 5'6", and he was a curious one in those rough-and-tumble days. He loved to sing, and even had a voice that approached professional status. And he must have had a certain endearing roguish *élan*. At the time of Sande's death, ex-jockey Sam Renick recalled a race against Sande in the 1930s. In those pre-photo-finish days, a common tactic was for one jockey to grab another jockey on the track and hold him back. Sande did that to Renick, causing Renick to lose the race. A week later, Renick and Sande competed again and Renick saw his opportunity to get even. He held Sande back, causing Sande to lose. Sande confronted Renick afterwards in the jockey's room: "Young man," Sande said, "you held me back out there." Renick admitted that, and reminded Sande of his own transgression a week earlier.

Sande replied, "Ah, yes. But I did it with finesse."

Earl Sande, Gallant Fox's jockey in 1930.
Later photo as a trainer. © *Collection of L. S. Suttcliffe, C. Ken Grayson, owner. Used by permission.*

Among all the Triple Crown winners, Gallant Fox's three-year-old racing season stands supreme, challenged by only one other horse. When compared to Gallant Fox in 1930, the others pale: Sir Barton, Omaha and Whirlaway were impressive, but erratic. War Admiral and Count Fleet were great but injury-shortened. Assault's record was hampered by illness. Seattle Slew in 1977 was good but too brief.

65

Affirmed's three-year-old season was stalked by the shadow of Alydar. Dare it even be contemplated? Heresy of heresies! Secretariat seems undependable when compared to Gallant Fox. His only challenger is Citation, whose racing style and demeanor were so similar to the Fox. Citation, like Gallant Fox, lost only one race in his three-year-old season, in circumstances very much like the Fox's only loss of 1930. The Fox's record in 1930 is simply incredible: the Wood Memorial; the Triple Crown; the Dwyer Stakes; the Arlington Classic; the Saratoga Cup; the Lawrence Realization; and the Jockey Club Gold Cup. Few, if any, horses can match that record of accomplishment.

On April 26, 1930, at the Jamaica track, the team of Earl Sande and Gallant Fox made their debut. The Wood Memorial was one mile, seventy yards, in distance. Then, as now, it was an important preparatory race for the Triple Crown. So in a very real sense, it was all on the line in this one: the winner of the Wood Memorial would gain a betting advantage for the races yet to come. Only five horses, Gallant Fox included, started. The horses broke well from the post, and Crack Brigade took an early lead. The Fox was hemmed in fourth place around the clubhouse turn by Desert Light and Gold Brook, the second and third place horses. Sande used all his skill to keep the Fox in contention, but it was tight all the way. At the beginning of the far turn, Sande tried to ease him past, but Desert Light pinched him back.

Now there was no way left for them. Sande took a wild chance and relied on Gallant Fox's great speed to go around Desert Light. Here a battle developed; Desert Light and his jockey, to keep Gallant Fox from passing them, also moved outward while still moving forward at top speed. The Fox responded; he pounded past Desert Light and drew up to face the leader, Crack Brigade. By the quarter pole they were even. Crack Brigade gave battle, and then Sande let the Fox go at full speed. He went by the leader and drew away. Sande and Gallant Fox crossed the finish line four lengths ahead of Crack Brigade in time of 1:43 3/5.

History points out matters odd to contemporary eyes. Modern racing fans are used to a predictable Triple Crown pattern: the Kentucky Derby on the first Saturday in May, then the Preakness two Saturdays later and finally the Belmont Stakes three Saturdays after that. It wasn't always that way. While the Kentucky Derby has usually been run on a Saturday, the Preakness has been run on every day of the week except Sunday. The Preakness early on acquired its own cachet of importance. In 1922, for example, the Kentucky Derby and the Preakness were held on the same day, thus preventing a Triple Crown winner for that year. In some years, such as 1930, the Preakness was held before the Derby. As a result Gallant Fox is the only Triple Crown winner to win the Preakness *before* winning the Kentucky Derby.

"The way the Preakness was run yesterday demonstrated how fine a horse Gallant Fox is. Had he broken in front he probably would have won by half a dozen lengths."
— Paul Menton,
Baltimore Evening Sun, May 10, 1930

The 1930 Preakness ran on Friday, May 9. Eleven horses contended, and Gallant Fox was the even money favorite. The track that day was fast and the horses went to the post at 5:02 P.M. Sande and the Fox were at the pole position. The race was delayed for a massive 6 1/2 minutes. After the horses broke, Gallant Fox was second, but almost immediately got into trouble. By the first turn, Sande and the Fox were eighth, trapped in the pack. Sande took him to the outside on the back stretch, and Gallant Fox relentlessly passed other horses: first Armageddon; then Snowflake, Swinfield, and Gold Brook. By the 3/4-mile mark, the Fox was in third, two lengths behind Crack Brigade and the leader, Tetrarchal. Sande and the Fox were not slowing down: Crack Brigade caught Tetrarchal, but so did Gallant Fox. Sande let the Fox cruise for a brief time. At the mile they were four lengths behind Crack Brigade. Then Sande let Gallant Fox go and he surged forward. At the head of the stretch he was a head in front of Crack Brigade, and the two dueled down Pimlico's homestretch. Crack Brigade faded at the end. Still, it was close — one of the closest Preakness finishes in Triple Crown history: Gallant Fox by 3/4ths of a length over Crack Brigade. (The close finish was due in part to the short length of the Preakness. Had the race been longer, Gallant Fox might have won by more. The Preakness notes state Gallant Fox "…was drawing away at the end.")

"How did I do it? It was easy!"
— Earl Sande on the 1930 Kentucky Derby,
Louisville Courier-Journal,
May 18, 1930

The Kentucky Derby was run eight days later. Gallant Fox was the bettors' preference at $1.19 to $1. This time there were fifteen horses, and the Fox was seventh from the post. Churchill Downs wasn't quite as favorable as Pimlico had been. The track was rated good, but it didn't make much difference to Gallant Fox. The horses went to the post at 5:00 P.M. and broke nearly three minutes later. A horse named High Foot vaulted into an early lead, but was quickly caught by Alcibiades. In many ways the Derby was like the Preakness; Gallant Fox was once again caught in the pack, and again, Sande sent him to the outside. On the backstretch, the Fox passed all ahead of him, and was in first by a length at the 3/4-mile mark. This was how Gallant Fox liked to run. Sande was the ideal jockey for him, and they seemed to have fused into one form. Jimmy Breslin many years later described the race:

"Earl rode perfectly so far. He had kept his horse out of trouble every foot of the way. He hadn't done a thing to use up any more of Gallant Fox than necessary. Now he came around the last turn with a ton of live horse under him and the big crowd began to roar as the great rider of his time hunched low on Gallant Fox's back, his body moving as if he were part of the horse, and the two of them came down the stretch with the rhythm of the big winner."

They moved up a little bit, and no other horse could catch them, or even offer a serious challenge. The notes to the official race chart say that the Fox "...held command under restraint thereafter and won with something in reserve." Gallant Fox won by two lengths in time of 2:07 3/5.

A half-hour later, Matt Winn poured champagne over Woodward and Sande. Sunny Jim wasn't there; instead of the celebration of his greatest triumph, he was across the track, all business, belying for once his nickname, checking on his horse. Gallant Fox had "pranced back to his stable," and a groom was hot-walking him. The groom said to Sunny Jim, "He's fine, boss. He's a great one, ain't he?" Sunny Jim replied: "Never mind the talk. Give him a little bit of water, then keep him walking. This ain't a popularity contest."

Up in the press box, Damon Runyon hammered out a new version of "A Handy Guy Like Sande":

> *Say, have they turned back the pages*
> *Back to the past once more?*
> *Back to the racin' ages*
> *An' a Derby out of the yore?*
> *Say, don't tell me that I'm daffy,*
> *Ain't that the same ol' grin?*
> *Why it's that handy*
> *Guy named Sande,*
> *Bootin' a winner in!*

> *Say, don't tell me I'm batty!*
> *Say, don't tell me I'm blind!*
> *Look at that seat so natty!*
> *Look how he drives from behind!*
> *Gone is the white of the Ranco,*
> *An' the white band under his chin —*
> *Still he's that handy*
> *Guy named Sande,*
> *Bootin' a winner in!*

Maybe he ain't no chicken,
Maybe he's gettin' along.
But the ol' heart's still a-tickin',
An the ol' bean's goin strong.
Roll back the years! Yea, roll em!
Say but I'm young agin',
Watchin' that handy
Guy named Sande,
Bootin' a winner in![2]

"There no longer exists any doubt about William Woodward's Gallant
Fox being the greatest 3-year-old of the year."
— Bryan Field,
The New York Times, June 8, 1930.

Only three other horses challenged Sande and the Fox in the Belmont Stakes. The race's outcome, though it seems predestined now, wasn't predictable at the time. The main challenger was Whichone, the leading juvenile in 1929, when he had beaten Gallant Fox in the Futurity that year. Whichone developed knee trouble in late 1929, but came back in 1930 to win the Withers. He was the insiders' choice, while the Fox was considered to have won the Preakness and the Derby over indifferent opposition. Moreover, Swinfield's jockey was the fine Raymond "Sonny" Workman. Now the Belmont was the equivalent of a match race between Workman on Whichone and Sande on Gallant Fox. The bettors made Whichone the 4 to 5 favorite. The Fox was at 8 to 5, and the other two horses, Questionnaire and Swinfield, were at 8 to 1 and 30 to 1 respectively. Sande had recently been in an automobile accident, but was patched up sufficiently to ride in the Belmont; this was one race he wasn't going to miss.

The Belmont track on June 7, 1930 was rated "good". The horses went to the post at 4:24 P.M. and this time, there was no significant delay; they broke a minute later. Gallant Fox was at the pole position and after the start, Sande took no chances. He and the Fox went right to the lead and stayed there through the whole race. Whichone challenged them briefly at the end; Workman used the whip on Whichone, but all Sande did was hand-ride Gallant Fox. Workman's efforts were in vain; Sande and the Fox won by three lengths in a new Belmont Stakes record, 2:31 3/5. As the official race notes put it, Gallant Fox finished

---

[2] Gallant Fox's victory meant that Sande tied a record set by the African-American jockey Isaac Murphy in the 1800s: three Kentucky Derby victories

"…with speed in reserve."

Twenty-two days later at Aqueduct, Gallant Fox with Sande up won the Dwyer Stakes. For some time, Sande's status was doubtful; he had been unseated by another race horse two weeks earlier and was still limping on the day of the Dwyer Stakes. The Fox was the 1 to 10 favorite of the bettors and was challenged by four other horses. Still, it was an exciting race: the Dwyer was a 1 1/2-mile race and there was plenty of room for surprises. Limbus, ridden by Laverne Fator, took the early lead in the race, while Bannerette was second and Gallant Fox in third. The Fox moved up to second and Sande sent him along the rail to challenge Limbus. Fator, a Hall of Fame jockey, wouldn't bite on that one; he moved Limbus over to the rail and forced Gallant Fox to come around on the outside. Fator hadn't ridden against the Fox in 1930, and didn't know what horse he was challenging: by the 3/4-mile mark the Triple Crown winner passed Limbus.

The Fox wasn't out of the woods: another horse, Xenofol, passed Limbus and moved up to take on Sande and Gallant Fox. Twice Xenofol moved up close and twice Gallant Fox pulled away. The Triple Crown winner crossed the finish line one length ahead of Xenofol in time of 2:32 2/5.

Gallant Fox had now become the first horse in history to win the Wood Memorial, the Triple Crown, *and* the Dwyer Stakes. The Dwyer's purse was $11,500. Added to the winnings from the first four races, Gallant Fox had won $210,230. The American one-year earnings record was $313,639, set by Zev in 1923. Could he break it?

The 1 1/4-mile Arlington Classic at Arlington Park in Chicago was the Fox's next race. On July 12, 1930, he and five other horses went to the post. He was the favorite in the betting at $1.32 to $1. When the race started, Sande took him into third place. Immediately, Sande moved Gallant Fox along and by the first 1/4-mile was in second. The leader, Maya, was moving along at high speed, but Gallant Fox was at full speed, too. He passed Maya easily. Sande was about to give him a breather when another horse, Gallant Knight, moved up quickly to challenge the Fox.

Other jockeys might have panicked when Gallant Knight drew alongside Gallant Fox. Not Sande; he was too good, too cool, riding too great a horse to make a careless mistake. Another jockey would have used the whip on the Fox, but not Sande: he knew that Gallant Fox hated that. There must have been a smile on Sande's face at that point. It was a battle now, and Sande knew that when Gallant Fox had competition, the horse would run his heart out. Gallant Fox and Gallant Knight stayed alongside each other, neither one giving an inch. Herman Schuette, Gallant Knight's jockey, lashed his horse. Gallant Knight responded, and for one infinitesimal moment, the challenger put his head in front of the Fox.

That was it: Gallant Knight made the Triple Crown winner mad. Sande just hand-rode him, still sparing the whip. In Bryan Field's words, "As smooth and easy as a railway express, Gallant Fox drove on to a continuous thunder of cheers from the stands. He was going the easier of the two under the wire." The Fox was also the first under the wire by a neck.

It was a memorable race and he had triumphed again. He was now the first horse to win the Wood Memorial, the Triple Crown, the Dwyer Stakes, and the Arlington Classic. He occupied second place on the list of money-winning American horses and fifth on the world's list of winning racers. Could any horse stop him? The imminent answer was yes, but not without a lot of divine intervention.

When racing experts discuss the Travers Stakes, one horse comes to mind: Gallant Fox. It is curious, even tragic, that America's oldest continuous horse race is remembered for one of racing's greatest upsets.

The Travers is held at Saratoga, and is often called the "Summertime Derby." The 1930 Travers was run on August 16, and Gallant Fox was the favorite. His old adversary from the Belmont Stakes, Whichone, was back, and many looked forward to another battle between the two. Whichone's jockey, Sonny Workman, had been given orders to challenge Gallant Fox every step of the race. Overlooked was another horse entered, Jim Dandy.

It rained heavily in Saratoga the night before the Travers Stakes. The track at Saratoga turned sloppy. The experts called it "Saratoga Mud," a deep, heavy goo that made going difficult. It was just what Jim Dandy liked: he was a "mudder," a horse that liked to run in the mud. In fact, he won the Grand Union Hotel Stakes at Saratoga on a muddy track the year before. Jim Dandy didn't deserve to be rated at 100-to-1 but those were the odds on him.

I have before me as I write a copy of the program from the 1930 Travers Stakes. Jim Dandy was entered in an earlier race that day against lesser opponents. He was scratched from that and entered in the Travers to run against Gallant Fox and Whichone. One suspects that Jim Dandy's owner, Earl Chaffee of Wilshire Stable, aware of the Saratoga Mud and his own horse's proclivity for muddy going, was out to sandbag Gallant Fox.

By the time of the Travers, the track was still in bad shape. Boards were laid out at right angles to the rail to keep the horses to the outside. Despite the conditions, the fans present looked forward to another round in the Gallant Fox-Whichone contest. The horses broke and Whichone immediately grabbed the lead. Gallant Fox was in second, but stayed close to Whichone. Jim Dandy was in third, well back of the Fox. Gallant Fox drew ahead of Whichone briefly on the backstretch, and somehow, through a magnificent effort, Whichone regained the lead. But to the inside, Jim Dandy had a clear shot. His jockey, Frank Baker, shot Jim Dandy past Gallant Fox and Whichone. The crowd fell silent for a moment; who could have believed that a 100 to 1 long shot could beat

Whichone, let alone Gallant Fox?

There was more incredulity: Sonny Workman eased up Whichone. He broke down from the mud on the track. Gallant Fox passed him, but never caught Jim Dandy. The long shot crossed the finish line six lengths ahead of Gallant Fox. Whichone made it through the race, but just barely. He finished three lengths ahead of the fourth horse in the race, Sun Falcon.

It was a terrible day for Woodward, Fitzsimmons, Sande, and Gallant Fox. The Fox ran a fine race, but the track conditions were against him. There was only the consolation that Gallant Fox had come through the muddy ordeal uninjured, and even *that* was tempered by the melancholy thought of Whichone's breakdown. Whichone was not injured so severely as to cause his destruction, but he never raced again. Woodward, a gallant sportsman, wrote later, "We killed [*sic:*Woodward spoke figuratively here] our adversary, which was unfortunate, and the whole thing was a fiasco and a very sad affair." It was Gallant Fox's only loss of 1930, and the Travers Stakes most remembered.

Disingenuously, Woodward wrote a few months later, "Up to this time [after the Travers] we had not thought much of the earnings of The Fox, although he had been winning the big races and his winnings amounted to a large sum of money. We had never expected him to be the big money winner of all time. However, at this time it dawned on us that this should now become our objective and that we must try to reach for the sake of the horse."

Oh, give me a break! Woodward was a banker, high in New York's financial circles. Bryan Field of *The New York Times,* for one columnist, kept track of Gallant Fox's earnings. It's simply impossible to believe that William Woodward *didn't* realize all along just how well Gallant Fox was doing.

Two weeks after the Travers came the Saratoga Cup again at Saratoga. It was a small field, just six horses. The Fox was entered and paired with a stable mate, Frisius, a four-year-old horse that had recently won the Merchants and Citizens' Handicap.

The two Belair Stud horses turned the Saratoga Cup into a match race: Frisius took an early lead while Sande kept Gallant Fox in third for much of the 1 3/4-mile race. At the 1-mile mark, Gallant Fox and Sande made the move: they passed Frisius and drew away to win by 1 1/2 lengths. That avenged the Travers defeat and pushed Gallant Fox closer to Zev's American earnings record of $313,639.

The races were longer in distance now, and Gallant Fox faced two of the longest in America: the Lawrence Realization at 1 5/8 miles, and the Jockey Club Gold Cup, at *two* miles. It had been a successful year for the Fox, but inevitably physically punishing. Could he stand up to the rigors of the imminent two long races? Could he break the American or even, the International winnings records?

As it turned out, the answer to both questions was yes, and with seemingly ridiculous ease. First was the Lawrence Realization at Belmont Park on September 10, 1930. It was a race for three-year-old horses and older. Many good horses should have been expected to enter it, but Gallant Fox scared off almost every other horse in the country. Only three horses challenged Gallant Fox: Questionnaire returned, and Yarn and Spinach were also present.

The Fox broke well, but Sande kept him in second place. Questionnaire led through 3/4 of a mile, but then Sande sent Gallant Fox to the outside. On the far turn, Questionnaire carried the Fox wide, but he recovered and drew even with the leader. Sonny Workman was riding Questionnaire, and it was said that "Workman [was] the greatest whip rider in the game and Sande the poorest." Both used the whip on their horses, but neither one budged into a lead. Sande went back to a hand ride and it was a great battle down the stretch. Gallant Fox responded as he had so often in the last five months: Relentlessly, he kept going, pricked his ears up at the finish line and won by a nose over Questionnaire.

After the race Workman claimed Sande had fouled him. The claim was disallowed and Gallant Fox remained the winner. The disallowed claim was too much for Sande; on top of Workman's moves on Whichone in the Travers, and his latest moves in this race, now Workman was using the last possible means to defeat the Fox. Sande was usually not much for re-fighting races in the jockey's room, but this time he boiled over. In Woodward's words, "They had a set-to in the jockey's room, resorting to fists, which was an unknown thing from Sande's point of view."

The Lawrence Realization paid Belair Stud $29,610. That brought Gallant Fox's winnings to $317,685. He passed Zev to become the all-time money winner of American racing. A French horse, Ksar, set the world's money-winning record some years earlier with a total of $335,340. Could the Fox surpass it?

Gallant Fox rested for eleven days and started in the Jockey Club Gold Cup at Belmont. Woodward also entered Frisius one more time, and only Yarn challenged the Belair horses. It was Gallant Fox's longest race of 1930, and in many respects, his easiest. Sande let him ease along in second place behind Frisius through the 1 1/4-mile mark, but then hit the Fox once with the whip. He responded immediately; he rushed to the front, passed his stable mate, and eventually won by three lengths. Yarn came on strong at the end to beat Frisius by thirteen lengths. It might have been just a two-mile warm-up for the Triple Crown winner; Sande dismounted the Fox and told the owner, "Mr. Woodward, this horse is just about ready to run."

The Jockey Club Gold Cup was Belmont Park's last major race of 1930. The advent of the race was bittersweet for racing fans. Many, Bryan Field of *The New York Times* included, sensed that it might be Gallant Fox's last race of all time. The Jockey Club Gold Cup purse was $10,500, bringing Gallant Fox's total winnings to $328,165. That was still less than Ksar's record, but then people analyzed the record. Ksar's total included breeder's allowances and the values of the trophies awarded. Immediately, the breeder's allowances and trophy values won by the Fox were factored into his winnings. The result: Gallant Fox had won $341,365. It was a new world's record. In 1930, Gallant Fox won:

> The Wood Memorial
> The Preakness Stakes
> The Kentucky Derby
> The Belmont Stakes
> The Triple Crown
> The Dwyer Stakes
> The Arlington Classic
> The Saratoga Cup
> The Lawrence Realization
> The Jockey Club Gold Cup
> The American record for winnings
> The world's record for winnings.

That was Gallant Fox in 1930. The gentle, friendly, curious horse from Belair Stud. Ridden by the comeback jockey, he triumphed over them all. The record stands out in sharp relief to all who came after him.

After the Jockey Club Gold Cup, Woodward and Fitzsimmons planned to enter Gallant Fox in the Hawthorne Gold Cup in Chicago and then the Latonia Championship at Latonia track in Kentucky. But at a workout just after the Jockey Club Gold Cup, the Fox developed a cough. Woodward and Fitzsimmons conferred; the cough meant his racing for 1930 was over. Still, there was next year to think about. Gallant Fox's ability meant that he would carry very high weights in handicap races. Like Man o'War ten years earlier, that also meant risking a severe or even fatal injury. Woodward didn't need the money. Gallant Fox didn't need any more victories. So, like Sam Riddle and Louis Feustel before them, William Woodward and Sunny Jim Fitzsimmons decided to retire their great horse. The announcement came on October 6, 1930. Gallant Fox would return to his birthplace, Claiborne Farm, for stud duty.

The Fox stayed at Belmont Park for three weeks before he was shipped home. Somehow he knew that he would not race any more, and he behaved differently: He was not mean, just more controlled and less exuberant. He returned to Kentucky by train, and as always, he was a good traveler, not giving any problems. People came to see him at every stop, little children came to pet him, and he enjoyed the attention. Once, the train's steam engine took on water and the Triple Crown winner got splashed by some of it. Gallant Fox turned around, indignant, determined to face and fight the intruder that soaked him. Bracing in stubbornness, he faced the incoming water until it ceased.

He reached Claiborne Farm and was put into a stall. Woodward was concerned about putting him out in a paddock the next day. It had been some time since Gallant Fox had been free and the people around him worried what the Fox might do once he was let loose in the paddock. Handlers stood in the corners of it to protect him from injury, and then the Fox was let out of the stall. He stayed put for some minutes, not sure what would happen next. Then it hit him: Gallant Fox threw his head back and raced around and around *his* paddock, exultant in his new-found freedom.

> *"Money and I are incompatible."*
> — Earl Sande.

After Gallant Fox, Sande's life went downhill. He was, in perspective, the most tragic of all Triple Crown jockeys. Sande sold his own stable in 1930. For some time, he was a fixture at a Long Island restaurant where the management allowed him free room and board in exchange for singing to the restaurant's patrons. It wasn't all penury: he trained horses for some years, and in 1938 was the leading money-winning trainer. Then he made a mistake: he went into horse breeding as well as training. He was underfinanced, and his horses were of poor quality. His other investments went sour, and soon he was reduced to living in one room over a bar on Long Island.

Sande hung around horse racing, and in 1953, he made yet another jockey comeback. He was racing, he said, "...for the creditors." He won one race out of ten starts, and then retired for good. His bad luck continued; he had little success in yet another attempt at horse training. He sold a small stable of horses in 1957. By the mid-1960s he was morose, quarrelsome, divorced from his second wife, and nearly penniless. His dinners were usually Spartan: as Gene Smith put it, "...a can of soup and a tin of salmon." Even his great love, horse racing, eluded him now. He couldn't afford a car and the bus schedule wasn't accommodating, so he rarely went to Belmont Park or Aqueduct. On many days he couldn't afford the 50¢ for a *Daily Racing Form*. He had a television set, but when it broke, Sande didn't have the money to fix it; he went to a nearby place that showed the races and watched them there.

Racing tried to help him, but he refused all job offers as a steward, publicist, or greeter at tracks. To Sande, you had to do it *your* way, not trade on what you were or what your name was. He was just too independent, too strong minded, to take a proffered hand.

Finally, people around Saratoga who knew him took up a collection to send him to his father, then in his nineties, in an Oregon nursing home. They raised $500, but Sande wouldn't accept it unless his benefactors took his promissory note for repayment. For four years he spent time with his father, and was in several Oregon nursing homes. On August 20, 1968, he died in Jacksonville, Oregon, at the age of sixty-nine. On hearing of the jockey's death, the reaction around Saratoga was, "Sorry to hear it, but he was such an odd guy."

Gallant Fox's career as a sire has been described in generally disappointing terms. But, the 1995 *Laurel/Pimlico Media Guide* notes that he fathered over ninety race winners and his first two crops were impressive: the Fox sired Omaha, the third Triple Crown Winner and a subject of the next chapter. Two other sons, Flares and Granville, accomplished what Omaha very nearly did: both won the Ascot Gold Cup in England. Granville also won the 1936 Belmont Stakes.[3] During the period 1934-1953, the Fox's offspring earned $1,788,648 in American purses and £25,597 in English winnings; not bad for horses that largely raced during the Depression and World War Two. He stayed high on the list of sires through the Thirties; thereafter, his siring record fell off. One offered explanation is that few top-quality mares were sent to him, and therefore, his foals were not top-quality. Claiborne Farm retired him from stud in 1952.

On November 13, 1954, around 1:00 P.M. Gallant Fox died of old age — Homerically, about one hour before post time for the Gallant Fox Handicap at Jamaica track in New York and also the Marguerite Stakes at Pimlico (named for his dam). He was the second horse to win the Kentucky Derby, the Preakness Stakes, and Belmont Stakes. Gallant Fox is buried near his sire and dam at Claiborne Farm.

The Fox is little-known or remembered now; perhaps it was just too long ago, lost in the shadows of time like the Great Depression and the newsreel era. But what Gallant Fox WAS is as important as what he DID: he was the trailblazer. Yes, Sir Barton won the three races eleven years earlier. But Sir Barton was a strange one, a classic case of the unknown that rose to brief stardom. Gallant Fox showed again that all three races of the Triple Crown could be won in a year. Not that it could happen just once; it could happen again. More than any other horse, he set the pattern for the Triple Crown champions to come.

Racing columnist Neil Newman, in *Famous Horses of the American Turf,* wrote a chapter on Gallant Fox. One line in that chapter has become the Fox's epitaph, quoted in books and videotapes. That line is used again here, because more than seventy years later, there's nothing better that has been or could be said about The Gallant Fox of Belair, Maryland:

---

[3] Granville was elected to the National Museum of Racing and Hall of Fame in 1997, joining his sire and his half-brother Omaha. That indicates *how* impressive Gallant Fox's first two foal crops were.

"He swept like a meteor across the racing sky in 1930..."

Sunny Jim Fitzsimmons, trainer of Gallant Fox and Omaha, at his last public appearance. He went to work at 6:00 A.M. at Belmont Park, then headed for his retirement ceremony (age 88) that afternoon at Aqueduct Race Track, New York. June 15, 1963. © *Collection of L. S. Suttcliffe, C. Ken Grayson, owner. Used by permission.*

III. VICTORIOUS PROGENY: OMAHA AND WAR ADMIRAL

Omaha — Triple Crown, 1935: Jockey, Willie Saunders
War Admiral — Triple Crown, 1937: Jockey, Charles Kurtsinger

Both Omaha and War Admiral ascended the throne in the kingdom of Thoroughbred racing when each won the Triple Crown. But at what price came their fame?

One of them died in exile, branded a failure at stud. When the track where he was buried was torn down, it was discovered his remains had been lost. The other died in his native state, a great sire, and underappreciated as a racer. His registration certificate was misplaced, and he was technically alive for fourteen years after his death.

The children of the famous have a terrible time of it; they are always being compared to their famous parents. It seems this is true of horses as well as people. Few horses have labored under the burdens of famous sires as much as Omaha and War Admiral. Omaha was the son of Gallant Fox. War Admiral carried a familial curse above all other horses; he was the son of Man o'War.

OMAHA

Omaha may be the least of all the Triple Crown winners. His racing career was short, and his winning percentage is the lowest of all the horses ever to win the Triple Crown. There was drama to Sir Barton, the unknown that came from nowhere to sweep racing and then returned to obscurity. Gallant Fox conquered all that opposed him. Omaha fit neither of those patterns. His racing fame is based on six victories in the spring and summer of 1935 plus an English epilogue the next year. Yet he cannot be ignored.

Omaha was one of Gallant Fox's first foals. He was a big horse, so big that he required extra-large stable accommodations. His jockey, Willie Saunders, recalled: "Everywhere we went with him, they'd have to give him two stalls. They'd take two stalls and knock the partition out in the middle to

79

make one huge stall."

He was bigger than his sire. And he was unlike Gallant Fox in another respect: Omaha was one of the most nervous horses ever to win the Triple Crown. If you watch a film of him racing, you will see that his jockey takes him to the outside away from other horses. There was a very good reason for that tactic. If another horse brushed him, Omaha immediately retaliated by reaching out and biting the offender.[1] His most famous jockey, Willie Saunders, kept that a secret for many years. Saunders said of him later that Omaha "…would have stopped [on the track] and went to fightin' instead of runnin'." Moreover, he was jumpy. One source reports that his trainer, Sunny Jim Fitzsimmons, called Omaha the most nervous horse he had ever trained.

Omaha resembled in style one successor, Triple Crown Champion Whirlaway. Both were strong horses, both started slowly, finished with a rush, and were nervous horses throughout most of their careers.

The third Triple Crown champion was born on March 24, 1932 at Arthur Hancock's Claiborne Farm near Paris, Kentucky. His sire was, as noted, Gallant Fox, and his dam was a mare named Flambino. Six months after he was foaled he was taken to William Woodward's Belair Stud in Maryland. There he was broken to saddle and trained to race. It was at Belair that he was named. There are two versions of how that came to be: one account says that Woodward followed a trend of naming horses that involved using the letter "O": "Bend Or," "Ormonde," and "Orme." "Omaha," then, was just another name in the trend. Another story has it that Woodward's friends were impressed by the colt's "beefiness," so names associated with beef and meat-packing were considered. "Chicago" was contemplated, but another horse had recently taken that name. "Kansas City" was also discussed, but apparently Woodward didn't favor that one. That left Omaha.

Omaha's two-year season was rather moderate. He made his debut at Aqueduct on June 18, 1934 in a 5/8 of a mile race. Fourteen horses started; Omaha was fourth from the post. He was fifth at the quarter-mile, and began to move up quickly on the outside. By the stretch he was in third and finished second by a nose to another horse, Sir Lamorak. It was not a bad race, and five days later he was entered again at Aqueduct. It was another 5/8-mile race, but the field was smaller: only five horses. Omaha was fourth after a quarter-mile, second by a neck at the stretch, and caught the leader, a horse called Allen Z., to win. It was Omaha's only two-year victory.

Over a month passed before Omaha started again. This time he ran in Saratoga. He placed fourth in the United States Hotel Stakes on August 4, 1934.

---

[1]That trait apparently only came to the fore on the track. Willie Saunders recalled forty years later that Omaha "Was fine around the barn…just don't bother him and he wouldn't bother you."[sic]

The 3/4-mile race normally wouldn't have much importance to this story: It was one of his four unplaced finishes that year. But the record points out his ability to come on strong in the final moments of a race. Omaha was one of the ten entries, and started ninth from the post. He was last through the half-mile, but gained steadily through the last quarter-mile to finish fourth. The notes to the *Daily Racing Form* chart says, "OMAHA, badly outrun to the stretch, closed with a rush."

Omaha finished fourth again one week later in the Saratoga Special. He showed little that was noteworthy in that race, but he showed again his come-from-behind talent eleven days later, in the 3/4-mile Sanford Stakes at Saratoga. He was in the rear for most of the race, but came on strong at the end to finish second. On September 1, he ran in the 6 1/2-furlong Hopeful Stakes at Saratoga. His jockey for this race was Charles Kurtsinger, who had won the Kentucky Derby, Belmont Stakes, Wood Memorial, Dwyer Stakes, Lawrence Realization, and Jockey Club Gold Cup on Twenty Grand three years earlier. (As will be seen in the next section of this chapter, Kurtsinger rode War Admiral to a Triple Crown three years later.) Omaha was ninth at the post and held no better than seventh place through the first four furlongs and the head of the stretch. Then he moved up again, closing quickly, and finished fourth. He did even better five days later at Belmont Park in the Champagne Stakes, another 6 1/2-furlong race. Twelve horses started, and Omaha was farthest from the post. He broke well, angled across the track, and stayed with Balladier, the winner, for the entire race. Balladier won by a neck. Again, the notes to the *Daily Racing Form* chart state, "OMAHA, close up and on the outside of the leader all the way, was gaining at the finish."

Two more races remained for him that year: the Futurity Stakes at Belmont on September 15 and the Junior Champion Stakes at Aqueduct on September 29. Kurtsinger rode him in those races. He was fourth in the Futurity Stakes, although he again showed a tendency to gain at the close of the race. He did better in the Junior Champion Stakes, staying in fourth for most of the race, but coming on strong at the end to finish second, only a head behind the winning horse. The *Daily Racing Form* chart notes say it well: "SAILOR BEWARE, well up all the way and in near pursuit of the pace, responded to urging in the stretch and outlasted OMAHA in the final drive. The latter was outrun in the early stages, improved his position steadily on the outside and finished with a rush."

Omaha started nine races that year, winning one, placing in four, and finishing unplaced in the other four races. Yet some of his losses were close, by such narrow margins that some called him a hard-luck horse. His tendency, to close with a rush was noted in several races. A few discerning track observers noted that two-year-old races are at a shorter distance than three-year-old races, and perhaps Omaha would come into his own over a longer course. Possibly

Omaha had been "shut down" too soon before his closing rush could take him to victory. In that case, the longer distance of three-year-old races would make a critical difference. In any event, fans would have to be "wait until next year" to see what Omaha could really do.

> *"I think Omaha is the best horse I ever rode...*
> *I'm sure he's the best horse I ever rode."*
> — Willie Saunders
> *Louisville Courier-Journal*, May 5, 1935

The jockey most identified with Omaha is William, "Willie" or "Smokey" Saunders. He was born in Bozeman, Montana, on April 13, 1915. Eight years later, Saunders' family moved to Calgary, Alberta, Canada, where Willie galloped Thoroughbreds at the local tracks. He hooked up with a Chicago horse trainer, L.T. Whitehill, and became a jockey. He won his first race at Tanforan on April 14, 1932, the day after his seventeenth birthday. Later, his contract was transferred to Sunny Jim Fitzsimmons, and Sunny Jim took Saunders under his wing. Naturally, he grew in ability.

He rode for Sunny Jim at Wheatley Stable, and that was how he happened to luck into riding Omaha. Saunders rode Carry Over in the 1934 Wood Memorial. Carry Over finished next to last. After the race, Saunders was blinded from the racetrack dust. A lady came up to him and wondered what had happened to her horse. Saunders thought it was some disappointed bettor, and snapped, "Lady, why don't you go home and cook your husband's meals and quit losin' his hard-earned money on these bad horses." Then Saunders stalked off to the jockey's room.

The disappointed lady bettor happened to be Mrs. Henry Carnegie Phipps, co-owner of Wheatley Stable and Saunders' ultimate boss. Sunny Jim came to Saunders the next day and told him he was fired as a jockey for Wheatley, but since the trainer also worked for Belair Stud, Saunders could ride for *that* stable. (And, when Mrs. Phipps was out of the country and unable to get the race results, Saunders rode again for Wheatley.) The next year, Saunders was ready to ride Omaha to the Triple Crown.

He acquired the nickname, "Smokey," at sixteen. The trainer Saunders worked for at that time discouraged smoking and drinking. One afternoon, smoke came out of the trainer's tack room. A foreman rushed in, thinking the room was on fire. It was only Willie Saunders, puffing on a cigar. The incident stayed with him: He carried the nickname "Smokey" for the rest of his life.

Omaha's first start of 1935 was in the South Shore Purse, at the Jamaica Race Track on April 22, 1935. Omaha and four other horses started the one-mile-and-seventy-yard race. The track was fast, and the horses went to the post at 4:03, breaking three minutes later. Omaha was second from the post. A horse named Thorson set the early pace; Saunders kept Omaha back during the early going. Omaha was third at the half-mile and three-quarter marks. He moved up a bit on the backstretch, and then settled back. In the home stretch he came on again and won by three lengths.

The South Shore Purse victory put Omaha in the spotlight. He and a stable mate, Vicaress, were favored at 5 to 2 for the Wood Memorial five days later. Here, however, fortune did not favor Omaha. Twelve horses were on the field at Jamaica. Omaha was again second from the post, but was quickly squeezed into a pack, far off the leader. Saunders eventually got him to the outside where he could get some running room. But Omaha's slow start and the immediate jam-up pretty well doomed his chances for victory. He finished strongly, in the words of the Associated Press "...[appearing] to be hopelessly out of all contention, but was taken to the outside and finished with a rush." Omaha was third, three lengths back of the winner.

Despite the loss in the Wood Memorial, Omaha went into the 1935 Kentucky Derby as one of the strong contenders. A poll taken of sportswriters two days prior to the Derby had nine writers picking Nellie Flag, a filly owned by Warren Wright, owner of the Calumet Baking Powder Company, as the favorite. Seven chose Omaha, and three writers chose Today, winner of the Wood Memorial. Three other horses each received one vote. On the morning of the Kentucky Derby, Today was rated the favorite at 3 to 1.

Of the horses other than Omaha, Nellie Flag would normally not even merit a footnote in racing history, except for two things: She was Calumet Farm's first Kentucky Derby entry and Eddie Arcaro's first mount in a Triple Crown race. Nellie Flag ran the one-mile Derby Trial at 1:40 2/5, and she was the favorite in the betting at $3.80 to $1. Omaha was second choice, at $4 to $1. But known only to her owner, trainer, and jockey was the fact that Nellie Flag was in season that weekend; she was unable to run her best. [2] There was some discussion about scratching her, but it was decided to let her run anyway.

---

[2] Eddie Arcaro wrote fifteen years later of Nellie Flag at this very moment, "...All our hopes — those of Mr. Wright, [owner of Calumet Farm] Mrs. Wright, Williams [Bert Williams, trainer], myself, and all the others who had worked so zealously to bring her up to razor sharpness for this one big effort — were dashed to the ground. It's unfortunate that mares are in season about the first of May."

OMAHA, third winner of the Triple Crown, 1935. Willie Saunders up.
© *Collection of L. S. Sutcliffe. C. Ken Grayson, owner. Used by permission.*

"Like father, like son."
— Bruce Dudley,
Louisville Courier-Journal,
May 5, 1935

It rained in Louisville most of Kentucky Derby Day, May 4, 1935. Despite the all-day moisture, the track was still rated as good. Eighteen horses went to the Churchill Downs starting gate at 5:13 P.M. that day. Omaha was tenth from the pole position, while Nellie Flag was ninth. At about 5:16 P.M. the race started. Nellie Flag broke to an immediate lead, but very quickly ran into interference by Plat Eye, another horse in the race. By the quarter-mile mark she was in eleventh place, although she and Arcaro would eventually come back to finish fourth. Omaha trailed at ninth by the half-mile mark, and then Saunders took him outside. By the three-quarter-mile mark Omaha was in fifth, behind Psychic Bid, Whopper, Boxthorn, and Plat Eye. Then Saunders sent Omaha to the front; he was alongside the leaders going into the far turn. Then he charged past Plat Eye and took the lead. Omaha never gave it up and won by 1 1/2 lengths in time of 2:05. Roman Soldier mustered a late dash to place second.

The Governor of Kentucky presented the trophy to William Woodward, who said, "I am very happy to win and expect to come back next year with another Derby winner." Postmaster General James Farley was also present, and that created a few problems. Farley was also chairman of the Democratic National Committee, and Woodward was a staunch Republican. Woodward kept telling Farley, "Jim, you're a fine fellow, but that Roosevelt, he is no good." The radio crew shut down the broadcast, restarted it, and tried to interview Woodward again. Back went Woodward to his anti-FDR remarks. So, the broadcast crew tried again, but every time, Woodward would continue in his anti-FDR vein. Sunny Jim Fitzsimmons declined an invitation to speak over the radio. Willie Saunders, then just twenty years old, said: "I knew I could win because this horse has come from so far back before and won so many races from behind. Sure, it's the biggest thrill of my life. It's always been my ambition to win a Kentucky Derby."

Immediately, the comparisons came: Gallant Fox and Omaha both won on a rainy day with a track rated only as "good." Omaha was always identified as the son of Gallant Fox. It was impossible to forestall. Like his sire, the morning after the Derby Omaha was shipped aboard the Cincinnati Limited to Pimlico for the Preakness.

Three days before the Preakness, Omaha ran the Preakness Trial, one mile in length, in 1:44 1/5 in heavy going. At the nine furlong mark (1 1/8 miles) he was recorded at 1:58 1/5. Obviously, he was a strong horse, and now, the one to beat. He was even money on Saturday morning, Preakness Day, May 11, 1935. Nellie Flag was second at 7 to 2.

Eight horses went to the post at 5:56 P.M. and broke three minutes later on a fast track. Omaha was sixth from the post and stayed in sixth position for the first quarter mile. Then he began to close up; by the three-quarter-mile mark he was fourth behind Brannon, Boxthorn, and Psychic Bid. After seven furlongs, Saunders moved Omaha to the outside and took the lead by half a length. During the stretch he drew away to win by six lengths, in the *Daily Racing Form* words, "...with much to spare." One sportswriter called it "...the easiest victory in this famous test since Man o'War won in 1920." His time was 1:58 2/5, just 1/5 of a second off the Preakness record set the previous year. "It is not too much to say that Omaha could not have done much better and that Saunders was supremely confident of the outcome," opined *The New York Times*.

OMAHA, Willie Sanders up.
© *Collection of L. S. Sutcliffe. C. Ken Grayson, owner. Used by permission.*

Omaha was shipped back to Aqueduct on the morning of May 12, 1935. Next would come the Withers at Belmont on May 25, 1935. He was the 1 to 2 favorite out of the nine-horse field, but this time, a horse named Rosemont came on to defeat him. Omaha broke well from the second position on the fast Belmont Park track, but the short length of the Withers (one mile) didn't allow him much margin for a slow start. Rosemont broke well, took the lead early, and held on throughout the race. Omaha was sixth at the half-mile mark, and made up ground throughout the race. He came on at the end but it wasn't enough. Rosemont won by 1 1/2 lengths.

Despite his loss to Rosemont in the Withers, Omaha went to the Belmont Stakes starting line the 3 to 5 favorite. A mere four other horses faced him; only two of them, Rosemont and Firethorn, were given any chance to beat the Kentucky Derby and Preakness winner. By this time, the experts were convinced: Omaha was the one to beat. The longer route of the Belmont would eliminate many of the difficulties that plagued him in the Withers.

It rained in New York on Saturday, June 8, 1935. The Belmont Park track was rated good for the first four races, sloppy for the fifth and sixth races, which included the Belmont Stakes, the Number 5 race.[3] The horses went to the

---

[3] The track condition created a problem for Saunders: Omaha's large size meant that he wasn't a good horse in the mud. Fortunately, that didn't seem to affect him in this race.

starting line at 4:22 P.M. and broke thirty seconds later. Omaha started third from the post. A horse called Cold Shoulder took the lead and held it through the 3/4-mile mark. Then he dropped back to eventually finished fourth. Rosemont was second at the start; he dropped back to fourth at the half-mile, moved up to third and stayed there to the finish. Firethorn was fourth at the start, and moved up to second by the half-mile. He stayed second through to the finish. Another horse, Sir Beverley, held fifth throughout the race.

Which leaves only Omaha. He was third at the start, and held third place through the half-mile. Saunders kept him out in the middle where the footing was firmer, not so mushy. At the 3/4-mile mark he was in fourth place by ten lengths. But on the far turn, Omaha began to close. He caught up with Firethorn on the outside. Rosemount passed Cold Shoulder. For a moment, it looked like a repeat of the Withers. Then Saunders turned his horse loose. Both Firethorn and Omaha speeded past Rosemont, "so fast," said *The New York Times,* "that it seemed almost as if the Withers winner had stepped in a hole."

Now the race was between Omaha and Firethorn. They were head and head for a furlong, but Omaha wore down Firethorn and very gradually pulled away. By the sixteenth pole Omaha had taken command. Firethorn was worn out by then, but managed to stay within a length and a half of Omaha at the finish. Omaha won in a time of 2:30 2/5. In the depths of the Great Depression, the winning purse was a healthy $35,480. Inescapably, Bryan Field of *The New York Times* wrote, "To his Kentucky Derby and Preakness victories *the son of Gallant Fox* has now added the grueling Belmont *to duplicate the feat of his sire.*" (emphasis added.)

But after that, Omaha displayed his racing inconsistency, first with a victory in the South Shore, then a third place finish in the Wood Memorial. The victories in the Derby and the Preakness were followed by the second-place finish in the Withers. Then came the Belmont Stakes and the Triple Crown. In keeping with his up-and-down pattern, Omaha lost the Brooklyn Handicap on June 23 at Aqueduct Race Track.

Woodward took a risk with that race. In fact, Woodward passed up the American Derby, run in Chicago the same day, to try the Brooklyn Handicap. Omaha had not previously raced out of his class. The Brooklyn Handicap was a race for three year olds and up, which meant that Omaha would face older horses. And, to boot, there was even a jockey change: Wayne Wright, not Saunders, rode Omaha. Six horses started in the 1 1/8-mile race, and Omaha was the even-money favorite in the betting. As usual, Omaha broke slow, sixth at the start. He trailed throughout the race, although by the half-mile mark, he was in third. There he stayed, failing to make up any ground. A horse named Discovery won in world's record time for the 1 1/8 mile, 1:48 1/5. The notes to the race results stated Omaha "Was a badly beaten horse at the end of the race." About the only consolation for Woodward was an announcement made after the race by the officers of the Queens County Jockey Club:

> *"We have voted* [so went the announcement] *Mr. Woodward
> our heartfelt appreciation for his support of New York racing. He
> passed up the $25,000 American Derby for horses of Omaha's age,
> which was at the mercy of the colt, in order to run in our $10,000
> race where his chances to win were problematical. We feel it is a
> practical example of sportsmanship which is rare in this present
> day."*

Take it for what it was worth.[4]

There was no shame in losing to a record-setter, but better had been expected of Omaha. His next start was the Dwyer Stakes at Aqueduct on June 29, 1935. Five horses contended, including Omaha. The weather was good and the track was fast. Wayne Wright again rode Omaha. The Triple Crown winner was second to a horse named Good Gamble at the start, and stayed in second through the half-mile and three-quarter-mile marks. He caught up with Good Gamble and took the lead at the head of the stretch. He won the nine-furlong race in time of 1:49 1/5. The purse was a princely (for 1935) $9,200.

Proving that he could run and win in the Midwest, Omaha won the 1-1/4 mile Arlington Classic at Arlington Park in Chicago on July 20. Wayne Wright was on Omaha, and the pair challenged nine other horses. As usual, Omaha started slowly (seventh at the start) and fell back to eighth at the quarter-mile mark. Wright had taken him to the outside, and he started to move up slightly on the backstretch. He started to pass the leaders on the stretch turn and was second by the three-quarter mile mark. He drew clear, took a 1 1/2-length lead, and held it to win.

It was his last race of the year. In fact, it was Omaha's last race ever in America. After the Arlington, Omaha was shipped to Saratoga in anticipation of more racing, including the Travers on August 17. But while training at Saratoga, Omaha pulled up lame. His third year racing season was over. He spent the rest of the year at Woodward's Belair Stud in Maryland. It was a curious third year; victories in the Triple Crown, the South Shore Stakes, the Dwyer, and the Arlington Classic as well as the losses in the Wood Memorial, the Withers, and the Brooklyn Handicap. He was the leading money-winner that year, but he had not swept away everything before him, as had his sire in 1930. Still, Gallant Fox and Omaha were the first, and to date the only, father-son pair to win the Triple Crown.

---

[4]At least that was better than what happened to Wright in the next race. He was suspended for two days due to a riding infraction in the race following the Brooklyn Handicap.

With the end of Omaha's American racing career, we must now say adieu to Willie Saunders. Saunders' image received a blow in the autumn of 1935. He was a major jockey, a racing idol, but a tragedy that autumn forever marred him. Evelyn Sliwinski, the 24-year-old wife of a Louisville tailor, was found dead on a Louisville highway on the morning of October 20, 1935. Another lady, Agatha Mackenson, said that she saw Sliwinski at a roadhouse party the previous evening. Mackenson said that she and Sliwinski left with two men. Evelyn Sliwinski, according to this report, became ill in the car, and one of the men struck her repeatedly. The driver threw Sliwinski out onto the road, then ran over the dazed woman. The driver drove about five miles, turned the car around, came back, and again ran over Sliwinski. Mackenson identified Willie Saunders as the man in the back seat during the incident.

When the word got out, Saunders turned himself into the Louisville police. In those pre-*Miranda* days, Saunders talked to the police freely. He admitted he was in the back seat during Evelyn Sliwinski's last ride, but stated he had no part in her death. Saunders identified Walter Schaeffer as the driver. Accordingly, Schaeffer was charged with murder and Saunders was charged with being an accessory to murder.

The trial was held in early January, 1936, at Louisville. The jury deliberated two hours and found Schaeffer not guilty on January 9. Under Kentucky law, if the principal to murder (Schaeffer) was found not guilty, the accessory (Saunders) could not then be convicted. The charges against Saunders were dismissed. The jockey was contrite: "I've been very much worried because it was the first time I was ever in trouble, but I promise you it will be the last," he said. [5]

Willie Saunders went back to riding. In the words of his obituary in *The Blood-Horse*, "He went on to distinguish himself in the Thoroughbred industry and as a cavalryman during World War II." Saunders won the 1936 San Juan Capistrano Handicap, and the 1937 Santa Margarita Handicap. His winnings for three years averaged more than $100,000 per year, healthy sums during the middle of the Depression. Fittingly, he served in the cavalry (by that time, mechanized, not mounted) in the Pacific in World War II. He returned to racing in 1946. We will see him again, albeit briefly, in the Citation saga.

Saunders retired as a jockey in 1950 and became a racing official. As a jockey he rode 3,401 mounts and won 401 races for a win percentage of 11.7%. He finished third or better 34% of the time. He was a racing official for twenty-seven years, retiring in 1977. One photo of the then-living Triple Crown jockeys, taken in 1976, shows Saunders in the middle of the group, Warren Mehrtens and John Longden on one side of him, Eddie Arcaro and Ron Turcotte on the other side. It is Saunders who is the focal point of the picture; the

---

[5] Evelyn Sliwinski's husband also filed a $100,000 damage suit against Schaeffer and Saunders. That case was settled out of court.

viewer's eyes are drawn immediately to Saunders' sheaf of white hair and the broad smile on his face.

Willie Saunders died of cancer in Naples, Florida, on July 30, 1986. He remains the least-known of all the Triple Crown-winning jockeys.

English racing had long appealed to American owners. Over the years, various American horses had gone to England to try racing there. As recently as 1929, the previous year's Kentucky Derby winner, Reigh Count, raced in England.[6] Woodward planned for Omaha to go overseas. The plan made some sense: Woodward had been at one time part of the American Embassy staff in London and had many English contacts. Omaha's clear strength and good recovery from the lameness indicated he might do well on turf, and the longer distances in English racing meant that Omaha's slow starts and impressive strong finishes made for likely success. In December, 1935, the announcement came: On December 6, Omaha would be shipped to England "...if his condition is reported good." On Christmas Eve, 1935, he was taken from Belair Stud to Aqueduct. A week later, the final announcement came: Omaha would race in England in 1936.

On January 8, 1936, the *Aquitania* of the Cunard White Star Line left New York harbor with Omaha. He arrived in Southampton on January 15, 1936 and was taken to Newmarket for training. He would be the only American Triple Crown winner to race in England.

His first English victory was on May 9, 1936, in the Victor Wild Stakes at Kempton Park. His jockey in England was Pat Beasley. The course was a mile-and-one-half in length, the same as the Belmont Stakes. For the first mile Omaha stayed back, just as he had under Saunders in the Triple Crown the previous year. Then Beasley let him go, and just as he had the year before, Omaha cut loose. He went from fourth place a half-mile from the finish to first within twenty yards. He won by 1 1/2 lengths.

Three weeks later, on May 21, 1936, Omaha won the Queen's Plate at Kempton Park. This time the race was *two* miles. Once again, Beasley kept Omaha in check throughout most of the race. A horse called Bobsleigh took the early lead, but Omaha stayed with him throughout the race. Again, Omaha put on his usual finishing show, and took the lead in the last quarter-mile. He won by a neck over Bobsleigh.

Omaha was rated the favorite for the Ascot Gold Cup on June 18, 1936, but it wasn't to be. The Ascot Gold Cup was at that time the world's longest race; two and one-half miles. Omaha was nervous at the beginning and may have burned up valuable energy. His jockey held Omaha in restraint behind a filly named Quashed for the first two miles. Then, with a half-mile to go,

---

[6] Reigh Count will appear again in this book; he sired the 1943 Triple Crown winner, Count Fleet.

Quashed and Omaha were let loose and took the lead head to head. For the last half-mile, it was a match race between Quashed and Omaha, with the lead alternating between them. But then the conformance of the Ascot course made a critical difference: an incline lead to the finish. Omaha hit the incline, broke stride, and dropped back a quarter of a length. He was never quite able to make it up. At the end, it was Quashed by a nose.

It may not have even been that much; many thought it was a dead heat between Omaha and Quashed. Even Quashed's jockey said, "I couldn't see anything between us at the finish." There was talk of a special match race between Omaha and Quashed, but the Woodwards put a stop to that. Mrs. Woodward said on June 19, 1936, "It is not like Mr. Woodward to do other than to accept a race as run. Horses are not machines and they do lose. Naturally, he was disappointed that Omaha did not win, but I feel sure there is no desire on his part for a special match race."

Omaha's last race was on July 2, 1936. He finished second in the 1 1/2-mile Princess of Wales' Stakes at Newmarket to a horse called Taj Akbar. Omaha had to concede eighteen pounds of weight, carrying 138 pounds to Taj Akbar's 120 pounds. Before the start Omaha was again nervous and sweating profusely in the paddock. Omaha stayed with the leaders throughout the race, and in the words of one account, "For a mile and a quarter of the 1 1/2-mile race he [Omaha] seemed the winner." He battled head-to-head with Taj Akbar during the last quarter mile. But the weight handicap proved too much for Omaha, and possibly, some bad handling by the jockey in that last portion. Omaha lost by a neck to Taj Akbar. The weight handicap made the difference: in the words of one report, "No horse in the world could win with such a handicap."

Still, it had been a good year for Omaha. Racing on foreign tracks, at longer distances, in the opposite direction from American racing, over uneven track surfaces, he had won two important races and finished second by the slightest of margins in two other races. One loss was very likely due to the weight he had to carry. He generated excitement in the British racing community, but no one knew then that the Princess of Wales Stakes was the last race Omaha would ever run.

Omaha spent the winter of 1936-1937 in England. Woodward planned to try the Triple Crown winner again in the 1937 Ascot Gold Cup. Omaha was entered in two English races, but was scratched in each of them in order to focus on the Ascot Gold Cup. Woodward entered him in the Gold Cup, but withdrew him due to lameness from a tendon injury in his left foreleg. On June 14, 1937, the announcement came from London: Omaha would be retired from racing and returned to the U.S.A. for stud duty. He was loaded on the *American Merchant* on September 3, 1937, and landed in New York City on September 13.

Omaha never raced after the 1936 season. He returned to Claiborne Farm in Paris, Kentucky, where he had been foaled. He joined his sire in stud duty.

Omaha has been regarded with Sir Barton and Citation as an unsuccessful sire.[7] This is not totally true: An item in the AK-Sar-Ben Racetrack files, the track where Omaha was buried, notes that Omaha's progeny won 565 races. He sired a few stakes winners, including South Dakota, Hidalgo, and Prevaricator. In the 1950s, an article appeared stating that Omaha's grandchildren were more successful on the track than his children were.

But Omaha has the last laugh — horselaugh, if you will — on history's assessment of him as a failure at stud. He has one major link to modern horses, an extremely important one that is little-known. Omaha foaled a filly named Flaming Top who in turn bore a filly named Flaring Top. Flaring Top in turn foaled a daughter named Flaming Page, who gave birth to Nijinsky II, the last winner of the English Triple Crown (through 1999) and one of the most important sires of recent times.[8] So without Omaha, the horse that was branded a failure at stud, we would not have many of the great racehorses of today.

But in the 1940s, all of that was in the future. In 1943, Woodward determined that Omaha was unlikely to sire successful racehorses. Accordingly, Woodward leased Omaha to the Jockey Club's Lookover Stallion Station in Avon, New York. That lasted seven more years, when a group of breeders in (appropriately) Omaha, Nebraska, bought him and shipped him west.

The trip from New York to Nebraska had its own tale. Omaha was not penned-up or crated, but was allowed to stand loose in the railcar. At every stop, Morton Porter, who accompanied Omaha, opened the car's door. Fifty-two years later Porter recalled, "Whenever the train would stop, I'd let Omaha walk around a little bit. That always drew a lot of attention because people weren't used to seeing a horse on the train." People came up to see the horse, and the visitors heard the story of the third Triple Crown winner, and the only one to race overseas. At the end of each stop, "...people would clap and wave good-bye to us," Morton Porter remembered. "They knew they were looking at a real special animal." *Indeed....*

He wound up as a pensioner at the farm of Grove Porter, Nebraska's then-racing commissioner, in Nebraska City[9]. The third Triple Crown winner remained a local celebrity until his death in 1959. He mellowed over the years, and he loved being groomed. Around visitors, he was usually easy to handle,

---

[7] "Success as a sire" means that the stallion sired horses that were themselves successful racers.

[8] At Nijinsky II's death in 1992, the horse was second on the list of all-time sires. Omaha's connection to Nijinsky II is more important than is commonly acknowledged.

[9] He was still turned out for stud occasionally. Any owner that wanted his mare to mate with Omaha needed only to contribute $25 to charity.

and he adored being fed apples. One day a small boy who visited Omaha regularly slipped over the fence and mounted Omaha bareback. The hose didn't mind; he stood patiently, unconcerned about anything.

But occasionally, his old orneriness returned; Morton Porter, Grove Porter's son, remembered that the old racer was "...a bit cranky in his last months, but he was really interesting, with a personality all his own. One below-zero morning, he bit my upper arm through several layers of heavy clothing. It did not break the skin, but my arm was black and blue, indicating the tremendous strength in his jaws." Porter also recalled that later he and Omaha "...had some words over that."

Now and again Grove Porter took Omaha out to the AK-Sar-Ben track at the Omaha Stock Show for the fans to see. The horse strutted with pride at every such occasion. At one Omaha Gold Cup race (named for him), it was terribly hot. Omaha sweated profusely in the winner's circle, and then finally rolled around in the sand like a colt. The crowd loved it. Morton Porter, holding Omaha's head, told track management that he didn't know how much longer he could keep Omaha from rolling over. Finally, J.J. Issacson, AK-Sar-Ben's General Manager, told Porter, "Well, let him roll. People aren't betting anyway. They are all watching Omaha, and let him put on his show." Morton Porter let the champion go, and Omaha "...rolled clear over on his withers and came up on the other side." The crowd went wild over that.

A few minutes later the race started, and Morton Porter remembered wondering how the old horse would behave. He found out: when the starting bell rang at the start of a race, Omaha "...almost jumped the track to get into the thing."

Omaha is the most difficult Triple Crown champion to assess accurately. In 1935 and 1936 he naturally attracted much attention from the press but unlike Man o'War or Secretariat, faded quickly from public view.[10] Omaha's racing record is spotty: nine wins out of twenty-two starts. In both raw numbers and win percentage, his numbers are the lowest of any Triple Crown Champion. But, he did win the Triple Crown, and ran very creditably in England. Different opinions have been offered about Omaha: racing expert John Hervey wrote of him: "In action he was a glorious sight; few Thoroughbreds have exhibited such a magnificent, sweeping, pace-annihilating stride, or carried it with such strength and precision. His place is among the Titans of the American Turf."

Whew! Marvin Drager said of Omaha in his book, *The Most Glorious Crown,* "The career of the third horse to wear the Triple Crown in the United States could be best summed up in a word as 'erratic.'"

---

[10] A telling example is Jimmy Breslin's 1962 book, *Sunny Jim: The Life of America's Most Beloved Horseman,.* Breslin devotes several pages to Gallant Fox, but only three paragraphs in the book mention Omaha.

It's not easy to reconcile those statements, but it can be done. Kent Hollingsworth wrote, "Omaha was one of America's great stayers." And there's the answer. He was a *distance* runner, more at home in a long race than a short one. His misfortune was to be born at the wrong time and then plagued by injuries. He raced at a time when races were shorter, and had little opportunity to show what he really *could* do in long races. In his two-year-old season, he showed his powerful ending stride time and time again. He was clearly the best in the Belmont Stakes. When he raced in England under heavy weight over a long distance, Omaha showed his true ability. Had he been born fifty years earlier, he might have been remembered as one of the great horses of all time.

WAR ADMIRAL

Most racing fans would summarize War Admiral in three sentences:
>He was the smallest son of Man o'War.
>He won the Triple Crown in 1937.
>He lost a match race to Seabiscuit in 1938.

Those statements are true, but to leave it there would diminish the Admiral. He was far more than just a mere recitation of those statements, and he deserves to be remembered as a whole. His statistics compare to the best of them: 26 starts, 21 firsts, 3 seconds, 1 third-place finish. His win percentage was 81%; his money percentage, 96%...and then came a magnificent stud career.

But there is more to War Admiral than a saga of an overlooked champion, the son of America's greatest horse. His story is one of greatness shadowed by bad luck. Injuries, illness, and an incredible miscalculation by his owner plagued his career. The Admiral deserves to be remembered as a great champion in his own right.

His story starts on May 2, 1934. By then, Man o'War had proven to be a pretty good sire. One son, Clyde Van Dusen, had won the 1929 Kentucky Derby, and two other sons, American Flag and Crusader, respectively had won the 1925 and 1926 Belmont Stakes races. In 1933, Man o'War mated with a filly named Brushup. Brushup had some good bloodlines and raced twice as a two-year-old, placing once and showing once. She didn't seem an auspicious choice for Man o'War, but who could tell? The formula was, and still is, "breed the best to the best and hope for the best."

This best son of Man o'War was born at Sam Riddle's Faraway Farm. Man o'War was powerful and tall (about sixteen hands); Brushup was smaller, about fifteen hands. Their colt, named War Admiral, never grew beyond 15.3 hands. The colt was the smallest son that Man o'War sired, and some nicknamed the Admiral "The Mighty Atom." Whatever the diminutive intent of "Atom", "Mighty" turned out to be one hundred percent accurate.

WAR ADMIRAL, fourth Triple Crown winner, 1937 Kentucky Derby. Jockey, Charles Kurtsinger. © *Collection of L. S. Sutcliffe. C. Ken Grayson, owner. Used by permission.*

War Admiral's trainer was George Conway, one of the best and simultaneously least-known trainers in racing. Conway was shy and avoided publicity; even his birth date is unknown. He was born about 1869, and entered racing around 1887 as a groom. By the turn of the century, he became a trainer. His winning horse was a filly named Evening who won a race at the old Gravesend Park in New York on June 8, 1905. A few years later, Conway hooked up with Sam Riddle and became Riddle's track foreman. From there, it was only a short step to becoming Louis Feustel's assistant trainer, and Conway helped train Man o'War. By 1926, Conway became the head trainer at Glen Riddle Farm. He trained Crusader.

Conway was a careful and patient conditioner of horses. He believed that a horse should not be run if the horse was not at its best. That belief dovetailed with much of Sam Riddle's thinking, and Riddle respected Conway's abilities. The synergy of like minds resulted in a good team on the track: War Admiral, trained by George Conway, usually ridden by Charles Kurtsinger.

WAR ADMIRAL. Winner, Triple Crown, 1937.
© *Collection of L. S. Sutcliffe. C. Ken Grayson, owner. Used by permission.*

"His chief assets as a jockey are his ability to judge pace; his strength, which allows him to hold a horse back if it wants to run out too early; his willingness and ability to obey the orders of a trainer, and above all, his coolness."
— Quentin Reynolds on Charles Kurtsinger,
"A Man and A Horse,"
Collier's, May 14, 1938.

Charles Kurtsinger was one of racing's greatest jockeys. He was born in Louisville, Kentucky, on November 16, 1906, not far from Churchill Downs. He started riding as a jockey in 1924. In 1931 he rode Twenty Grand to victories in the Wood Memorial, Kentucky Derby, Belmont Stakes, Dwyer Stakes, Lawrence Realization, and Jockey Club Gold Cup. The following year he rode Head Play to victory in the Preakness. He was one of Omaha's jockeys in 1934. By 1936 he was riding for Glen Riddle Farm, and he got the chance to ride the small colt foaled by Man o'War. The Admiral and Kurtsinger became one of racing's greatest horse-jockey combinations. Charles Kurtsinger has been overshadowed by his contemporaries Earl Sande, George Woolf, and John Longden, to name a few, and is not well-known except to racing experts. But his record as a jockey speaks for itself.

> *"He's the most beautiful horse I ever saw. Man O'War wasn't beautiful.*
> *Man O'War was magnificent-looking, but he lacked the sharply*
> *etched, almost feminine beauty of the Admiral."*
> — Quentin Reynolds,
> "A Man and a Horse," *Collier's,* May 14, 1938

War Admiral was so small that only his head and neck resembled that of his sire. But that small size meant he was "power packed", and harbored a highly concentrated version of his father's desire to race. Like his sire, War Admiral was friendly around the barn, and it was only as he approached the starting gate that his intense desire to race came to the fore. Of all the horses that have won the Triple Crown, he was the most obstreperous at the starting gate.[11] Sometimes the starters allowed War Admiral to start from outside the gate, at the farthest position. (This practice has been stopped. If a horse won't enter the gate, the racing stewards are empowered to scratch the horse then and there.) It should have been an impossible handicap, starting from so far out, but War Admiral was the classic "catch-me if-you-can" horse, taking an early lead and holding it all through the race. He inherited his sire's speed, and most of the time that was enough. His trademark: a near tantrum at the starting gate followed by a wire-to-wire victory. After the start, it was smooth going. He didn't need blinders and was easy to handle on the track. Only the starting gate gave him trouble. John Hervey noted that foible, and wrote of War Admiral, "Otherwise, he is a faultless racing machine."[12]

Most of Man o'War's foals (including War Admiral) didn't inherit his father's two-year-old speed. They were all good, yes; better than most. But in general, they didn't have his youthful power. The records of most of Man o'War's foals at age two seem disappointing when compared to their sire.

War Admiral's first race was on April 25, 1936, at a 4 1/2-furlong maiden race at Havre de Grace, Maryland. Ten horses were entered, and the Admiral ranked third choice in the betting. He ran second for most of the race, but took the lead in the stretch and finished first by a neck. The *Daily Racing Form* chart notes say, "WAR ADMIRAL, a keen factor in the early running, came courageously when straightened into the stretch and outfinished SONNY JOE

---

[11] Grantland Rice once wrote, "War Admiral was no picnic at the start, but he couldn't hold a candle to his old man." Thank God for small favors: the starting gate hadn't been invented when Man o'War was running, but one shudders to think what would have happened if anyone had even TRIED to put Big Red in a starting gate. The result would have been too horrible to contemplate.

[12] Kurtsinger once explained War Admiral's behavior at the starting gate as, "He likes to run, he's anxious to get going, and he isn't going to let some goat get the jump on him. That's all. The Admiral and I like to get away first and let them chase us."

under a vigorous drive."

Like Man o'War, War Admiral had broken his maiden (won) in his first race. His next race occurred at Belmont Park on May 21 in the $900 Brightwaters Purse race. He opposed seven other horses, and it was in this race he set the pattern. The race was 5/8 of a mile. War Admiral jumped immediately to the lead, held onto it, and finished first by two lengths.

The National Stallion Stakes at Belmont Park rolled around on June 7. Ten horses ran. The Admiral had some trouble in it; he broke well and was second at the start. But his jockey in that race, John Westrope, let him swerve inside to the rail. That cost him ground and time. He battled back to finish third by a nose. The winner was Pompoon, of whom more later. The notes to *The New York Times* race chart pay tribute to War Admiral's character: "He ran a good race under poor handling."

Charles Kurtsinger's first race on War Admiral took place on July 1, 1936, at the Great American Stakes at Aqueduct. The Admiral was second choice in the betting behind a colt named Fairy Hill. The race was a good one: War Admiral was in first place by the 1/4-mile mark, but another horse, Top Radio, challenged him. Top Radio took over first under encouragement from his jockey's whip. Kurtsinger, too, went to the whip on War Admiral and regained first place. But into the stretch, the Admiral tired. The challenge by Top Radio had taken some energy out of him, and with a furlong to go, he swerved. War Admiral was solidly ahead of the pack, but Fairy Hill came on, passed him, and won by two lengths.

Up to that point, War Admiral had a decent record: four starts, two victories, one second, and one third. But remember, he was a Man o'War colt, and much was expected of him, especially after his victories in his first two races. Then the first incident in a string of bad luck occurred: A coughing virus affected racehorses that summer, and War Admiral caught it. He rested for two months, missed the Saratoga meet that summer, and was ineligible to run in the Belmont, Pimlico, or Narragansett Futurity races for two-year-old horses. (In retrospect, it was unfortunate that War Admiral missed the Pimlico Futurity. Future races would show that War Admiral and Pimlico Racetrack were not meant for each other. A loss in the 1936 Pimlico Futurity might have gotten that message home early and at low risk.)

He came back on September 19, 1936, in the Eastern Shore Stakes at Havre de Grace. It was a massive field of fifteen horses in a 3/4-mile race. Kurtsinger hustled him right to the lead, as in the Brightwaters Purse, and he never gave up. He finished five lengths in front of the pack in time of 1:11. It was a new record for that race, and the Admiral regained some luster.

He ran his last race as a two-year-old at Laurel on October 10 in the 3/4-mile Richard Johnson Handicap. The track was muddy, and War Admiral carried the most weight: 124 pounds. No other horse carried more than 119 pounds. These factors made the difference. Kurtsinger put him immediately in the lead, but at the 1/2-mile, he was caught by a horse named Bottle Cap. Kurtsinger kept the pressure on the Admiral, but it wasn't enough; the combination of the weight and the muddy track put War Admiral in second, 1 1/2 lengths behind Bottle Cap.

The raw numbers show that War Admiral had a good rookie year. He ran six races, won three, was second in two, and third in the remaining race. He was never out of the money, and had a creditable fifty percent win record. His winnings of $14,800 were low by today's standards, but good when it is remembered that the nation was still caught in the Great Depression, causing purses to be low in general. Moreover, the virus caused him to miss most of the *good* two-year-old races. The virus hampered him, to be sure, but there was really little to complain about. Pompoon was named champion two-year-old, while War Admiral was well-regarded. 1937 promised a showdown between the two horses.

War Admiral began the 1937 racing season where he started the year before, at Havre de Grace. He ran on April 14, 1937, in the $1,000 Calvert Purse. It was only a six-furlong race with five other horses. The track was fast, and War Admiral broke well. He went straight to the lead and never gave it up: He finished three lengths ahead of his nearest competitor. At one point, Kurtsinger asked the Admiral for full speed, and he responded, in the words of *The New York Times,* "apparently without effort." His time of 1:11 2/5 was the best time posted for that distance in Maryland that spring.

The victory was impressive. It qualified him immediately for the Kentucky Derby. But there would be no long rest for War Admiral before the Derby; ten days later, he won the 1 1/16-mile Chesapeake Stakes at Havre de Grace. He ran against six other horses, but "…none showed the ability to run with the trim brown son of Man o'War."

He was the favorite in the betting, and didn't disappoint his backers. Kurtsinger again let him go right to the front, but kept him in check for most of the race. The Admiral was never more than two lengths in front through the 3/4-mile mark, and two horses, Court Scandal and Fairy Hill, challenged him. Kurtsinger let him go, and War Admiral "drew away, hit the home stretch with plenty of reserve, and speedily lengthened his lead." The Admiral crossed the line six lengths ahead of Court Scandal in time of 1:45. Conway was jubilant: "He ran like a champion," the trainer said. The Kentucky Derby lay ahead.

"60,000 SEE WAR ADMIRAL DEFEAT POMPOON IN DERBY"
–The New York Times
Sports page headline, May 9, 1937

To modern racing fans, it seems curious that Sam Riddle entered only one horse in the Kentucky Derby in his long involvement in racing: War Admiral in

1937. Riddle preferred to race his horses in Maryland and New York. Moreover, he had a sound reason, one that is still shared by many horse owners and trainers. Riddle felt that 1 1/4 miles in early May was just a bit too far too early for a three-year-old horse. Not that it really mattered. The only horse he ever started in the Derby won it.[13]

War Admiral was the favorite for the 1937 Kentucky Derby to be run on May 8. He was rated at odds of $1.60 to $1.00. The track was fast, and the horses went to the post at 4:42. True to his heritage, the Admiral's fractiousness held up the race start for an incredible 8 1/2 minutes. He was at the pole position, and at the break, immediately led the field of twenty horses. It was a reasonably close race for some time. War Admiral never had more than a 1 1/2-length lead through the mile, but after that, he increased his lead. At the beginning of the stretch, he had a three-length lead over Pompoon, the number two horse. Pompoon was a stretch runner, and he made his run in the home stretch. It wasn't enough; Kurtsinger piloted War Admiral home 1-3/4 lengths ahead of Pompoon with a time of 2:03 1/5.

The newsreel of the race focused on the Admiral headed for home. Kurtsinger is on him, not letting go, only using the whip once, not steering him, just letting his horse do the work. The Admiral seems to be running like a horse possessed: His ears are pricked up, and his legs claw the air in front of him. The velocity and totality of the image are of complete, ferocious determination and absolute fire: *"Don't get in my way,"* he seems to say. The viewer is left with the unsettling thought: could any horse, even his daddy, have been better on the track...?

"WAR ADMIRAL DEFEATS POMPOON BY HEAD IN PREAKNESS"
— *The New York Times*
Sports Page headline, May 16, 1937

The Admiral was shipped to Pimlico that night for the Preakness slated for one week later. That race was a different story.

The Preakness field was much smaller, only eight horses. The horses went to the post at 5:25 P.M., and the Admiral was on his best behavior this time, only delaying the start 3 1/2 minutes in this race. Kurtsinger and he were at the post again, rated favorite at $0.35 to $1.00. The start was good. Again Kurtsinger took the Admiral to the lead. But two things were different: Two other horses in the race, Jewell Dorsett and Flying Scot, didn't allow War

---

[13]This raises the question: Why *did* Sam Riddle enter War Admiral in the 1937 Derby? One answer may be that he was jealous of William Woodward. Woodward's father-son entries Gallant Fox and Omaha each won the Triple Crown and attracted much attention. One way for Riddle to regain the limelight was to have his own father-son team of Man o' War-War Admiral capture the headlines.

101

Admiral to get away from them in the Preakness's early stages. And, there was Pimlico's geometry to contend with: The turns are tighter at Pimlico than at other tracks. Kurtsinger let the Admiral go wide on the first turn, costing him ground and time. While they were in the lead the entire race, it was always close. For most of the race War Admiral only led by a length, and never more than 1 1/2 lengths. At the 3/4-mile mark, Pompoon moved up to just one length behind War Admiral. It looked like the Admiral was in trouble.

To make matters worse, Kurtsinger took the Admiral wide again on the far turn. This move forced Pompoon farther to the outside. Kurtsinger explained later, "I went as wide as I did to pick the best footing for War Admiral. I was never worried." Perhaps the jockey wasn't worried, but almost everyone else at Pimlico that day *was*: Pompoon came on with his late run, and at the beginning of the home stretch, was only a head behind the Admiral. Pompoon's jockey, Wayne Wright, went to the whip, and Pompoon and War Admiral battled down the stretch. At times, Pompoon was in a nose in front; then War Admiral edged ahead. Kurtsinger kept cool and didn't panic. He just waved the whip at the Admiral, never touching him. It was enough; however good Pompoon was, War Admiral was the better horse. He crossed the finish line a mere head in front of Pompoon. It remains the closest Preakness victory of all the Triple Crown winners.[14]

Back at Faraway Farm, Will Harbut, Man o'War's groom, was more romantic about War Admiral's Preakness victory. In Harbut's version of the race, the close finish was more of a deliberate challenge than a near victory. With a reference to Man o'War's epic finish over John P. Grier in the 1920 Dwyer Stakes, Harbut told visitors about War Admiral, "He won mos' all the races his daddy won. In the Preakness he went wide and let Pompoon run up to him, den he looked over Pompoon and he said, 'Pompoon, my daddy broke John P. Grier's heart! Come on!'"

"WAR ADMIRAL WINS BELMONT STAKES FOR TRIPLE CROWN"
— *The New York Times*
Sports Page headline, June 6, 1937

Their respective owners made War Admiral and Pompoon skip the Withers Stakes in order to save them for Round Three: the Belmont Stakes on June 5. Seven horses entered the race, the track was fast, and War Admiral was on the outside, seventh from the post. He was the favorite in the betting, at 4 to 5. Pompoon was there, and was second choice at 3 to 1.

---

[14] Really, Kurtsinger *wasn't* worried in the Preakness. Later, he said, "The Preakness was an easier race for War Admiral than the Derby, for in the Derby I did hit the colt a couple of times and shook him up a time or two, but in the Preakness, I rode with more coolness and more confidence and did not lay the whip on him."

The horses went to the post at 4:22 P.M., and the Admiral was up to his old tricks again. He delayed the start with his fractious behavior for seven and a half minutes.[15] Finally the race started, and Kurtsinger took War Admiral right to the lead. There was no serious challenge: Pompoon was never better than fourth and the Admiral maintained a steady lead of three or four lengths throughout the race. One horse, Sceneshifter, moved into second but never came close. The Admiral cruised to a three-length victory in an official time of 2:28 3/5, a new track record.

Even more remarkable about the Admiral's record victory was the condition he ran it in. At the start of the race, War Admiral had stumbled and trod on his own right forefoot. The shoe on his right rear hoof caught the right front hoof and sheared off of a bit of his hoof. It was a severe injury: he ran the race bleeding all the way and went into the winner's circle trailing blood. The previous record for a 1 1/2-mile race was 2:28 4/5, set by Man o'War. On only three good hooves, spattering blood on his underbelly from the cut, War Admiral broke his father's record.

A veterinarian pronounced the hoof injury serious but neither fatal nor permanent. It was clear War Admiral would be out for some time. There was no possibility that he could run in the Dwyer Stakes or Arlington Classic but some hoped he might be able to run in the Lawrence Realization at Belmont in late September. The Admiral was shipped to Saratoga for summer recuperation. True to his off-track nature, he was a good patient, easy to work with and not fractious at all. His small size worked in his favor. There was less stress on the injured hoof, and that aided his recovery.

The Admiral made one appearance at Saratoga. On August 14, the day of the 1937 Travers Stakes, he was paraded before the crowd. He didn't run in the Travers, or in any other of the races at Saratoga that summer: Riddle and Conway knew he was too great a horse to risk an injury by a premature return to racing. The summer passed, and the leaves at Saratoga started to turn. War Admiral improved, but he was still not quite ready. He was sent back to Glen Riddle Farm in Maryland for some rest during the last bit of warm weather.

He had started the racing year in Maryland, and he would finish it there. On October 26, 1937, War Admiral returned to racing in the $1,200, 1 1/16-

---

[15] A quartet of photos taken at the 1937 Belmont Stakes clearly illustrates War Admiral's antipathy to the starting gate. Several times, the Admiral was led into the gate, only to go out through the front, even dragging a handler with him. One of the photos shows the Admiral's ears down and a look of clear disgust on his face. The author showed these photos to his father, who remembered the Admiral from his teenage years. The father's immediate comment was, "The sonsofbitches! Trying to make him go into the starting gate! What the hell were they thinking of!" Dad, the world is a far less interesting place without you.

mile Church Hill Purse at the Laurel track. Despite the long layoff, he was the favorite in the betting at odds of $0.40 to $1.00. He had changed little in the last five months. He still hated the starting gate and delayed the race for 6 1/2 minutes. It was a classic War Admiral race: Kurtsinger took him right to the lead, and put him out in the middle of the track where the going was easier. The Admiral was only challenged in the first quarter-mile. On the backstretch he demonstrated that the layoff had cost him nothing in speed. At the start of the stretch, he was four lengths ahead of the number two horse. Kurtsinger eased him up some, and he finished 2 1/2 lengths ahead of the pack.

He was his old self, fractious at the gate and swift on the track. Only five days separated him from his next race, the $19,100 1 1/4-mile Washington Handicap at Laurel. He carried the most weight in the race, 126 pounds, but that didn't make any difference. He led all the way and won by 1 1/2 lengths. The purse made him the leading money-winner of the year.

Sam Riddle and George Conway entered him in a new race, the Pimlico Special, to be run on November 3, 1937 at Pimlico. The race was a 1 3/16 mile race, the same distance as the Preakness. Somehow, War Admiral's Preakness finish was forgotten in the planning for his final race. Three other horses challenged him, and it was his toughest race of 1937. The track was fast and he just couldn't seem to get a grip on the track surface. He was second at the start, third at the 1/4-mile mark, third at the 1/2-mile, and was still in third at the 3/4-mile mark. A horse named Masked General was in the lead, but fortune favored the Admiral. On the far turn, Masked General went very wide, to the extreme outside of the track, and Kurtsinger shot War Admiral through to win by 1 1/2 lengths. He was the leading money winner of the year up to that point. The notes to *The New York Times* chart state ominously, "War Admiral scored a very lucky victory."

Enough was enough. With the Pimlico Special victory in hand, Sam Riddle announced immediately that the Admiral would be retired for the remainder of the year. War Admiral was named "Horse of the Year." He had earned his reputation as of Man o'War's best son and brought home $181,300 for Sam Riddle. It had been a perfect season; eight races, eight victories, and the Triple Crown. Of all the Triple Crown winners, only Count Fleet matched that accomplishment. None of the others — such "minor leaguers" as Gallant Fox, Whirlaway, Citation, Secretariat, and Seattle Slew included — have gone through a three-year-old Triple Crown season undefeated.

But someone in War Admiral's camp should have noticed over the winter what racing author John Hervey wrote in *American Race Horses: 1937:* "That the footing at Pimlico [did] not suit him." There was his close finish in the Preakness, followed by the "very lucky victory" in the Pimlico Special. If the Admiral was to run at Pimlico a third time, he might not be so fortunate.

War Admiral started his 1938 racing season at Hialeah in the 7/8 mile

Heather Purse on February 19. He had only three and a half months of rest, but it didn't affect him. The crowd of 25,000 was Hialeah's greatest crowd to date. They had come to see the previous year's Triple Crown winner race. The Admiral was the bettor's choice, at 0.3 to 1, and five other horses challenged him. He was fractious at the gate, lunging through it ten times before he was removed to the outside. Two horses, Sir Oracle and Stubbs, set the early pace, but Kurtsinger kept War Admiral relaxed, racing to the outside of the track through the half-mile mark. On the far turn Kurtsinger let him go, and he took the lead with a quarter-mile left. At the stretch he led by four lengths, and Kurtsinger let him relax. Sir Oracle challenged, but with too little, too late; War Admiral won by 1 1/2 lengths and extended his winning streak to nine races.

Sam Riddle was jubilant: "He's a great colt. I'm proud of him. After the Widener, I'm going to take him to Maryland, and then to Belmont Park."

The Widener Handicap, two weeks later, was one of the premier Florida races. Riddle and Conway entered the Admiral in it, and quickly came up against an unpleasant fact: the Admiral, being the champion, had to carry high weight penalties. Riddle had avoided that with Man o'War eighteen years earlier by simply retiring him. But Riddle was bound by his promise to run the Admiral.

On March 5, the day of the 1938 Widener, it didn't matter very much. War Admiral had to break from outside again, and in a field of thirteen horses, that was very far out from the post. He carried 130 pounds, sixteen pounds more than any other horse in the race. But the Admiral was the Admiral: Kurtsinger put him right into the lead and nothing mattered; not the weight, not the outside start. He won the 1 1/4-mile race by 1 1/2 lengths in a time of 2:03 4/5. The race was worth $49,500 to Riddle. The notes to the race chart state, "At the far turn, allowed to have his head, he bounded away and opened a wide lead as they swung into the stretch and won easily."

Riddle wasn't stupid: he knew he had one of the great horses of all time in War Admiral. The Admiral was just too good to risk an unnecessary injury. He was small: not more than 15 1/2 hands high and less than 1,000 pounds in weight. Racing under a weight handicap, given the Admiral's stature, was taking a *big* risk. Accordingly, Riddle announced that War Admiral would *not* be started when, in his opinion, the weight handicap would be excessive for him. He withdrew the Admiral from a number of spring races in Maryland.

At the same time, Seabiscuit emerged as a contender.[16] Seabiscuit had been tearing up tracks around the country and the pressure increased for a match race between War Admiral and Seabiscuit. A race had been set for May 30, but that race was canceled by Seabiscuit's handlers. Riddle then announced that

---

[16] Laura Hillenbrand recently recounted Seabiscuit's saga magnificently in her 2001 best-seller, *Seabiscuit: An American Legend.* The reader is referred to that work for Seabiscuit's life and career, including the Seabiscuit-War Admiral match race.

War Admiral would run in the Suburban Handicap at Belmont Park two days earlier instead. But a heavy rain fell on the night of May 27-28 that left the track muddy. Riddle himself was ill and was under doctor's orders not to be disturbed. George Conway took it on himself to scratch the Admiral.

That did it. The racing community's reaction was hostile. Riddle and Conway, and by extension, the Admiral, came in for vituperation. Neither the owner nor the trainer ever uttered a word in apology or self-defense. (Actually, none was needed. Conway had done the right thing.) But they had to do *something* to stem the criticism. They entered the Admiral in the Queens County Handicap, a one-mile race at Aqueduct, on June 6.

The record varies. One account says War Admiral was booed when he went to the Aqueduct post, while another account says he was applauded when he paraded before the fans. And history played its part: eighteen years earlier, John P. Grier had challenged Man o'War in the Dwyer, almost beating him. Now it was the Admiral's turn to race at Aqueduct.

Three other horses started that day: Snark, Rudie, and Danger Point. For once, War Admiral was calm in the starting gate while Rudie was the troublemaker. The Admiral carried 132 pounds; six more than Snark, twenty more than Danger Point, *twenty-three* more than Rudie.

War Admiral broke well, and Kurtsinger eased him into second. Rudie took the early lead, and was still holding first at the quarter pole. Kurtsinger led the Admiral go and he quickly overtook Rudie. Snark, ridden by John Longden, made *his* move and passed Rudie to challenge the Admiral. Now history seemed to repeat itself: just as John P. Grier and Man o'War had battled down the Aqueduct stretch in 1920, so too did Snark and War Admiral battle down the same track. With one furlong left, Snark drew even with War Admiral. Longden used the whip on Snark, but while Kurtsinger drew his whip, he just waved it at the Admiral. War Admiral crossed the wire one length ahead of Snark. Here the record is clear: War Admiral was cheered as he entered the winner's circle. He carried six more pounds than Snark, was a year younger, and still won impressively. His winning streak now tallied eleven races.

War Admiral rested for three weeks, and then was taken to New England to run in the Massachusetts Handicap at Suffolk Downs. Seabiscuit was entered as well and now it appeared that the much-touted race between the two would finally come off. But heavy storms left the track muddy. Seabiscuit was scratched at the last moment, and Riddle and Conway were left "holding the bag." The Admiral went to the post carrying 130 pounds, twenty-three to twenty-nine pounds more than the other horses. One horse, Menow, was a good mudder and jumped quickly to the lead. War Admiral tried valiantly through the race, but the weight and the mud were too much. Menow won, and the Admiral finished fourth behind Menow, Busy K., and War Minstrel. It was the only time in his career that he finished out of the money.

It was disappointing, but understandable. War Admiral had been in training for nearly six months, ran four races, and won three of them carrying weight. The loss, as bad as it looked in print, was due to fatigue, mud, and weight. It was time for another rest.

Riddle and Conway rested the Admiral for a month, and brought him back to racing at Saratoga. On July 27, he won the Wilson Stakes. As at Suffolk Downs the month before, the track was muddy. He was fractious at the gate, but broke well. One horse, Flying Fox, immediately took the lead but went wide, out to the outside fence at the backstretch and Kurtsinger drew the Admiral into the lead. Flying Fox came back, but the Admiral was just too far ahead to be caught. He won by eight lengths.

Three days later Riddle and Conway entered War Admiral in the Saratoga Handicap. It was a 1 1/4-mile race and again the track was muddy. The owner and trainer were pushing things: War Admiral had received only three days rest after a major race, and now raced on a bad surface. War Admiral was carrying 130 pounds to boot. Kurtsinger still rode him, and the Admiral went right to the lead. But Esposa, a filly that had done little in the Wilson Stakes, suddenly came alive. Esposa only carried 116 pounds, and she stayed with War Admiral the entire way. War Admiral had a three-length lead in the stretch, but Esposa challenged him. At the wire, War Admiral was only a neck in front of his challenger. It had been close, very close.

The Admiral was rested for three more weeks and raced again in the 1 ¼ mile Whitney Stakes at Saratoga. In the interim, Kurtsinger was badly injured in a race at Saratoga and was laid up. Wayne Wright rode the Admiral and again Esposa challenged him. The Admiral carried no more weight than he had in the Derby (126 pounds), and this time, the track was fast. Esposa carried 121 pounds and she used that lighter weight advantage all the way. War Admiral took the lead from the beginning, but Esposa again stayed with him. Still, there was no doubt as to the best horse: Wright kept the Admiral under restraint for most of the race, and when Esposa challenged at the end, Wright just hand-rode the champion. He won by a length. Wright said afterwards: "He ran just like a machine. All I had to do was sit there and guide him." Was there ever a time when he thought they might lose the race? "No," said the jockey.

Man o'War won $249,265 in his career; War Admiral winnings now tallied $251,700. The son raced more than the sire; but the purses were smaller due to the Depression. It was a truly great accomplishment.

A week later came the Saratoga Cup, the Admiral's last race at racing's summertime headquarters. Kurtsinger was still not riding and Wright had been suspended, so Maurice Peters got the mount. Esposa challenged the Admiral again, but it was never a contest. War Admiral went right to the lead, and drew away to win by four lengths. Bryan Field of *The New York Times* said of the race: "Peters...was so much at ease aboard Samuel D. Riddle's colt that he spent much of his time looking back over his shoulder at Esposa."

Now there was another month's rest before the 2-mile Jockey Club Gold

Cup at Belmont Park. Only two horses challenged the Admiral, who was the 1 to 10 favorite in the betting. Kurtsinger was still unavailable, but Wayne Wright had finished his suspension. It was really not much of a contest. As usual, War Admiral went into the lead, stayed there, and was never threatened. He won by three lengths.

It had been a near-perfect year for War Admiral: nine races, eight wins, and only the loss in the Massachusetts Handicap. He won $156,160 that year, and there seemed to be no reason why he would *not* be named "Horse of the Year" for 1938.

A new and prickly factor entered the equine equation, and ironically, it was a relative. All of his life, War Admiral had been compared to his sire; now he was being challenged by a nephew. Seabiscuit was a grandson of Man o'War, a nephew, then, of War Admiral. He had originally been trained by Sunny Jim Fitzsimmons at Wheatley Stable, and raced for two years for Wheatley and Sunny Jim. His record was indifferent, and eventually, Charles Howard of San Francisco purchased him. That was the turning point; under Howard's trainer, Tom Smith, Seabiscuit enjoyed success in races across the country. He would be a horse that, though never winning a Kentucky Derby, Preakness, or Belmont Stakes, would be elected to the National Museum of Racing and Hall of Fame. There was a great deal of rivalry between eastern and western racing: War Admiral was the champ of eastern racing, while Seabiscuit was the premier western racer. The fans of eastern racing stated the Admiral was best, while westerners just as enthusiastically plumped for Seabiscuit. Like Sir Barton and Man o'War, the pressure grew for a match race between Seabiscuit and War Admiral.[17] The occasion finally chosen was the 1938 Pimlico Special. It was the third defining moment in War Admiral's life.

The race was scheduled for November 1, 1938. Kurtsinger was to ride the Admiral, who was the favorite. Moreover, Sam Riddle dictated most of the terms for the race, even down to the race announcer. One item stands out: the race was to be run at Pimlico.

PIMLICO! Certainly, one of America's great tracks — but it was the worst possible track for War Admiral. When one looks at his close finishes in the Preakness and the 1937 Pimlico Special, it's not hard to conclude that he had a problem whenever he ran at "Old Hilltop."

So, why did the match race occur at the Admiral's least-favorite track? After many failed attempts to arrange a race between Seabiscuit and War

---

[17] The negotiations between Sam Riddle and Charles Howard (Seabiscuit's owner) started the year before. The lead-in to the November 1, 1938 match race is so complicated and involved that the reader is best referred to the chapter on War Admiral in Marvin Drager's book, *The Most Glorious Crown*. And again, for the "Seabiscuit point of view", Laura Hillenbrand's *Seabiscuit: An American Legend* is the book to read.

Admiral, Alfred Gwynne Vanderbilt, Jr. intervened. Vanderbilt pushed Riddle and Seabiscuit's owner, Charles Howard, to hold the race at Pimlico. Howard really wanted to run at Belmont Park; Riddle didn't want War Admiral to run against Seabiscuit at all.

But Vanderbilt kept at it. He flattered Riddle, even at one point assuring Riddle that War Admiral would handily beat Seabiscuit. Gradually Riddle came around. With Vanderbilt as mediator, Riddle dictated most of the terms of the race. Howard finally agreed, but Riddle remained recalcitrant. Finally, Vanderbilt tracked Riddle down in New York City, found Riddle at Penn Station, and blocked Riddle from boarding the train until he signed the contract. Riddle agreed, but he should have stuck to his guns. It was the worst decision Riddle ever made in his career.

That was bad enough, but at this point, fate intervened. Seabiscuit's usual jockey, Red Pollard, had broken a leg recently at Narragansett Park in Rhode Island. The replacement jockey was George Woolf, one of racing's greatest jockeys. Woolf, in the late 1930s, was probably the best jockey in racing. He was nicknamed "The Iceman" for his cool, controlled style. Kurtsinger wasn't far behind The Iceman in the jockey ratings, but he would be riding against a superstar. So, there it was: the two best horses of the year ridden by the two best jockeys of the year in what would be called racing's all-time greatest match race.

Race day for the 1938 Pimlico Special in Maryland sparkled under a brilliant autumn sun. There would be no further delays of this race. Woolf was his normal cool self; one source says Kurtsinger looked nervous and the Admiral, "A bit tucked up." Because War Admiral hated the starting gate so much, Riddle demanded and got a walking start, where the horses walked up to the start line without being held in a gate. To compensate, Woolf used a trick borrowed from quarter-horse racing: the jockey kept Seabiscuit's head turned towards the Admiral, determined to leave War Admiral no room to dart past him. After two attempts, the race started on the third try.

The Admiral was on the inside, and jumped off on the wrong foot. Woolf went to the whip and Seabiscuit was in the lead by a length as the two horses passed the stands the first time. Seabiscuit got to the rail and pulled four lengths ahead going into the back stretch. Kurtsinger went to the whip on the Admiral and the two horses raced side by side for about a half mile. Then the Admiral caught Seabiscuit on the far turn and got a nose ahead. Woolf went back to the whip, shouted to Kurtsinger, "Get that whip ready, because I'm going to make you run," and managed in a furlong and a half from home to get a half length ahead. By then the Admiral tired; Woolf yelled, "Goodbye, Charley," Seabiscuit drew ahead, and won by four lengths. Seabiscuit broke the track record time of 1:56 3/5. To his dying day, and even today, the Admiral's reputation was shattered by this loss to Seabiscuit.

The Admiral raced once more in 1938, winning the nine-furlong Rhode

Island Handicap at the Narragansett track on November 12, 1938. (Seabiscuit was eligible for that one, too, but his owner decided to pass). The bettors seemingly ignored the result of the Pimlico Special; the Admiral was the favorite of the six horses entered at odds of 1 to 20. War Admiral was again fractious in the starting gate; he had to be moved outside. Kurtsinger broke the Admiral smartly at the start. A horse called Mucho Gusto took the early lead. Kurtsinger kept the Admiral back, but moved up on the backstretch and took the lead by the halfway point. Then Kurtsinger let him go, and he left the others behind. At the far turn War Admiral was six lengths ahead of the rest. Kurtsinger took him under restraint in the last furlong, and he won by 2 1/2 lengths. Riddle was plainly proud of the small horse that had such a great season: "It is time he had a rest. His has been a long campaign, and we are all proud of him."

The Rhode Island Handicap victory wasn't enough to redeem his reputation: when the sportswriters met, War Admiral just missed Horse of the Year honors, which were awarded to Seabiscuit. But Bryan Field said it best when he called the Admiral, "The little horse with the big heart."

SEABISCUIT beats **WAR ADMIRAL** at Pimlico, November 1, 1938.
© *Collection of L. S. Sutcliffe. C. Ken Grayson, owner. Used by permission*

Only one final race remained before the end of Admiral's racing career.

After the Rhode Island Handicap, War Admiral went to Glen Riddle Farm in Maryland for a couple of months. He was shipped to Hialeah in January, 1939, in contemplation of that year's Widener Handicap. The Admiral won one preparatory race, the Fort Pierce Purse, on February 18. The race was worth $1,100. He won it in his style, staying in first all the way. It was his last race.

He developed a fever and was sent north to Belmont Park. He remained in training, but by May the fever had developed into what was called "a rheumatic ailment." He was retired to stud on June 6, 1939. (As an aside, trainer Conway had been in ill health during most of War Admiral's four-year-old season. Conway passed away shortly after War Admiral's retirement. As we shall see, 1939 was therefore the end of racing for all three; War Admiral, Kurtsinger, and Conway.)

War Admiral turned out to be as good a sire as he was a racer. He started out fourth in line from Man o'War in the stalls at Faraway Farm, but worked his way up to the stall of honor next to his sire. Sam Riddle didn't restrict the mares brought to the Admiral, which helped War Admiral's siring record. War Admiral's greatest progeny was Busher, one of the great fillies of all time. From 1944 to 1958, he was consistently in the twenty leading sires of North America and his offspring won nearly $7 million in purses. The Admiral was the leading North American sire in 1945. For seven years in the 1960s, after his death, his grandchildren were successful. He was twice the leading broodmare sire, twice the second-leading broodmare sire, twice the third-leading broodmare sire, and once the fifth-leading broodmare sire of that decade. He appears, albeit far back, in the bloodlines of both Seattle Slew and Affirmed. His name could still be found in 1993 in the pedigree of winning horses. He lived a phenomenal life, and no horse could have done better.

But time changed everything. Sam Riddle died at age ninety in 1951. Seven years later Faraway Farm was sold, together with the stock. Included in the sale were the last four stallions that originated at Glen Riddle Farm, War Admiral among them. The Admiral was sent to Hamburg Place in Kentucky. Ironically, this was the birthplace of Sir Barton, whose career was so intertwined with Man 'o War's.

Well, the Sire giveth, and the Sire taketh away. War Admiral was great in part because he *was* Man o'War's son. But that hobbled him forever: no matter how great the Admiral was, he would always be compared to his sire. It would have taken a perfect racing career to be divested of that burden. No matter how good he was, no matter how many races he ran and won, he would always have been compared unfavorably to Man o'War. He was the horse he was, and his bloodline manifested both his greatness and his burden.

Much has been made of his loss to Seabiscuit. That loss sparks three comments:

1. First, in match races, it is rare that both horses come to the race in top condition. Usually one horse is at peak form while the other is "off his pace." Therefore, the race winds up as an unequal contest between the horses. This was one factor in Sir Barton's loss to Man o'War in 1920, and could have been the story in the Seabiscuit-War Admiral match.

2. Next, even great horses finish second. Citation finished second 10 times; Whirlaway, 15 times; Secretariat, 3 times; Exterminator, 17 times; Count Fleet, 4 times. Enough said.

3. Finally, what disgrace was there in finishing second to Seabiscuit?

War Admiral started more races than Man o'War, won more races than Man o'War, won more money than Man o'War, and won the Triple Crown, which Man o'War, no matter what the explanation, did not win. The Admiral's win percentage remained the highest of all the Triple Crown winners for forty years, until Seattle Slew, with nine fewer career starts, sneaked by him by a mere percentage point. The Admiral set a record in the Belmont Stakes and was a magnificent sire. He places second to no other horse, but no matter what, will always be ranked below his father. Such are the injustices of life.

In the spring of 1939, George Conway retired. He suffered a physical breakdown in May, 1939, and his doctor ordered a long rest. Conway had been in racing (in one job or another) for over fifty years, approximately twenty-five of them with Sam Riddle. Conway went to his brother's home in New Jersey to recuperate, but it was too late. On June 19, 1939, while War Admiral was being transported from New York to Kentucky, George Conway died at Oceansport, New Jersey.

During the 1938 Travers at Saratoga, Kurtsinger had taken a spill. He emerged with only slight injuries, but the mishap changed matters. The next year, Sam Riddle decided to replace Kurtsinger with another jockey for War Admiral. The combination of the spill and the jockey change resulted in Kurtsinger's retirement from racing in 1938. He had second thoughts about that and came back to ride in 1939. It was his last year; he never rode again after 1939. In addition to his Triple Crown on War Admiral, he won one Derby, one Preakness, two Belmonts, two Jockey Club Gold Cups, and a Belmont Futurity, as well as many other victories in his fifteen years of racing. In all, he rode 5,651 races in sixteen seasons. He won 721 of them, placed in 742, and showed in another 742 races. He had a creditable win percentage of 13 and a money percentage of 39.

Kurtsinger returned to Louisville to become the proprietor of two farms and the owner of several brood mares. He also went into horse training. In September, 1946, he fell ill and entered a Louisville hospital. He was treated for ten days and underwent blood transfusions. Nothing worked. Charles Kurtsinger died on September 24, 1946, at the age of thirty-nine.

> *"War Admiral must be the best horse I have ever ridden.*
> *He has done everything asked of him, and done it with such ease."*
> — Charles Kurtsinger on War Admiral, 1937

The two horses trapped by their heritages died within six months of each other in similar circumstances. In the winter of 1958-1959 old age caught up with Omaha. On the morning of April 24, 1959, Morton Porter found Omaha dead in his stall. The third Triple Crown winner was buried at the AK-Sar-Ben racetrack in Omaha, Nebraska, near a large plinth of polished grey granite bearing the inscription: "Omaha, One of the Immortals of the American Turf."[18]

On the evening of October 30, 1959, War Admiral fell ill in his stall, unable to rise. He died at 10 P.M. the following day[19]. Even in death, War Admiral could not escape his patrimonial burden. He is buried at the Kentucky Horse Park in Lexington, five feet away from his sire.

---

[18] Omaha was first buried under the granite plinth. In 1974, the AK-Sar-Ben track enlarged its clubhouse over Omaha's gravesite. The plinth was moved, but Omaha was not moved with it. The clubhouse addition was built over Omaha's remains. This was discovered when AK-Sar-Ben was torn down in 1997 for an office park. The third Triple Crown winner rests under a concrete slab, the exact location of his remains being unknown.

19 War Admiral's death caused yet another slight to his memory. When a racehorse dies, its registration certificate is returned to the Jockey Club, which takes the horse off its books and then declares the horse officially dead. For some reason, War Admiral's certificate was never returned to the Jockey Club. Even though his death was widely publicized, he was not taken off the Jockey Club's books for fourteen years. Secretariat's 1973 Triple Crown win caused a resurgence of interest in Triple Crown winners, and a researcher discovered that War Admiral was still "alive." When the omission was publicized, War Admiral was finally declared officially dead fourteen years after his passing.

IV. THE IRON HORSE: WHIRLAWAY

Triple Crown, 1941. Jockey, Eddie Arcaro.

"His name was Whirlaway, and he was variously described
as crazy, stupid, ornery, nervous —and brilliant.
— Jim McKay, 1988

He was the ultimate come-from-behind horse. To see him in the old newsreels even now, more than sixty years after his Triple Crown season, more than fifty years after his death, is to sense a certain excitement and thrill. To imagine once again the long tail flip skywards and then streak like a meteor to the finish line is to experience what thrilled the fans so long ago: Whirlaway, Mr. Longtail, running twice as fast as any other horse.

Some Triple Crown champions can be written-about straightforwardly: Gallant Fox, Count Fleet, Citation, or Secretariat, for example. But to write about Whirlaway? Whirly was ...ah, well, Whirly was Whirly.

William Wright founded the Calumet Baking Powder Company in the 1880s. It was a success, and the Wright family branched into other areas. In 1910, William Wright bought a farm in Libertyville, Illinois, for training trotting horses. He named the farm after his company, Calumet. Later, the farm enterprise was extended into Lexington, Kentucky, and that facility, too, was named Calumet Farm. William Wright died in 1931, but before that, operating control of Calumet Baking Powder and the Wrights' other ventures passed to his son, Warren.

Warren Wright was an historic Thoroughbred owner. His father, William Wright, brought trotting races to Kentucky. Warren considered trotting races to be too slow. He moved Calumet Farm in Kentucky into Thoroughbred racing in the early 1930s. Success came fairly quickly; in the space of six years (1932-1938) the Calumet record went from one win (a comparatively meager $1150 purse) to fifty-eight wins and $100,320 in purses. But somehow, it still wasn't enough. Wright achieved basic success, but his ultimate goal, the Kentucky Derby, or even the Triple Crown, remained out of reach.

During the early years of Calumet, Wright made astute equine purchases;

115

1936 was an especially good year. That year, Wright bought a brown colt named Bull Lea. Bull Lea sired Citation, Coaltown, Armed, and many other horses and proved to be one of racing's great sires. Also in 1936, he purchased a quarter-interest in Blenheim II, a stallion considered Europe's most successful sire, and to boot, the winner of England's 1930 Epsom Derby.

In 1937, Wright bred a mare named Dustwhirl to Blenheim II. The foal, born on April 2, 1938,[1] was named Whirlaway, a name in keeping with his dam.

WHIRLAWAY as a yearling, 1939.
© *Collection of L. S. Sutcliffe, C. Ken Grayson, owner. Used by permission.*

Wright got more than he bargained for when he bought a quarter-interest in Blenheim II. He got a great horse, all right, but there was just one thing wrong with the Blenheims: they were crazy. The Blenheim line had a streak in it, the likes of which is still not understood, that made them gifted runners but harder than hell to control on the track. Whirlaway was the most famous of the Blenheims, and his idiosyncrasies were publicized extensively in newspapers and magazines.[2] A Blenheim II grandson, Hill Gail, illustrates the crazy streak

[1] Appropriately, it was the day after April Fool's Day.

[2] While the crazy streak of the Blenheim II line has justly been given attention by writers, it is possible that Whirly's dam, Dustwhirl, contributed to the situation. Marvin

well: in the 1952 Kentucky Derby, Hill Gail was so obstreperous in the paddock that Ben Jones, the Calumet horse trainer, grabbed Hill Gail's halter and punched the horse in the nose. That seemed to settle him down some, but the race began, and Hill Gail acted up on the track. The jockey, Eddie Arcaro, sensed that the horse was about to throw a tantrum right on the track during the middle of the race. Arcaro redirected the colt's temperament and ran him to the point of near-exhaustion to win the Derby.

"...he had some kind of an intuitive understanding of what the horses needed. I guess that's what made him such a wonderful trainer as he was."
— Margaret Glass,
long-time Calumet Farm employee,
on Ben Jones, 1996.

The Hill Gail anecdote introduces another player in the Calumet saga: Ben Jones. Ranking racing's greatest trainers and jockeys is much like ranking football's greatest quarterbacks or baseball's greatest hitters: there's plenty of room for disagreement. But two names in this era stand out above all others: Sunny Jim Fitzsimmons and Ben Jones.

He was called Plain Ben Jones, and sometimes just by his initials, B.J. Perhaps he cultivated a plain image, but he was an imposing figure, tough and smart. He knew how to train horses, and some still call him the greatest Thoroughbred trainer of all time. He was born in Missouri in 1882, and worked on his family's cattle farm.

"When I was a boy, I was crazy about horses and Holstein cows. Couldn't decide which I liked better. When I got big enough to help with the milking, I made up my mind," he told an interviewer. It was a fortunate decision for him, for Calumet Farm, and for horseracing. He got into training; his first Derby winner was Woolford Farms' Lawrin in 1938. Eventually, he officially trained six Kentucky Derby winners[3], two Preakness Stakes winners and one Belmont Stakes winner. He worked at Calumet until 1960 at age seventy-seven, and passed away a year later. His most famous horse, undoubtedly, was Whirlaway.

Three things about Whirlaway are most remembered: his speed, his tail, and his temperament. The speed will be seen in the races. Whirly's tail was

---

Drager, in his book, *The Most Glorious Crown*, cites an article in *The Blood-Horse* which stated that Dustwhirl was "marked by a distinct willfulness, which may have been the cause of her failure to race and for her retirement..." If that was true, then Calumet faced a behavioral double whammy when dealing with Whirlaway's foibles.

[3] "Officially" is the key word here. He is listed as Citation's trainer in the 1948 Derby, but Citation was actually trained by Ben's son, Jimmy. Ben Jones was listed as the trainer so he would be credited with the "win."

certainly the longest of any Triple Crown Winner and one of the longest horse tails in the entire history of Thoroughbred racing. Mordaunt Milner, the English racing expert, wrote "I myself have never seen a longer one." It was thick and reached nearly to the ground. It was a key to tracking him in a race: you looked for that great chestnut tail streaming out in the breeze, and you found Whirly. That earned him the nicknames, "Mr. Longtail," and "The Little Horse with the Big Tail." Then there was his temperament...

To say that Whirly was a problem horse would be an understatement. No one could control or train the strong-minded colt. At times it took several men to saddle him. He scared at the crowd noise at a race track, spooked at the sight of steeplechase jumps.[4]

Ben Jones took over the job of training Whirlaway, and he had his hands full. Jimmy Jones, Ben's son, was also a trainer at Calumet and recalled his father's labors: "He just took that horse and wore him down. He'd be gone two or three hours. Whirlaway was a bastard in the paddock. So they just went to the paddock every day. He stood in there and stood in there until Whirlaway got so he was the best horse you ever saw in the paddock.

"That was one of the greatest jobs of training I ever saw, really. He was a peculiar horse in that he had a very stubborn disposition, but he learned. He would respond to habit-building, and that's what really made the horse go."

Ben Jones had to be *absolutely* consistent with Whirlaway; if Jones took him through one route to the racetrack, Jones had to take the same route every day. If Jones changed the route, it was back to square one: change the route and give Whirlaway time to get used to the change. It was arduous and time-consuming, but it worked beyond anyone's dreams.

Jones addressed Whirly's other anxieties through the application of hard work. He moved groups of people around Whirlaway to get him used to a crowd. He spent much of the day with Whirly, riding alongside Whirly on a white pony. Jones walked the chestnut colt around a track to get him used to the crowd noise and the track layout. Some days Jones ran Whirlaway on grass and other days ran Whirly on dirt. Whirlaway was repeatedly saddled and unsaddled to get him used to the process of race preparation. It was an unusual and intensive training program for a Thoroughbred.

Another problem proved more difficult: Whirly just wanted to run to the outside rail. That was serious, because a horse running along the outside runs along the outside diameter of the track and has farther to go. That habit was never completely corrected, and it plagued Whirlaway (or more correctly,

---

[4] The author's father saw Whirlaway in newsreels in the 1940s and was always a fan of Mr. Longtail. When Whirly's aversion to steeplechase jumps was related to him, the author's father remarked, "Whirlaway wasn't stupid. He knew those things were dangerous."

118

WHIRLAWAY during a workout.
© Collection of C. Ken Grayson,. Used by permission..

Warren Wright, Ben Jones, and all of Whirly's jockeys) throughout Whirlaway's racing career.[5]

> *"...at that time, I wrote to some of my friends who were here in the East, and I had heard that Calumet was going to send him to Saratoga, and I wrote them, and I said, "Look out for a horse called Whirlaway. Before the season is over he's going to win something."*
> — Racing historian Tom Gilcoyne
> on Whirlaway's Two-Year-Old Season

Ben Jones skipped the New York races for two-year-olds and started Whirlaway in Chicago. His first race was a five-furlong affair at Lincoln Fields near Chicago on June 4, 1940. Whirly ran to the outside rail, and in spite of himself, won by a nose. It was an omen.

Three weeks later he raced again, this time at Arlington Park. It was the

---

[5] Oddly, Whirlaway's behavior in the barn was exemplary. He was a nice horse, liked visitors, and enjoyed attention. Unlike War Admiral, he was well-behaved in the starting gate. Truly, he was a mass of contradictions.

119

Oak Park Purse, and Whirly finished third. But his race was better than the results indicated: he started very slowly and was outrun for most of the race. At the beginning of the stretch, Whirlaway took off and "…was racing boldly at the close." The Oak Park Purse was short, only 5 1/2 furlongs. If it had been a longer race, he might have caught the leader.

Ben Jones let him rest a week and then started him in the Chicago Heights Purse at Arlington Park on July 2. He did it again: the race was also a 5 1/2 furlong affair, but Whirlaway stayed back, and let go at the head of the stretch. He won by one length.

Jones only gave him three days' rest before starting him again at Arlington Park in the 5 1/2 furlong Hyde Park Stakes. He was the bettors' favorite, at 3.4 to 1, but the size of the race was large: thirteen horses. Whirly was squeezed back early into eleventh place, and never made up the ground. He came on towards the end to finish fourth. Like Omaha before him, Whirly wasn't at his best in the short races for two-year-olds; there just simply wasn't enough room for a come-from-behind horse to win in the late stages.

At the Nedayr Purse on July 20 at Arlington Park Whirlaway tried it again. He stuck in fifth place for most of the 5 1/2 furlong race, and moved strongly in the stretch. But when it came time, there was just no room; the horses bunched up, and there was no way Whirly could maneuver around them. He finished in fourth place.

His last race at Arlington Park was the 3/4 mile Arlington Futurity a week later. John Longden rode him. Longden is most identified with Count Fleet (see the next chapter) and other great horses, but he also rode Whirlaway as a two-year-old in 1940. In fact, Longden rode Whirly ten times, the third highest total of any jockey to ride Mr. Longtail. Longden let Whirlaway break slowly (last in the twelve-horse race) but quickly found his stride. He ran fourth again, but it was a close race and he finished well, a length behind the second horse.

Jones took Whirly and Longden to Saratoga for the summer races. It was a long train trip for Whirlaway. At his first race there, the United States Hotel Stakes, he showed what he could do: one horse, Attention, vaulted into the lead in the stretch but Longden and Whirlaway moved up on him. It was a 3/4-mile race, and again the short distance made the difference. The race notes state Whirly "Closed going fastest of all at the end." Attention had won by only a neck. But had it been a longer race....

At Whirlaway's death in 1953, some racing writers said that his greatest race came on August 10, 1940, in the 3/4-mile Saratoga Special. It marked the first victory for the Longden-Whirlaway team. Whirly was squeezed back at the start and trailed last for most of the race. At one point, early on, he bore out and even struck the *outside* rail.

Longden finally got him straightened out, and with a quarter-mile left in the race, Whirly took off. With an incredible rush, Whirlaway swooped around the pack and won by a length. It really was the formula for the great jockey

Longden on Whirlaway: the run to the outside, straighten him out, and then an incredible final rush to victory.

Ben Jones and Eddie Arcaro, **WHIRLAWAY'S** trainer and jockey. Photograph taken at the 1952 Kentucky Derby. *Courtesy Ken Grayson Collection. Used by permission*

Whirlaway's record had been spotty up to then: eight races with three firsts, one second, two thirds, and two fourth-place finishes. But the Saratoga Special was *so* impressive a win that some called him the sure two-year-old champion. Maybe he would be, but there was much racing left in the year.

Whirlaway raced in the Grand Union Hotel Stakes on August 25 and finished second. This was another short race (3/4 mile), and again distance made the critical difference. Whirly trailed in fourth or fifth place for most of the race, but then he took off again in the stretch. He was quickly boxed in by the other horses, and when he got clear it was too late. He made his usual valiant end rush, but lost by 1 1/2 lengths.

Whirly rested six days and ran again in the 6 1/2 furlong Hopeful Stakes at Saratoga. It was a rainy day, and the track was sloppy. Only three other horses challenged Whirlaway. Longden took him slowly out of the gate and he stayed in fourth place for most of the race. At the 5/8 pole, Longden let him go. He responded with a great rush. He quickly passed the other horses and won easily. During the race the horse was struck in one eye by a small stone. The consequent injury could have been severe; some thought it might cost Mr. Longtail the sight in that eye. Ben Jones even called in human eye specialists to assist the veterinarians treating the horse.

Whirlaway's incredible constitution showed itself. The injury was serious, but with three weeks' rest, Whirlaway returned to racing. On September 25 at the Futurity Trial for the Belmont Futurity at Belmont Park[6] Longden rode him again, and they took the immediate lead. Then, as usual, Whirlaway fell back, as far as ninth in the ten-horse field. He made his late move but never climbed above fifth.

Three days later at the Belmont Futurity Longden again let him fall back as far as eleventh in the fourteen-horse race. Once again, Whirlaway responded at the close of the race. He made another great closing rush to cross the wire in third place.

The losses could have been explained as the result of the injury and the hiatus from racing. Ben Jones wasn't ready to quit. He shipped Whirlaway out to Kentucky to compete in the fall racing meet at Keeneland. (It was very convenient. The Keeneland Race Track is literally next door to Whirlaway's home at Calumet Farm.) The Calumet horse won the Myrtlewood Purse on October 8 in his style. Longden let him loaf at the start, and he took the lead in the stretch to win by two lengths.

Ben Jones gave him a comparatively long rest this time: ten days. On October 19, Whirlaway showed that the neighboring track agreed with him: he won the Breeders' Futurity by a length. The notes to the official race chart say it well: "WHIRLAWAY, slowest to start and steadied along until well into his best stride, improved his position on the outside, engaged the leaders approaching the final eighth, and won drawing away."

He was almost through for the year. Jones shipped him back east to Baltimore to catch the last few races at Pimlico. Whirlaway ran in the Pimlico Futurity on November 2 and was the heavy favorite in the betting. A win was not to be. Whirlaway bore to the outside after the first turn. Longden let him go, and he moved up valiantly through the backstretch and far turn. Then he did it *again*: at the beginning of the stretch, Whirlaway bored outward a second time. He finished third.[7]

---

[6] A definition must be given. For various major races, such as the Kentucky Derby, or here, the Belmont Futurity, there is often a "warm-up" race a few days beforehand. This is called the "Trial" race (hence, the Futurity Trial) but is not a mere practice race. The results are included in the entrants' racing records for the year.

[7] This was John Longden's last race on Whirlaway, for Longden signed a contract with John Hertz to ride for his stable. (See the next chapter.) In racing history, the

His final race for 1940 came twelve days later, at the Walden Stakes at Pimlico. George Woolf, "The Iceman" of Seabiscuit-War Admiral fame, rode Whirlaway for the first time. Eight horses were entered, and Woolf let Whirlaway run his own race. The race was his longest to date: 1 1/16 miles. Woolf let him run easily in the backstretch, and then turned him loose. He won by four lengths.

That was it for the year, and a good record it was: sixteen starts, with seven firsts, two seconds, four thirds, and three unplaced finishes (a 44% win record, an 81% money record.). He won $77,275 in purses, a very good earning for a two-year-old horse racing at the end of the Great Depression. Tied with Our Boots, Whirlaway was named Best Two-Year-Old colt of 1940.

Still, there was his nasty habit of running to the outside. No matter how hard Ben Jones tried, Whirlaway always wanted to bear out. Jones himself spoke the valediction for all his efforts: when sportswriters Grantland Rice and Red Smith came to visit him, Rice alluded to Whirlaway's temperament: "I hear you've got a half-witted horse there, Ben." Jones responded: "I don't know, but he's making a halfwit out of me."

Whirlaway spent the winter of 1940-1941 in Florida. Warren Wright kept a winter home in Florida and raced some of his horses at Hialeah and Tropical Park in Coral Gables during the colder months. Mr. Longtail didn't get much of a rest: less than three months. Jones announced that Whirly would start racing in February, 1941. The critics and experts weighed in: wasn't that too short a break? Well, in Jones's eyes (with some justification) Whirlaway was an "iron colt." He loved to race, needed to race, and he was going to do just that.

On February 8, 1941, at Hialeah, Calumet Farm's jockey Wendell Eads rode Whirlaway in a six furlong race, the Coconut Grove Purse. He was the favorite in the betting, and didn't disappoint the bettors. Eads was light even for a jockey, about 102 pounds, and some thought he was too small to handle such a powerful horse. (Of that, more later.) Eads's lightness didn't seem to matter; Whirly broke slowly, and the pack left him far behind for the first two-thirds of the race. In the last third, Whirlaway cranked up to full steam, bore to the outside, and won by a head. He hadn't changed his tactics over the winter. Warren Wright said simply, "Of course, I'm satisfied with the race. Who wouldn't be."

Whirlaway got ten days' rest and ran in the Arcadia Purse, a 7/8-mile race at Hialeah. This time, Basil James rode him. The race didn't go well; James kept him under restraint early on (a VERY bad thing to do with Whirlaway) and

---

Longden-Whirlaway period might seem just a note in the careers of both the horse and the jockey. It is worth more than that: Longden rode him ten times, the third highest total of any jockey on Whirly. Longden became Whirly's first Hall of Fame rider and rode Whirly to most of his impressive two-year-old victories.

while he ran well at the end of the race, he finished third. Jones had no excuses: "He just ran a bad race, I guess. Horses do, you know." Warren Wright was defiant: "He will start Saturday, barring injury."

The Saturday start that Wright referred to was the Flamingo Stakes, four days off. Florida racing has always had an important "prep race" for the Kentucky Derby. Today it is the Florida Derby at Gulfstream Park, but then it was the Flamingo Stakes at Hialeah. Jones knew Whirly was tough, but there were limits. The Flamingo Stakes was 1 1/8 miles, and Jones thought that was too far, too soon. (Shades of Sam Riddle and Man o'War in the Kentucky Derby!) Under pressure to race Whirlaway, Jones thought fast.

A splint occurs when a horse's leg bone becomes enlarged, indicative of leg problems. The treatment at that time for a splint was to apply a chemical much like a mustard plaster, which would aid the blood flow and speed healing. The compound, however, also would singe the hair on a horse's leg. Ben Jones applied some of the compound to one of Whirlaway's legs which was perfectly sound, and of course, it singed the hairs on the leg. *Voila!* Instant evidence of a splint. Jones informed Warren Wright of Whirlaway's "leg ailment", showed him the "affected" area: '...see, Mr. Wright, this is where the hair singed....' Whirlaway was withdrawn from the Flamingo Stakes.

That bought Jones time; Whirlaway didn't run again for nearly a month. His next race was at Tropical Park at Coral Gables on March 22. The occasion was the Miami Springs Purse, a $1,200, 3/4-mile race. Basil James flew in from California to ride him again. The track was muddy, and that made a difference. Whirlaway never caught fire; he flattened out and finished third.

On March 28, Whirlaway ran in the Silver Springs Purse, a $1,200, 5 1/2-furlong race at Tropical Park. As always, he came from behind. He was third out of six horses at the head of the stretch and was forced wide at the far turn. His jockey for this race, R.L. Vedder, recovered and Whirlaway put on his closing rush to win by a neck. Jones was very pleased. He announced that Whirlaway would be shipped to Keeneland in Kentucky, the site of his previous autumn's triumphs, to race the next month.

The A.J.Joyner Handicap on April 11, a 3/4-mile, $1,500 purse race, was Whirly's three-year-old debut in his home state. Wendell Eads rode him again, and it was again a classic Whirlaway race. He held in third or fourth place for most of the race, put on his end rush, and won by a neck.

On April 24, Whirly, again with Wendell Eads up, ran in the Blue Grass Stakes at Keeneland, Kentucky. The Blue Grass was then, as it is now, an important preparatory race for the Derby. Jones thought he had Whirlaway's nasty habit of running to the outside under control, but it came back in this race. Mr. Longtail bore out, could not make it up, and lost by six lengths.

The Derby Trial at Churchill Downs ran five days later on April 29. Whirlaway, again with Eads up, broke slowly and spent the first half-mile in fifth place, then came on with a rush. By the head of the stretch he was in first by a half-length. But then he ran to the outside. Another horse, Blue Pair, came on to win.

Even now, over sixty years later, one can almost hear the "Oh, My God's!" that must surely have been uttered by Ben and Jimmy Jones. In the Silver Springs Purse and the A.J. Joyner Handicap, Whirly had been steered to the outside. That may have given him the idea that was the way to run. It was just four days until the Derby, and Whirly reverted, possibly permanently, to his old habit of running outside. Time was short now, and it was apparent that Eads wasn't the jockey for Whirlaway. Eads recalled in 1991: "I was so small that I couldn't hold him. He was just too much for me."

Clearly, something had to be done. Ben Jones talked to the Wrights at Calumet. Jones called Greentree Farm's jockey. The jockey later said, "I had seen too many good riders that couldn't handle him [Whirlaway]. I didn't know why they thought *I* could." So, the Wrights then talked to Mrs. Joan Payson, the daughter of Greentree Farm's owner (she was later the first owner of the New York Mets baseball team), and *she* got involved. Mrs. Payson asked the jockey to ride Whirly for Calumet. The jockey responded: "But I don't want to ride him."

In those days of a close-knit fraternity of racing owners, matters were frequently handled on the basis of handshakes, verbal commitments, and repayment of favors. Joan Payson came back with: "Well, you're doing me a favor. And I owe Mrs. Wright a favor."

That settled it. Reluctantly, Greentree's jockey, Eddie Arcaro, went off to Calumet Farm to ride Whirlaway in the Kentucky Derby, four days hence.

> *"Kid, drop that bag and go home! You'll never make a caddy as long as you live. A little runt like you ought to be a jockey."*
> — golfer and racing fan to the 13-year-old Eddie Arcaro,
> Eddie Arcaro, *I Ride to Win!*, 1951

The jockey who would win five Kentucky Derbies, six Preakness Stakes, six Belmont Stakes, including two Triple Crowns, was born on February 19, 1916, in Cincinnati, Ohio. Eddie Arcaro's mother was only sixteen when she gave birth to him, and he weighed just three pounds. A doctor came daily for two months to check on him and bathed the future champion in warm water with whiskey in it. Arcaro's mother was never quite sure of that treatment, and for the first four months of Eddie Arcaro's life, the infant was wrapped in cotton flannel strips and was called "the shoe box kid." (Similar infant care was given to another future jockey, Bill Shoemaker, some fifteen years later. Shoemaker weighed only 2 1/2 pounds at birth, and wasn't expected to live very long. Shoemaker's grandmother thought otherwise. She put the new-born in a shoe box, warmed some wraps in an oven, and put the wrapped Shoemaker in the shoe box on the opened oven door. Shoemaker retired as the champion winning jockey of all time. Is there a causal connection between wrapped-up infants in shoe boxes and later champion jockey status?)

Arcaro grew up in Cincinnati and northern Kentucky. His formal education was cut short when he quit school at thirteen and started to work as a caddy at a local golf course. One of his better clients was connected with horse racing, and used to call Arcaro "my jockey." That put an idea in Arcaro's head. Later, he threatened to leave home and change his name. To calm things down, his father took him to Latonia Race Park. It would go down in history as perhaps racing's most portentous visit to a track.

Latonia track had a porch just off the jockey's room. Arcaro saw it, stood on it, and stayed there for two or three hours, listening to the jockeys talk and watching them in their silks. He remembered later, "When I heard how they traveled, and the big races they won, I had to have it."

For three months he repeatedly asked his father to take him back to Latonia. When he finally returned to the track, his father introduced Arcaro to two trainers. No horse racing job was available then, and the future jockey waited. Eventually, a job came open with T.H. McCaffrey's stable, and Arcaro grabbed it. Each morning Arcaro got up at 6:00 A.M., took three trolleys to work, and spent the day doing whatever needed to be done: hot walking, filling buckets, cleaning tack, rubbing down horses, etc. After a while he got to exercise the horses. From there it was onward and upward.

He became a jockey with a small stable, and rode his first race at fifteen in Bainbridge, Ohio. He finished sixth; he rode forty-five times before he finally won. Some of his early racing took place at Agua Caliente in Mexico, and very quickly he got a thorough hard-knocks education in the school of *real* riding. We saw Eddie Arcaro on Nellie Flag, challenging Omaha in 1935, when the jockey was just nineteen. His first Triple Crown-level win was in the 1938 Kentucky Derby, aboard Woolford Farm's Lawrin. Lawrin's trainer was Ben Jones, and it was Arcaro that Jones thought of when things became critical for Whirlaway.

When Arcaro arrived at Calumet Ben Jones told him, "I know you've heard so many stories about him, but you know that I wouldn't send for you if I didn't think that I could correct it. This is the fastest horse in America, and with you riding him, we'll win the Derby." So, they worked during what little time was left. On the day before the Derby, Jones stationed himself on a pony about six feet out from the inside rail at the head of Churchill Downs' homestretch. The plan was for Whirly to hug the inside rail, charge around the turn, and storm between the rail and Jones astride the pony. Arcaro recalled later, "I just said to myself, 'if the old man is game enough to stand right there, I guess I'm game enough to run him down.' Ben Jones never moved a muscle, and Whirlaway slipped through the narrow opening as pretty as you please. I'll tell you, he was flying, too. If he had ever hit Ben Jones, neither one of us would have been around to talk about it."

The best was yet to come. On Derby Day, what Ben Jones did would have landed him in the National Museum of Racing and Hall of Fame even if he had never done anything else in his long training career. He remembered a suggestion his son Jimmy had made. Years earlier, they had a horse that kept running to the outside, much like Whirlaway. Ben and Jimmy cut the left blinker off the horse, and the problem was cured. So, hours before post time for the 1941 Kentucky Derby, in the paddock, Ben Jones took a knife and cut off Whirly's left blinker. Arcaro recalled, "I came down to the paddock before the race, and B.J.'s asking everyone around if they've got a pocketknife. Someone finally finds one for him, and right there he cut off the inside [left] blinker."

This was a neat bit of equine psychology: what a horse can't see, he won't run to. By cutting off the left blinker, Whirlaway could see the inside rail. By leaving on the right blinker, Whirly could *not* see the *outside* rail. Therefore, he would run to the inside, but not the outside. But it was a risk. Arcaro asked Jones, "Have you ever done this before?" Jones responded, "No, but I've seen it done. I did it when I was around trotters." This was just hours before the Kentucky Derby, and Arcaro said it was a hell of a time to be experimenting. Jones replied, "Don't worry about it, it'll work."

Would the one-eyed blinker indeed work? There was no time to find out. Arcaro had some confidence built up in Whirlaway, and they were the favorites at $2.90 to $1. Jones was taking no chances; he walked Whirlaway around the track one last time. He gave Arcaro his last minute instructions: "Don't start him too soon. Don't let him break too fast. You have one run with him, and wait until the tail end of the race. He can run three-eighths faster than any horse in the country."

Eleven horses went to the Derby Post on May 3, 1941. The track was fast, and the horses broke cleanly. Whirlaway was sixth at the start, and eased back into eighth at the clubhouse turn. Then Arcaro turned him loose and Whirlaway responded. "A clocker told me, 'That horse did something I've never ever seen a horse do, or thought a horse could do. He ran an eighth of a mile in a little over ten seconds,'" Arcaro recalled. Whirlaway just kept going, and was fourth after a mile. Whirly flew down the stretch, the great chestnut tail straight out and streaming full in the breeze. Arcaro later wrote: "I had never seen such power exhibited as when we hit the three-eighths pole and I called on him for his speed. He literally took off, nearly catapulting me out of the saddle. As he stretched his legs, I felt as if I were flying through the air. That final rush he showed was stunning." Whirlaway stormed to the front and ran the final eighth mile in 23 3/5 seconds (only 2/5 of a second slower than Secretariat's final eighth of a mile in the 1973 Derby). Arcaro didn't look back until it was all over, and found he had won by eight lengths.[8] Whirly's time was a record: 2:01 2/5 for the mile and a quarter. It stood for twenty-one years. In the jockey's room after the race, Arcaro said: "He was the runningest son of a bitch I ever sat on. I wouldn't say the best, but the runningest."

To some, it just couldn't have happened; the owner of a losing horse maintained that Whirly surely *must* have been doped. The post-race tests were negative: the Kentucky Derby victory was 100% pure, unadulterated Whirlaway.

WHIRLAWAY wins the Kentucky Derby, May 3, 1941, Arcaro up. Photograph autographed by Eddie Arcaro.
© *Collection of L. S. Sutcliffe, C. Ken Grayson, owner. Used by permission*

"He wasn't the greatest horse that ever lived, but he was just about the most exciting. Every time he stepped on a track you knew that some time during the race you were going to see that breathless, blinding, tremendous burst which was as stirring a spectacle as any field of sports could produce. "He was Babe Ruth, Jack Dempsey, Bill Tilden, Bobby Jones — not just a champion but a champion who was also the most colorful figure in his game."

---

[8] Whirly's eight-length margin matched the record set by Old Rosebud (1914) and Johnstown (1939.) Assault also won the Derby by eight lengths in 1946. No horse has ever won the Kentucky Derby by more than eight lengths.

— Red Smith,
"The Swiftest Halfwit." 1953.

WHIRLAWAY under the roses, 1941 Kentucky Derby, Arcaro up. Ben Jones, trainer, holding.
© *Collection of L. S. Sutcliffe, C. Ken Grayson, owner. Used by permission*

Thoroughbred racing fans will long dispute which race was the greatest single performance in racing history. Modern fans will root for Secretariat's 31-length victory in the 1973 Belmont Stakes; others might claim honors for Count Fleet's 25-length victory in the 1943 Belmont Stakes. But for sheer audacity, it is hard to beat Whirlaway's victory in the 1941 Preakness.

Eight horses contended for the Preakness on May 10, 1941. The track was good, and the horses went to the gate at 5:58 P.M. Whirlaway was at the post. The pack broke at 5:59 P.M., and the race is, to modern viewers, alternately incredible and hilarious. Whirly was even money in the betting, and Arcaro let him go. The field broke quickly, and Whirlaway was dead last through the first quarter-mile.

And not just dead last: The film of the race shows him more than five lengths behind the pack through the clubhouse turn. He was *so* far out of it that the dust from the other horses was literally blowing across the track when

129

Whirly rounded the turn.

Still, Arcaro bided his time. At the beginning of the backstretch, Whirlaway did it again. He put on a magnificent burst of speed, and in one of the truly incredible performances of all time, hurtled down Pimlico's backstretch. Arcaro said ten years later: "Around the first turn the leaders seemed to be at least a mile away. I didn't dare start Whirlaway moving too soon and I had to gamble on his finishing speed. I could not tell at the time whether he was in a running mood or not. But I found out after I had turned him loose and told him to go. I thought then I was riding a blinding tornado."

At the half-mile mark Whirly was seventh, and within the next quarter-mile had caught up and gone through the pack. Jockey Johnny Gilbert, riding the lead horse, heard a *whoosh* and Arcaro's voice shouting, "So long, Johnny!" Gilbert shouted back, "So long, Eddie." There was nothing else Gilbert could have done as the chestnut streak thundered by Gilbert to take over first by a length. Then Whirly pulled away: At the beginning of the stretch he had a three-length lead, and ultimately won by five lengths. Arcaro said afterwards: "There are no other three-year-olds, just Whirlaway."

Ben Jones thought that four weeks between starts was too long for Whirlaway, so he entered Whirly in the 1 1/4-mile Henry of Navarre Stakes on May 20, 1941, at Belmont. This posed a major problem. Arcaro was riding for Greentree Stable and had been "loaned" to Calumet. Greentree entered a horse named Hash in the Henry of Navarre Stakes, and Arcaro was contractually bound to ride Hash for Greentree. Back went Eads onto Whirlaway. Whirly was the 3 to 4 favorite in the betting, and Eads rode Mr. Longtail properly. Whirlaway won by 2 1/4 lengths. Hash, with Arcaro up, crossed the wire third.

> *"...He was not a horse that could be managed well. When he wanted to turn in his run, you just had to let him go. He wanted to go all out or not at all."*
> — Eddie Arcaro, *I Ride to Win!*, 1951.

Somehow, it doesn't seem necessary in retrospect to have even run the 1941 Belmont Stakes, but it had to be done anyway. On June 7, 1941, only three horses showed up to challenge Whirly in the Belmont: Itabo, Robert Morris, and Yankee Chance. The track was fast, and Whirlaway, again with Arcaro as his jockey, was the 1 to 4 favorite in the betting. The challengers had a strategy: keep Whirly to a slow pace and hope they could challenge him in the stretch. The plan was obvious to Arcaro, too. On the way to Belmont, he told his wife: "If they don't run the first half mile better than forty-nine seconds, I'm gonna let him go to the front. I can't hold him slower than that."

Whirly was at the pole position, and the field broke from the gate at 4:57 P.M. Itabo grabbed the lead at the start, but Arcaro, who had a stopwatch in his head, knew what to do and when. The half-mile was run in 49 4/5 seconds, and

Arcaro called out to the other jockeys, "The hell with this, fellas, I'm leaving." Whirlaway seized the lead and pulled away. At the mile Whirly was five lengths ahead, but then he started to loaf the rest of the way. Arcaro said fifty years later: "He was a drunk dude. I could have outrun him myself from about the eighth pole home. He was just a mixed-up kid, really."[9] Whirlaway crossed the finish line three lengths ahead of the pack in time of 2:31. Eddie Arcaro and Calumet Farm rode to victory on the four legs of the most certifiably insane horse that ever won the Triple Crown.

Now Whirlaway became a media star. He was good copy, and few horses since Man o'War received the press attention he got. He became a national figure amid some pretty tough competition: Joe DiMaggio and Ted Williams were setting records in baseball that year. Bob Feller of the Cleveland Indians was capturing headlines with his fast ball, and Joe Louis commanded the boxing ring. Parts of the country were still mired in the Depression, and now it seemed inevitable that America would get into what was then called "The War in Europe." So here came this horse with blinding speed, a huge tail that streamed out like a ship's pennant, and an unpredictable temperament. He was irresistible.

Arcaro rode him again in the Dwyer Stakes at Aqueduct on June 21, and again, they triumphed. The Dwyer was the same length as the Kentucky Derby, 1 1/4 miles, and the race was very much like the Derby. Arcaro kept him under control for most of the race, and with a half-mile left, let him go. Whirlaway bounded to the lead and stayed there. There was an objection by another rider, and a few tense minutes followed while the stewards investigated. The objection was denied. Eddie Arcaro and Whirlaway had won the Dwyer Stakes.

That was Arcaro's last ride on Whirlaway for 1941; Arcaro was plagued by suspensions and other riding commitments for the balance of the year. It was disappointing for Ben Jones and for Arcaro, but Whirlaway had to be ridden, Arcaro or not. There were other jockeys available.

Ben Jones sent his Triple Crown horse back to Chicago, where the horse had started racing the previous year. The Arlington Classic was not far off, and Jones thought Whirlaway would be perfect. But first, a warm-up was in order: Arlington Park had a new race, the 1 1/8-mile Special Event Purse on July 15. Eads rode the Triple Crown winner against three other horses. Whirly was of course the favorite at $0.10 to $1, and he didn't disappoint his backers. He took

---

[9] Arcaro's present-day comment must be tempered in the light of history. Forty years earlier, in his 1951 book, *I Ride To Win!*, Arcaro defended Whirlaway's race by saying that it was not the kind of race the horse liked. Arcaro had managed Whirlaway in that race, but it wasn't Whirly's style of racing. As Arcaro said, "He wanted to go all-out or not at all."

over first at the half-mile mark, and went wide into the stretch. This time, Eads took a strong hold on him, got him straightened out, and finished first by 2 1/2 lengths.

Whirlaway had now won six races in ten weeks. It was time for a good rest, but Warren Wright and Ben Jones entered him in the Arlington Classic on July 26. He carried 126 pounds (only one other horse entered carried that much) and to boot, yet another jockey would ride. Arcaro had been scheduled, but Arcaro was under suspension. Jones didn't feel comfortable asking Eads to ride Whirlaway in this race, so he contacted a free-lance jockey, Alfred Shelhamer, to ride Whirly in this most important race. Jones briefed Shelhamer on how to ride Whirly: don't take too strong a hold, let him stay back, go in the stretch.

Whirly ran last for most of the race. He challenged the leader, Attention, in the stretch, and steadily began to close on him. But fate intervened: a clump of dirt thrown up by Attention struck Mr. Longtail in the eye. That, coupled with the great exertion, caused Whirly to come up short. Shelhamer and Whirlaway finished 1 1/2 lengths back of Attention.

The loss could be forgiven. It was a blow to an eye, much like the one he had suffered the previous year. But it wasn't as serious, so Ben Jones sent him back to the races. He shipped Whirly to Saratoga for the summer races there, and immediately entered Mr. Longtail in the Saranac Handicap on August 6. Arcaro was Jones's first choice to ride Whirlaway, but Arcaro was still under suspension, so Jones looked around for another jockey. He found Alfred Robertson, a fine Scottish jockey who rode against Whirlaway in the Arlington Classic. (At this point, Whirlaway had raced with six different jockeys in fifteen different races on nine different tracks in five different states in six months. No jockey rode him more than three consecutive times in 1941. Counting the Saranac Handicap, he had a different jockey in each of his last four races. Other horses might have cracked from all the traveling, the various tracks, and all the different riders. Not Whirlaway.)

Only four horses challenged Whirlaway in the Saranac Handicap, but one of them was War Relic, the last great son of Man o'War. (As a tribute to his ability, War Relic is buried next to War Admiral at the base of Man o'War's grave at the Kentucky Horse Park in Lexington.) Basil James, who rode Whirlaway earlier in the year, now rode War Relic against him. The Triple Crown winner and the last great son of Man o'War turned the one-mile race into one of the most memorable races of all time. Both Whirly and War Relic hung back for much of the race: War Relic in third, Whirly in fifth. War Relic took over first at the 3/4-mile mark. In the stretch, War Relic held first, Whirly trailed in fourth place. When Robertson let his horse go, the result was predictable: Whirlaway drifted out, but closed fast in a photo finish. The photo showed War Relic's nose was *on* the finish line, but Whirly's nose was just a bit *over* the line. The race went to Whirlaway.

Sam Riddle, War Relic's owner, was present at the race. He had won his share of races with Man o'War, War Admiral, and so many other horses, and had lost his share, too. But *this* one was too much. Riddle stood up in his box, protested the decision, and waived his cane over his head. The officials scurried in all directions, but their decision stood.

Jones was impressed enough with Robertson to hire the Scot as Whirlaway's jockey for the rest of 1941. They raced again ten days later in the Travers Stakes, the race wherein Gallant Fox had been upset by Jim Dandy eleven years earlier. Whirly was the favorite, at $0.15 to $1.00, and only two horses challenged him. The track was muddy, almost as bad as in 1930, but there was no Jim Dandy to come from behind. John Longden rode Fairymant, while Basil James rode Lord Kitchener. (Both of the challenging jockeys had previously ridden Whirlaway. Their prior experience didn't help them much.) Fairymant took the lead, but Robertson kept Whirlaway under restraint. In the stretch, the Scottish jockey let his horse go. Whirlaway splashed past Fairymant to win by 3 3/4 lengths. Through 2003, Whirlaway remains the *only* Triple Crown winner to win the Travers Stakes as well.

Ben Jones didn't waste any time after the Travers. He sent Whirlaway and Robertson on the road again back to Chicago, to run in the 1 1/4-mile American Derby at Washington Park one week later. The Travers and the train trip didn't seem to affect him one bit. He was the favorite, at odds of 0.20 to 1.00, and he didn't disappoint the bettors. He took the lead early for him, with 1/2-mile to go in the race, and just pulled away to win by 2 3/4-lengths. The Associated Press writer said it succinctly: "Whirlaway convincingly demonstrated his undisputed hold on the three-year-old championship of the American turf today by galloping, with amazing ease, to victory in the $60,900 American Derby at Washington Park."

Whirlaway rested three weeks this time, and another train trip. Jones sent him to Narragansett Park in Rhode Island to run in the Narragansett Special on September 13. War Relic was there waiting for him, and got his revenge for the Saranac Special. Sam Riddle's horse took the lead from the start and lead all the way. Whirly moved from fourth to second in the race, but could never catch War Relic. The son of Man o'War beat Whirlaway by *4 1/2 lengths.* (War Relic had been rested since the Saranac Handicap, while Whirlaway had been raced continuously. War Relic was accustomed to the Narragansett track, while Whirly was a newcomer to it. Finally, Whirly carried 118 pounds, while War Relic carried only 107 pounds. Everything was in War Relic's favor. But we note again that not even the greatest horses like *every* race track. We saw that War Admiral did not do well at Pimlico. Narragansett Park was *not* Whirlaway's favorite track.)

Jones sent Whirlaway back to Belmont for the Lawrence Realization on September 20, and the Jockey Club Gold Cup seven days later. Whirlaway was again the favorite for the 1 5/8 mile Lawrence Realization. He carried 126 pounds, the same as the Kentucky Derby weight, but twelve pounds more than the nearest horse, Fairymant.

Under Robertson's reins, Whirly's racing style had changed. He took the lead early, with 1/2-mile to go, and held onto it all the way. He won by *eight* lengths. Bryan Field put it well: "Whirlaway's streaming tail and flashing heels were about all the others saw in the Forty-ninth Lawrence Realization Stakes...."

Whirlaway's last race of 1941 was the two-mile Jockey Club Gold Cup. He lost, but by the slightest of margins. He stayed back for the first mile, was in first at the stretch, but then another horse, Market Wise, came on strong to beat him by just a nose.

With that, Jones called it a year. In twenty starts, (thirteen firsts, five seconds, two third-place finishes) Whirlaway was never out of the money. He won $272,386, the Triple Crown, the Dwyer Stakes, the Travers Stakes, the Saranac Handicap, and the Lawrence Realization, to hit the high points. He had six different jockeys over nine months (Wendell Eads, Basil James, R.L. Vedder, Eddie Arcaro, Alfred Shelhammer, and Alfred Robertson,) raced at nine different tracks in six different states, and traveled over 7,000 miles by train. It stands as an amazing record of stamina and adaptability that is unlikely ever to be equaled by another Triple Crown winner.

He was named Horse of the Year and Best Three-Year-Old Horse. What other horse could have been? Remember Arcaro's words after the Preakness: "There are no other three-year-olds. Just Whirlaway." The jockey was correct: there *were* no other three-year-olds but Whirlaway in 1941, and everyone knew it.

Jones sent Whirlaway back to Calumet for a rest. The plan was to give the horse a month in Kentucky, then ship him to California for the March 7, 1942, Santa Anita Handicap at Santa Anita Park. Jones sent him to California on October 24, and he arrived at Santa Anita to a crowd of 3,500 some four days later. He was the first Triple Crown winner to be raced in California. He trained well, was doing well, and then came December 7, 1941. Now the whole world, Whirlaway included, was at war.

The advent of American participation in World War II changed everything in sports. Baseball was most affected, but football, basketball, all sports, including horse racing were impacted. The U.S. Army gave orders to cancel the Santa Anita Handicap, and so it was. There was some thought that Whirlaway might be stranded in California "for the duration," and who knew how long *that* would be?

Fortunately, *racing* would not be cancelled: curtailed, yes; oriented to fund-raising drives, yes; but, not cancelled completely. Somehow, Jones got Whirlaway back to Kentucky in time for the races at Keeneland in April, 1942.

On April 9, he ran in the 3/4-mile Phoenix Handicap at Keeneland.

Ironically, Greentree Stable entered a three year old, Devil Diver, in the race Eddie Arcaro, still bound contractually to Greentree, rode Devil Diver. Whirly carried the most weight: 128 pounds. (The four other horses carried weights of 112 to 114 pounds.) Arthur Craig rode him. Whirly broke well, had a slow start, and then picked up horses throughout the race. He was gaining on Devil Diver, but he didn't start his rush quite soon enough. Arcaro and Devil Diver finished a head in front of Whirlaway.

That wasn't too bad: Seven months had passed since Whirlaway's last race. He carried much more weight than any other horse in the Phoenix Handicap, and it was a short race. He probably would have won a longer one. He ran again six days later at Keeneland in another 3/4-mile race, the Sesquicentennial Handicap. Again, he carried the most weight (126 pounds) and faced six other horses. Craig rode him again, and the race was much like the Phoenix Handicap. Sun Again, another Calumet horse, took the lead. Whirly was back through much of the race, gained steadily on the backstretch, and finished half a length behind Sun Again.

Whirly needed to win again. On April 25, he won the 1 1/16-mile Clark Handicap at Churchill Downs. Wendell Eads, still a Calumet contract jockey, rode him. The notes to the race chart could have been a composite of all his previous races: "WHIRLAWAY dropped far out of contention in the first eighth, was kept in contention in the first eighth, was kept in the track after reaching the back stretch, started up before reaching the final half mile and closing strongly after losing additional ground on the stretch turn, was up in the final stride." In other words, Whirly did it again, his way.

So he was back after all. Now it was time to go east to Baltimore, back to Pimlico, for the 1 3/16-mile Dixie Handicap. Arcaro was able to ride him again, and they avenged their defeat by Attention in the 1941 Arlington Classic. Whirlaway broke slowly, and stayed in last place for much of the race. After 3/4 of a mile Arcaro let him go and Whirly rocketed past the other horses. The Associated Press report stated that "He passed them all — Challedon, Mioland, and Attention — so easily he made it look more like fun than work." Whirlaway finished 3/4 of a length ahead of Attention to win.

Now he had won two of Pimlico's most important races: the Preakness and the Dixie Handicap (the third big race there, the Pimlico Special, would not occur until later in the year.) Moreover, there was something else to consider: Gallant Fox's earnings record of 1929-1930 lasted only one year before it was broken by a horse named Sun Beau, who won $376,744 over five racing seasons. In turn, Seabiscuit broke Sun Beau's record in winning $437,730 between 1935 and 1940. After the Dixie Handicap, Whirly's winnings totalled $371,811. That was less than $5000 away from Sun Beau, less than $66,000 away from Seabiscuit. Could he do it? The way he was going, who would bet against him?

From Pimlico he was sent north to Belmont to run in the 1-1/4 mile

Suburban Handicap on May 30. Arcaro was free from contractual obligations to Greentree for that race, so once again he rode Whirlaway. It started out as a replay of the previous year's Preakness: Arcaro let him break slowly, and they were last by nearly twenty lengths after a half-mile. Then Arcaro turned him loose. Just as he had at Pimlico the year before, Whirlaway came rushing down the backstretch, around the far turn, and passed horses one after another. But the late rush fed Whirly's tendency to run to the outside: entering the stretch he was out in the middle, and that proved critical. Arcaro and he could never quite catch up to the eventual winner, Market Wise. He finished second, two lengths back.

It was still a good race with a classic Whirlaway finish. He earned $6000 for his troubles. That moved him ahead of Sun Beau to second place in the money rankings. Whirly stayed in New York to run in the Carter Handicap, a 7/8 mile race at Aqueduct slated for June 13. But here was a predicament: Calumet couldn't find a jockey for him. Eads was under a suspension. Greentree had a horse, Swing and Sway, entered, and that took care of Arcaro. George Woolf rode another horse in that race, Pictor, for W.L. Brann. Even John Longden was booked for the Carter Handicap. Finally, a lesser-known jockey, Leon Haas, was booked.

Haas' major distinction is that he happened to ride Whirlaway in one race. So, Whirly found yet another rider up, his fourth in sixth races. And of course, the Horse of the Year carried extra weight: 130 pounds, the most weight carried by any of the nine horses in the race. Consider it, then: a heavy weight penalty, a jockey unfamiliar with him, and three other jockeys in the race that had ridden Whirlaway in the past. Haas let him stay in last place for most of the race, then let him go in the stretch. He opened up again and passed six horses easily. Had it been a longer race, it would have been Whirlaway's race. As it was, Doublrab finished first, a mere head in front of Swing and Sway. But Whirly closed fast. He was 3/4 of a length behind Swing and Sway and only a length behind Doublrab. Bryan Field of *The New York Times* put it well: "The handicaps the little horse [Whirlaway] had assumed were too much. He ran gallantly and gained new glory. But it was Doublrab who got, and earned, the victory."

The Brooklyn Handicap, one of the most important handicap races, was two weeks away. But instead of resting Whirly, Jones felt it was time to get even. He entered Whirlaway in the $2,275 Celt Purse, a 1 1/8-mile race at Aqueduct just five days prior to the Brooklyn Handicap. George Woolf was available, and he rode Whirlaway, the horse's fifth rider in seven races. Attention was also entered, as was Swing and Sway. Whirly still carried the most weight, but this time it was only 122 pounds. As usual, Whirly broke slowly, stayed far back, and started to move up in the back stretch. He was blocked in by Swing and Sway and Attention, so Woolf had no choice but to take the chance of sending Whirly outside. The rider went to the whip and Whirly responded by passing Swing and Sway. He came up next to Attention.

They battled down the stretch to a photo finish at the wire. A few minutes later, the results were posted: Whirlaway got his nose across the line first.

John Longden (left) shakes hands with Eddie Arcaro at Belmont Park, May 4, 1955. Both jockeys rode Whirlaway, and both rode different winners to Triple Crown victories. © *Collection of C. Ken Grayson. Used by permission.*

Other horses would have been exhausted from all the racing, but not Mr. Longtail. He seemed possessed of endless reserves. Five days later Woolf and Whirlaway ran in the 1 1/4-mile Brooklyn Handicap, He carried 128 pounds, six pounds more than his nearest competitor, but again, it didn't make any difference. When the race started his rider let him loaf near the back of the pack. On the backstretch, Woolf let him go. Once again he pounded past the competition. Swing and Sway was in the lead, but not for long; Whirlaway flashed past him and finished first by 1 3/4 lengths. The purse was $23,650, bringing his total winnings to $404,486. Now he was just $33,244 behind Seabiscuit.

The 1 3/16- mile Butler Handicap at Empire City on July 4 was next for him. It was a special day, America's first Independence Day celebration during World War II. By this time Woolf was getting most of the rides on Whirlaway, and they went off as the favorite at 3 to 4 odds. Here Whirlaway had a massive weight handicap, *twenty* pounds more than any other horse in the race. Whirly

137

was in seventh and last place for most of the race, and moved up in the stretch. Now the weight, and fatigue from all the past races, caught up to him. He was tired, *very* tired. He bore out badly in the home stretch. His tendency to run to the outside emerged from sheer fatigue. Still, he passed all the other horses but one: Tola Rose, ridden by Warren Mehrtens, and carrying only 103 pounds. Swing and Sway finished third, ridden by John Longden.

Whirlaway won $6000 for his troubles, and now lagged only $27,244 behind Seabiscuit. Jones didn't give him much rest, but gave him a change of scenery. He ran eleven days later in the 1 1/8-mile Massachusetts Handicap at Suffolk Downs. He was even money, 1 to 1, in the betting, and Woolf rode to a classic Whirlaway victory: last for most of the race, a magnificent closing finish, and first over the line by 2 1/4 lengths. He ran the race in 1:48 1/5 to set a new track record. The purse was $62,600. He smashed Seabiscuit's record by $35,000. He was now the world's champion money-winning horse.

One of the remembered images of World War II is the war bond drive to raise funds to finance the war effort. Most sporting events held a war bond event at one time or another. Racetracks were no exception. Naturally, Whirlaway was eagerly sought after by every track. Warren Wright and Ben Jones accepted as many invitations as possible. Arlington Park near Chicago was the next stop on Whirlaway's travel itinerary for precisely that reason. The tracks in the east had seen Whirlaway run on war bond day; now it was Chicago's turn. Travel restrictions or no, Whirlaway was shipped to the Midwest to run in the Arlington Handicap on August 1. Arcaro was Whirly's jockey in this race, and the leading money-winner carried 130 pounds, by far the most weight in the race. Add in a track that was sloppy from summer rain, and here was a perfect recipe for a defeat: a thoroughly tired horse with heavy weight on a bad track. Still, he did it his way: last for most of the race, and thundering with his usual magnificent closing rush. It wasn't enough. He finished second, 3 1/2 lengths behind the winner.

The loss has been attributed to fatigue, the weight, and the track, but recent research has revealed something else: during the race, a small object, a stone or clump of dirt, struck Whirly's right eye. The incident might have happened when Whirly started his stretch run, for he never closed up tight to the finish line. That would throw off any racer, equine or human. For the next few weeks, Whirlaway wore an isinglass blinker to protect his right eye.

It was also Arcaro's last race on Whirlaway. Arcaro's racing schedule for Greentree, plus the earlier suspensions, kept him from riding Whirlaway more often. In September, 1942, he was suspended again for riding infractions, this time indefinitely. The suspension lasted a year and by the time Arcaro returned to the turf, Whirlaway had been retired. It was a pity that things worked out that way, for the 1941 Triple Crown races demonstrated that Arcaro was perfect for him. It is useless to imagine what might have resulted had he been available more often to ride Mr. Longtail. All we can do is watch the old newsreels, sit back, and savor the long-ago image of racing greatness as Eddie Arcaro smoothly steers Whirlaway to yet another victory.

Thanks to the eye injury and all the press reports about his fatigue, Whirlaway got what he needed most: a four week break. Jones thought he could run anytime, anywhere. That was true, but even an iron horse needs rest.

Whirlaway didn't run again until August 29, and then he went to Garden State Park at Camden, New Jersey, for the 1 1/8-mile Trenton Handicap. Eads was off suspension and rode him. Whirlaway had never run at Garden State Park before, and there was some speculation that the layout of the track (an unusually short homestretch) would cause Whirly problems. Because of that, Eads would have to send Mr. Longtail to the front sooner than usual.

But bless his heart: Somehow, Whirlaway knew what to do. Last through the quarter-mile, without any prompting from Eads, he bolted to the front in the backstretch. He captured the lead at the half-mile mark, and won by one length. His time of 1:50 4/5 was only 1/5 of a second of the track record. Eads said afterward: "Whirly got excited and was full of running. I couldn't hold him anyway, so I just sat back and let him go. He ran a great race."

Whirly's one month hiatus had done the trick. A Rhode Island venue was next, at Narragansett Park. On September 12 Woolf rode him to victory in the 1 3/16-mile Narragansett Special. He carried 130 pounds again, and it was a typical Whirlaway race: far back for most of the race (sixteen lengths at one point!), but then Whirlaway decided to run. *The New York Times* said at that point, the race became "just a romp." He won by two lengths. With every race, Whirlaway was breaking his own records: Including the $25,000 Narragansett Special Purse, he had won $491,136. No horse before Whirlaway had won a half-million dollars in purses.

Every Triple Crown winner seems to have had a challenger. First it was Man o'War against Sir Barton; then it was Seabiscuit versus War Admiral. To this august pair of challengers is added the name of Alsab.

The colt owned by Albert Sabath of Chicago (hence his name, "Al-Sab") was one of the most incredible bargains in racing history. Sabath purchased the horse at the 1940 Saratoga yearling sales for a mere $700. Sabath raced him hard, an incredible twenty-two times at age two, and twenty-three times at age three. Alsab ran the mile in the 1941 Champagne Stakes in record time. He followed that up with a record victory in the 1942 Preakness, as well as second-place finishes in the Kentucky Derby and Belmont Stakes. So here it was, in shades of Man o'War and Sir Barton: the best three-year-old horse, Alsab, challenged the best four-year-old horse, Whirlaway.

Alsab had been entered in the Narragansett Special, but Sabath had withdrawn him. The reason given was that Alsab had arrived at Narragansett too late to train properly. The fans on September 12 were disappointed; they had been awaiting a head-to-head contest between Alsab and Whirlaway. But James E. Dooley, president of the Narragansett track, came to the rescue: he announced that on the following Saturday, September 19, 1942, there would be a $25,000 special 1 3/16-mile match race between the two horses. Jones liked the idea and got Warren Wright's approval. The trainer told the press they would stay there for the week and Whirlaway would "run even if it snows."

In the race, Alsab led all the way. Whirly, ridden by Woolf, stayed near the challenger, never falling more than two lengths behind. In the stretch, Woolf let him go, and the cry, "Here comes Whirlaway" shot up from the crowd. It was an epic finish, both horses seemingly glued to each other as they passed the wire in a photo finish. The camera awarded the victory: Whirlaway's head was cocked down slightly, while Alsab's was more level to the ground. The slight angle differential made all the difference. Alsab put his nose over the wire just before Whirlaway did.

There was no disgrace in losing like that. Ben Jones sent him back to Belmont for the 1 1/2-mile Manhattan Handicap one week later. Whirlaway carried 132 pounds, again more than any horse entered. Moreover, there was yet another jockey crisis: Arcaro was suspended, Woolf was unavailable, Eads was riding for Calumet in other races that day, and even Andy Craig, Leon Haas, and John Longden were riding other horses in the Manhattan Handicap. Jack Westrope was hired to ride Whirlaway.

It really didn't matter *who* was on Whirlaway that day; he ran his standard race, far back seventh or eighth in the eight-horse field, and then put on his usual memorable stretch run. But one of the horses, Bolingbroke, also stayed back, and he carried only 115 pounds. When Whirly made his move, so did Bolingbroke. The weight penalty Whirlaway carried (seventeen pounds more than Bolingbroke) proved decisive. Bolingbroke finished 1 1/2 lengths ahead of Whirlaway.

John Hervey wrote of the Manhattan Handicap, "Whirlaway was great in defeat, perhaps never greater." The pattern was clear now: glorious victories alternated between equally glorious defeats.

There were a couple of important races left in the 1942 racing season, the Jockey Club Gold Cup at Belmont one week after the Manhattan Handicap, and the Pimlico Special a month later, as well as a host of minor races.

Whirlaway had just missed winning the two-mile Jockey Club Gold Cup the previous year and now was time to win it once and for all. He was the favorite in the betting, but there was some good competition. Alsab and Bolingbroke were entered, as was The Rhymer, a horse that had raced against Whirlaway in other races that year. Woolf was available to ride Whirlaway, and the two set out for revenge. Ben Jones and George Woolf *knew* Whirlaway could go the distance; not so Alsab or Bolingbroke. Whirlaway trailed either fourth or third in the four-horse field for most of the race, and with a half-mile to go, Woolf turned him loose. He moved up beside the leader, Alsab, and it was close for a moment. Woolf let him ease back for just a moment to conserve Whirlaway's strength. Then, with an eighth of a mile to go, it was suddenly all over: Whirlaway pounded to the lead and held it for the rest of the race. He beat Alsab by 3/4 of a length; Bolingbroke by nearly nine lengths; The Rhymer by twenty-four lengths. The purse was $18,350. That put his winnings up to $511,486. Whirlaway became the first horse in history to top $500,000 in career earnings.

Alsab got his revenge on Whirlaway the following week in the 2 1/4-mile New York Handicap at Belmont Park. Johnny Westrope rode Whirly again, and this time, the jockey got a different set of instructions: Take Whirlaway to the lead early. The race was long, and the Triple Crown winner carried 130 pounds; again, the most in the field. Jones thought that the long race would prove too much for him to use his come-from-behind tactic, so Westrope was told to get him in front early, and hold onto the lead. It almost worked. Whirly took the lead by the first mile, and held onto it for most of the race. But with an eighth of a mile to go, Whirly faded and dropped back. Alsab, carrying nine pounds less than Whirlaway, and another horse, Obash, carrying only 106 pounds, both caught Mr. Longtail to finish first and second respectively. He carried *such* a high weight over a *very* long distance. His victors ran the same distance, but with much less weight. Whirlaway could be forgiven.

Now Whirlaway got a two-week rest and another trip, this time to Laurel in Maryland. He ran in a more normal race, the 1 1/4-mile Washington Handicap, on October 24. Woolf was back on him, and it was a standard Whirlaway victory: a slow break from the gate, far back for most of the race, and then the heart-stopping closing finish to victory. *The New York Times* headline said it well:

> "TURF'S GREATEST MONEY-WINNER
> ADDS ANOTHER VICTORY TO HIS LIST."

He had now won $528,336 in purse money.

Four days later, he ran in the $10,000, 1 3/16-mile Pimlico Special, the race that saw Seabiscuit defeat War Admiral four years earlier. But there would be no defeat for a Triple Crown winner in this race. No one, *no one,* entered a horse against Whirlaway. It is incredible. Not even Man o'War had faced *no* opposition in a race[10]. Woolf let him break from the gate and kept him under restraint for the first mile — no use risking an injury in a walkover. Then Whirlaway turned rank. He wanted to go, and Woolf had no choice. Whirlaway finished, all alone on the track, with his usual burst of speed. His time was 2:05 2/5, about seven seconds behind his Preakness time the year before. Not bad for a horse that had no opposition and was held back for most of the race.

---

[10] This is called a "walkover" because the unopposed horse has only to walk around the track and "walk over" the finish line to win the race.

The Riggs Handicap, a 1 3/16-mile race at Pimlico worth $9,225, was Whirlaway's next race. It was five days after the Pimlico Special walkover, and Whirlaway carried 130 pounds again, the most in the race. He was far back for most of the race. He came on strong at the end to challenge the leader, Riverland. But that horse, ridden by Johnny Gilbert, carried only 116 pounds. He was even behind Whirlaway during part of the race. But the weight factor again was decisive. He passed Whirlaway in the stretch and beat him by 2 1/2 lengths.

Whirlaway's last eastern race of 1942 was at Pimlico on November 11, in the 1 5/8 mile Governor Bowie Handicap. Eads was on him this time, and it was no contest; Whirlaway took the lead early around the 3/4-mile mark and stayed there to win by three lengths.

His last race of 1942 was on December 12 at the Fair Grounds in New Orleans, Louisiana, in the 1 1/8-mile Louisiana Handicap. Tony Pelletier, Vice-President of the Fair Grounds track, needed a drawing card. The Fair Grounds had a dismal 1941 racing season, and 1942 hadn't been much better. A request went from New Orleans to Calumet. To Pelletier's great joy, Ben Jones announced that Whirlaway would go to Louisiana for the race.

Whirlaway's entry worked: the Fair Grounds packed in a record crowd of 20,000 souls to see Mr. Longtail. Eads rode Whirlaway in his only Louisiana appearance, and the chart is an exercise in *deja vu:* Whirlaway was last in the race for the first mile, moved up after that, and won again in the stretch. He had now won $560,911. It was a record.

With that, Ben Jones put Whirlaway away for the winter of 1942-1943. He was named Best Handicap Horse and again, Horse of the Year. In one year he had run twenty-two races — more races than Man o'War or Gallant Fox ran in their entire careers. He won twelve of them, finished second in eight, and took third in two. He never finished out of the money. He raced under crushing weight burdens and was truly an iron horse. He set the world's record for winnings. It is a racing year that stands up well in comparison to any other horse.

It was tragic that Jones let him run "just one more time." In the weeks after the Louisiana Handicap, Jones discovered that Whirlaway had somehow injured his left foreleg. He had a bowed tendon, the worst injury a racehorse can suffer short of a broken leg. Where had it happened, and how? Probably it happened at the Fair Grounds, but no one could be sure. He was not a colt any more. Time had caught up with him. He was never the same after the Louisiana Handicap.

But it was also fortunate that the end was now in sight. Mr. Longtail had recovered from many minor ailments, but the bowed tendon took more out of him than any previous injury had done. Whirlaway was five years old in 1943, and had run an impressive fifty-eight races. Jones treated him unsuccessfully over the winter; the races and workouts had taken their toll. A sound Whirlaway would have tempted Ben Jones to keep him racing as long as possible, until he might have broken a leg in a race and had to be destroyed.

Jones entered Whirlaway in several races in the spring of 1943, but Whirly was scratched in all of them. He was taken to Chicago, where he had started racing three years earlier. At Washington Park on June 22, he finished third in the War Admiral Purse. He didn't seem to be hurting, so Jones entered him in the Equipoise Mile four days later at Washington Park. Whirly finished fifth and came up lame when he returned to the barn.

On June 28, 1943, Warren Wright announced Whirlaway's racing career was over. Ben Jones said: "He pulled up noticeably sore. He didn't respond to treatment. I called Mr. Wright this morning and after a conference he agreed with me that the only logical course was retirement. After all, it would be little short of inhumane to continue training such a great horse and run the chance of permanently maiming him."

So there it was, the end of his racing career. And what a career it was! the Triple Crown; a Kentucky Derby record; twice Horse of the Year; best two-year-old in 1940; best three-year-old in 1941; best handicap horse in 1942; 60 starts with 32 victories, both more than any other Triple Crown Winner; and winnings totaling a record $561,161, all earned at the tail end of the Great Depression and the beginning of World War II. Twelve different jockeys rode him on seventeen different tracks in nine different states; more individual jockeys than any other Triple Crown horse. He did something still unequaled: He won the Travers Stakes in addition to the Triple Crown.

Four of his jockeys, Eddie Arcaro, John Longden, Alfred Robertson, and George Woolf, were later named to the National Museum of Racing and Hall of Fame. In most of his races, he carried far more weight than any other horse on the track, and usually beat all of them. All that was now history. Never again would a spectator cry, "Here comes Whirlaway!" and then watch the chestnut tail straighten out as Whirly forged from behind to drive past the other horses to victory.

Ben Jones added: "It's just like losing my best friend."

Whirlaway was paraded at Washington Park in Chicago on July 5, 1943. It was his last track appearance, and the crowd was appreciative. He returned to Lexington eight days later, and was honored with "Whirlaway Day" on August 8, an occasion replete with speeches from local dignitaries.

Whirly returned to Calumet to join his sire in stud duty. He turned out to be a good sire. Eighteen of his foals were stakes winners, and through 1951, his offspring earned $1,631,330, but none ever approached his greatness. (Few horses could; with few major winners in his siring record, Whirly's bloodline faded away fairly rapidly after his death.) In 1950 he was leased to Marcel Boussac, a French businessman, and Whirly was accordingly shipped to

Europe. He stood at a farm in Normandy, and later, Boussac purchased the Triple Crown Winner outright from Calumet.

Whirly's end was both Homeric and ribald: a Frenchwoman got him. (Well, sort of.) On April 6, 1953, he died in his stall of a ruptured nerve tissue shortly after breeding a mare in Normandy. (*C'est Magnifique!*) His remains were later returned to Calumet Farm, and he is buried in the Calumet horse cemetery.

We have not seen the last of Eddie Arcaro, but here it is appropriate to note what he felt about his first Triple Crown horse, Whirlaway. It must be remembered that Arcaro later rode Citation, Assault, Nashua, and Kelso (among *many* other horses) and may have been "spoiled" by them. Arcaro's later feelings about Whirly were interestingly negative: "It was never any picnic to ride Whirlaway. Once he started to climb you just couldn't slow him down. It was always like stepping on the accelerator of a big Cadillac. How he could pour it on!"

In a 1991 *Sports Illustrated* article on Whirlaway, Arcaro was quoted as saying: "I don't think any horse is great that has the idiosyncrasies he had." Yes, Whirly had his crazy moments, and few knew those better than Eddie Arcaro. But earlier Arcaro had expressed affection for and pride in Whirlaway. In his 1951 book, *I Ride to Win!*, Arcaro called Whirlaway the "red fellow" and said that he and the horse had developed a "true affection" for each other. Whirly's legacy to Arcaro, like his legacy to racing, was mixed.

After Man o'War's death in 1947, sportswriters voted Whirlaway their favorite living racehorse. He was loved by the crowds that watched him come from behind, by the press agents that wrote about him, and by Ben Jones. Too many times, it seemed that Whirly lost interest if he couldn't win. The "idiosyncrasies" that Arcaro spoke of endeared him to the crowd, if not to the jockeys and handlers that worked with him. The spectators saw nothing of the hard work, the tight hold, and the ever-present threat of bolting to the outside; what they saw was Whirlaway's chestnut tail streaming out full in the wind he sliced with his incredible kick to come from behind to victory.

We are left with his name, Whirlaway, as the most melodic one of any Triple Crown winner, and with the memories of his idiosyncrasies. It would be fascinating to know what caused them. Was he indeed crazy, as so many have said? Or maybe, just maybe, he was really brilliant, an "evil genius" who knew exactly when to make his move, able to come from behind faster than any other horse. Only he knew, and he didn't tell us.

Whirlaway is a champion in his own right, yet he is linked with his successor Triple Crown Champion from Calumet Farm, Citation. They came from the same stable, were each ridden in their Triple Crown seasons by Eddie Arcaro, and won their Triple Crowns only seven years apart.

144

In the spring of 1992, when Calumet Farm was sold at a bankruptcy auction, the second line in a *Wall Street Journal* article about the sale stated, "Saddled with Debts, Breeder of Whirlaway and Citation is Up for Auction." They are forever joined in comparisons, and Whirlaway inevitably comes off second-best. Yet, for all the controversy, Whirlaway remains a compelling racehorse. Even today, the viewing of an old newsreel, with Mr. Longtail flipping his tail into the air and speeding for the finish line, is as riveting as it was in 1941. Whirly is, with Count Fleet, Citation, and Secretariat, one of the Big Four of Triple Crown Winners. It is no surprise to realize that in 1941, the four greatest sports figures in America were two baseball players, Joe DiMaggio and Ted Williams; one boxer, Joe Louis; and one iron Thoroughbred: Whirlaway, the little horse with the big tail.

WHIRLAWAY. Portrait taken 1948.
© *Collection of C. Ken Grayson. Used by permission*

*"His name was Whirlaway,
and he was variously described
as crazy, stupid, ornery, nervous — and brilliant."*
— Jim McKay, 1988

V. THE UNVANQUISHED: COUNT FLEET

Triple Crown, 1943. Jockey, John Longden

Count Fleet's jockey, John Longden[1], said of him in the Belmont Stakes, "Going into the race, I thought he'd have to fall down to get beat. Then I thought he could get up and win, he was that good. He was, what you'd say, a kind of a freak horse. He could do anything..."

Grantland Rice, the great sportswriter, called the Count one of the four best Thoroughbreds he had ever seen. Count Fleet is one of the Big Four of Triple Crown winners, with Whirlaway, Citation, and Secretariat, and is one of racing's greatest, with Man o'War, Citation, Kelso, and Secretariat. Count Fleet's career was sandwiched between the celebrity of Whirlaway and Citation. He raced during World War II, when media and sports fans' attention were focused on matters other than Thoroughbred racing. Moreover, his racing career was truncated. Count Fleet may be the least-known of all the great Thoroughbreds. But, look at his record: 21 starts, 16 firsts, 4 seconds, 1 third-place finish. He was never out of the money. Only one phrase is proper for him: The Unvanquished Horse.

John Hertz was a Czech immigrant and Chicago businessman who founded Yellow Cab and the Hertz Rent-A-Car Company. He and his spouse enjoyed horse racing, and they went into it. In the late 1920s, Hertz, as part of an investment group, bought the Arlington race track near Chicago. Hertz himself had been a boxer, and one day saw a two-year-old colt called Reigh Count race in Saratoga.

The colt was spunky, even biting another horse in a race. Reigh Count's fighting instinct appealed to the ex-boxer, so Hertz bought him. The next year, 1928, Reigh Count won the Kentucky Derby. On March 24, 1940, a brown colt was born as a result of a mating between Reigh Count and a mare named Quickly at Hertz's Stoner Creek farm. The foal was given a name in keeping

---

[1] When he was racing, he was generally called Johnny Longden. He preferred John Longden and will be so denominated here.

147

with his sire: Count Fleet.[2]

The horse trainer at Stoner Creek was Don Cameron, who had been a balloon pilot in World War One. He was a decent trainer, and knew many jockeys. When Hertz needed a jockey, Cameron recalled one who had raced for him previously in Canada. He wrote to that jockey a letter in 1942 asking him to come to work. The jockey was John Longden.

John Longden. In Triple Crown racing there are a few jockey/horse combinations that could be called "perfect", where a good or great jockey is ideally matched to his mount: Sande on Gallant Fox; Kurtsinger on War Admiral; Arcaro on Whirlaway; Arcaro again, on Citation; Turcotte on Secretariat — and John Longden on Count Fleet.

John Longden was born in Wakefield, England, in 1907. In 1912, his family emigrated to Taber, Alberta, Canada.[3] Longden grew up there, and when he got older, he worked in the coal mines around Taber. He always liked horses, and got the idea of race riding. He read anything he could find about horses, jockeys, and racing, and he made up his mind to be a jockey. Meanwhile, he dug coal and handled the mine mules. He started hanging around the horses at the county fairgrounds and saw his first races there. One day, he approached a horse owner and asked if he could ride one of the man's horses. First the answer was negative, but Longden kept after him until the owner said yes. Longden pushed his luck, and asked if he could ride the horse in a county fairground race. He won it: his first race, his first victory.

For three years, he alternated working in Taber's mines in the winter and riding in the fair races in the summer. The fair circuit got extended south of the border into Montana. In the autumn of 1927, he went down to Salt Lake City and stayed for a while with family friends. He went to the track in Salt Lake and got a job exercising a couple of horses. On September 27, 1927 he rode his first Thoroughbred race at Salt Lake City aboard a filly named Mary Phema. He

---

[2] Mention should be made of Count Fleet's dam, Quickly. She earned her name, having set one track record and tied two others. She was distantly related to Man o'War. Quickly started an immense 85 races, winning 32, placing in 14, and showing in 13 races (a win percentage of 38%, a money percentage of 69%.) She ran in small-purse races during the Depression, but managed to earn $21,350. Count Fleet had some pretty good bloodlines in him from both parents.

One other thing: *Mrs.* John Hertz is formally listed as Count Fleet's owner, but it appears that John Hertz made many important decisions regarding the Count.

[3] Here was Longden's first brush with fateful history: his family's journey to Canada was delayed, because an unforeseen delay caused the Longden family to miss sailing with their first ship. A fortunate thing, for the ship they missed was *RMS Titanic.*

finished third. He posted his first Thoroughbred victory on a horse called Hugo K. Asher on October 4, 1927. He went back to Taber and the coal mines for the winter, but he was hooked on racing.

In the spring of 1928 Longden talked the coal mine manager into giving him a small stake so he could go to Calgary and try his luck in racing there. He got hired as an exercise boy and soon was promoted to jockey. He learned how to race, and the victories came — not quickly, but steadily.

He married a Calgary girl in 1929. In 1930 he decided to try racing in California. He had no luck finding a jockey's job there, so he tried Mexico. No luck there, either. He and his pregnant wife started back to Canada. They got as far as Spokane, and Longden was forced to send his wife back to Calgary alone. He worked odd jobs in Spokane until he could join her in Calgary.

His career started to grow in 1930. He emerged as the leading rider in British Columbia that year. In the next few years, things went better for him. He raced in central and western Canada, returned to California; and even raced in 1932 in Mexico against the legendary Australian racer Phar Lap. Longden had paid his dues.

John Longden (1907-2003).
Courtesy Grayson Collection

By 1937, he was working for Sunny Jim Fitzsimmons, trainer of Gallant Fox and Omaha. Sunny Jim is most associated with William Woodward's Belair Stud, home of the father and son Triple Crown team, but he also worked for Mrs. Ogden Phipps' Wheatley Stable. Longden went to ride for Wheatley and won the 1937 Wood Memorial on Melodist, but finished fourth to Charles Kurtsinger on War Admiral in the Kentucky Derby that year.

He was a tough jockey, determined to win. Bill Shoemaker, a contemporary rival and a later friend, said of Longden, "When he was at the top of his game, he would shut off his best friend to get home first." But he was an honest rider on the track. He picked up his share of riding infractions (It happens to every successful jockey), but no one ever claimed John Longden cheated to win a race. He cared a great deal about people; many were the times he helped out other jockeys. And if a jockey was severely injured, Longden was ready to help in any way he could. In short, John Longden was a gentleman.

As his career grew, his home life changed. Divorced in 1939, Longden kept racing to stay busy, and spent the early summer of 1940 at Hollywood Park in California. (Also in 1940, as we have seen, he was one of Whirlaway's jockeys.) He met a lady, Hazel Tarn, and they were married in 1941.

In the spring of 1942, he went east to ride for Don Cameron and John Hertz. Longden's introduction to his greatest horse was appropriately casual, with no hint as to what was to come. Don Cameron one day asked Longden to ride a brown colt: "Gallop him, John. I don't know much about him but his old man could run some."

Longden asked, "Who is he?"

"A Reigh Count colt. Name's Count Fleet."

Count Fleet as a colt was a bit like his father; in John Longden's words, "a rogue." The colt just wanted his own way. As far as the Count was concerned, that meant running whenever and wherever he felt like it. In fact, Count Fleet nearly killed Longden and himself at a morning workout at Belmont Park. The Count was running as he chose, and Longden saw two other horses coming directly at them. "Somehow I managed to steer between them, but how I'll never know," Longden recalled thirty years later. The story got around, and no one else wanted to ride the seemingly incorrigible colt. (Thus by default the job of riding Count Fleet fell to Longden. No other jockey ever rode the Count in any races or trials.) This, and other offenses, nearly caused Count Fleet to be sold at a near-bargain basement price.

If there was an award for the "Worst Possible Decision Fortunately Reversed", a strong contender for it would have to be John Hertz's attempt to sell Count Fleet. Hertz decided he didn't want the scrappy little colt, so he put the Count on the market for $4500. (The numbers vary. Longden said in 1994 that Hertz's asking price was $3500, while other sources say it was $4500. No matter; Hertz wasn't asking very much.) Longden went into the barn and saw the Count being walked around. Longden knew the Count could run, and asked someone in the stable what was happening. Longden found out that the Count was up for sale. The jockey knew better than to let *that* happen, so he took action.

He had to speak to John Hertz immediately. It was at the beginning of World War Two, and gasoline rationing was in effect. "I got on my bicycle...I went to the first phone I could get and told him, 'Please don't sell him because I think he's a good horse.'" Hertz replied, "Well, he might hurt you." Longden answered, "No, he won't hurt me. He just likes to run." The call worked; by the time Longden returned to the barn Count Fleet had been taken off the market.

John Longden in Hertz yellow silks speaks with Mrs. John Hertz, Count Fleet's owner. *Courtesy Grayson Collection.*

It is only necessary to know a five word phrase to understand Count Fleet: *He just loved to run.* That's it. Really, it is.

He just loved to run. The Count wasn't a big, powerful-looking, magnificent animal, like Man o'War or later, Secretariat. Count Fleet was about fifteen hands high and not very impressive in his build. He was, in his jockey's description: "a gentleman" in the starting gate. He liked people, he tolerated other horses. But first and foremost, *he just loved to run.* If Longden just let him run, things would turn out fine. Only when Longden tried to rein him in would the Count get rank; he would bolt to the outside. (One mark of a great jockey is knowing when *not* to do something.) After a race, it took two handlers to cool Count Fleet down: after thirty minutes of walking, the Count was still ready for more. By that time, the handler walking him was worn out. So, a second handler had to come out and walk the Count for *another* half-hour.

In his two-year-old season, he was considered hard to handle, but he was

151

young. Eventually Longden found a way to handle him. The Count always wore blinkers, was thought difficult on the turns, and believed to be sometimes uncontrollable. Yet he had speed to spare. Longden worked with him to the point that Count Fleet would let no other rider mount him. He may have been aloof later in his life, but Longden saw nothing of that during the Count's racing days. Count Fleet wasn't vicious, neurotic, or a loner. *He just loved to run.*

Count Fleet was Count Fleet to the end of his life. In the early 1970s, shortly before his passage, several articles appeared on the then-only living Triple Crown winner. One reported that after a long and truly successful career as a sire, and having been retired from stud for several years, he still had an eye for the mares at Stoner Creek. Another article, done about six months prior to his passage, reported the Count was still in generally good shape, his coat richly colored. As his groom put it, "Shoot, one day last week he ran like a two year old...there were bones poppin' and crackin' but when he got straightened out, why you shoulda seen him go!" *He just loved to run.*

> *"Someday he is going to be one fine racer.*
> *When that leggy brown colt wants to run, he can just about fly."*
> — Sam Ransom, Stoner Creek stable hand,
> on Count Fleet

Count Fleet's two-year-old season was impressive: fifteen starts, ten wins, four seconds, one third. His first race was on the Widener course at Belmont Park on June 1, 1942. It was a five-furlong maiden race with sixteen horses entered. Longden told the starter Eddie Blind, "He's nuts, Eddie, but he's going to the Derby just as sure as I'm sitting here."

At Widener Longden and Count Fleet were far out on the track, thirteenth from the pole. The Count ran fifth at the start, third after a quarter-mile, and finished second, 1 1/2 lengths behind the victor. To a modern reader, the notes to the race chart are full of portent. The chart simply said of the second-place horse, "Count Fleet ran well." If the other horses and jockeys had known what was about to hit them, they might have just stayed in the paddock.

Two weeks later, on June 15th at Aqueduct, the results were the same. The Count was entered in a 5 1/2-furlong maiden race with thirteen other horses. He was seventh at the start, and got tangled up in the pack. Still, by the half-mile he was second, and stayed there to the finish, 1 1/2 lengths behind the leader. The next day's *New York Times* again hinted at what was to come: "Count Fleet, away in a tangle, improved his position on the outside and finished well."

The third time was the charm. Count Fleet's first victory was on June 19, 1942, in a 5 1/2-furlong, $1,500-purse race at Aqueduct. Ten horses challenged, and the Count was third from the post on a fast track. He went wide around the turn and was third at the quarter-mile; Longden brought him in and by the half-mile, moved him into first. He never let up; he stayed in first, winning by four lengths. The notes to the race chart say the Count "Won in a romp." Bryan Field of *The New York Times* noted of the winner of that race: "Count Fleet must be put down as a keen two-year old. He ran out yesterday in the third race thereby losing many lengths. Even so, he came on so powerfully that he was four lengths to the good at the end."

On the Fourth of July, 1942, America's first Independence Day in World War Two, the Count won fittingly the $2,000, 5 1/2-furlong, Army and Navy Purse at the Empire City Track at Yonkers. Five other horses were on the track, and Count Fleet was at the sixth pole position. The track was fast and the start was good. The Count was fourth at the quarter-mile, moved up to second by the half-mile, was in first by three lengths at the top of the stretch, and won by four lengths.

You can't win 'em all: Count Fleet finished second in the East View Stakes at Empire City on July 15, 1942. The Count was again on the outside and broke slowly. Longden sent him up on the outside, but it was never quite enough; he finished a mere length behind the victor, Gold Shower.

Count Fleet got even one week later in the 5 3/4-furlong, $5,000 Wakefield Stakes, also at Empire City. Gold Shower was there with two other horses, and again Count Fleet was at the outside. This time he jumped into the lead at the beginning, was back in third at the quarter-mile, but by the half-mile, was back in first. Longden and the Count just drew away, winning by four lengths. Gold Shower finished third.

From there, Hertz sent Longden and the Count to Chicago to run at Washington Park. They won the $1,200 Willow Springs Purse in a 3/4-mile race on August 11th, but the Count had some trouble in that race. Count Fleet was third by the quarter-mile, and second at the half-mile. But entering the stretch, he was forced wide. He won by a neck; the closest victory of his career. Four days later, the Count ran in the Washington Park Futurity. He finished second to Occupation (ridden by jockey George Wooll.) Count Fleet ran well, but was taken to the outside fence by War Knight. Still, the Count overcame that and finished second by a nose.

Then it was back to New York for Longden and the Count. They won the 6-furlong, $2,500 Mars Purse at Aqueduct on September 15. They followed that up with another victory on September 24 at Belmont. It was the $2,000 Morello Purse, another 6-furlong race. At the half-mile Longden and the Count were ninth in a twelve-horse field; then Longden let him run. They pulled ahead to win by three lengths. Count Fleet was made a favorite for the Belmont Futurity.

Here nature intervened: Count Fleet finished third in that race, this time for the oldest and most forgivable of reasons. Longden recalled, "I was about to go by the filly, Askmenow, when the Count decided he didn't want to leave her. She was in that delicate condition which appealed to him. I couldn't budge him. He just galloped along beside her and let Occupation steal the race." (Translation: Askmenow was in season that weekend, and Count Fleet's mind

153

was on matters other than racing. It was the only third-place finish of his career. Let's give him that one.[4])

It also was the last time Occupation beat Count Fleet. Longden bet Woolf two hundred dollars that Occupation would never again beat the Count. Longden collected that autumn in the Pimlico Futurity; when Count Fleet again met Occupation. In Longden's words, "It was no contest." Count Fleet finished first.

In the 1942 Champagne Stakes held on October 10 at Belmont Park, Longden found the solution to Count Fleet: "He was acting up behind the gate that day. I got tired of his nonsense and belted him a couple with my whip. It was the only time I ever used it on him. [A fast learner, that Count Fleet: Longden *never* used the whip on the Count again, anytime, anywhere, before or during a race.] It got his mind on his business and we broke on top and were never headed. He set a mile world's record for two-year olds, going the distance in 1:34 4/5. And he was never beaten again. I'd found the key to him: get him out on top, give him the race track and let him run. It was what he loved to do more than anything else." There were seven other horses in that race; the Count took an early lead and never gave it up, to win by six lengths. His race time set a new record for two-year-old horses at a mile, 1:34 4/5, and, as Longden said, the Count never lost again.

His last race in New York that year was the 1-mile, 70-yard Thunderclap Purse at Jamaica on October 20. Count Fleet was part of an eight-horse field, and at the break, Longden sent him to the outside. They took the lead by the half-mile, and no other horse seriously threatened. The Count won by six lengths.

His last two-year-old races were at Pimlico in Baltimore. Occupation was the favorite for the Pimlico Futurity on October 31, and here John Longden collected on his bet with George Woolf. Occupation, with Woolf up, and Count Fleet, with Longden up, were the contenders. Occupation took a slight early lead, but the Count stayed with him into the backstretch. They were even through the backstretch and into the turn, but then Longden called on Count

---

[4] One account of the race is more humorous. Trent Frayne wrote, "Count Fleet, rushing up on the outside, suddenly was on the very brink of propping all four feet to keep from sailing past Askmenow. Then he galloped contentedly along, his head never straying from the lady's side.

"Askmenow's jock, pinned to the rail and able to go nowhere, hollered at Longden.

"'Dammit all, John, get your horse offa me!'

"'I'm tryin' to get him offa you, but the son-of-a-buck won't budge,' Longden yelled back."

According to Frayne, at the conclusion of the race, "Longden had to climb down and haul the Count away from Askmenow, whose answer must have been a constant demurrer."

Fleet for more speed (Poor George Woolf had *no* idea what Longden calling on Count Fleet for more speed would mean.) The Count pulled away on the turn and moved to a three-length lead at the top of the stretch. Woolf tried to challenge Longden, but Longden never even used the whip on Count Fleet. The Count just kept pulling away from Occupation and won by six lengths.

For his two-year-old finale, Count Fleet won the $9,700 Walden Stakes on November 10. Here is a curious foreshadowing of the future: Count Fleet had little opposition in his last race of 1942. He was the heavy favorite, and won by *thirty* lengths. A wire service report stated: "The big Reigh Count colt, with Johnny Longden aboard, went out in front from the starting gate and held a two-length margin by the time he hit the first turn. From then on the only questions were how big his final margin would be and which of his nondescript rivals would take second money..." This could have been a description of the next year's Belmont Stakes.

When the sportswriters gathered that autumn to select the best racehorses of the year, Count Fleet received the greatest number of votes for best two-year-old horse.[5] Due to a wartime ban in Florida on racing, Count Fleet wintered in Hot Springs, Arkansas. His three-year-old season, and the Triple Crown races, was on the horizon.

Few horses ever dominated the Triple Crown so thoroughly as did Count Fleet in 1943. The Count won six races in eight weeks: the St. James Purse, the Wood Memorial, the Kentucky Derby, the Preakness, the Withers, and the Belmont Stakes. He had no special moves. There was no special plan to win the races. The strategy was simplicity itself: *just let him run*. It would be all that was needed.

Just let him run. The first race he won that spring was the St. James Purse, on April 13, 1943, at the Jamaica Race track. Eight horses started that day on a sloppy track. The Count was the favorite, at 3 to 20, and started in the eighth position. He broke slow, and went wide into the first turn. A horse named Bossuet took the lead and held it into the stretch. Count Fleet moved up to second at the half-mile mark, and stayed with Bossuet into the homestretch. Then the Count passed him and opened up a four-length lead to win. (We note here the first of three leg injuries that happened to Count Fleet in 1943. He received a minor cut on his left foreleg in the St. James Purse. It healed quickly. The two future injuries would increase in their severity, the last one causing his retirement from racing.)

---

[5] As a further indication of Count Fleet's success that year, he was assigned a weight of 132 pounds in The Jockey Club's Experimental Free Handicap. This is not a race, but a performance ranking system of two-year-old horses by a group of racetrack secretaries. The greater the weight they assign, the higher the value of the horse being rated. This practice continues to this day. To date, *no* horse has ever been assigned a weight equal to Count Fleet's weight assignment.

Just let him run. On April 17, 1943, Count Fleet won the Wood Memorial at Jamaica. Seven other horses challenged him that day, and the competition was first-rate: George Woolf, on Vincentive; Conn McCreary, on Slide Rule; and Ted Atkinson, on Blue Swords, were among the seven. But it really didn't matter who else was on the track that day; it was all Count Fleet. Blue Swords was first by a head at the start, Count Fleet in second. By the half-mile mark, the Count took over first place by four lengths. Longden and the Count never had anything really to worry about. The next day's account said: "At the end he was just breezing along." The Count won by four lengths and came within 2/5 of a second of breaking the track record. Slide Rule and McCreary would finish third; Woolf, on Vincentive, would place eighth. Atkinson and Blue Swords tried valiantly, but could not catch up. As *The New York Times* put it, "Blue Swords did his gallant best but it wasn't nearly good enough, as Count Fleet went serenely on his way to score just about as he pleased."

Only one thing marred the Wood Memorial victory: Count Fleet suffered a gash to his left rear hoof. Another horse, probably Vincentive, nicked the Count. The wound bled somewhat, but it was packed with a sulfa dressing. Longden and the crew traveled from New York to Kentucky, soaking the Count in epsom salts and also holding ice on the wound to reduce the swelling. The treatment was successful, but the wound cast some doubt on Count Fleet's ability to run in the Derby.

> *"For my money, the Fleet's in. I think the Count will win 'by hisself'..."*
> — Sportswriter Mike Barry
> on the 1943 Kentucky Derby.

It was wartime; gasoline was rationed and travel was discouraged. There was talk about canceling the 1943 Derby altogether. Matt Winn stood firm; it was vital, he declared, that the unbroken tradition of the Kentucky Derby remain unbroken. Two wars had been fought since 1875, and still the Derby had been run during each. His final statement: "The Kentucky Derby will be run, even if there are only two horses in the race and two people in the stands." But Winn made a concession: out-of-town spectators were discouraged. Hence, the Derby that year would be remembered as the "Streetcar Derby," as some 61,209 spectators, mostly locals, reached Churchill Downs by whatever means were available: bus, streetcar, even horse and buggy.

On May 1, 1943, Count Fleet, with Longden up, both of them wearing bright Hertz-yellow silks ("Like the Yellow Cab," said Longden,) stepped onto the course at Churchill Downs. Fifteen years earlier Count Fleet's sire won the Derby; eight years hence one of Count Fleet's sons would win the Derby. But now it was Count Fleet's race.

The Count was rated at an incredible 4 to 10, meaning that a $2 bet would pay $2.80. There were nine other horses on the field, three being ridden by jockeys who would be elected to the National Museum of Racing and Hall of Fame: John Adams on Blue Swords, Conn McCreary on Slide Rule, and Ted Atkinson on Gold Shower. So, despite the incredibly favorable odds, the 1943 Kentucky Derby wasn't necessarily a cakewalk for Count Fleet and John Longden.

Just let him run. After it started, there was really no contest. Count Fleet grabbed the lead at the beginning and never stopped. At the half-mile mark he was first by a head. At the three-quarter pole he was ahead by two lengths, and he maintained that lead into the homestretch. At the stretch turn, Blue Swords moved up very briefly just behind the Count. Longden saw Blue Swords, and said to Count Fleet, "Let's go, son." That was that. Count Fleet pulled away a bit more and won by three lengths. Atkinson's horse, Gold Shower, was second through the half and three-quarter marks, but then faded and finished eighth. John Adams on Blue Swords was second. Conn McCreary on Slide Rule finished third. The Count's time was 2:04 2/5 on a fast track.

The Preakness was on May 8. Like the Derby, wartime travel restrictions and gasoline rationing caused most of the spectators to arrive by bus or street car. Longden and the Count arrived in Baltimore on May 7, but the jockey made an immediate overnight trip to New York City: his wife had given birth to a son.

Just let him run. Only three other horses challenged Count Fleet in the Preakness: Blue Swords was back, also Vincentive, ridden by George Woolf, and a horse called New Moon. The Count was the 1 to 9 favorite in the betting. Like the Derby, there was no contest anytime during the race. The middle starting gates were used. The Count and Blue Swords broke in the center of the track, but went to the rail on the first turn. The Count started to pull away in the back stretch. Vincentive was nearby, and Longden told Woolf, "Well, goodbye." Blue Swords took over full command of second place. At the far turn, Longden looked back, saw the horses well behind the Count, and just sat down. They breezed home to an eight-length victory.[6] The Count's time was 1:57 2/5, only 2/5 of a second off the record set the previous year. After the race, Woolf told Longden, "He's a racehorse." Wayne Wright, New Moon's jockey, said afterwards, "I don't know what happened. I never saw the race after the first twenty yards."

Just let him run. Count Fleet won the Withers on May 23, 1943. The Withers is little-known now, but in the 1940s, it was a race of great importance. Only two horses challenged Longden and the Count, who was the 1 to 20 favorite. The track was muddy, and the solution was simple: take the horseshoes off the Count. ("He could run over any type of racetrack. It just didn't make any

---

[6] Count Fleet's eight-length victory margin remained the modern Preakness record until Funny Cide shattered it in 2003. Although the first Preakness winner, Survivor, won by ten lengths in 1873, that race was a different length. The Preakness standardized its length of 1 3/16 miles in 1925, and no horse from 1925 until 2003 had won by a greater margin than Count Fleet.

difference to him," Longden said. Indeed, taking his horseshoes off didn't make any difference to Count Fleet in this race.) Slide Rule with Conn McCreary returned, and another horse, Tip-Toe, also appeared. The Count broke cleanly, immediately went to the front, and just kept going. By the three-quarter mile mark he had a four-length lead; he increased it to five lengths by the start of the stretch; at the finish, he had won by six lengths. For most of the race Longden ran the Count in the middle of the track in search of firm footing, about midway between the rails and nearly forty feet off the inside rail. *The New York Times* report says, "Count Fleet was much the best."

Just let him run. The most one-sided Belmont in Triple Crown history occurred on June 6, 1943. Only two horses showed up to take on the Count; the number-two rated horse, Fairy Manhurst (whom Longden would ride later that year in the Lawrence Realization), was 29 to 1 in the betting odds. The third horse, Desoronto, was 53 to 1. The Count hung in at his normal 1 to 20. The horses went to the post at 4:18 and broke a minute later. The Count grabbed the lead, and there was absolutely no doubt as to which horse was the best. By the half-mile, he had a five-length lead, by the three-quarter mile mark, a ten-length lead, and then he opened up and decided to *really* run. At the beginning of the stretch the Count had a *twenty*-length lead. Actually, there wouldn't have been much to write about[7], but for...

During the race, Count Fleet injured a tendon in his right front leg. Longden felt the Count bobble, and tried to bring the Count up, so as not to cause further injury. The unstoppable Count Fleet took the bit and drove for home. He finished twenty-five lengths ahead of the field to post a record that stood for thirty years.[8] On only three good legs at the end, Count Fleet set a Belmont Stakes record for 1 1/2 miles in 2:28 1/5. It was 2/5 of a second faster than War Admiral's previous record and further broke Man o'War's Belmont victory margin record by five lengths.

The morning after the Belmont Stakes, the Count could hardly rise. Fortunately, the injury was treatable. It was not severe enough to cause Count Fleet's destruction, but his third-year racing season came to a premature end. Despite that, Count Fleet was named both Horse of the Year and Best Three-

---

[7] The notes to *The New York Times* chart of the 1943 Belmont Stakes state: "Count Fleet opened a long lead and just galloped along to win very easily. Fairy Manhurst outgamed Desoronto for the place."

[8] Here is a mystery: While the official results say the Count won by twenty-five lengths, Longden, and *The New York Times* the morning after the Belmont, state the Count won by thirty lengths. Trent Frayne has supplied the solution: "He [Count Fleet] won by what the race-caller decided was twenty-five lengths, although it might even have been more." So Longden and the press may have been right, after all: Count Fleet may have won by thirty lengths. But we must use the official race records.

Year-Old horse in 1943. The Count and War Admiral are the only two Triple Crown Winners to date to have been undefeated in their three-year-old seasons. He was treated over the winter, but at a workout at Belmont the next spring, it was apparent that he would never be the old Count Fleet. The announcement came on July 22, 1944: Count Fleet would return to Stoner Creek for stud duty. He never raced again.[9]

Just let him run. The Count's racing days were over, but he was the Unvanquished Horse. He was as successful in stud as he was a racer (difficult to believe, but true). He may have been the greatest sire of all the Triple Crown winners: one son, Count Turf, won the Kentucky Derby in 1951; another, Counterpoint, won the Belmont the same year. Count Fleet has the distinction of siring two different horses that won elements of the Triple Crown during the same year.[10] Still another son, One Count, won the Belmont in 1952. Counterpoint and One Count were named Horses of the Year for 1951 and 1952, respectively. Let us not forget the distaff side of Thoroughbred racing: one of Count Fleet's daughters, Kiss Me Kate, was named best three-year-old filly in 1951. And, as if to drive the point home, one of his daughters foaled Lucky Debonair, winner of the 1965 Kentucky Derby, while another of his daughters foaled Kelso.[11]

That only tells the glamorous part of the Count's siring career. He led the list of sires in 1951, was the second leading sire in North America in 1952, and was fifth leading sire in North America in 1953. He led the list of broodmare sires in 1963, and was never lower than fifth-rated broodmare sire during all the other years of the 1960s. Count Fleet was the fourth-ranked broodmare sire in 1971, two years before his death. As late as 1993, his name still appeared in the pedigree of winning racehorses.

Count Fleet lived on in the gentle retirement of Stoner Creek for nearly thirty years, until the magnificent age of thirty-three. He was in hailing distance

---

[9] Count Fleet's racing career was, indirectly, a casualty of World War II. Between races, tracks are leveled and watered to provide an even racing surface. But in 1943, Belmont was conserving water and gasoline and only graded and watered the track at the beginning of the day. By the time of the Belmont Stakes the track was rough. Count Fleet stepped in a hole left by an earlier race, which caused his injury.

[10] Further, Count Turf's victory in the Derby marked the first time there have three generations of Derby winners: Reigh Count (1928), Count Fleet (1943), Count Turf (1951). It's only been done one other time to date: Pensive (1944), Ponder (1949), Needles (1956).

[11] Kelso, like Exterminator and Seabiscuit, deserves a book of his own. Suffice it to say that he was five times named the Horse of the Year, from 1960 through 1964. No other horse has been given that award that many times. His closest competition, Forego, only won Horse of the Year three times. No horse written about in this book won Horse of the Year honors more than twice.

of his thirty-fourth birthday when, in early December, 1973, his front legs gave out. For two days, the Unvanquished Horse tried unsuccessfully to stand up once again. Finally, at 2:00 P.M. on December 3, he quietly passed away. He is buried at the only home he ever knew, Stoner Creek Farm.

With great pride John Longden remembered in 1994, "That other great horse we had, Secretariat...they [Count Fleet and Secretariat] compare pretty close together." This sounds like rank heresy to a modern racing fan, but in truth, Count Fleet and Secretariat do compare closely. Looking at the newsreels from 1943 and the videotapes from 1973, one is struck at how swift and powerful they both are. It is like watching brothers race. Both won sixteen out of twenty-one races; both won the Belmont by huge margins. Which one was better? We'll never know. But imagine, just imagine, the Count versus Big Red. It would be one hell of a match race.

COUNT FLEET, Longden up. *Courtesy Grayson Collection.*

In thirty-nine years of racing, Longden rode against Phar Lap, Citation, Assault, and War Admiral; he rode Whirlaway, Swaps, Noor, Busher, and the Count. But of all his mounts, Count Fleet was his greatest. Longden visited the Count on every trip to Kentucky. Count Fleet seemed to recognize his jockey and would come over for sugar and to nuzzle Longden. Their last visit occurred about two years before the Count's death. When the Count died, Stoner Creek Farm (which had long before passed out of control of the Hertz family) didn't notify his jockey; he read of it in a newspaper. "It was," said Longden years later, "like losing an old friend."

After his jockey career ended in 1966, Longden became a horse trainer. He trained Majestic Prince, the 1969 Derby and Preakness winner. To date, John Longden is the only individual to have both ridden and trained Kentucky Derby and Preakness winners. He was elected to the National Museum of Racing and Hall of Fame in 1958, still an active jockey. He retired as the jockey with the most wins in racing history, 6032. His record stood for four years until Bill Shoemaker passed him. He retired from training in the early 1970s to live in California.

Longden had a long and wonderful retirement; he remained active well into his nineties, gave interviews often, and loved to reminisce about Count Fleet. But inevitably the infirmities of age took their toll. In August of 2002 he suffered a stroke, and was bedridden for several months. At 1:25 P.M. on February 14, 2003, his ninety-sixth birthday, John Longden died quietly in his sleep.

In his last time at bat, baseball great Ted Williams hit a home run. In his last race as a jockey, John Longden rode a horse to victory.

Count Fleet never finished out of the money. He won the Triple Crown. He set records as a two-year old, a length record in the Preakness, and length and time records in the Belmont Stakes. He was best two-year-old colt in 1942. He was best three-year-old horse in 1943. He was Horse of the Year. He sired a Kentucky Derby winner and two Belmont Stakes winners, two of which were each named horse of the year. He was a grandsire of the great Kelso. He was an outstanding sire. He had done it *all*.

And there was something else: "He knew he was royalty", said Stoner Creek's farm manager. Indeed, Count Fleet *was* royalty, for he had outlived them all: Man o'War died in 1947; Gallant Fox in 1954; both Omaha and War Admiral in 1959; Whirlaway in 1953; Assault in 1971; Citation in 1970. When he died, six months after Secretariat's Triple Crown, Count Fleet was the last link between modern racing and the great horses of the 1930s and 1940s.

The most telling comment about Count Fleet came from his jockey: "Nobody really knew how good he was outside of myself, and even I don't know," John Longden said.

VI. THE OBSCURITY TRIUMPHANT: ASSAULT

Triple Crown, 1946. Jockey, Warren Mehrtens.

"Now there was a horse for you. He had a great heart, could run any distance you wanted him to and he was a fine competitor."
— Bill Egan, Assault's handler at King Ranch.

Some Triple Crown teams seem predestined to be Triple Crown winners: Gallant Fox/Earl Sande; War Admiral/Charles Kurtsinger; Whirlaway/Eddie Arcaro; Count Fleet/John Longden; Citation/Eddie Arcaro; and Secretariat/Ron Turcotte. At the other end of the spectrum are the "Improbables", those from whom little was expected but much was achieved: Sir Barton/John Loftus, for example. Perhaps the most improbable pair ever to win the Triple Crown came in 1946 out of the far-off King Ranch in Texas: Assault and his Brooklyn-born jockey, Warren Mehrtens.

Robert J. Kleberg, Jr., General Manager of King Ranch, wanted to start a racing stable and as well improve the bloodlines of the ranch horses through interbreeding with Thoroughbreds. Bold Venture, a racehorse for M.L. Schwartz in Kentucky, attracted his interest. Bold Venture was a chestnut colt who had won the 1936 Kentucky Derby and the Preakness Stakes. He had a short racing career; eleven starts in his second and third years, six firsts, two seconds, no thirds, three unplaced finishes. He was a fine racer; certainly not an all-time great one, but far from bad.

When the horse was sold to King Ranch in Texas, Bold Venture became the founding sire of King Ranch Thoroughbred racing. He was a better sire than a racer. One son, Middleground, won the 1950 Derby and Belmont and placed second in the Wood Memorial, the Derby Trial, the Withers, and the Preakness. Middleground nearly won the Triple Crown. However, it is with an earlier foal of Bold Venture we are concerned with here. In 1942, Bold Venture was bred to a rather sickly mare named Igual. The resultant foal entered the world on March

163

26, 1943, and was named Assault.

ASSAULT: Triple Crown Winner, 1946. *King Ranch: Max Hirsch, Trainer, W. Mehrtens, jockey . © King Ranch, Inc., Kingsville, Texas. Used by permission.*

Unlike Bold Venture, Igual was not a particularly healthy horse. She was on the verge of being destroyed when the King Ranch veterinarian, Dr. J.K. Northway, discovered an abscess on her leg. The abscess affected her whole condition. Treatment cured the abscess, but Igual never raced. Her foals were unlucky; her first two foals were not much as racers. A full brother of Assault, Air Lift, showed promise, but he broke his leg in his first race and was destroyed.

> *"That clubfoot was an ugly looking thing, but he learned to handle it."*
> — Eddie Arcaro, 1996.

Assault shared the bad luck of Igual's other foals. He was a frisky colt and that temperament that nearly caused his early death. As a weanling, Assault was off grazing, prancing around a King Ranch pasture. One day he stepped on a sharp surveyor's stake. The stake penetrated the soft tissue of the colt's right front hoof and went right through the top of the hoof. The pain he suffered can only be imagined.[1]

---

[1] The injuries suffered by American GIs in Vietnam from *punji* stakes (hidden

Dr. Northway treated the stake wound as best he could, including performing a hoof operation. Despite all the treatment, Assault's right front hoof was permanently deformed. It looked dried out and shrunken, in Joe Palmer's words, "...like a piece of very old, dry wood which keeps its shape but seems to have no solidity." He always walked with a slight limp, a rolling gait to compensate for the injury, and looked as if he was always about to fall down. In addition, the right front hoof was thin and brittle.

Shoeing Assault was always a challenge. One inexpert farrier could have ended Assault's racing career permanently with a misplaced nail. So King Ranch permanently assigned one farrier, John Dern, to Assault. The horse needed a special shoe with an upturned tip to anchor it. While the hoof apparently didn't affect his running, it earned him the nicknames, "The Club-Footed Comet," and the "Horse with Three Legs and a Heart."

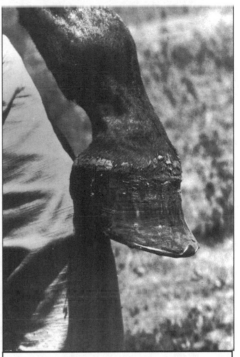

ASSAULT'S right front hoof.
© *King Ranch, Inc., Kingsville, Texas. Used by permission.*

His trainer, Max Hirsch, told Joe Palmer in 1946: "When he came up from Texas I didn't think he'd train at all. When he walked and trotted you'd think he was going to fall down. It wasn't hurting him any more but he'd gotten in the habit of favoring and protecting it with an awkward gait, and now he keeps it up. But he gallops true. There isn't a thing wrong with his action when he goes fast."

A graph of Assault's racing career graphed resembles a pair of high mountain peaks, linked by a narrow valley, and finishing with a long, uneven, ungentle and painful slope to retirement. The first part is the upward climb of his two-year-old season when he won some races. It gives little indication of what was to come. The first peak comes in the spring of 1946, when he won the Triple Crown and three other important races. Next follows the narrow valley in the summer and early autumn of 1946, when he was set back due to an ailment. During the glorious second pinnacle from November of 1946 to the Butler

sharpened stakes that easily penetrated a combat boot sole and human foot) are a close comparison to Assault's stake wound.

Handicap in 1947 he was the best Thoroughbred on the turf. Finally, there is a long 3 1/2-year slope downwards, when he was retired twice and brought back twice to racing, hampered by injuries before retiring for good. Assault took on some of the best horses of his day, Stymie, Gallorette, Lord Boswell, Natchez, Rico Monte, Armed, and Noor among them, and more often than not emerged victorious. Assault's is a glorious story: the story of The Obscurity Triumphant.

In the 1950s, baseball fans perpetually argued about which of the three centerfielders of New York-area baseball teams was best: Mickey Mantle of the New York Yankees, Duke Snider of the Brooklyn Dodgers, or Willie Mays of the New York Giants. Similar arguments occurred in racing circles about Thoroughbred horse trainers in the 1940s, namely, which one was best: Sunny Jim Fitzsimmons of Belair Stud, Ben Jones of Calumet, or Max Hirsch of King Ranch.

Max Hirsch was born in Fredricksburg, Texas in July, 1880 (the exact day is unclear.) He started racing quarter horses at age ten at the Morris Ranch. (A bit of racing trivia here; the Morris Ranch has the oldest silks registered with the Jockey Club.) Two years later he traveled east with a load of Morris horses. Wyndham Walden, the Morris Ranch racing director, noticed Hirsch and made him an exercise boy. Two years later, at age fourteen, Hirsch became a jockey. He started 1,117 races and won 123 of them. But then he grew too big to be a jockey and became a horse trainer. One of his clients was M.L. Schwartz, Bold Venture's original owner, and Hirsch also advised Robert Kleberg about the purchase of horses, including the fateful purchase of Bold Venture.

Early 1936 found Hirsch back in Texas, working for Kleberg full-time as a trainer. Hirsch could spot talent, an ability that he retained to his death in 1969. He discovered Bold Venture, Assault, Middleground, and other horses such as Grey Lag and High Gun. His record in spotting jockeys was pretty good, too. He found Ira Hanford, who rode Bold Venture in the 1936 Kentucky Derby. Hirsch also found Bill Boland (who won the 1950 Kentucky Derby and Belmont Stakes on Middleground), Doug Dodson, and Warren Mehrtens, who rode Assault to the 1946 Triple Crown.

Warren Mehrtens, Assault's Triple Crown jockey, was born in Brooklyn in 1920. He was a diving star in high school. That wasn't his first love. Mehrtens had dreamed about becoming a jockey since age seven; a nearby shoemaker had advised Mehrtens to try the jockey's life. In 1938, he started to race and finally won his first race in 1940. Max Hirsch saw him ride, and offered Mehrtens a job. Mehrtens' parents opposed it; they thought little of racetrack people. Mehrtens' father went to see Hirsch, and the Texan convinced him. Hirsch said he made his jockeys go to church on Sundays, and the father signed the contract immediately. That made Warren Mehrtens a contract rider for King Ranch. As a rider for King Ranch he met the chestnut colt with the strange gait, but at that first meeting Assault was just another horse to be ridden, trained, exercised, and fed.

In 1945, King Ranch sent Assault to New York to begin racing. His two-year-old season was inauspicious. His record that year resembles Sir Barton's and Omaha's two-year-old records. Moreover, his wobbly gait inspired little confidence in his racing ability.

Assault's first three races were at Belmont Park. He raced for the first time on June 4, 1945, and finished twelfth. Jimmy Stout rode him in that race, but Warren Mehrtens took over after that. Eight days later Assault ran again, this time with Mehrtens up. He improved somewhat, to finish fifth. Then, after an eleven-day break, Assault finished second in his third time at the track. He next ran at Aqueduct, where he broke his maiden in the $1,915 Gowanus Purse race on July 12. Assault raced well in that one. He was second throughout the race and won the race in the stretch, finishing half a length ahead of the rest of the horses. He ran six days later in the East View Stakes at the Empire City meeting at the Jamaica track, in a race that Count Fleet finished in second place three years earlier. Assault did little of note in that race: He finished fifth.

In his only memorable race that year he captured the $11,505 Flash Stakes on August 5 at Belmont Park. That race was normally held at Saratoga, but these were the waning days of World War II; America had been at war for three and one-half years. Although Hitler had been defeated, the Pacific War was still raged and travel restrictions were still in effect. Therefore, the race moved to a New York City venue. Assault went off at 70 to 1 odds in the betting. The track was muddy and the result was a four-way photo-finish. The track officials awarded the race to Assault.

Three races remained for Assault that year: he finished third in the Babylon Handicap at Aqueduct on September 5, fourth in the Cowdin Stakes a week later at Aqueduct, and finally, drew down second in a purse race at Jamaica on October 8. His winnings that year were $17,250; he had two firsts, two seconds, one third, and four unplaced finishes. It wasn't an outstanding first year, but he showed promise.

Assault's first start of 1946, the first start of his two "glory years", was the Experimental Free Handicap No. 1[2] at Jamaica on April 9. The betting favorite was Count Speed, a full brother of the last Triple Crown winner, Count Fleet[3]. Assault was third choice in the betting for the six-furlong race. Mehrtens

---

[2] This is a real horse race, not to be confused with the Jockey Club's Experimental Free Handicap, which is a theoretical performance ranking. (See the previous chapter.)

[3] John Longden rode Count Speed. However, Longden did not have anywhere near the success on Count Speed that he had on Count Fleet.

rode him, and the pair was in the sixth pole position. The horses went to the gate at 3:40 and broke four minutes later in a good start. Assault moved to fifth at the start, but by the quarter-mile he was only a head behind the leader. At the half-mile he was in first by a head, and then he began to pull away. He was ahead by three lengths in the stretch and finished four lengths ahead of Islam Prince, ridden by Eric Guerin. (The hapless Count Speed threw Longden in the starting gate. Longden rode him, but finished ninth.) The Experimental Free Handicap paid King Ranch $7500, and Assault, now nominated for the Kentucky Derby, boosted his reputation. He was a curiosity: Surely, the horse from Texas with a deformed hoof wasn't a *real* contender for the Derby, much less the Triple Crown....

The 1946 Wood Memorial made racing fans notice Assault. Before the Wood, Assault was simply an odd-walking horse from Texas; after the Wood, he was on the path to the Triple Crown. The track at Jamaica on April 20, 1946 was fast. Thirteen horses contended for the Wood Memorial that day; then as now, the winner of the Wood was considered a contender in the Kentucky Derby. The pack broke at 4:05 P.M.; Assault was eleventh from the post. He was seventh at the start, but within a quarter-mile, took third. Mehrtens and Assault stayed in third through the three-quarter-mile mark, and then Mehrtens took him to the outside. At the sixteenth pole he was first by a head and drew away to win by two lengths. His time was 1:46 3/5 for the 1 1/16-mile race. The victory in the Wood Memorial made people aware of the Texas horse, but Assault was not the favorite for the Kentucky Derby.

The doubters' feelings were confirmed at the Derby Trial on April 30. Assault finished fourth. There were some extenuating circumstances: the Churchill Downs track was muddy that day, and the bandages Hirsch wrapped around Assault's legs waterlogged and filled with mud, which created an impossible obstacle. Still, the obscure Texas Thoroughbred with the brown *cafe con léche* silks bearing the white "Running W" of King Ranch was regarded as a contender. Assault was not the favorite in the Derby, but neither was he a long-shot.

> "...then when they turned for home, all of a sudden, I saw this — they were coming fairly close to head on — one horse bolt to the front, and as they came closer to me, I could see it was King Ranch, and I knew it was Assault."
> — Racing historian Tom Gilcoyne,
> spectator at the 1946 Kentucky Derby

The 1946 Kentucky Derby was run on May 4. A record 100,000 spectators attended, and the winner's purse was a record $96,400. Seventeen horses started that day, and the favorite was the Maine Chance Farm entry, a trio of Lord Boswell, Knockdown, and Perfect Barham, at odds of 1.10 to 1. The field was very competitive: Eddie Arcaro rode Lord Boswell. Ted

Atkinson, a future Hall of Fame Jockey, rode Perfect Barham. Also on the track was John Longden, who rode Spy Song for Dixiana. (Arcaro had won the Derby on Hoop Jr. and the Belmont on Pavot the year before, while Longden rode Count Fleet to the Triple Crown just three years earlier.) Ranked sixth, at odds of 8.2 to 1, and with three future Hall of Fame jockeys up against them, Assault and Mehrtens had their work cut out for them that day.

No Triple Crown victory came to Assault without difficulty. On Derby Day, the track at Churchill Downs was slow. Assault was second on the pole position, and after the start held third behind Lord Boswell and Spy Song. At the half-mile, Spy Song was in first, Knockdown was second, a horse named Dark Jungle was third, a horse named Rippey was fourth, and Assault, fifth. At the 3/4-mile it was still Spy Song in the lead, followed by Knockdown and Dark Jungle, and then Assault in fourth place. At the mile, Assault was third behind Spy Song and Knockdown, but on entering the stretch, Assault and Mehrtens saw an opening on the inside rail. They drove through it and took the lead. Assault pulled away to win the Kentucky Derby by eight lengths.[4] Portentously, the notes of the race chart of the 1946 Derby say that Assault "...drew out to win with little left."

The Derby's statement pointed to something: just like Whirlaway, Assault had one powerful run per race in him. That run had to be well-timed because, otherwise, Assault would burn out too early. That trait spelled near- disaster for Assault one week later in the Preakness.

Today, two weeks elapse between the Derby and the Preakness. This was not so then, and the short respite between the two races might have been critical. No one knew that at the time; for the first time in his career Assault was ranked as the favorite horse at 7 to 5. Lord Boswell had a jockey shuffle; Arcaro was taken off him and Doug Dodson, normally a jockey for Calumet, rode the horse in this race. Lord Boswell and Knockdown were rated second at 2.25 to 1. Arcaro rode a horse called Hampden for William duPont.

---

[4] No horse has won the Kentucky Derby by a greater margin, although Old Rosebud (1914), Johnstown (1939), and Whirlaway (1941), all won as Assault did, by eight lengths. Assault's time in the Derby was fairly slow, however, 2:06 3/5. That was more than five seconds slower than Whirly's record time five years earlier.

ASSAULT wins the Kentucky Derby by eight lengths, May 4, 1946. Max Hirsch, trainer. Warren Mehrtens up. Spy Song 2nd, Hampden 3rd.
© *King Ranch, Inc., Kingsville, Texas. Used by permission.*

On Preakness Day, May 11, 1946, the track in Baltimore was fast. At the start, Assault broke cleanly but was quickly squeezed back into the pack. Rounding the first turn, Assault was stuck in the middle. At the half-mile mark, he was sixth. He broke out of the pack and by the three-quarter mile mark he was in third. At the end of the mile Assault was in the lead and clearly in control. But getting out of the pack and into the lead had cost Assault some vital reserves; Mehrtens had called on Assault for a burst of speed to break out and take the lead. Warren Mehrtens was criticized for what was called a too-early move, but he had to make a split-second decision.

ASSAULT is led to the winner's circle at the Kentucky Derby, May 4, 1946.
King Ranch: Max Hirsch, trainer, Warren Mehrtens up. *Photo by Bert Morgan, N.Y.*
© *King Ranch, Inc., Kingsville, Texas. Used by permission.*

The film of the 1946 Preakness shows Assault and Mehrtens solidly placed in
the pack. Mehrtens said later, "I didn't want to make my bid when I did, but I
was afraid to wait for the turn for fear of getting pocketed." Assault maintained
the lead in the back stretch, through the far turn, and into the home stretch. And
then the early burst of speed took its toll...

Assault tired, and Doug Dodson on Lord Boswell sensed a "kill" coming.
As Assault slowed, Dodson called on Lord Boswell for full speed. Inside the
eighth pole Mehrtens looked back over his shoulder and saw Lord Boswell
charge. Mehrtens gave Assault a whack with his whip; the blow surprised
Assault and the horse swerved towards the rail. It cost him precious ground and
opened up the track for Lord Boswell. The horse's reaction surprised Mehrtens,
too; the jockey thought that Assault might just stop if he used the whip again.
Mehrtens believed Assault could beat Lord Boswell to the wire, so he hand-rode
Assault and prayed that his horse had enough left to win.

ASSAULT: Preakness at Pimlico, May 11, 1946. King Ranch's Max Hirsch, trainer; Warren. Mehrtens up. Lord Boswell running 2ⁿᵈ, Hampden 3ʳᵈ·· © *King Ranch, Inc., Kingsville, Texas. Used by permission.*

Down the home stretch they thundered, Dodson whipping Lord Boswell furiously, Mehrtens coaxing every last bit of energy out of the tiring Assault. At the wire, it was Assault by a neck in front of Lord Boswell. Assault and Mehrtens won, but to use another's phrase, "It was a damned close-run thing."[5]

On the train ride home, Mehrtens expressed confidence in Assault. "Boswell isn't half the horse mine is." Eddie Arcaro sniffed: "Can you imagine what Whirlaway would do to this bunch? It would be pathetic. He'd run right over them." (Maybe so, Eddie. But Whirly wasn't running that year.)

Assault's win in the Preakness was better than War Admiral's victory over Pompoon nine years earlier, and not much worse a showing than Gallant Fox's Preakness win. Assault skipped the Withers, at that time a very important race, to rest for the Belmont. But even with the Withers break, the "what abouts" accumulated; despite the Wood Memorial, despite the Derby, despite the Preakness, there were doubts: *What about* the deformed hoof; *What about* the slow time at Churchill Downs; *What about* the almost-staggering finish at Pimlico; *What about* the mile-and-a-half at Belmont Park...Lord Boswell was the favorite for the Belmont Stakes at 6 to 5, while Assault was rated a slight second, at 7 to 5.

For the Belmont, Assault and Mehrtens once again faced heavy

---

[5] Arthur Wellesley, the Duke of Wellington, on his victory at the Battle of Waterloo.

competition. Ted Atkinson was back, this time on Cable. Arcaro was again on Hampden, and Conn McCreary rode Natchez for Mrs. Walter Jeffords. Lord Boswell had yet *another* rider: Eric Guerin. Even John Longden made a return appearance to ride Mahout, another horse owned by Mrs. Jeffords.[6]

On June 1, 1946, the weather was cloudy, and the Belmont Park track was fast. The horses went to the post for the 1946 Belmont Stakes at 4:40 P.M., and broke almost immediately. Assault stumbled out of the gate and nearly threw Mehrtens. They recovered and moved to the inside. On the far turn and back stretch, Assault stayed well back. Assault was fourth at the mile, and moved up to third by the mile-and-a-quarter mark. At the beginning of the stretch Hampden was in the lead, followed by Natchez; Assault was third. Into the stretch, Natchez took the lead, but for this race, Mehrtens and Assault held something in reserve. Midway through the homestretch, Assault made his move: he passed Natchez. Mehrtens recalled that Assault "went flying by him," and drove home to win the Belmont by three lengths. For all their troubles, the Improbable Pair had triumphed.

> *"In those times, in that year, he was the best of the crop. He was just better than all the horses around. They were all good. They just weren't good enough to beat Assault."*
> — Warren Mehrtens, 1996.

The Lone Star Flag flew on all Texas state office buildings in honor of Assault after the Belmont. There was talk of a state holiday in the horse's honor, but someone realized that "ASSAULT DAY" probably wasn't a good idea. Mehrtens and Hirsch, the Triple Crown jockey and trainer, respectively, received a cut of the winnings. Kleberg had the first non-Kentucky-born horse ever to win the Triple Crown. Assault received a special reward: A cook baked a cake in the King Ranch colors of *cafe con léche* (the King Ranch's brown and white silks) and the newest Triple Crown winner gobbled it.

Two weeks after the Belmont, Assault triumphed again. He won the Dwyer Stakes at Aqueduct on June 15. Assault carried ten more pounds than any other horse in the 1 1/4-mile race. He was the 2 to 5 favorite and was sixth from the post, the outside for the race. He broke fairly well, was fourth going under the wire the first time, but throttled back into fifth place at the half-mile.

---

[6] For the statistically-minded reader, Arcaro won 5 Derbies, 6 Preaknesses, and 6 Belmonts; Atkinson, 1 Preakness and 1 Belmont; Guerin, 1 Derby, 1 Preakness, and 2 Belmonts; Longden, 1 Derby, 1 Preakness, 1 Belmont; and McCreary, 2 Derbies, and 2 Preaknesses. The jockeys arrayed against Assault and Mehrtens in the Belmont won the staggering total of thirty-one Triple Crown-level races. Additionally, Arcaro, Atkinson, Guerin, Longden, and McCreary would *all* be elected to the National Museum of Racing and Hall of Fame.

173

He moved up to third by the three-quarter mark, held in third at the mile. Once again, Mehrtens sent him. Assault closed with a rush, taking over first place at the start of the stretch. Assault finished three lengths ahead of the rest of the pack, and in the notes to the race chart, "Was only galloping at the end."

The Dwyer victory meant that Assault became the leading single-season money-winner. From his six victories in seven races so far that year, Assault won $339,720, topping Gallant Fox's record.

After the Dwyer, Assault went into a slump. He ran in the Arlington Classic in Chicago on July 27, but finished sixth — dead last. Mehrtens rode him, and they were 7 to 10 in the betting. Assault broke second out of the gate and was third down the backstretch. The fans thought Assault was up to his old tricks: a powerful closing rush at the far turn and then victory. It wasn't to be; Assault faded on the far turn and came in last. During the race, Mehrtens used the whip to prod Assault on, but Assault failed to respond. The horse returned to his stall in pain. It turned out that the Triple Crown winner had a kidney ailment and was simply unable to run his best. (It is remarkable that Assault could even walk, let alone race a mile-and-a-quarter, carrying 126 pounds on his back, and being hit with the whip not far away from the ailing kidneys.) He recuperated for a month and came back on September 7, to run in the Discovery Handicap at Aqueduct.

Hirsch decided to run Assault in Handicap races. The Triple Crown winner bore some heavy weight penalties: in the Discovery Handicap, Assault carried eleven extra pounds over the nearest competitor. He finished third, and the show was chalked up to the two-month layoff and the extra weight. He finished second a week later in the Jersey Handicap by a half-length. Again, he carried twelve pounds extra weight. On September 25, Assault ran in the 1 1/2-mile Manhattan Handicap at Belmont, and finished third. He ran two races in October, 1946, finishing second by a half-length in the Roamer Handicap on October 19, and showing in the Gallant Fox Handicap on October 26. In retrospect, this was a turning point: Assault was well placed for much of the 1 5/8-mile race. With five furlongs to go, Mehrtens sent Assault to the lead. That was easily accomplished, but Stymie, another contender, came up with a late rush and caught Assault. The South American horse, Rico Monte, was also on the track and *he* came up late too, catching Assault for the place.

None of the losses were bad results in and of themselves, but Assault, was, after all, that year's Triple Crown winner. King Ranch felt something had to be done, and done quickly. Had Mehrtens lost confidence in his Triple Crown horse? Was he favoring Assault after the kidney attack? The Gallant Fox Handicap loss had brought matters to a head; Assault had one powerful run in him, and it was critical not to use it too soon, as had happened in the Gallant Fox Handicap. The trainer told the jockey, "Flesh and bone can only stand so much. You're asking too much out of this horse." Max Hirsch felt the trouble was in the jockey, not the horse. Ironically, King Ranch brought in Eddie

Arcaro, Mehrtens' rival on Lord Boswell and Hampden, to ride the Triple Crown champion.[7]

> *"Assault was fun to ride. He moved up on you quick,*
> *then exploded."*
> — Eddie Arcaro, 1996

It worked: Assault's next victory was in the Pimlico Special at Pimlico on November 1, 1946. Assault and Arcaro turned it "Into a one-horse race." Three horses challenged Assault, and his major opponent was Stymie.[8] Hirsch knew Stymie was a slow-starting horse, so he told Arcaro to stay back and not get caught from behind by a late charge from Stymie. Assault and Stymie were last going under the wire for the first time, and the other two horses, Bridal Flower and Turbine, set the pace. Things stayed pretty much in that form until the half-mile pole, when Stymie and Assault went after the leaders. Assault was on the rail, Stymie on the outside. Arcaro shot Assault through Bridal Flower and Turbine to take the lead; he left the other horses behind at the beginning of the stretch. Just to be sure, Arcaro used the whip on Assault a couple of times, but the result was unlike the Preakness. Assault was firmly in control and crossed the finish line six lengths ahead of Stymie. Assault's winnings increased to a record $402,845. Arcaro wrote a few years later, "Like many other skeptics, I did not realize what kind of horse this son of Bold Venture-Igual was until I rode him for the first time. Then, I might add, I really did know."

Assault's last start of 1946 was in the Westchester Handicap on November 9. Five horses challenged him (the great filly Gallorette included) with Arcaro once again the jockey. It was a 1 3/16-mile race, and Assault was fourth from the post. He broke well and settled back into last place through the half-mile. Arcaro moved him up gradually and turned him loose at the far turn.

---

[7] This is both an echo of the past and a precursor of the future: Arcaro was brought in to ride Whirlaway only four days before the 1941 Kentucky Derby. Arcaro in late 1946 ended his career as a contract jockey for Greentree Stable and was at that time a free lance jockey. Now, he was brought in to ride Assault only four days prior to the 1946 Pimlico Special. In 1948, as will be seen, Arcaro was brought in to ride Citation at short notice. This raises more racing trivia: Arcaro rode Citation to the 1948 Triple Crown, making him the only jockey to win two Triple Crowns. However, his races on Assault in 1946-50 also make Arcaro the only jockey to ride three Triple Crown horses: Whirlaway, Assault, and Citation. No other jockey rode more than two Triple Crown champions.

[8] Stymie was, ironically, a product of King Ranch but was lost to another stable when Max Hirsch entered Stymie in a claiming race. Stymie was claimed, and went on to be one of the great racehorses of all time. During this period, he was one of the leading money winners and Assault's chief rival on the turf.

James Roach of *The New York Times* said, "Arcaro steered around horses, passed them one by one — and it became apparent to every last customer in the park that he was home by the time they straightened out for the run down the straightaway." Assault was second at the mile, first by two lengths at the head of the stretch, and maintained that lead to the finish line.

Assault went back to Columbia, South Carolina for the winter. It had been a good year for the Texas horse: 15 starts, 8 firsts, 2 seconds, 3 thirds, 2 unplaced finishes. His winnings for the year were $424,195. That set an all-time record, surpassing Gallant Fox's 1930 winnings record.

What was he? Was Assault a great horse? Yes, he won the Wood, the Triple Crown, and the Dwyer. Yes, he broke the one-year winnings record. But his times were unimpressive, his winnings concentrated in the Triple Crown races, and his ability at a distance uncertain. On the other hand, he improved as the year went on, gave away massive weight allowances to older horses, and even beat Stymie. And, he raced beautifully until the July kidney ailment flared; anything like that would almost certainly knock out any horse for a time. In all, the writers named him Horse of the Year for 1946. So, was he a great horse? The consensus was that he was very good, but not great. At least, not yet.

Assault accomplished one other thing in 1946; he brought Thoroughbred racing back to Texas. Texans had raced horses for years, on ranches, in county fairs, or wherever, but Thoroughbred racing — well, that was some other world.[9] Then Assault came out of nowhere to win the Triple Crown. Assault and later, Middleground, were the only Texas-bred horses to date to win the Kentucky Derby and Belmont. Assault proved that a Texas Thoroughbred horse was every bit as good as a Kentucky or Maryland horse.

Over the winter of 1946-1947, Assault's personality began to fill out. Early in 1946, he had been a very "...matter-of-fact kind of colt" (Joe Palmer's phrase,) but he seemed to know something about his status. He wasn't mean in the barn or fractious in the starting gate. He liked people and was a friendly horse. Assault didn't act up much before a race, but once in a while, he threw his head back in the post parade and popped his rider in the mouth. (That trait caused Warren Mehrtens to need dental work later on. Assault loosened nine of Mehrtens' teeth.) He had become king of the stable over the racing season, and he sensed it. His appetite developed enormously; his groom eventually had to bring him a handful of grain before entering the stall, or else Assault had a fit. Once, the Triple Crown winner stuck his head outside the stall fifteen minutes before feeding time and spied his dinner just out of his reach. The horse threw such a tantrum that dinner that day was fifteen minutes early.

---

[9] Texas formerly had three Thoroughbred tracks: Epson at Houston, Alamo Downs at San Antonio, and Arlington Downs at Arlington. All had gone out of business by 1940.

Assault wasn't a mean horse, *ala'* Sir Barton, but he possessed a mischievous streak that came out that winter. He realized he could play a trick on his exercise rider. As the result of favoring his bad hoof, he developed the habit of moving slowly back from exercises. Assault noticed that the exercise boy relaxed a bit at that point and did not pay close attention. So, Assault would leap to one side, throw the exercise boy on the ground, and go tearing off rider-less through the stable area at King Ranch, enjoying a bit of freedom. Hirsch put a stop to that by having a groom lead Assault back to the stables on a line.

And, there was always the bad hoof. The front part of it was cut out early in 1947. It grew back somewhat — not normally, but improved. The hoof wall was a bit thicker, but still a problem. But overall, Assault was in good shape. On May 3, 1947, one day before the anniversary of his Kentucky Derby victory, Warren Mehrtens rode him in the 1 1/8-mile Grey Lag Handicap at Jamaica.

Assault's four-year-old season proved as good a year as could be found anywhere: seven starts, five wins, one second, one third. Stymie and six other horses challenged Assault and Mehrtens in the Grey Lag Handicap. Assault was second from the post, third at the start, and Mehrtens eased him into seventh. There Assault idled for the first half-mile. Mehrtens sent him, and Assault passed the other horses steadily. By the beginning of the stretch he was third and caught the leader, Lets Dance, to win by a head. *The New York Times* race chart noted his racing tactic: Assault "...closed with a rush, and won in the final stride."

Assault returned to Pimlico for the Dixie Handicap on May 9. Arcaro rode the Triple Crown champion again, and the main challenger was the South American horse, Rico Monte. It was a 1 3/16-mile race, and Arcaro timed Assault's run perfectly. James Roach of *The New York Times* wrote that Assault "...moved with a rush to the far turn, went outside horses on the bend, was third to the stretch and was in front at the sixteenth pole. So powerful was his charge (Arcaro did not have to urge him a great deal) that there was hardly a doubt about who was going to win once he hit the straightaway." Assault beat Rico Monte by a half-length, and in the process won $24,700 for King Ranch. He won Pimlico's three great races, the Preakness, the Pimlico Special, and the Dixie Handicap. The last victory moved Assault into third place on the world's money-winning list.

Assault and Arcaro were unstoppable that spring. Assault rested three weeks and returned with Arcaro to Belmont Park for the Suburban Handicap on May 31. Once again Assault's properly-timed closing charge decided the race; he ran fourth for most of the 1 1/4-mile race. Again Arcaro sent him on the back stretch. At the mile he was second; he caught the leader, his old adversary Natchez, in the stretch and won by two lengths. Stymie, also on the track, finished fourth. Rico Monte finished fifth.

Three more weeks passed, then with Arcaro up, Assault ran and won the

Brooklyn Handicap on June 22 at Aqueduct. It was another 1 1/4-mile race. By this time, Arcaro had it down pat; Arcaro carefully kept him in fourth place through the 3/4 mile mark, some six lengths back of the leader, Windfields. Arcaro turned on Assault's speed, and again the chestnut horse from Texas passed the rest. He was in first by 1 1/2 lengths at the stretch and just pulled away to win by four lengths. The notes to *The New York Times* race chart said "At the end he was only galloping." Stymie again challenged Assault and finished second.

The victory in the Brooklyn Handicap brought $38,100 to King Ranch. With that victory, Assault took over Whirlaway's spot as the leading money winner of all time.

Arcaro and Assault had another three-week interlude before the $36,700, 1 3/16-mile Butler Handicap at the Jamaica track on July 12, 1947. The handicapper assigned Assault 135 pounds to carry that day, and it made a difference. Stymie and Rico Monte were present again, as was Gallorette.

Assault cruised in fourth place for much of the race. When it was time to make his move, he found himself squeezed into the pack — not unlike his situation in the previous year's Preakness. This time there seemed no way out. He was ahead of Stymie, but Gallorette and the other horses were solidly in front of him. At that point Stymie made his move, passed Assault, and took the lead. Other horses were firmly placed around Assault. To everyone watching, Assault's chances to win seemed hopeless.

Hopeless, that is, to everyone except Assault --and he was the only one that mattered. The horse took control of the race, surged forward, saw an opening considered impassable by Arcaro, and pushed through to draw near Stymie. Arcaro remembered later, "He went through by himself with me hanging on."

Assault and Stymie battled down the stretch, and with every stride Assault gained ground. Arcaro had a winner now, and he made the most of it. At the finish line Assault was a neck in front of Stymie.

Max Hirsch congratulated Arcaro on a powerful race; the jockey now respected the Thoroughbred he had the year before included as part of a "pathetic" bunch." "I rode," Arcaro said, "a powerful horse." Racing historians have called the 1947 Butler Handicap Assault's finest race.[10]

Had Assault been retired at that point, his reputation would be far higher

---

[10] Joe Palmer, in *American Race Horses, 1947*, states that Arcaro said during 1947 that Assault was the best horse he ever rode. I have not found the actual quote, but it's certainly possible; Arcaro rode Assault when the horse was at his best. While Assault's place in Arcaro's pantheon was taken the next year by Citation, the Texas horse remained high in Arcaro's memory. Arcaro remembered in 1996: "Until I got on him, I underestimated him. But I'd have to say he's No. 3 of the ones I rode, right after Citation and Kelso." Pretty great company to be in.

than it is today. He had won the Triple Crown, beaten Stymie repeatedly, and became (for a brief time) racing's leading money winner. Assault, the Texas horse with the deformed hoof, the obscure racer that was never a favorite in a race until the Preakness, had taken on the best of his time and beaten them consistently. He was at the height of his career.

But now the long, painful, slow denouement began. A week later, in the 1 5/8-mile International Gold Cup at Belmont, Stymie got even with his tormentor. Assault was again in fourth through most of the race, but Stymie was in fifth, almost stalking Assault. After the 1 1/4-mile mark, Arcaro sent him again. He moved up to second, but then began to falter. Stymie and his jockey, Conn McCreary, had a bit more in reserve; they passed Assault to win. Assault finished third. Arcaro said afterwards: "It might have been a little far for Assault. He did his best."

It might also have been a little too much racing for him. In 1947, three great Thoroughbreds graced racing: Assault, Armed, and Stymie. All three would be elected to the National Museum of Racing and Hall of Fame, and each was for a time the leading all-time money winner of Thoroughbreds. Pressure was building for a match race between the three.

Hirsch was initially against it. He told Grantland Rice, "I'll run against either of those horses but not both together. A come-from-behind horse will beat a sprinter every time. Why stick Assault in there to beat himself [*sic*] whipping a fast horse like Armed only to get nailed from behind by a plodder like Stymie?"

During the summer of 1947, Assault, Armed, and Stymie all traded places for the honor of leading money-winner. Armed, a gelding from Calumet Farm, had started very late. He didn't even race in his two-year-old season and really didn't come into his own until his fourth year. He won ten of fifteen races as a four-year-old, eleven of eighteen races in 1946 as a five-year-old. Assault's victories over Stymie eliminated the need for a match race between Assault and Stymie, or even a three-way race including Armed. But still, there was Armed for Assault to contend with.

Shortly after the Empire Gold Cup, Kleberg and Warren Wright of Calumet began to negotiate a match race between Assault and Armed. The initial idea was for a $100,000 purse match race at Washington Park in Chicago on August 30, 1947. Arcaro was supposed to ride Assault. The match almost came off. Almost; after his final workout before the race, Assault came back limping on his left foreleg, the "good" one. An examination revealed a badly placed nail in the shoe, and the Chicago race was called off.

Kleberg then approached George Widener, President of Belmont Park, to host a rescheduled match race. Widener agreed, as did Warren Wright, and it was set for September 27. Joe Palmer put it very succinctly in *American Race Horses, 1947:* "By the time of the race, everyone was sorry."

Assault trained very well throughout much of September, but on

September 22, he came back from a workout lame. Max Hirsch thought that an old leg splint (an enlarged leg bone) was to blame. Hirsch even asked Ben and Jimmy Jones, Calumet's trainers, to inspect Assault. Racing had taken its toll on Assault; he still had his determination to win, but his legs had become fragile. Kleberg and Hirsch painted themselves into a corner; Assault had to race somehow, and Kleberg and Hirsch could only hope he wouldn't be injured or beaten too badly by Armed. Press releases were issued, and even the local S.P.C.A. got into the act, showing up at Belmont on September 27 and demanding proof that Assault was fit to race.

In September, 1947, $100,000 was a fortune, but Robert Kleberg of King Ranch and Warren Wright of Calumet Farm didn't need the money. Because of all the unfortunate publicity surrounding Assault, Kleberg and Wright announced that the purse would go to various charities.

The race itself wasn't much; Armed took the lead from the start and never let it go. Arcaro kept Assault in the race, but the horse just didn't have it. Arcaro, not wishing to risk an injury to Assault, pulled him up at about the sixteenth pole. Nearly fifty years later, Arcaro remembered: "He [Assault] started badly, but the poor guy, he was all heart. He wanted to go hard. But I didn't let him. You don't do that to someone you respect." Armed won by six lengths. It was Assault's last race of 1947 and an unfortunate end to one of the best years any Thoroughbred race horse ever had.

Hirsch returned Assault to Columbia, South Carolina, for the winter and treated the splint. Assault ran seven races in 1947 with five victories, one third-place finish, and one second-place finish in a match race which shouldn't have been run. That didn't matter to the critics. "Horse of the Year" honors went to Armed. The lingering bias against Assault remained.

King Ranch still had confidence in Assault. He won the seven-furlong fifth race at Hialeah in Miami on February 14, 1948. Warren Mehrtens, still King Ranch's stable jockey, rode Assault again.

He ran a race in preparation for the Widener Handicap the following week. Three other horses challenged the field. Assault was at the post and was fourth at the start. He stayed in fourth through the quarter-mile and moved up to third at the beginning of the far turn. He drew even with the second-place horse, Star Pilot, halfway through the far turn and took over second place at the beginning of the home stretch. Assault moved into first at the sixteenth pole and held on the rest of the way to win by a head. The finish was close, reminiscent of the 1946 Preakness, but Mehrtens said: "He could have won by as far as I wanted. He's even better than he was in the Derby."

The euphoria didn't last very long. King Ranch brought in Eddie Arcaro again to ride Assault in the $50,000 Widener Handicap on February 21. He performed well at a workout, but finished a very disappointing fifth in the

Widener. The following day, Assault was sore and an osselet (a bony growth indicative of leg problems) had popped out on one ankle. Kleberg and Hirsch decided to retire Assault to stud at the King Ranch property in Kentucky.

Assault's stud book filled up quickly but now came another setback: He tested sterile. Bold Venture had not been a prolific sire; was it a family trait? A second test gave the same result. On March 27, King Ranch announced Assault's bookings were cancelled. That raised the interesting question: What does one do with a sterile Triple Crown winner? The answer was to send Assault back to racing as soon as possible.

By the summer of 1949, Assault recovered sufficiently from the leg ailments to return to the turf. His first start that year was the Glengarry Purse at Aqueduct on June 24. He carried 118 pounds in the 7/8-mile race, and finished second by a nose.[11] It was a good race for an older horse after a fourteen-month convalescence.

Assault's last major career victory was in the 1949 Brooklyn Handicap at Aqueduct, on July 2. Dave Gorman rode the Triple Crown winner in that race. In one of the curious twists that abounded in Assault's career, Warren Mehrtens rode against him. Assault was fifth out of ten horses at the start and moved up to fourth at the half-mile. He moved up steadily, and by the mile, was in second. At the top of the homestretch, he took command and opened up a 1 1/2-length lead. He slowed down the stretch, but hung on for a 3/4-length victory. "Old men come back once in a while, don't they," gloated Max Hirsch.

Assault started four more races that year. He finished third in one, the Edgemere Handicap at Aqueduct on September 10th and had three unplaced finishes. In addition to the deformed hoof, the past kidney ailment, and all the old leg problems, Assault began to drip blood from his nose after a workout or race. The analogy is a beloved old automobile with 120,000 miles on it; the brakes give out, then a new radiator is needed, then a new water pump, then a replacement windshield wiper motor, then various leaks develop. Assault, like an old automobile, had just been run for too long. In the Massachusetts Handicap on August 13 the dripping blood caused him to choke up and finish fourth. Assault rested a month. He came back in the Edgemere Handicap and he didn't bleed. Considering his finishes in the Glengarry Purse, the Brooklyn Handicap, and the Edgemere Handicap, perhaps he had something left in him. Arcaro rode him in that race, and said afterwards, "He was himself today."

On September 24, Assault, ridden by Dave Gorman, finished dead last in the Manhattan Handicap at Belmont Park. Hirsch tried one more time: Arcaro

---

[11] Bill Boland, his jockey in that race, was an apprentice, not yet sixteen years old. It was a heady moment for Boland, getting to ride a Triple Crown horse at such a young age. Boland understood the significance of it; the jockey was awfully nervous. Boland recalled in 1997: "If I had been a little more experienced, he [Assault] would have won that day."

rode him in the Grey Lag Handicap at Jamaica on October 15, 1949. Assault bled in the race and never got above eighth place in a twelve-horse field. "I guess the old horse just isn't there," Arcaro said sadly.

Assault's 1949 winnings totaled $45,900. It was a creditable enough year for a six-year-old horse with leg problems, but not for a Triple Crown Champion who had once been the leading money winner of all time. On October 17, Max Hirsch wired the Maryland Jockey Club that Assault would be permanently retired, and unable to run in the forthcoming Pimlico Special. Unnamed "other ailments", not leg problems, it was said, caused his retirement.

But once again, Assault's racing career was not quite over. Middleground, Assault's stable mate, won the Kentucky Derby and Belmont in 1950, and received most of the attention from King Ranch that year. Even so, King Ranch sent Assault back to racing.

There had been another incredible turn in the life of Assault. Assault was allowed to run with a group of Quarter Horse mares in 1950 and he apparently got two of them in foal. It could only have been due to a genetic quirk: repeated examinations of his semen gave the same result as before: Assault was sterile. But with rest and an absence from racing came a slight improvement in his fertility; only to vanish when Assault began race training. To everyone's surprise, he was able to sire some colts.[12]

After that strange news, the Triple Crown winner was sent to California in late 1950 to boost his winnings.[13] Assault was put on a train from King Ranch to El Paso, thence to be shipped on to Los Angeles. Groom Pastel Garcia and King Ranch assistant veterinarian Monte Moncrief accompanied Assault on the trip. At El Paso, a situation occurred that would have been *opera bouffe'* had not the results been so potentially tragic.

When the train reached El Paso, Dr. Moncrief was advised the train's departure would be delayed. Moncrief went to make a telephone call (He remembered it wasn't a long one.) When he returned the train had departed, taking Assault and Garcia with it. Frantically, the veterinarian chartered a plane,

---

[12] This is still a subject of debate. Dr. Monte Moncrief stated in a 1996 interview that he truly doubted whether Assault had *any* siring ability. Other, earlier, sources state that he did sire Quarter-horse/Thoroughbred horses. Even if Assault had sired the mixed-breed horses, they wouldn't have been eligible for Thoroughbred racing.

[13] It is not clear why Assault was sent back to the track, but Middleground may supply the answer. Middleground had a good spring in 1950, winning the Kentucky Derby and Belmont Stakes, but he trained poorly during the summer. Then he broke his leg in a morning workout on October 11, 1950. Fortunately, he was saved, but his racing career was over. Therefore, King Ranch's "flagship" horse of 1950 was first doing poorly and then out of commission. In light of those facts, Hirsch may have *had* to send Assault back to racing, if only briefly.

got to L.A., and met the train when it pulled in. Garcia had a suitcase of medicines for Assault, but didn't know how to administer them. Moreover, the truss bar across the railcar door locked it open, and they rode across New Mexico, Arizona, and the California desert vulnerable to the cold, hobos, and whatever. Despite the threat of a cold or pneumonia, Assault came through the arduous train ride none the worse for it.

Assault did boost his winnings slightly in 1950: he ran three races that year and won the $2200, 7/8-mile Hyde Park Purse at Hollywood Park on November 22 by two lengths. Arcaro rode Assault for the last time and Assault's last victory. He looked like the old Assault of 1946-47. He broke well and sprinted immediately to the lead. Assault drew away; at one point during the race he was four lengths in front. In the middle of the stretch, Arcaro eased him up, but the lead was so great there was never any doubt of the outcome. Assault finished first by two lengths.

Eight days later he was entered in the Westwood Purse, also at Hollywood Park. Bill Boland, the King Ranch jockey who rode Middleground to victory in the Kentucky Derby and Belmont Stakes, was on Assault. The competition was too great; the great Irish horse Noor, ridden by John Longden, also ran. Noor and Longden bedeviled even Citation that year[14]; now it was Assault's turn to lose. Assault ran a decent race: he again broke well, and held in first during the middle of the race. Noor came on in the stretch to pass Assault, and Assault started to bleed. Boland remembered, "He actually gushed." Assault finished third and won $750. His total winnings in 1950 were $2,950. It was a far cry from his winnings of 1946-1947.

On December 9, 1950, Assault ran in the Hollywood Gold Cup at Hollywood Park. The Noor-Longden team was in that race and finished first. Assault was fifth through most of the race. At the stretch, he made a charge and moved up to fourth; then he tired. Assault finished seventh out of eight horses. The Associated Press report said it was "...doubtless his last race...."

> *"He always persevered in spite of his lame foot.*
> *He was a great old champion among champions."*
> — J.K. Northway, veterinarian,
> of Assault, September 1, 1971.

This time, Assault's retirement stuck. Hirsch returned him to Texas and he never raced again. He spent a comfortable retirement; Pastel Garcia, the groom, was there, and Doctors Northway and Moncrief looked after him. He

---

[14] An account of the Citation-Noor battles of 1950 will be found in the next chapter. Suffice it to say here that Noor beat Citation in four races that year, although Noor had to work for those victories. In any case, having beaten one Triple Crown winner that year, Noor then took on another, albeit older, Triple Crown winner.

got plenty of feed, room to exercise, and attention from King Ranch. He was Texas' great horse. People came to visit him, and he enjoyed all the attention visitors gave him. He had his own special paddock, about twelve acres near Middleground. Every day he waited for children to come by after school and pet him, which they unfailingly did. Fan mail came to the ranch for Assault, and at times a temporary secretary was hired to help with it. Once an envelope arrived addressed simply, "ASSAULT, TEXAS." Every letter was answered with a picture of the Triple Crown winner.[15]

The Fifties passed, as did the Sixties; then the Seventies came: all the time the old racer grazed on the plains of King Ranch. By 1969, it was apparent that old age had caught up with Assault. He started to show signs of senility, and his coat lost its luster. King Ranch wanted people to remember him as he had been, not as an old horse. So, in late 1969, visitors and photographers were no longer allowed to see the seventh Triple Crown winner. Still, Assault was active, had a good appetite, and was alert, docile, and friendly. He lived into his twenty-eighth year. On September 1, 1971, while being transferred from one pasture to another, Assault stumbled and fell, fracturing his left foreleg near the shoulder. Dr. J.K. Northway, the same veterinarian who had long ago treated the stake wound, watched as Dr. Monte Moncrief put down the "great old champion among champions."

Later that day a small group gathered around a freshly-dug grave near the King Ranch offices. Assault's body was on a veterinary gurney, and a tractor pulled it off the gurney and into the hole. Assault was placed so that he was facing west, in keeping with the cavalry tradition. Dr. Northway said a eulogy, and Pastel Garcia reached into the grave and put the racer's legs forever in a running position. The story of the seventh Triple Crown winner, a horse that by all rights should never even have been on a race track, ended where it began, at King Ranch.

Of the two jockeys most associated with Assault, Eddie Arcaro's career will be related in the next chapter. As for the jockey that rode Assault to the Triple Crown...

Warren Mehrtens kept riding, and remained a good jockey throughout his career. He rode some good horses, including Kiss Me Kate, a Count Fleet filly named the Best Three-Year-Old Filly of 1951 ("She was very good," the jockey remembered.) Mehrtens retired as a jockey in 1952 and worked as a racing steward at various tracks in the northeast. He retired from that in 1982 and moved to Sarasota, Florida. Warren Mehrtens died on December 29, 1997; one

---

[15] Assault has not been forgotten by his native state. In 1999, with horse racing enjoying a renaissance in Texas, Retama Park in San Antonio created the "Texas Horse Racing Hall of Fame." The first horse named to the Texas Horse Racing Hall of Fame was, naturally, Assault.

of the most underappreciated jockeys in racing history. His remains were cremated, and a part of the ashes was scattered in the Belmont Park infield.

For many years, Mehrtens kept his King Ranch racing silks packed away in a trunk. But in April, 1996, two weeks prior to the fiftieth anniversary of Assault's Kentucky Derby victory, Mehrtens went into the trunk, brought the silks out, and draped them over a living room chair for his friends to see.

Mark Twain said there are three types of prevarications: lies, damned lies, and statistics. He meant, of course, that numbers can be interpreted to suit almost any purpose. Assault's win percentage (43%) and his money percentage (74%) are tepid compared to other Triple Crown Winners. But bald numbers can mislead. Assault raced into his seventh year, a longer racing career than any other Triple Crown winner. He started forty-two races: double the number of races that Man o'War, Count Fleet, and Secretariat each ran and more races than any other Triple Crown champion except for Whirlaway and Citation. His record in his third and fourth years was exceptional: third year — 15 starts, 8 wins, 2 seconds, 3 thirds (a 53% win record, an 87% money record); fourth year — 7 starts, 5 wins, 1 second, 1 third (a 71% win record, a 100% money record). In his three-year-old racing season, he set a one-year winnings record: $424,195 in purses. Six of his wins that season were the Wood Memorial, the Kentucky Derby, the Preakness Stakes, the Belmont Stakes, the Dwyer Stakes, and the Pimlico Special (surely a case of winning when it counted most).

Assault's place in racing history is muted; like Count Fleet, his career falls between the celebrity of Whirlaway and Citation, and he stands in the shadow of the Count. Assault is remembered today mainly for his deformed hoof and his Triple Crown. He should be remembered for more than that; from the outlands of King Ranch, Assault is The Obscurity Triumphant.

VII. THE ICON:
CITATION

Triple Crown, 1948. Jockey, Eddie Arcaro

"He was the kind of horse, though, that wasn't flashy. He didn't win by extraordinarily wide margins. He didn't win in dramatic fashion, rushing up from the rear. He wasn't a golden chestnut so that his coat shone in the sun. He just beat everybody around, and then went home and ate his meal."
— Racing historian Tom Gilcoyne on Citation.

His image is blurred now, forever trapped in the black and white newsreels of the late 1940s. His record, also in black and white, is clear: 45 starts, 32 firsts, 10 seconds, 2 thirds. In his third-year season, he was almost perfect: 20 starts, 19 firsts, 1 second. Citation was the greatest racehorse between Man o'War and Secretariat.

Man o'War and War Admiral carried on at their starts, impatient to race; Count Fleet and Secretariat broke from the gate and were not seen again by human eyes until they entered the winner's circle. Not so with Citation. He had neither the fiery temperament nor the blinding power. All he did was win with grace. "Frictionless Stride" was what he was said to possess. He made racing look easy, although assuredly it was not. Citation was, and remains, racing's Icon.

"...he was so sweet."
— Margaret Glass,
long-time Calumet Farm employee,
on Citation, 1997

Citation, like the predecessor Triple Crown winner he resembles most, Gallant Fox, was accused of being lazy. Permit another opinion to be ventured: Citation, like Gallant Fox, *knew* he was the best of his time, and that no other horse could beat him if he was sound. He didn't seem to worry, to break out in sweats, or refuse to enter a starting gate. He was not a fiery horse, just very calm and highly intelligent. He rarely acted up, and on those few occasions, his

187

misbehavior was limited to kicking his stall after a race. But he was never mean, aggressive, or aloof. At Calumet he was curious as to what went on around him at the farm and this carried over to his racing. Sometimes in a race Citation looked around at the scenery. His very calmness, his unyielding confidence, has been confused with indolence. That wasn't it.

Watch old newsreels of him racing and you will see the very image of authority. In 1947 and 1948, the years for which he should be remembered, no other horse really could challenge him. Citation went out, generally broke well, took charge, and won the race.

He wasn't like Whirlaway, running far back and coming from behind. He didn't have the dominating power of Secretariat, but Citation was incredibly fast, fast enough to win solidly and impressively. Nor was Citation like the Admiral or the Count, taking the lead from the start and challenging the other horses in the race to catch him. No, Citation was something else. Like Gallant Fox, he commanded the turf. Regardless of what the track was like, regardless of how far behind he was, Citation was always the horse to beat.

In the same year that Warren Wright of Calumet Farm purchased Blenheim II, Whirlaway's sire, he bought another horse, Bull Lea, at the Saratoga Sales. Bull Lea was a reasonably good racer, but not much at a distance. When Bull Lea was retired to stud, Wright wanted an English horse from Lord Derby's stable, Hydroplane II, for Bull Lea, but there was a problem in timing and transportation: it was during World War II, and trying to ship a mare across the Atlantic was asking for the freighter to be sunk by a German U-Boat. Undaunted, Wright shipped Hydroplane II to the USA via a then-safer Pacific route. The mare arrived in the USA in July, 1941. Her first two foals were not much on the track, but number three was born on April 11, 1945, the result of a mating with Bull Lea. A friend of the Wrights was given the honor of naming the new foal. By this time, the USA had been engaged in the war for nearly 3 1/2 years, and a word commonly heard then, "citation", came to the friend's mind. Citation it was.

Citation's trainer was Jimmy Jones, the son of trainer Ben Jones. He had come to Calumet Farm with his father in 1939, and assisted Ben in the epic of Whirlaway's training. After Pearl Harbor, Jimmy spent most of World War II in the U.S. Coast Guard. He returned to Calumet and horse training afterward. Ben Jones had decided to "throttle back" some, and one day in 1947, a story appeared in the *Daily Racing Form* reporting that Ben Jones had named Jimmy the head trainer at Calumet. Warren Wright heard about it, and got Ben Jones on the telephone. Wright had not been consulted and was naturally agitated. But Ben Jones stuck to his guns in the face of his boss' ire. When the telephone conversation ended, Warren Wright said, "Well, how can you argue with somebody that's done the job he's done and the kind of fellow he is?" Jimmy's

188

promotion stayed intact.

Officially, Ben Jones was listed as Citation's trainer in the 1948 Kentucky Derby, but that was a bit of subterfuge to give Ben a shot at getting credit for another Derby winner. Jimmy was Citation's primary trainer, and is so listed in the Preakness and Belmont records. Jimmy was as good a trainer as his father and oversaw the "glory years" of Calumet in the late 1940s and 1950s.

> *"On November 1, 1947, word came to Pimlico that Man o'War had died in the fullness of his years at Faraway Farm, and the news set many a veteran horseman to recalling the red flame that had flickered through American racing in 1919 and 1920.*
> *At the end of each tale there would be a sage wag of the head and some form of, 'We'll never see another one like him.'*
> *"Across the race track, the slanting rays of a yellow November sun were falling on the green barn which housed Citation..."*
> — Joe H. Palmer,
> *American Race Horses, 1948*

If Citation struggled in any way, it was simply to get a crack at the track. This was the prime of life for Calumet racing. Although Whirlaway was retired, Calumet had plenty of fine horses in its stable: Armed, Assault's match race challenger, plus promising newcomers such as Bewitch, Faultless, and Coaltown. Citation, though he might have been immediately spotted for greatness at another horse farm, was just one more horse; promising, perhaps, but at Calumet, just one of many fine Thoroughbreds.[1]

His first start was at Havre de Grace, Maryland, on April 22, 1947. It was a small race, a 4 1/2-furlong purse race worth $2,500. Al Snider, a Calumet stable jockey, rode him. The start was good. Citation started slowly. For most of the race he was in third place, but entering the stretch, Snider put pressure on him. He drove up along the inside and won by a half-length. It was a win; not auspicious in and of itself, but it followed in the steps of Man o'War, War Admiral, and Whirlaway: He broke his maiden in his first race.

On May 3 he raced again, this time at Pimlico. It was another small race, 5/8 of a mile with a purse worth $3,500. This time Citation took the lead at the start. He never gave it up and won handily. Now he was two for two.

On May 21 he was back at Havre de Grace for the Perry Point Purse. The race was only 5/8 of a mile and again worth only $3,500. Snider rode him, and kept him in second place for most of the race. But he was never far back, not

---

[1] Calumet was, during this time, much like the New York Yankees baseball team. The Yankees had so much talent that fine players who would have been stars on other clubs were second-stringers on the Yankees. Calumet horses were in an analogous position. Calumet had so many fine Thoroughbreds that horses that would have been stars at other farms were just "ho-hum" at Calumet.

more than three lengths. Snider got after him early in the stretch. Citation responded and drew away to win by two lengths.

He was three for three, and perhaps he could have run in the Arlington Futurity at Arlington Park near Chicago. Apparently the powers that were felt Citation was not quite ready. Moreover, Citation's stable mate, the filly Bewitch, was tearing up the track. There was little need to fire yet another Calumet cannonball.[2] Still, he raced once at Arlington, in the Sealeggy Purse, a 5/8-mile race worth $4,000. Doug Dodson, the jockey that bedeviled Assault and Warren Mehrtens in the previous year's Preakness, rode Citation. This time, Dodson let him break slowly and he was fourth out of eight horses for most of the race. In the stretch, Dodson sent him: he ran between horses and pulled away to win by a half-length.

The Arlington Park meet was over, and the Bull Lea colt was now four for four. He had come from behind, taken the lead, traveled across country, and been ridden by two different jockeys. It was a *very* promising start for a green horse. Calumet judged him ready to run in more important two-year-old races.

The Elementary Stakes at Washington Park on July 30 was his next race, and his first big one: 3/4 of a mile, and a $20,000 purse. Dodson rode him again, and Citation held command throughout the race. He was second at the quarter-mile, and took over first during the next quarter-mile. He never relinquished the lead, and finished first by two lengths.

His only loss of 1947 occurred on August 16 in the Washington Park Futurity, and it was not much of a blemish on his record. His stable mates Bewitch and Free America were also entered, and the three-horse Calumet entry was the favorite, at 0.20 to 1. Dodson rode Bewitch in that race. Steve Brooks was on Citation, and Jack Westrope was on Free America. Jimmy Jones thought his horses would finish one-two-three in that race, and so instructions to the three jockeys were simple: "If it comes up that way, there's no sense in you fellows beating these horses. It makes no difference to us which one of the three wins. If they are in front, let 'em finish on their own courage."

Jones's judgment was unerring. Bewitch took the lead early and never gave it up. Citation, in fourth place during the race, came on strong at the end. He finished only a length back of Bewitch. And Free America challenged Citation strongly to finish third by a head. Calumet Farm swept the race.

Now it was back east for Citation, to Belmont Park for the Futurity Trial on September 30. Fourteen horses were entered and Citation was second choice in the betting. Doug Dodson had been suspended for ten days following a bad ride on Bewitch the week before, so Al Snider got the call again. The horses

---

[2] Bewitch went on to a distinguished racing career and was one of the great fillies of all time. However, she was overshadowed by the Calumet stars, Citation and Coaltown.

broke well and Citation dropped back into the middle of the pack. On entering the stretch, Snider got on him, and he rapidly passed the other horses. He won by a length. *The New York Times* lead on page 41 the next day read:

"CITATION TAKES FUTURITY TRIAL AT BELMONT PARK."

It was the first time he had made the *New York Times* headline. It would not be the last.

The 6 1/2-furlong Futurity at Belmont was held four days later. Again there were fourteen horses, and again Snider rode him. Citation broke well and took the lead by the half-mile. Snider kept after him, and he won by three lengths. Bewitch finished third. The eastern racing establishment took notice of what kind of a horse had come out of Calumet *this* year.

Citation's ran his last race of 1947 on November 8, back in Maryland where he had started six months earlier. He ran in the Pimlico Futurity, and Dodson was back on him. Citation broke well, stayed in second or third, and then sprinted to the lead in the last quarter-mile. He won by 1 1/2 lengths.

With that, it was time to rest Citation over the winter. He had won eight races and placed in one, which he might have won had his jockey been told to push him. His winnings totaled $155,680, He had shown he could sprint, stay the distance, run in the mud, and travel, all without adverse effect. He was named Best Two Year-Old Horse and went to Florida as the early favorite for the 1948 Kentucky Derby.

Horses, like people, have their definite likes and dislikes Al Snider and Doug Dodson rode Citation most often, but Citation ran better for Snider than Dodson. Jimmy Jones put Snider on Citation, not knowing *why* Citation performed as he did. Jones recalled, "It wasn't until later in Citation's career that I realized he had a 'hole card.' Citation wanted his jockeys to have their hands very close together in his mane. If they spread their hands apart, as jockeys can do when taking a long hold, he wouldn't run as willingly." That wasn't Dodson's riding style, but it *was* Snider's.

The horse didn't get much rest (only three months) before running the February races at the Hialeah track in Florida. They ran for the first time in 1948 in the 3/4-mile Ground Hog Purse at Hialeah. Citation broke in second, took over first after the half-mile and won by a length. The race normally wouldn't mean much, but Citation was still two years old, the youngest horse in the race.[3] The other horses were four, five, six, and seven years old. Included in

---

[3] For purposes of consistency and simplicity, all racehorses born during a given year are arbitrarily assigned the birth date of January 1 of that year. Therefore, a horse actually born in, say, April, is listed as three months older than it really is. This prevents having to sort horses out by birth date for a specific race. However, that means that a three-year-old horse may actually still be two years old at the start of his three-year-old

the field was Calumet's own Armed, another son of Bull Lea and the 1947 Horse of the Year. Citation had beaten the Horse of the Year, and all the older and more experienced racers.

Nine days later, at the 7/8-mile Seminole Purse at Hialeah, again he was the youngest horse in the race, and was competing again against Armed. Another Calumet horse, Faultless, was also in the scene. Citation broke fast, went into second at the 3/16-mile mark, and stayed there through the 5/8-mile mark. Then Snider sent him and he finished first, a length ahead of the number two horse, Delegate. Armed finished third. (Snider had a very good day; he won four consecutive races on February 12.)

He was simply the best horse around, and he showed it again on February 18 in the 1 1/8-mile Everglades Stakes. The word had gotten around, and only two horses, Hypnos and Silverling, challenged him. Hypnos took an early lead, but Snider on Citation stayed with him. After three-quarters of a mile they were in first and never gave it up. The margin wasn't great (only one length), but that wasn't the buzz. Citation was simply in command for the whole race. The notes to the race chart say it well: "CITATION, taken under steadying restraint when HYPNOS sprinted to the front going to the first turn, moved up readily when asked, displaced the leader and won with speed to spare."

Hialeah's premiere three-year-old race was the Flamingo Stakes. It had become a major preparatory race for the Triple Crown races to come. Jimmy Jones couldn't resist entering Citation in its 1948 running, and Citation was the bettors' favorite at 0.20 to 1. The race on February 28 was 1 1/8 miles in distance. Six other horses were entered. Citation broke well and settled into fourth place by the quarter-mile. He didn't stay there long: He moved into first by the half-mile and held it. Things were close for a bit: sometimes he was only a head in front. But Snider rapped him with the whip in the stretch and he pulled away to win by six lengths. His time, 1:48 4/5, was only 3/5 of a second off the track record.

There it was, and it was impressive: four races in twenty-six days and four victories. Again Citation had beaten the previous year's best horse, and other, older fine horses. Even at that early date, he emerged as the horse to beat.

Citation's triumphs at Hialeah have been remembered. A large plaque with his name on it appears on a fountain outside the track commemorating the first Flamingo Stakes winner to go on to win the Triple Crown. (Seattle Slew was similarly honored with a large plaque nearly thirty years later.) A bronze statue of Citation stands in a nearby reflecting pool. Small bronze plaques around the base of the pool mark the races he won in 1948. He is the only horse

---

season.

192

honored with a statue at Hialeah [4]

After Citation's successes at Hialeah, the plan was for Citation to go north to race at Havre De Grace, Maryland, before the Kentucky Derby. Fate intervened: Al Snider went on a fishing trip in the Everglades. Something happened; his fishing boat was found, but Snider's body never was. Once again, as in 1941, Calumet called for help. Now the stage was set for the most evocative combination of horse and jockey of all time: Citation and Eddie Arcaro.

> *"Man and boy, I had been on fast horses beyond number. But this Citation was a horse apart from anything else I had ever ridden. His stride was frictionless; his vast speed alarming. You could call on him at any time and, as Ben Jones said of him, he could run down any horse that ever breathed...In addition to everything else, he was intelligent. He knew his business when he got out there on the track. He seemed to have a way of knowing what was demanded of him, and he gave without stint. Riding him was like being on a machine equipped with a throttle. You opened it up and away you went. That was Citation."*
> — Eddie Arcaro,
> *I Ride to Win!*, 1951.

Nearly fifty years later the combination of Citation and Eddie Arcaro stands in vivid contrast to any other. Name any horse and jockey pairing you like; we have seen many of them already, and others are yet to come: Longden on Count Fleet or Noor; Loftus, Sande, or Kummer on Man o'War or Sir Barton; Sande on Gallant Fox; Kurtsinger on War Admiral; Arcaro on Whirly, Assault, or later, Nashua or Kelso; Turcotte on Secretariat. Name any of them, and yet you never get by Arcaro on Citation. It just can't be done. There have been jockeys as great as Arcaro. There have been horses as great as Citation. But after all is said, there never was, and probably will never be, a better example of perfection in racing than the combination of Citation with Eddie Arcaro up.

Much had happened to Eddie Arcaro since 1941. Since Arcaro's Triple Crown on Whirlaway, he had been suspended for roughness[5], then came back to

---

[4] Though the Hialeah track itself is still beautiful, the neighborhood around it has deteriorated dramatically. That deterioration is in part the reason why few races are now run at Hialeah. Should the Hialeah Track ever go under the wrecker's ball, it is fervently hoped that Citation's statue and pool will be saved and moved to another Miami-area track such as Calder or Gulfstream Park.

[5] The story of Arcaro's suspension is, with the perspective of time, amusing. He was cut off by another jockey in a 1942 race. Arcaro got mad, and when he got mad, the results were immediate and volcanic. Eddie caught up with the offender, and sent the

win the 1945 Derby on Hoop, Jr., as well as the Belmont that same year on Pavot. He ended his long connection with Greentree Stables and became a free-lance jockey. That change in status enabled him both to oppose Assault in the 1946 Triple Crown and later ride him in other races. Arcaro had well earned the reputation, "The Master", but for him the best was now to come. It almost didn't happen; Al Snider had invited Arcaro to go along on the fateful Everglades fishing trip, but Arcaro's wife became ill at the last moment and Arcaro left Florida to return to New York. It turned out to be a fortuitous illness.

Besides Citation Calumet that spring had another horse, Coaltown. Coaltown was a great horse, later elected to the National Museum of Racing and Hall of Fame. But remember Napoleon's dictum for choosing generals: "I choose lucky ones." Until the epic duel of Affirmed and Alydar thirty years later, Coaltown might have been the unluckiest horse of all time: He raced at the same time as Citation.

Arcaro went to Calumet and was more impressed with Coaltown than with Citation. But Ben and Jimmy Jones pushed for Citation nonetheless. Still, Arcaro's doubts persisted. He had a bad experience six years earlier in the 1942 Derby. He was riding for Greentree Stables that year, and chose to ride Devil Diver instead of another Greentree entry, Shut Out. Shut Out won the Derby, and Arcaro had no wish to repeat *that* mistake. Moreover, Coaltown had just won the Blue Grass Stakes and Coaltown, not Citation, was the idol of Kentuckians. All their talk about Coaltown's greatness kept Arcaro from having complete confidence in Ben and Jimmy Jones' judgment and Citation's capabilities. Even on the morning of the 1948 Derby, Arcaro asked Ben Jones, "Are you sure I'm on the right horse?" "You are," was the immediate reply. The team of Citation and Eddie Arcaro became The Immortal Pair.

Looking back, it all seems so easy. We now think that any horse and jockey that challenged the Immortal Pair that spring of 1948 must have been crazy. But time can distort as well as clarify, and on April 12, 1948, at Havre de Grace, Maryland, it wasn't apparent that things would work out as they did. It was Arcaro's first start on Citation, and the occasion was the Chesapeake Trial. The track was muddy, and one horse in the race, Hefty, kept carrying Citation and Arcaro wide. Another horse, Saggy, went on to win. It was Citation's only loss of 1948.

It seemed an inauspicious start to a great partnership, but Arcaro knew better than to risk injury to Citation by going all-out on a muddy track. The big races were yet to come, and it was worth a loss to preserve Citation for them.

---

other jockey flying off his horse and into the infield. Of course, an inquiry followed. Arcaro was asked what he thought he was doing. Eddie replied: "I was trying to kill the sonofabitch". After a suspension that involved a year of contemplation and reflection, Arcaro was reinstated.

194

Five days later, the Immortal Pair avenged that defeat by winning the Chesapeake Stakes. Saggy was on the track again, and Citation took revenge. He won by four lengths, but it was worse than it looked. Before the race, Citation's special snaffle bit broke, and the start of the race was delayed for an equipment change to a standard D-bit. That didn't sit well with Citation; he went wide on the turns, wandered around the track, and was hard to control. Yes, he had won, but Arcaro asked Jimmy Jones later, "Does this bum always do these things?" Jones told Arcaro that the problems were due to the replacement bit and that they would go away with a new snaffle bit. The next day, Jones went to a boatyard at Havre de Grace and had a new ring welded.

> *"Citation will win—because he can catch any horse he can see
> — and there is nothing wrong with his eyesight."*
> — Ben Jones, Calumet trainer
> on the 1948 Kentucky Derby

Ten days later, properly equipped, and on a good track, the Immortal Pair won the Derby Trial.[6] Were they unstoppable? On May 1, Kentucky Derby Day, Citation was paired with his stable mate, Coaltown, as the favorites at odds of $0.40 to $1, the same odds as Count Fleet five years earlier. Only win betting was allowed. Citation and Coaltown were *that* strong.

The Derby track was sloppy. Coaltown had the pole position, Citation was number two. Four other horses were on the track, but there was only one real race: the pair from Calumet. Coaltown took the lead at the start and held it through a mile, even opening up a five-length gap on the back stretch. Arcaro's orders were to let Coaltown take an early lead and not burn out Citation too quickly. But even so, Arcaro was, in his own words, "Plenty scared" when Coaltown took the five-length lead. Arcaro remembered what Ben Jones had told him: "The horse that Citation could not run down had not yet been born." Citation hung back of Coaltown in second place. Then in the far turn, Arcaro remembered later "...[I]asked Citation for it. As if gifted with steel springs for legs, he bounded after his stable mate. At the three-sixteenths pole we drew even. Just clucking to him, I could feel him continue to surge ahead with that blazing speed."

It is one of the most enduring images in all racing: Citation hurtled around the far turn at Churchill Downs at full speed, frictionless, ears pricked up, totally calm and completely collected, looking around at the infield scenery, drawing even with Coaltown. Famed sportscaster Clem McCarthy was at the radio mike that day, and his call of the 1948 Kentucky Derby became a sports classic:

---

[6] Through 2003, Citation remains the only Triple Crown winner to have won both the Derby Trial and the Kentucky Derby.

Jimmy Jones (left) and Ben Jones (right, in white hat) lead **CITATION** into the winner's circle at the 1948 Kentucky Derby. Arcaro up.
Photo courtesy Grayson Collection. Used with permission.

> *"And they're turning for home, Coaltown and Citation head and head, and it looks like Eddie Arcaro's got his Derby. They're coming in there just like they were the enemy. Riding each other close and...it is Citation coming to the front. He's everything they said he was. He's going to win with his ears pricking. It is Citation by two. The other horse, Coaltown, is hanging on gamely, but that's all he can do is hang on gamely to be second. Citation wins..."*

The Immortal Pair won the Derby by 3 1/2 lengths. Arcaro wrote later, "I doubt that any horse ever received the ovation that was extended Citation that day as he was brought into the Winner's Circle."

> *"He had it. I could have ridden him and won it, I think. But Arcaro, I think, was the best rider. In the Preakness he was simply the best."*
> — Jimmy Jones, 1997,
> remembering the 1948 Preakness Stakes

Jimmy Jones holds **CITATION** with Arcaro up after winning the 1948 Preakness. *Courtesy Grayson Collection. Used with permission.*

The Preakness followed on Saturday, May 15, 1948. Only three horses challenged the Immortal Pair: Vulcan's Forge, with Doug Dodson up; Bovard, with Willie Saunders (Omaha's Triple Crown Jockey) up; and Better Self, with Warren Mehrtens (Assault's Triple Crown Jockey) up. And again, only win betting was allowed. Citation was the betting favorite at odds of 1 to 10. It really wasn't much of a contest: Citation grabbed the lead at the start and stayed there to the finish line. Arcaro tried to hold him back, so as not to tire out, but that didn't matter to Citation: he won by 5 1/2 lengths. The closest any other horse got to him was Vulcan's Forge, who came within 1 1/2 lengths at the half-mile. The official race results say "CITATION sprinted to the front while under stout restraint, was without serious opposition, merely galloping along in front to the stretch, felt the sting of the whip twice, and easily increased his advantage." At least the other horses and jockeys were present to look like there was competition.[7]

---

[7] Warren Wright did very well financially that day. Citation won $91,870 for the Preakness, but at the Jamaica Track in New York the same day, Citation's stablemates Faultless and Fervent were entered in the Gallant Fox Handicap. Faultless and Fervent finished one-two in that race, winning $60,300 and $15,000 respectively for Calumet. The day's total of $167,170 in winnings was the largest one-day total for any stable to that date.

When the jockeys were asked their opinions of the race. Arcaro said, "It was even easier than the Derby. It's a privilege to ride such a horse." Dodson got right to the heart of the matter: "Nobody's going to beat him." Mehrtens said nothing, but Willie Saunders had the best statement on the Preakness. Both Mehrtens and he had been there with Triple Crown winners, and while Saunders' horse, Bovard, was a good one, Saunders knew what he was up against. After the Preakness, Saunders was asked for his opinion. "What a horse! Citation, I mean," Omaha's jockey said.

Many trainers would have rested Citation between the Preakness and the Belmont. Not so Jimmy Jones. As his father entered Whirlaway in the Henry of Navarre Stakes between the 1941 Preakness and Belmont, so Jimmy Jones entered Citation in the Jersey Stakes on May 29. It was no contest; Arcaro and Citation won by "only" eleven lengths.

> *"I said in the paddock, 'Eddie, the only way you're going to get beat is to fall off the horse.'"*
> — Jimmy Jones,
> 1997, remembering the 1948 Belmont Stakes

Unlike Whirlaway or Count Fleet, the 1948 Belmont Stakes wasn't considered a total blowout for Citation. He was the betting favorite at 1 to 5, but there was a hitch. Bull Lea, Citation's sire, was not a distance runner. Accordingly, seven other horses lined up to challenge Citation and Arcaro; perhaps the Bull Lea line would finally show itself in the 1 1/2-mile Belmont. Perhaps, just perhaps, there was a chance to sneak by the Immortal Pair.

Hah! The Belmont Stakes was run on June 12, 1948. As in the Preakness, the jockeys opposing Citation and Arcaro were among the best. Arcaro's competition that day: Warren Mehrtens on Better Self; Doug Dodson on Vulcan's Forge; Eric Guerin on Salmagundi; and Ted Atkinson on Faraway (the last horse that Sam Riddle, owner of Man o'War and War Admiral, ever entered in a Triple Crown race.) The track was fast, and the horses went to the post at 4:45 P.M.. They broke a minute later.

Citation drew the pole position and stumbled at the start.[8] It didn't make

---

One other fact should be noted: Pimlico's track was sloppy that day, and the time was slow. Citation's victory time in the Preakness was 2:24 3/5, curiously, the slowest winning Preakness time of any Triple Crown winner in history.

[8] Citation's Belmont Stakes starting stumble is one of the most famous missteps in racing history. It came about in an odd manner: Atkinson and Faraway were in the stall next to Arcaro and Citation. Atkinson looked over and saw Citation resting his left foreleg on a ledge in the gate. Atkinson told Arcaro about it, and Arcaro smacked

198

much difference; the Immortal Pair recovered and took the lead almost immediately. Still, it was a tight race at the beginning. Citation was ahead of Better Self at the quarter-mile. Then Mehrtens and Better Self faded and Ted Atkinson on Faraway challenged; they closed within a head of Arcaro and Citation at the half-mile, and stayed within a length of Citation to the mile mark. Then Faraway faded very badly (He finished last.) and Citation pulled away. Arcaro let him go for a moment, but then quickly took back control of his horse: "He ran so fast he scared me," Arcaro said afterwards. (If Citation could run fast enough to scare Arcaro, then the horse was *really* moving.) At the 1 1/4-mile mark they were four lengths ahead. At the finish Citation was a solid eight lengths ahead of Better Self, who had regained second. Citation's time of 2:28 1/5 was identical to Count Fleet's record of five years earlier. A few minutes later, Eddie Arcaro beamed as a blanket of white flowers was draped over Citation. They had swept the Triple Crown. It would not happen again for twenty-five years.

For the rest of 1948 Citation was unstoppable. For Eddie Arcaro, the years of 1947 and 1948 must surely have been "The Golden Ones." In 1947, as we have seen, he rode Assault to many impressive victories. Now, in the remainder of 1948, he repeated that performance on Citation. The Immortal Pair proceeded from the Triple Crown to put on one of the most incredible displays of consistent greatness in racing history.

The next stop was Chicago's Arlington Park. They raced in the Stars and Stripes Handicap there on July 5. They took on eight other horses, but the results were predictable: Arcaro kept Citation back for most of the 1 1/8-mile race, and sent him in the final eighth-mile. Citation sprinted to the lead and won by two lengths. His time of 1:49 1/5 tied the track record. He had won $38,000, and his career winnings totaled $427,020. With that, he passed Whirlaway on the money-winner list. Only Assault, Armed, and Stymie were ahead of him.

He should have run in the Arlington Classic, but a hitch developed. One morning while Citation was out for a walk, a manure truck came by and hit a tin feed tub. The resultant great clatter startled Citation. He jumped up in the air and landed dully. He was injured, and at first, no one knew how badly. It turned out to be only a pulled muscle in his right leg. It could have been fatal.

The muscle pull ended his chances to run in the Arlington Classic. He was out of training for a month. By early August, he had recovered sufficiently that Jimmy Jones wanted to enter him in the American Derby at Washington Park in Chicago on August 28. He needed some work and a prep race. Jones was in Saratoga in the middle of August, and learned that the Buckingham Purse, a six-furlong race at Washington Park one week before the American Derby, had an

---

Citation's leg with his whip. The blow startled the horse, and just then the gates opened. The combination of circumstances caused Citation to stumble upon leaving the gate.

opening. He moved fast and entered Citation in it. That left one small problem: Citation needed a jockey. Arcaro was unavailable to ride Citation in that race, so Jones found Newbold L. Pierson, the jockey that had ridden Coaltown in the Kentucky Derby. Pierson was a competent jockey; not in Arcaro's class, certainly, but a good one.

The jockey change made little difference to Citation. Pierson broke his horse well, kept Citation in second place, close to the leader, and took the lead by the stretch. They won by 2 1/2 lengths.

Arcaro was available one week later for the American Derby. Citation still needed some work after the injury-caused rest, but Jimmy Jones ran out of time. As insurance for Calumet, Jones also entered Free America, one of Calumet's other fine horses, in the 1 1/4-mile American Derby. The combination of the two drove the betting odds down to the minimum bet of $0.10 to $1.00. He had the two best horses, but Jones had some concerns. Papa Redbird, the winner of the Arlington Classic, was also entered. Citation had been off for six weeks, with only the Buckingham Purse to tune him up. Jimmy Jones told Arcaro to go after Papa Redbird early and not let him get away with a lead.

Arcaro and Citation ran the race exactly as Jones planned. Papa Redbird took the lead by the half-mile mark, but Citation galloped a mere 1 1/2 lengths behind. (Papa Redbird's jockey, R.L. Baird, should have known it was over at that point.) At the beginning of the far turn, Arcaro sensed it was time. He turned Citation loose, and the Immortal Pair thundered into first place.

But it wasn't over: another horse, Volcanic, passed Papa Redbird and drew close to Citation. Then Volcanic faded, and Free America, ridden by Newbold Pierson, came down the middle of the track and passed Volcanic. At the wire it was Citation by a length over his stable mate.

Citation was tired after the great race, but he was back. Jones' insurance of Free America proved to be a wise move. The American Derby paid $66,450 to the winner. With that purse, Citation passed his Triple Crown predecessor Assault to take over third place on the money winners' list.

Jimmy Jones gave him a month's rest and took Citation back to Belmont. Jones thought, he needed a tune-up before the Jockey Club Gold Cup on October 3, and Citation *had* to run in *it*. Jones chose the Sysonby Mile on September 3. There were some good horses entered in it: Coaltown was back, as were Assault's old adversaries, Spy Song and Natchez. Again, it really didn't matter: Arcaro kept Citation in fourth place behind Coaltown, Natchez, and Spy Song throughout the half-mile. Then Arcaro took him to the outside, and it was immortal: Citation veritably blew by those three horses to take command easily. He won by three lengths.

Jones was upset after the race: Had Arcaro pushed Citation too hard? Had he now jeopardized the Jockey Club Gold Cup to win the far less important Sysonby Mile? Jones confronted the jockey after the race: "Why did you move so soon," Jones asked.

Arcaro's answer was classic, and a tribute to the magnificent horse he had just ridden: "The so-and-so just took off on me," Arcaro replied.

In the face of such overwhelming logic, what else could Jimmy Jones do but smile? Later, Jones recalled, "He just kind of ran off with Eddie."

Jimmy Jones needn't have worried about the Jockey Club Gold Cup. It was a two-mile race, and Citation was the bettors' favorite, despite his exertion at the Sysonby Mile. In fact, he was *so much* the favorite that Belmont canceled "show" betting on the race; it was either bet to win or to place.

Belmont's management was prescient. The Jockey Club Gold Cup was over the moment the gates opened. Arcaro sent Citation right to the lead and no other horse ever got closer to him than four lengths. After the first mile, Citation decided to run even faster: he eventually crossed the finish line *seven* lengths ahead of the pack.

Arcaro brought him in tired, but how could he have been otherwise? The horse ran three miles in four days, and won both races by the combined total of *ten* lengths. Arcaro simply said afterwards, "You've got to ride that colt to realize how good he is. *I get a thrill every time I ride him.*"[Emphasis added.]

Jimmy Jones rested Citation for two weeks and ran him again in the regular Gold Cup race at Belmont on October 16. Once again Citation was the favorite, at $0.15 to $1. He broke well and wanted to go straight to the lead. Arcaro held him in restraint for the first half-mile of the 1 5/8-mile race, but after that, let him go. He rushed into the lead and never gave it up. He won by two lengths. The first paragraph of James Roach's story in the next day's *New York Times* stated: "Citation, who is certainly the horse of the year, probably is the horse of the decade, and may be the horse of the century, did it again at Belmont Park yesterday. He won the $111,700 Gold Cup race in a romp."[9] (The only blemish on the race came in the winner's circle. Citation, as the winner, was draped with a blanket of chrysanthemums. He didn't like to be covered with flowers and Jimmy Jones had to cover his great horse's eyes as the floral blanket was applied.)

> *"Citation has mowed down his opponents with such consistency that today he finds all of his foes conceding his supremacy."*
> — Joseph B. Kelly,
> *Baltimore Sun*, October 29, 1948,
> on the 1948 Pimlico Special.

One of the major autumn races at that time was the Pimlico Special. Of

---

[9] The historical response to Roach's statement: he was, he was, and he may still be.

course, Citation was the leading entrant, and as it turned out, the *only* entrant. The Pimlico Special was a winner-take-all invitational race for winners of certain stakes races, but after the Triple Crown, the Sysonby Mile, the Jockey Club Gold Cup and the Gold Cup, *nobody* was willing to challenge Citation in the Pimlico Special. The purse was the easiest $10,000 that Citation ever earned.

So, on October 29, 1948, the fans at Pimlico were treated to a rare sight, one that had been seen only once before, six years earlier with Whirlaway: a walkover in the Pimlico Special. As in 1942, no horse and jockey challenged the champion from Calumet Farm. Arcaro brought Citation out for the solo post parade and led him up to the starting line. (There was no starting gate used for just one horse.) The horse wanted to run, but Arcaro saw no point in tiring Citation or risking an injury. Arcaro's muscles surely must have been sore from holding back Citation. He kept Citation under tight restraint for most of the race, but let him go in the final quarter-mile. Citation finished the 1 3/16-mile race in time of 1:59 4/5. (Whirly ran the race in a leisurely 2:05 2/5.) He had now won $830,250 and had moved to second behind Stymie, with $911,335. The Associated Press account stated, "...Citation shouldn't have trouble becoming the first $1,000,000 winner in turf history." As it turned out, the press report was half right. Citation became the first equine millionaire, but not without *a lot* of trouble.

Jimmy Jones planned for Citation to run in the Santa Anita races in the coming winter. Gene Mori, Jones's friend, had just purchased the Tanforan track in the Bay Area, and wanted Citation to run at his track. Mori called Jones, stating: "Look, we're trying to make San Francisco a big racing center. And I don't know of a better way to start. You're going right by here to Santa Anita. What about stopping off and running [Citation] in our Tanforan Handicap?"

Jones resisted at first, and then gave in. He shipped Citation to Tanforan and entered him in one race, the Challenge Purse, a race worth $5,000, on December 3. With Arcaro up, they tore up the northern California track as they had tracks in Kentucky, Maryland, New Jersey, Illinois, and New York. In the race, Bold Gallant, ridden by John Longden, took an early lead. But Arcaro kept Citation in second, and by the stretch, let him go into first. Bold Gallant hung on, but it was really no contest. Citation won by 1 1/2 lengths, and as the notes to the race chart put it, he "drew out to win as his rider pleased."

His last race of 1948 was on December 11 in the Tanforan Handicap, a 1 1/4-mile race with a $50,000 purse. He made it look easy. Arcaro put him in second at the very beginning, but by the half-mile, they had taken over first. It was no contest; Citation breezed home, five lengths in front of every other horse, in time of 2:02 4/5. It was a new track record.

Citation had now won fifteen straight races, but Arcaro had noticed something odd about how he ran in the Tanforan Handicap: he just didn't seem to have his usual speed. Yes, they set a track record, but Arcaro used the whip on him more than in any other race. He mentioned that to Jimmy Jones, but the trainer was not overly concerned.

The beginning of the end came a few days later. An osselet, a bony growth indicative of leg problems and the same condition that forced Assault into retirement earlier that year, popped out on one of Citation's legs. That meant any racing was out of the question for the immediate future. There was no sense in keeping him in California. Citation was shipped to Hialeah for the winter.

What happened? Jones supplied the answer nearly fifty years later: Tanforan was built near a mountain. The runoff from the mountain came down and at one point, rose up on the track. Farmers would call it a "seep spot"; not a puddle, but a soft, weak place in the dirt. Citation ran through the seep spot and injured his ankle.

Despite the ankle injury, Citation had a glorious year. He put up nineteen victories in twenty starts, captured the Triple Crown, and banked $709,470, a record for one-year earnings. He was named Best Three-Year-Old horse and Horse of the Year. Of all his Triple Crown predecessors, only Gallant Fox had dominated racing as thoroughly as Citation. His total winnings were $865,150, and Warren Wright now wanted fervently for Citation to become the first racehorse to win $1 million.

But that was the trouble: Warren Wright *was* the boss, and he what he said was law. Citation should have been retired for good at that point, and his standing in racing history would be unquestioned. But less than $135,000 stood between Wright and his goal, and maybe two victories would do the trick....

Citation was treated over the winter of 1948-49, but the leg ailment hung on, refusing to go away. The fourth year of a racehorse's career is often the best. The horse is more experienced, and a year older and stronger. It was first hoped he could race at Belmont in the early summer of 1949, then it was hoped he could race at Arlington and Washington Park later, then finally, Belmont in the autumn. None of that happened. Citation missed it all due to the osselet. He stayed first in Florida, then Kentucky, and didn't race at all in 1949. Not that Calumet Farm had to worry: Coaltown and Bewitch took over, and they filled in magnificently. When Citation finally came back, in January, 1950, he was now in the five-year-old horse class, a year away from racing, heavier, and sorer.

The story of Citation in 1950 is paradoxical: The record shows only nine races, a mere two wins, seven places, and earnings of $73,480. At first blush, it seems a tragic record for the greatest horse of mid-century. But look further: 1950 was the year of one of racing's greatest rivalries, Citation-Noor. When the record is analyzed carefully, Citation was still the best on the track.

Arcaro was often unavailable to ride Citation, so Calumet picked Steve

Brooks. It was hardly a demotion for the horse; Brooks won the previous year's Kentucky Derby on Calumet's own Ponder. Brooks was eventually elected to the National Museum of Racing and Hall of Fame. He was a fine jockey and a fine choice to ride Citation in his comeback.

The team of Brooks-Citation started in the state where Arcaro-Citation had left off exactly thirteen months earlier: at Santa Anita in southern California. The occasion was the six-furlong Belmont Purse race on January 11, 1950, worth $5000. The day was rainy and the track muddy, but Citation looked as if he had not been out of training. He carried only 124 pounds (less than his Derby weight of two years earlier, but still the most of the four horses in the race). He was the favorite at $0.15 to $1. Brooks let him break well and settled him into third place. In the backstretch, one horse, Chutney, carried him wide, but Citation quickly overcame that. He moved along easily, and Brooks hit him just once. Citation responded, gaining ground: despite the muddy track. Bold Gallant was in first, and as Citation challenged, Bold Gallant bore out slightly and carried Citation wide. It didn't matter: Citation sprinted into the lead and won by 1 1/2 lengths.

The result pleased Jimmy Jones. A year's layoff and a new jockey apparently had little effect on the Triple Crown horse. "I'm not worrying so much now. I think he's going to be all right. Naturally, I am well pleased and am satisfied with the way he ran. I thought Steve handled him just fine," Jones said after the race.

Citation's victory set a record of sixteen straight wins. Not until 1994-1995-1996 would another horse, Cigar, tie that record. To date, it has never been broken.

Fifteen days later, reality set in when Citation finished second in the La Sorpesa Handicap at Santa Anita on January 26. Brooks was up and broke him well. Brooks kept him back, in second or third. A 14 to 1 long shot, Miche, an Argentine horse, took the lead. In the stretch, Miche and Citation hooked up for a blistering duel, but the long shot got his neck in front of Citation's at the wire.

It was an upset, yes; but those things happen. No matter what the outcome, Citation ran a fine race.

As so often happens in the Triple Crown saga, another horse entered the picture to bedevil the champion. It is time to meet Noor, an Irish horse, ridden by none other than John Longden. Longden was a great jockey, and Noor was a great horse.

Count Fleet was the best overall horse that Longden rode (*naturally!*); Busher, a War Admiral filly, was the best filly he ever rode. The title of Longden's best Handicap horse goes to Noor. This was high praise, indeed, coming from one of the greatest jockeys of all time. During the next four months, Noor and Citation battled each other five times and only once did Citation finish ahead of his Irish tormentor. (Charles S. Howard, Seabiscuit's owner, owned Noor as well. Too much can be made of coincidence, but this was the second time a great Howard horse challenged a Triple Crown winner.)

In their first challenge, the San Antonio Handicap on February 11 at Santa Anita, the paired favorites (at $0.45 to $1) were the Calumet Farm entries Citation and Ponder (the previous year's Kentucky Derby winner.) As punishment for losing the previous race, Brooks was taken off Citation and put on Ponder. Calumet again called on Eddie Arcaro to ride Citation. Portentously, the Longden-Noor combination was the second choice in the betting.

Citation and Ponder both stayed back. Citation made his move earlier than his stable mate: at the 3/4-mile mark, he was only two lengths behind the leader. But Brooks sent Ponder with a mighty sweep; Ponder came from seventh to first at the wire by a length over Citation.

It was the first time Citation ever lost two consecutive races. Still, there wasn't much cause for alarm; Ponder had run *such* a fine race that the defeat was forgiven. Citation carried the most weight, 130 pounds, while Ponder carried 128 and Noor only 114. But sixteen pounds or none, someone should have looked at the third horse, Noor. Longden kept him back until the stretch and he closed rapidly, finishing only a mere half-length behind Citation.

The Citation-Noor rivalry of 1950 remains controversial. Did Noor beat a sore, creaky horse past his prime that should have been retired? Or, did Noor beat Citation at the top of his game, fair and square? Both sides have proponents: Citation's backers say that the Triple Crown winner had been away for a year, usually carried more weight, and really *should* have been back at Calumet Farm. Jimmy Jones later said, "We probably shouldn't have kept going with him. We never really gave him enough time. You know you have to give a cripple more time to come back, and I was always pushing him, always two weeks behind where I should have been, and Noor kept improving."[10]

But when Longden was told that Citation in 1950 was past his prime, Longden responded immediately: "How could he have been? No way. He [Citation] set a world's record for a mile up at Golden Gate, fitting in that performance in between his meetings with Noor." Longden remembered some of the Noor-Citation battles, his own thrills in racing, and then leaped to Noor's defense. "I don't think it's quite fair to say Citation was far from his best when Noor defeated him, particularly in the final meeting when we gave him one pound in the Golden Gate Handicap," the jockey opined.

It is probably most accurate to say that while Citation was not the champion of 1947-48, he was still *the* horse to reckon with.

Two weeks later at the Santa Anita Handicap, Citation was entered along

---

[10] This statement appeared in the 1970 book, *The Great Ones*. It is very politically incorrect by today's standards but profoundly true. Citation was just not completely ready to race.

with Ponder and a great filly, Two Lea, from Calumet. Miche was back, and But Why Not, one of King Ranch's great horses, was entered. Again there was Noor and Longden. The 1 1/4-mile Santa Anita Handicap was an important race, and Warren Wright had pointed Jimmy Jones and Citation to win it. Jones had reservations about that. He felt the horse still wasn't ready for that particular race, but Wright was the boss.

Jones felt that Ponder was past his peak performance and wanted the jockey to ride Two Lea. He gave Steve Brooks his choice: Brooks chose Ponder, and Jones engaged Johnny Gilbert to ride the Calumet filly. That left Citation with Eddie Arcaro.

That put Longden on Noor with 110 pounds versus Arcaro on Citation with *132* pounds. Of a later race between the two stellar jockeys, Longden recalled, "I knew I had to out-guess Eddie Arcaro, and believe me that is not an easy thing to do."

Longden did it in the Santa Anita Handicap. The start was good, and Noor, Ponder, and Citation settled back for most of the race. Two Lea took the lead by the half-mile, and held onto it for most of the race. But Noor came up with a furlong to go and caught Two Lea. Citation rallied, passed his stable mate, and challenged Noor. The weight penalty was decisive: Noor finished 1 1/4 lengths ahead of Citation in track record time of 2:00. (Ponder was fourth behind Two Lea, proving out Jimmy Jones's prediction.)

> *"He was like an extension of me out there.*
> *He was the perfect extension of the trainer on the horse.*
> *And nobody had his sense of the way the race was being run."*
> — Jimmy Jones on Eddie Arcaro,
> quoted in *The New York Times,*
> November 15, 1997

It was the last time Eddie Arcaro rode Citation. The partnership that conquered racing in 1948 ended in 1950 with two second-place finishes. We shall not see Eddie Arcaro as a jockey again in this book. Arcaro won one more Derby (Hill Gail, in 1951); four more Preaknesses (Hill Prince, 1950; Bold, 1951; Nashua, 1955; and Bold Ruler, [Secretariat's sire] 1957). He won and two more Belmonts (on One Count [Count Fleet's son] in 1952; and Nashua, 1955). In all, he won five Derbies, six Preaknesses, and six Belmonts: more Triple Crown-level victories than any other jockey. He was elected to the National Museum of Racing and Hall of Fame in 1958 and retired in 1961 as the first jockey to take home $1 million in career winnings. He rode 24,092 races and won 4,779 of them. Included in that number were a record 549 stakes wins. Arcaro also was President of the Jockey Guild from 1949 to 1961. His Triple Crown on Citation was the last for twenty-five years, and Arcaro remains the only jockey to win two Triple Crowns. For a time he appeared in various promotions for Buick, Seagram's, and New York State's Off-Track Betting. He also did racing commentary for ABC sports. He retired to the Miami area, where he played golf with Joe DiMaggio, relaxed, visited Gulfstream Park, and appeared at an occasional racing function. After a long battle with liver cancer, Eddie Arcaro died at his home on November 14, 1997.

What can one say about Eddie Arcaro? Only a few others in racing history come close to him: Isaac Murphy in the 1800s; Earl Sande and Charles Kurtsinger in the 1920s and 1930s. His contemporaries come close: Longden, Shoemaker, and Hartack. But no other jockey quite measures up to Eddie Arcaro. Perhaps no other jockey ever will.

"He was simply smarter than everybody else on the track."
— William Nack on Eddie Arcaro,
Sports Illustrated, November 24, 1997

Citation and Noor immediately resumed their rivalry. They were still at Santa Anita on March 4, when they met again in the 1 3/4-mile San Juan Capistrano Handicap. Brooks was back on Citation and the horse carried 130 pounds to Noor's 117. Citation broke well and early on moved into second place. At the 1 1/2-mile mark he was running in first. But Noor, back for the first mile, moved into second place only a head behind Citation. It was a great duel for the next 3/8 of a mile: Brooks and Citation, Longden and Noor, neither pair giving an inch. In the very last stride down to the wire Noor got a nose in front. The time was 2:52 4/5. Noor had to set a new track and American record for a 1 3/4-mile race to beat Citation by a nose.

Citation rested for two months and traveled to northern California to race at Golden Gate Fields near Oakland. He ran in a six-furlong sprint, the Surprise Purse, on May 17. Gordon Glisson rode Citation in that race. Citation carried the most weight, 120 pounds, and his chief competition was Roman In. The race was a good one: the Triple Crown winner ran well, but Glisson ran him to the outside. Roman In took charge on the inside, and held on to first. Citation came close, but Roman In finished 3/4 of a length in front. The time of 1:08 2/5 tied the world record for a six-furlong race.

Citation had now been beaten four straight times, but in the last three, the victors had to run record times to beat him. It speaks volumes about the quality and speed of the racehorse: even with the layoff, extra weight, and leg trouble, beating him required record-setting times. To this point, Citation had won $910,080, and the Golden Gate Mile Handicap on June 3 was next. It was worth $23,300. If he won it, he would move that much closer to the $1 million mark.

Six horses started the race with Citation. Bolero, ridden by John Longden, took an early lead. Brooks, on Citation again, hustled Citation into second place. At one point, Bolero took a three-length lead. Brooks didn't panic: he let Citation run nice and easy. He set up to challenge Bolero at the stretch.

At the far turn, Brooks let Citation loose. The horse responded and relentlessly drew even with Bolero. Then he edged first a nose, then a head, then a neck in front. It was close for the last sixteenth of a mile, but Citation and Brooks crossed the finish line 3/4 of a length in front of Bolero. The time was 1:33 3/5. It was a new world record.

Citation seemed to be back: his last four races had broken records. But it was really all over. The victories had taken too much out of him. Jimmy Jones admitted that autumn, "I shouldn't have run him in those last two races. I knew he wasn't right. Actually he was a broken-down horse. But he was still so good that I thought he might do it, and he very nearly did."

The races Jones referred to were the Forty-Niners Handicap and the Golden Gate Handicap (a different, longer race than the Golden Gate Mile Handicap.)

On June 17, Noor and Citation renewed their rivalry at Golden Gate Fields in the Forty-Niners Handicap, a 1 1/8-mile race. Noor, Roman In, On Trust, and Stepfather also started. Citation carried 128 pounds, while Noor carried 123. The start was good and Brooks kept Citation in second for the first half-mile. At the 3/4-mile mark they were in first. But Noor and Longden made a move to challenge Citation and Brooks in the stretch. Once again, it was a bitter fight for a sixteenth of a mile. Noor finished a neck in front of Citation. Noor had set another world record time of 1:46 4/5 for the distance.

Citation's final race in 1950 was the Golden Gate Handicap a week later. Now *he* had a weight advantage, 126 pounds, versus Noor's 127. For most of the race Brooks kept Citation in third. When Noor, who had been farther back in the race, made his move, so did Citation. The challenge didn't last long: Citation faded in the stretch and Noor won by three lengths in another world record time of 1:58 1/5.

California racing was over for Citation for the year. He was shipped to Arlington Park at Chicago. Calumet hoped he could run in the Arlington Handicap, but on July 22, Citation came back lame. He was scratched from the race and Jimmy Jones doubted publicly that Citation would race again. He seemed to improve, feeding a faint hope that he could race at Belmont in the autumn. But the treatments didn't succeed, and Citation returned home to Calumet for the winter.

Nine starts, two firsts, seven seconds. With the exception of his last race, none of the defeats were by much. Citation set one record, and forced his challengers to set five more records to beat him. Joe Palmer was absolutely right when he wrote, "A simple study of the weights shows that, in four of his five meetings with Noor, Citation was the better horse. If Noor was good, then Citation was very good. Is this 'disappointing?' No: Citation was magnificent, and in some ways more heroic than in 1948."

Citation again should have been retired for good, but there were the numbers to consider. His winnings of $938,630 fell short of the $1 million mark by $61,370. Moreover, Warren Wright died on December 28, 1950. Now his wish to see Citation become the first equine millionaire took on a special impetus.

Looking back, it all seems so tragic. Jimmy Jones hoped Citation could race at Santa Anita in southern California in the winter, but the horse still wasn't ready. Finally, he was taken to the Bay Meadows Track at San Mateo in northern California. On March 18, Jones said that Citation was "four weeks away from a race." It was an accurate prediction: Citation went back to racing on April 18, 1951, in the Uncle Tom's Cabin Purse at Bay Meadows. Steve Brooks rode him again. Citation ran fourth through much of the race, but then moved into third by the stretch. There he finished, and it was his worst race to date. But Brooks was pleased: Citation carried 120 pounds and had been away from the track for ten months. The winning horse, A Lark, had carried only 109 pounds. The lameness was nowhere in evidence. It was an honorable result for a six-year-old horse with leg problems. The show paid only $430. It brought his winnings to $939,060.

He ran again at Bay Meadows eight days later in the Veterans Hospital Day Purse. He was the favorite, but as in the previous race, never was a serious factor. He finished third again, and won only $400. How different it all was from 1947 and 1948....

Jimmy Jones took him south to Hollywood Park where he would finish his racing career. He ran in the Hollywood Premiere Handicap on May 11. Citation and Brooks stayed far back for most of the race, but moved up in the stretch. The pack bottled them up and they finished fifth. It was the worst finish of Citation's career, the only time he ever finished out of the money. Could he *ever* break the $1 million mark?

At the Argonaut Handicap on May 30 Coaltown and Bewitch were also entered. The Calumet entry, as so long before, was favored. Citation was the star of the three: he broke in eighth place out of ten horses, but again made his move late in the race. He finished second, three lengths back. It wasn't a good race for Calumet: Bewitch ran fourth, and Coaltown finished ninth. Still, Citation took home $5,000 and that raised his total to $944,460. The way he was going — four races, no victories, and purses of only $5,830 — it might as well have been another million dollars away.

By June, Citation seemed to will a comeback. He started winning again, and the long, painful, slump ended. He won the 1-mile Century Handicap on June 14 by a half-length and won an $8,250 purse. On the Fourth of July, he won the American Handicap by a length, and took home $33,050 for Calumet Farm. Now there was just $14,240 left to win....

On July 14, 1951, Steve Brooks rode Citation in the Hollywood Gold Cup at Hollywood Park. Citation broke well, and was in third at the quarter-mile mark. He sprinted to the front, looking like the Citation of 1947-1948. He took over first by the half-mile and stayed there for the rest of the race to finish four lengths in front of the pack. A film clip of the race's finish has been preserved on the videotape, "Thoroughbred Heroes", and the viewer is momentarily puzzled: is Citation racing at Hollywood Park in July, 1951, or at Pimlico in May, 1948?

The purse was $100,000.00, which drove his winnings tally up to $1,085,760. Citation was the first horse in history to win more than $1 million in purses. He was doing better, running better, and Jimmy Jones entertained the notion of entering Citation in more races.

The night following the Hollywood Gold Cup, the telephone rang in Jimmy Jones's room. Mrs. Warren Wright was on the other end of the line. She told the trainer, "Jimmy, I wish you'd do me a favor. I wish you would call the press tomorrow and tell everyone that Citation has run his last race and will be retired. A million dollars was the goal of Mr. Wright for the horse, and now he has achieved it." The long struggle was over. It was time for Citation to go home for good.

"Almost every nice horse has one good move in him; the really good ones, you can move with them twice. With Citation, you could call on him at any time in a race; he had about eight moves in him."
— Eddie Arcaro on Citation,
The Blood-Horse Interactive Edition,
November 20, 1997.

A twenty-five year-gap ensued between Citation's Triple Crown and Secretariat's. During that time, the aura of the Triple Crown grew. Seven horses won the Triple Crown between the 1930 racing season and the 1948 season, inclusive, which is a little less frequently than one Triple Crown every three years. With the gap between Citation and Secretariat, the Triple Crown became the Holy Grail of Thoroughbred racing. In part, the greatness of Arcaro on Citation contributed to the mystique. Great horses ran during that quarter-century: Nashua, Swaps, Native Dancer, Bold Ruler, Tim Tam, Carry Back, Northern Dancer, Majestic Prince, and Riva Ridge, to name a few. But none of them ever quite made it. All of them, as well as Secretariat, had to contend with the legendary image of the Immortal Pair flying effortlessly across the finish lines at Churchill Downs, Pimlico, and Belmont Park.

Both Jimmy Jones and Citation were elected to the National Racing Museum and Hall of Fame in 1959. In 1964, Jones left Calumet Farm to be the racing director at Monmouth Park in New Jersey. He stayed there until 1976, when he retired for good. In retirement he split his year between Florida in the winter and Missouri in the summer. He usually stopped by Churchill Downs for the Kentucky Derby on his way to Missouri. He was a gracious man, eager to share his reminiscences about training. His love for his horses, especially Citation, and his admiration for the jockeys like Arcaro, Al Snider, and Steve Brooks, were ever-present.

Triple Crown Trainers: (left to right) Ben Jones (Whirlaway), Sunny Jim Fitzsimmons (Gallant Fox, Omaha), and Jimmy Jones (Citation). Photographed at Hialeah, Florida, 1958. *Courtesy Grayson Collection. Used with permission.*

On September 2, 2001, Jimmy Jones died at Saint Francis Hospital in Marysville, Missouri, at the age of 94. His career spanned fifty-six years. He had witnessed the Sir Barton-Man o'War match race in 1920; helped with Whirlaway; helped train Armed for the match race with Assault; trained Citation and so many others like Coaltown and Bewitch. A lot of racing history passed away with him.

Following a farewell appearance at Arlington Park in Chicago, Calumet Farm returned Citation to Kentucky, and it is there that the legend ends. It would have been better if he been retired after the osselet was discovered, as Count Fleet was retired after his injury in the Belmont. But Citation was close, SO close to that magic million mark…. He was sent back to racing repeatedly in its pursuit, and along the way, the inevitable, inescapable defeats he suffered tarnished him. Still, he was the first equine millionaire, the first horse ever to win a million dollars in purses.

Another unforeseeable development further tarnished his reputation. The image of greatness largely ended with him. Popular history over-simplifies: Citation has been compared to Sir Barton and Omaha as a failure at stud. This linkage is *very* far from the truth. One of his sons, Fabius, won the 1956 Preakness. Only two other Triple Crown Winners, Gallant Fox (Omaha, 1935,) and Secretariat (Risen Star, 1988,) sired Preakness winners.[11]

Appendix VI of this book lists the Triple Crown winners that in turn sired Triple Crown-race winners. Citation appears on that list; other Triple Crown winners aren't on it. Fabius and three others of Citation's offspring each won more than $100,000 in purses. A daughter, Silver Spoon, was named Champion Three-Year-Old Filly of 1959. She was elected to membership in the National Museum of Racing and Hall of Fame in 1978. Citation's last foal was born on April 19, 1970, a bright, alert, spindly-legged colt with a white blaze.

In all, he sired 263 named foals, of which 229 were starters. As of July 1, 1970, a month before Citation's death, 162 of those 229 horses (70%) had won one or more races. His progeny to that date had earned $3,528,269 in North American races. In 1969, he was in the top ten percent of all stallions. This is a siring record of good, solid, accomplishment, not a record of failure. But remember which horse we are dealing with here: Citation. Even more than any other Triple Crown winner, he was expected to produce offspring every bit as good as he was. Count Fleet came closest to meeting that expectation; most of the other Triple Crown winners, Citation included, didn't.

Citation died of old age on the evening of August 8, 1970. He rests near his sire and dam at Calumet Farm.

Eddie Arcaro said, "He was the best I ever rode."

---

[11] Even more remarkable is that Fabius came from Citation's first crop of foals. The odds against a Triple Crown-winning horse siring a winner of a Triple Crown-level race in his first crop of foals are astronomical.

Eddie Arcaro weighing in. Photo taken in 1955. *Courtesy Grayson Collection.*
Used with permission.

VIII. THE NATIONAL HERO: SECRETARIAT

Triple Crown, 1973. Jockey, Ron Turcotte

By any standard, 1973 was a veritable garbage can of a year for America. The nation's painful disengagement from the Vietnam War, inflation, the Arab Oil Embargo, and the Watergate Scandal made the year painfully impossible to forget. But the year brought one piece of good news for the country in 1973: a chestnut horse named Secretariat.

In 1950, the Thoroughbred Racing Association ordered nine silver trophy cups from Cartier's. The cups were triangular, with each side symbolizing a Triple Crown race. At an awards banquet that year, the first cup was awarded to J.K.L. Ross for Sir Barton, and at each following banquet for the next seven years, one cup was awarded for each of the other Triple Crown horses from Gallant Fox through Citation.

One trophy cup was left over, and that cup was never presented to a Triple Crown winner. It was a long time, sixteen years after the last presentation, until another horse qualified for the Triple Crown cup. By that time, the remaining cup was too scratched and battered to present to anyone. When finally a horse did qualify for the cup, a new cup had to be ordered.

Racing fans differ as to which ten horses were the greatest Thoroughbreds in American racing history. But three names will be found in anyone's top ten list: Man o'War, Citation, and Secretariat.

The greatest racehorse of modern times was foaled on the night of March 30, 1970, at Meadow Stable near Doswell, Virginia. Meadow Stable had a long and interesting history: the Chenery family built a home on the premises in 1810. The Civil War devastated the Chenery property; a large dike, built by slaves to hold back a bend of the North Rivanna River, had been damaged, and the family had no means of repairing it. The Chenery family kept trying to raise crops on the land, but in 1922, the effects of nature and the bank's mortgage finally prevailed. The property went into foreclosure.

Skip ahead to 1936, and C.T. Chenery, a self-made utilities millionaire, purchased the property at Doswell to fulfill a long-held promise he had made to

215

himself to restore the property to family ownership. The Meadow was in disrepair in the middle of the Depression, but Chenery embarked on a rebuilding and remodeling program. Quickly, the old, run-down, antebellum property became a showplace.

Chenery, like many wealthy people of the time, liked horses. He had worked around horses as a child. He began to assemble a stable, and over time, his stable became an impressive one. Meadow Stable produced Hill Prince, the Horse of the Year in 1950, and that year's Preakness winner. First Landing, another Meadow Stable horse, was the leading two-year-old colt of 1958, and Cicada was named Best Filly of 1961, 1962, and 1963. For a number of years, Cicada was the leading money-winner among fillies. Though lacking the cachet of Claiborne or Calumet, C.T. Chenery's Meadow Stable produced top-quality racers.

One particular Chenery purchase, Imperatrice, was an excellent broodmare. She foaled several stakes winners. With her good record of foals, Imperatrice was bred to Princequillo, who for a time was the champion broodmare sire. Out of that mating came a filly named Somethingroyal in 1952.

At the age of seventeen, Somethingroyal was mated to Bold Ruler, winner of the 1957 Preakness and one of the great sires of all time. Here is a story in itself: Ogden Phipps owned Bold Ruler, and Phipps had a rule: a cash stud fee was waived if the mare bore two foals by Bold Ruler. Phipps would then take one of the foals in lieu of the cash. C.T. Chenery regularly sent mares to Ogden Phipps's stable. Inevitably, Bold Ruler bred a Chenery mare. Through a complicated set of circumstances involving mares in 1968, and Somethingroyal and another mare in 1969, as well as a coin toss, C.T. Chenery "won" the foal by Bold Ruler that Somethingroyal was carrying.

When Bold Ruler's foals raced at age two they were often successful in the short lengths of two-year-old races. When the Bold Ruler horses turned age three and ran in longer races, they were often disappointing. The Princequillo line was another story: they tended to mature later and were known as distance runners.

The breeders Phipps and Chenery applied a time-tested maxim: breed the best to the best, and hope for the best. The idea was to mix the best qualities of Bold Ruler and Princequillo. It doesn't always work out as planned, but one time it did, and that made up for all the rest.

> *"...But the thing that caught you about him was his eyes.*
> *He had great presence, even as a baby.*
> *You'd look at him and he'd look back and not in a menacing way,*
> *not like, 'You can't catch me,' but in a way that said, 'I'm content with*
> *myself and if I permit you to come over, just be nice.'"*
> — Penny Tweedy,
> 1998, on the youthful Secretariat.

Howard Gentry, Meadow Stable's farm manager, was called away from a late-night pool game on the evening of March 29, 1970. Gentry headed to the foaling barn and found Somethingroyal about to give birth. The foal was good sized, and Gentry wondered if its hips would clear Somethingroyal's breech. Gentry and an attendant tugged at the emerging forelegs, and at 12:10 A.M., March 30, 1970, the entire foal entered the world. Gentry's immediate reaction was "There is a whopper!"

Within twenty minutes the new-born was on his feet. He began nursing twenty-five minutes later. (He would always be a big eater, and he showed it right from the start.) Meadow Stable decided to keep the colt, and sent in three names to the Jockey Club: Sceptre, Royal Line, and Something Special. Those were rejected, and Mrs. Penny Tweedy, C.T. Chenery's daughter, sent in three more prospective names: Games of Chance, Deo Volente ('God Willing' in Latin), and a third, which was approved: Secretariat.

From 1917 to 1989 there was a wonderful continuity to racing. When Man o'War was breathing his last, Citation was racing at Pimlico as a two-year-old. Ben Jones once said, "Citation was the greatest of them all...Maybe we'll never see his likes again in our time." Not in Ben Jones's lifetime, certainly; but when Citation was put to rest at Calumet Farm in August, 1970, the colt of Bold Ruler and Somethingroyal was playing in the fields of Meadow Stable. He was broken to saddle the following year. In January, 1972, Meadow Stable vanned Secretariat to Hialeah in Florida, where he was given into the hands of Meadow Stable's trainer, Lucien Laurin.

Lucien Laurin was born in 1912 in Saint-Paul de Joliette, Quebec, Canada. As a youngster, he was interested in horses. In his teens he became an exercise boy at Delormier Park in Montreal. In 1928, he rode his first race. It took two years for him to win, in 1930. He garnered some limited early success riding Sir Michael to victory in the King's Plate in 1935. But then controversy knocked his career away from the rail: in 1938, racing stewards at Narragansett Park in Rhode Island found an electric buzzer (used to shock a horse and thus spur it on to greater speed) in Laurin's jacket before a race day. Laurin protested that someone planted the buzzer in his coat (quite possible in those days) but the explanation didn't satisfy the stewards. He was banned from jockeying for life. He found a job exercising horses for Alfred Vanderbilt.

The "lifetime" ban was lifted in 1941 and Laurin went back to riding. The next year he turned to training and spent time racing horses on small tracks in New England, Ohio, and West Virginia. In 1950, he met Reginald Webster, a businessman who owned horses. In Webster's employ Laurin moved into the big-time with racing horses at Aqueduct, Belmont Park, and Saratoga. In 1958, Laurin finally achieved the success he had sought for thirty years: He trained Quill, the champion two-year-old filly of 1958.

Quill put him on the map; he continued to train for Reginald Webster, and also trained Amberoid, the winner in the 1966 Belmont Stakes. Laurin also worked for A.B. Hancock, and trained such fine horses as Dike, Jay Ray, and Drone. But still the ultimate goal, a Kentucky Derby, a Preakness, or even a Triple Crown, eluded him. It was time for a change.

In the early 1970s, Laurin got his chance. He was hired by Meadow Stable, to train an excellent horse, Riva Ridge. Riva Ridge became champion two-year-old of 1971; winner of the 1972 Kentucky Derby and Belmont Stakes; and in 1973, was named Best Handicap Horse. But Laurin could not focus all his attention just on Riva Ridge; Meadow Stable had other horses to run.

Secretariat had been galloped a few times at Meadow Stable. He hadn't been overly difficult to break and displayed a quiet, even temperament. The exercise boys liked him and he worked well. In Florida, his training proceeded satisfactorily, and he grew both in strength and confidence. By the summer of 1972, it was time for him to start racing. The *Daily Racing Form* noted one of his recent workouts: "…six furlongs in 1:12 4/5; excellent time for a never-raced horse." Laurin decided to start him in a 5 1/2-furlong race worth $8000 for maiden colts and geldings at Aqueduct on July 4, 1972.

The regular jockey for Meadow Stable had a previous commitment, so Paul Feliciano, an apprentice jockey, rode Secretariat in his first race. It was an inauspicious start to his career. Secretariat broke well but was almost immediately bumped by Quebec. That caused Secretariat in turn to bump another horse, Big Burn, and Secretariat found himself pinned between Quebec and Big Burn. Somehow Feliciano got his horse out of the mess, through the pack, and back into the race. Secretariat finished fourth, but was only about 1 1/2 lengths out of first. Given the initial problems, he ran a great race. It was the only time Secretariat finished out of the money.

Laurin hadn't seen the catastrophe at the start, and exploded at Feliciano after the race. When he and Mrs. Tweedy watched the race film, they saw the disastrous beginning and apologized to Feliciano.

The regular jockey for Meadow Stable had been injured, so Feliciano rode Secretariat in his second start, a six-furlong, $8000-purse race at Aqueduct. Ten horses started, and Secretariat hung back on the outside for the first quarter-mile. Both jockey and horse were determined not to be trapped this time. They started to move and passed one horse after another. About two hundred yards from the finish line, Secretariat took the lead and kept it. He crossed the finish line six lengths ahead of the pack. Feliciano, vindicated, stood up in the stirrups.

The apprentice jockey and two-year-old horse had done well, chalking up one unavoidable defeat and one victory. But now Meadow Stable's regular jockey, Ron Turcotte, took over.

"Oh, I have never seen a stallion, or any top horse, with such a good

nature, I have ridden a lot of them, a lot of good horses, and I have never seen one as kind as he was...He was very maneuverable...I could have headed him through a wall...He never refused and never shied from anything. He was an all-around horse. He could just do anything and everything."
— Ron Turcotte
on Secretariat, 1997

Ron Turcotte on Secretariat joined the Big Four of Triple Crown horse/jockey combinations: Earl Sande on Gallant Fox, John Longden on Count Fleet, and Eddie Arcaro on Citation.

Ron Turcotte was a French-Canadian from New Brunswick who worked as a lumberjack in his youth. Deep in the woods of Nouveau-Brunswick Turcotte got to know horses by working with draft horses that hauled logs. At age 18, the lumberjack life began to wear on Turcotte; he joined his older brother, Camille, in the big city of Toronto. The only employment they could find was picking night crawlers on a golf course until 3:00 A.M. for a bait company.

One day, Turcotte saw his landlord watching the 1960 Kentucky Derby on television. During the race the landlord suggested, "Why don't you become a jockey?"

The man who, thirteen years later, would ride perhaps the greatest horse of all time, replied: "What's a jockey?"

On the following Monday Turcotte headed out to Toronto's Old Woodbine Racetrack (it was later renamed the Greenwood Raceway.) *Anything* was better than picking worms at 3:00 A.M., and besides, he knew a bit about horses from his days in New Brunswick. Turcotte couldn't get in the gate without a pass. He tried again the next day, and the guard suggested he try the *other* Toronto track, the new Woodbine, as it was in its race meet. There he struck pay dirt. A racing official took Turcotte to Windfield Farms Stable, which was on the backstretch at Woodbine. He immediately got a hot-walker's job, and stayed the night at a simple room on the backstretch that the housed stable hands. He went back to his old room the next day, packed his things, and bade worm-picking farewell.

He did all sorts of jobs at Windfield Farms. He brushed the horses, mucked out stables, hot walked, changed water and feed, whatever was required of him. A few months later he started to gallop horses. By March, 1961, horse trainer Gordon Huntley offered Turcotte a job. Huntley noted Turcotte's work ethic and his talent with horses. Within a month Huntley made a jockey out of the ex-lumberjack.

Ron Turcotte's first ride was on June 21, 1961, aboard Whispering Wind in the second race at Woodbine. He finished sixth. It wasn't until April 9, 1962 that he won his first race. From there he shot upward to finish 1962 as Canada's top jockey with 180 wins. The racing season in Toronto at that time lasted only seven months, so Turcotte's win total was impressive. 1963 was just as good for him, and then he went south of the border to race.

His first stop was Maryland, and he took top rider honors at Pimlico and Laurel. Turcotte won 250 races in 1964, and placed third on the money-winning jockey list, ahead of the likes of Bill Shoemaker and Bill Hartack. Warren Mehrtens, Assault's Triple Crown jockey, was a racing steward at Delaware Park. He suggested Turcotte should go on to New York.

Turcotte ran his first Kentucky Derby on Tom Rolfe in 1965, and placed third behind Willie Shoemaker on Lucky Debonair and Ishmael Valenzuela on Dapper Dan. He avenged that finish two weeks later, when he and Tom Rolfe won the Preakness. Then they placed second in the Belmont Stakes.

The next year, mounted on Rehabilitate, Turcotte finished sixth in the Derby. The Kentucky Derby did not see him again until 1972, when he rode Riva Ridge to victory. Turcotte and Riva Ridge were also first in the Hibiscus Stakes, the Blue Grass Stakes, the Belmont Stakes, and the Hollywood Derby that year. In fact, were it not for a miserably sloppy track at Pimlico on Preakness day that caused Turcotte and Riva Ridge to finish fourth, Turcotte might have been the first jockey to win two *consecutive* Triple Crowns. But, there are no second chances at the Triple Crown. So, there it is: two successive Derby victories, two Preakness victories, two Belmont victories. A great jockey? Absolutely. A superstar jockey, like Sande, Longden, Arcaro, and Shoemaker? Indeed so.

Turcotte later recalled his first impressions of his greatest horse, Secretariat: "I just asked Mr. Laurin, 'Who is this pretty boy?'" Laurin told the jockey that the "pretty boy" was a colt by Bold Ruler out of Somethingroyal. Laurin told him to saddle Secretariat and work him. The horse was clumsy; in Turcotte's words, "It seemed like he didn't know which leg to put down first." But he soon straightened out, and Turcotte worked him before his first race at Belmont: Secretariat went 5/8 of a mile in fifty-eight seconds. *That* impressed Turcotte. He told Lucien Laurin, "Well, Mr. Laurin, I think we really got something here." In light of events to come, that was a masterpiece of understatement.

They made their debut at Saratoga on Monday, July 31, 1972, in a six-furlong purse race worth $9000. Secretariat was the bettor's favorite, at odds of $0.40 to $1. It was a small field of only seven horses. Secretariat was last at the quarter-mile mark, and then Turcotte sent him. He passed other horses and finished 1 1/2 lengths ahead of the pack.

The close followers of racing had tracked Secretariat, but he was still unknown to the public before the Sanford Stakes. Appropriately, the 1972 Sanford brought Secretariat into the spotlight. He did well, ate well, filled out, and worked better all the time. Three days before the Sanford, he worked 5/8 of a mile in 0:59, his second fastest time to date.

The race itself was a different story. On Wednesday, August 16, 1972, Secretariat ran in the Sanford. He broke well, but Turcotte noted that Secretariat did not quite have it at the start. He was in last place at the quarter-mile mark, blocked by two other horses. Secretariat and Turcotte bided their time and waited for a hole to open up. It looked edgy for a few seconds, but then a hole opened up. Turcotte turned him loose. Secretariat just accelerated past the leaders to win by three lengths.

"Secretariat exploded, driving through whatever room there was," William Nack wrote later. In the Sanford Stakes, one of the important two-year-old races, Secretariat gave Man o'War his only defeat.

It was a great race and Secretariat showed a running style typical of older, far more experienced horses. He could run, all right, and he wasn't afraid to take a chance.

Secretariat stayed at Saratoga another ten days and ran in the Hopeful Stakes on the final day of the 1972 Saratoga meet. The Hopeful, along with the Sanford Stakes, the Futurity at Belmont, and the Champagne Stakes, is a major race for two-year-old horses. It was the logical next race for him.

He made the most of it in inimitable Secretariat fashion. Nine horses were entered, and as in the Sanford, Secretariat broke from the gate poorly. Somehow, he had trouble with the Saratoga track. It made a difference: he fell back to last place in the first quarter-mile. Turcotte wasn't nervous; he knew Secretariat was still green. But as the turn came closer, Turcotte became alarmed. He needn't have worried; the horse got it together, pulled at the bit, and took off. His jockey swung him to the outside.

Now he had room to race and it was all over. Secretariat moved on his own accord, knowing exactly what to do. With magnificent strides, Secretariat passed all the other horses in 110 yards and took the lead by a head. He stretched it to three lengths going under the wire and timed only 3/5 of a second off the track record.

Turcotte remembers he was far more powerful than any other two-year-old that he rode. The observers were incredulous; two-year-olds just didn't run like that. What was he? What had hit racing? They were finding out.

Secretariat kept going. The 6 1/2-furlong Futurity at Belmont Park was next, on September 16, 1972. He was the favorite at $0.20 to $1.00. Now he developed a pattern: break, drop back, and close strongly. He followed it in this race too. Turcotte let him drop back to sixth place for the first quarter-mile. At the half-mile pole, Secretariat took off and went into the lead. Turcotte thought he was loafing some, and the jockey chirped to his horse. Secretariat quit looking around, buckled down, got back in business, and won by 1 1/2 lengths in time of 1:16-2/5.

Secretariat had now won the Sanford Stakes, the Hopeful Stakes, and the Belmont Futurity: three of the most important two-year-old races. The Champagne Stakes, the centerpiece of two-year-old racing, came next on October 14, 1972 at Belmont Park. It was a typical Secretariat race: far back for the first part of it, then a dash around the other horses to win. But on the far turn, things went awry. One horse, Linda's Chief, started to drift out. Then another horse, Step Nicely, pushed Linda's Chief into Secretariat. Turcotte gathered his horse up, but then more disaster struck. Yet *another* horse, Stop the Music, bumped into Secretariat, but Secretariat's head was oriented in such a way that it looked as if *he* was heading into Stop the Music. Finally, they untangled and Secretariat went on to win by two lengths.

The race stewards immediately looked into the race; Stop the Music's jockey lodged his own objection. The way Secretariat was faced when Stop the Music hit him made the difference. The objection was sustained and Secretariat was disqualified. Stop the Music was named the winner. To this day, Turcotte refers to the race as the "Shamepagne Stakes."

Secretariat ran two more races that year: the Laurel Futurity at Laurel Track near Baltimore on October 28, and the Garden State Stakes at Garden State Park in New Jersey on November 18. Secretariat won both of them, and each race had its own story. For the Laurel Futurity, the story lay in the layout of the track hardware. Laurel had at that time *two* finish lines: the regular finish line, which was also the starting point for one-mile races, and an auxiliary line 1/16 of a mile farther down for longer races, such as the Laurel Futurity. Turcotte let Secretariat run his normal race: lay back for most of the race, then execute a blazing dash to take the lead. But when Secretariat and Turcotte got past the usual wire, the horse noticed it and thought he had won. The finish was still 1/16 of a mile off. Secretariat kept running and widened his margin to win by eight lengths.

Question: "And Garden State, do you remember that?"

Answer: "Oh, yeah, that's probably the worst race I ever rode in my life. I was probably much too overconfident with that horse, the way he was doing things."

— Ron Turcotte, 1997,
on the 1973 Garden State Stakes.

Even the best can get cocky and make a mistake sometimes. Turcotte let Secretariat break quickly in the Garden State Stakes. The jockey took hold of Secretariat and let him drop far back out of contention. The lead horses were far ahead of Secretariat, about ten lengths through the first half-mile.

Turcotte noticed that one horse, Impecunious, tried to get outside. He moved Secretariat a little earlier than he had wanted so Secretariat would not be carried to the outside. As he did so, Impecunious lightly brushed Secretariat. But the room to maneuver put Secretariat in command. He charged by the other horses. They got to the quarter pole, where Turcotte's brother Rudy was riding Angle Light, the lead horse. Galloping at forty miles per hour, Turcotte said to Rudy, "How you making out, Bro?" Rudy replied appropriately and there was a brief exchange of pleasantries. Then Turcotte said to his brother, "Goodbye, I'm gone." (Turcotte explained, "We have conversations throughout the race, unless we don't like the jockey next to us, and then we don't talk to each other.") Secretariat just galloped to win by 3 1/2 lengths. Afterwards, Laurin complimented Turcotte on the race. The jockey, remembering how casually he had taken the early part of the race, said, "Mr. Laurin, that's the worst ride I ever gave a horse in my life." A victory covers a multitude of errors.

The major two-year-old races were over. Why keep him racing? Secretariat had the two-year-champion title locked up. There were the great races on the horizon: the Wood Memorial, the Triple Crown, the Arlington Classic, the Saratoga meet in the summer, why risk anything more? It was time to call it a year.

There it was: nine races, seven wins, one win which was disqualified, one fourth place. Secretariat was named "Horse of the Year" for 1972. He was the first two-year-old horse so honored.

Since the development of racing in Florida and California, the common way to prepare horses for the Triple Crown has been to race them in one of those warm-weather states, then send them into Triple Crown country. That involves the risk of shipping horses first to Florida or California, then to Kentucky, Maryland or New York. Penny Tweedy had shipped Riva Ridge to California in 1972, and some felt that hurt him. Laurin prepared to ship Secretariat for the Flamingo Stakes at Hialeah with some trepidation. The death of C.T. Chenery altered all the plans.

Secretariat was still working well, but now there was a *lot* of pressure for offspring. Penny Tweedy put together a financing group over the winter and syndicated Secretariat's breeding rights for *$6 million,* the record to date. He was to race only until November 15, 1973, then be sent to the stud barn. C.T. Chenery had died during the winter of 1972-73, and Mrs. Tweedy needed money to pay estate taxes. Moreover, the press comparisons between Secretariat and past champions: Man o'War, Gallant Fox, and Citation, among others came hot and heavy, driving up the value of the breeding rights. (Such focus was high praise for a horse that had run only nine races in his career.) It was heavy stuff, indeed, for the people involved with Secretariat.

The horse himself was unconcerned with such matters. He was the nicest of Thoroughbreds; friendly, playful, and gentle. He was ready for what was coming; looking back, he must have known it.

Turcotte said he had "such a good nature." Well, the horse *was* big-hearted, figuratively and literally. At his death in 1989, his necropsy revealed a startling fact: Secretariat's heart was twice as big as a normal race horse's heart. His heart was not abnormally enlarged; its chambers and valves were normal. It was just twice the size of a normal horse's heart. That may explain in part the results to come, and particularly, the outcome of the eighth race at Belmont Park on June 9, 1973.

In light of everything that was going on, Laurin decided on a less-common New York route to the Triple Crown: first the Bay Shore and Gotham Stakes at Aqueduct, then the classic Wood Memorial at Aqueduct, then the Kentucky Derby. It was an uncommon route to Churchill Downs, but then, this was an uncommon horse. And the world was about to find out just *how* uncommon he was.

The Bay Shore Stakes on March 17, 1973, was a seven-furlong race worth $27,750. The track was sloppy, and Secretariat fell back as usual at the start. He bided his time until Turcotte saw a hole develop so big that he "...could have drove [sic] a Mack truck through it." Turcotte steered Secretariat through and the hole closed up. Secretariat got bumped by the two horses. The other two horses "Just ricocheted" off Secretariat and he went on to win by 4 1/2 lengths. A jockey lodged an objection but it was disallowed. Mike Venezia, one of the losing jockeys, said later, "My horse ran a good race but the winner was much the best."

Three weeks later at the Gotham Stakes Secretariat showed again how powerful he was. The Gotham was a one-mile race worth $55,550. Turcotte tried something new with his horse. They had always come from behind. Now, Turcotte wanted to see what would happen if they took the lead early. Lucien Laurin never gave Turcotte orders; "He always told me to ride the race as I see fit," the jockey remembered. It was something to try out for the bigger races to come....

Secretariat broke well and was third by the quarter-mile. Then Turcotte "just picked his head up. All you had to do with this horse was just pick his head up." Secretariat responded quickly; he went right to the lead and stayed there. Halfway through the stretch, the horse gawked a bit, as if, in his jockey's words, he was saying, "Hey, what am I doing in the lead here so long?" Then another horse, Champagne Charlie, came up close to him. Turcotte tapped Secretariat with the whip — a rare occurrence. The horse took off again. Secretariat finished three lengths ahead of Champagne Charlie. Their time of 1:33 2/5 tied the track record for the mile. Turcotte's experiment had paid off handsomely.

With due respect to the Blue Grass Stakes at Keeneland, the Wood Memorial at Aqueduct was at that time the premier preparatory race for the

Triple Crown. As we have seen, Gallant Fox, Count Fleet, and Assault won the Wood Memorial. Omaha was defeated in it. Secretariat went into the Wood the clear favorite. He was paired with Angle Light (also trained by Lucien Laurin but owned by another stable) at odds of $0.30 to $1. But something happened on April 21, 1973.

Secretariat came out of pole position six and broke reasonably well. As was his custom, he stayed back for most of the race. In the stretch, he passed other horses, but never seriously challenged. He finished a bad third behind Angle Light and Sham. Turcotte said afterwards, "He just didn't have his punch today."

What had happened? The recriminations started. Mrs. Tweedy accused Laurin of setting up Secretariat in favor of Angle Light. Turcotte kept replaying the race in his mind. One thing stuck out, but Turcotte couldn't identify the cause: Throughout the race, every time Turcotte pulled on the reins, Secretariat threw his head back and didn't respond. That was the clue.

Secretariat had developed an abscess in his mouth, most likely due to a sticker in his feed. A New York Racing Association veterinarian had discovered it on the morning of the Wood Memorial. The veterinarian told Laurin and Eddie Sweat (Secretariat's groom) and instructed them to keep monitoring it and see what happened.

But incredibly, *neither Laurin nor Sweat told Turcotte or Mrs. Tweedy about the abscess.* Every time Turcotte went to the bit in the Wood Memorial, he pulled it right over the abscess. Secretariat naturally objected by throwing his head in the air. The horse felt poorly anyhow, and the race just made it worse. Why hadn't the jockey been told of the problem? "It was one of those things you don't advertise," the veterinarian said later.

"Put one finger at the side of one's mouth and the thumb on the other side and pull back," Turcotte said years later, describing what the effect of a bit in a horse's mouth would be like for a human. It was a pretty clear description.

Wait a minute. Secrecy has its place, indeed, but if any two people *should* have been told about the abscess, they were Ron Turcotte and Penny Tweedy. And more incredibly, they still hadn't been told *after* the race.[1] Now Mrs. Tweedy, Turcotte, and Laurin had a strategy conference. Six million dollars in syndication money depended on Secretariat. The question was: should he run in the Kentucky Derby? Fortunately for horse racing, the answer was affirmative. Turcotte said later: "I was confident he could outrun a horse going a mile, any horse going a mile, and all I had to do was gallop him the first quarter of a mile and let him take his time."

Meadow Stable sent Secretariat to Louisville for the Derby, abscess and all. The abscess hadn't come to a head and a veterinarian was going to lance it if

---

[1] There was one *good* thing about the defeat in the Wood Memorial: it took some of the pressure off Mrs. Tweedy, Laurin, Turcotte, and Secretariat.

it didn't break on its own. One night, Sweat looked in on Big Red. The horse was listless, and worst of all, hadn't enjoyed his dinner — a *very* bad sign for him.

But worst was over. "The next morning I goes *[sic]* out there to give him his breakfast like four o'clock, and I could see all this stuff was splattered on the wall, and he was feeling good and yelling for his food and all of that. He was tearing his stall down. He wanted to eat. [*Author's comment:* Secretariat was himself again.] He felt *so* good. He was all right after that. He was trying to tell me, 'I feel pretty good.' So I give *[sic]* him the amount of food he was supposed to have and he ate it up," Sweat remembered.

Now he was on the road to recovery, but he still had a sore mouth. Unbelievably, *no one had yet told Turcotte of the abscess.* He worked Secretariat the day after the abscess broke; the horse again threw his head back. (Naturally, the abscess hadn't completely healed.) Turcotte was bothered, and just couldn't figure out what was going on. His confidence in Secretariat was shaken, and he flew back to New York to ride after the workout in Kentucky.

One day at Aqueduct, NYRA veterinarian Manuel Gilman mentioned Secretariat's abscess to Turcotte, and it all came together: the listless Wood Memorial, the dull workouts later, throwing his head back. "Had I known this before the race, we still would have won [the Wood Memorial]," Turcotte said later. Now fully informed, the jockey returned to Louisville for the 1973 Kentucky Derby.

> *"Getting back to the Wood, he [Secretariat] knew when he was beaten. And he sulked in the corner...And after the race, he just turned his tail on us, and said, 'you know, bummer.' And I think he just figured he wasn't going to do that again."*
> — Penny Tweedy, 1998, on Secretariat
> after the 1973 Wood Memorial

> *"...he [writer Bill Nack] came down to the Jockeys' Room, and he says, 'Well, what do you think, Ronnie?' I say, "Well, Bill, it's practically in the book.' And he says, 'Ronnie, I'm afraid to tell you this.' He said, 'I don't think you can win.' I said 'Well, Bill...I'll see you in the winner's circle.' That's how confident I was."*
> — Ron Turcotte, 1997,
> on his prospects for the 1973 Kentucky Derby

Secretariat was the favorite in the Derby at odds of 3 to 2. He broke from pole position ten on a fast track. As the field of thirteen horses broke out of the gate, Secretariat dropped back into last place. Then Turcotte swung Secretariat to the outside. The move eliminated all other horses in this race and the next one. They passed the pack quickly; at the half-mile they were sixth; at the 3/4, fifth; at the mile, second.

A horse named Sham, ridden by Laffit Pincay, Jr., was in the lead. Secretariat pulled even at the top of the stretch. Pincay saw the challenge and lashed Sham. Turcotte lashed Secretariat, one of the very few times that was ever required. Sham and Secretariat stayed even for a hundred yards. Then Secretariat drew away as Turcotte switched the whip to his left hand, flashing it slightly. When it was all over, Secretariat had won by 2 1/2 lengths and set both a Derby and a track record time of 1:59 2/5.

How he broke the record was even more impressive: he ran the first quarter-mile in 25 1/5 seconds. Startling enough, but it didn't stop there: he ran the second quarter-mile in 24 seconds, the third quarter-mile in 23 2/5, the last quarter-mile in *23 seconds flat*. Instead of tiring through the race, he ran faster.

> *"The horse told me it was time...It was a slow pace and I asked him,*
> *'Do you want to go,' and he said, 'Yeah, let's go,' so we did."*
> — Ron Turcotte on Secretariat
> in the 1973 Preakness,
> *Baltimore Sun*, May 20, 1973.

Secretariat worked out steadily over the two week interval before Pimlico and the Preakness on May 19, 1973. He acted as if he couldn't run enough. He was as ready for the Preakness as he was ever going to be, and was touted again as the favorite.

At the start of the Preakness Stakes, Secretariat was last out of the gate and trailed into the clubhouse turn. Turcotte looked ahead and detected trouble: the horses were bunching up. The jockey thought, "There's something cooking up ahead." Turcotte nudged the right rein very slightly; Secretariat took a slight leap and then went to full-speed around the first turn. The tighter turns at Pimlico have often spelled doom for horses going too fast around them; not so with Secretariat. Turcotte pulled Secretariat once again to the outside of the pack, into the middle of the track. Secretariat was moving in first gear, but because he was on the outside coming in, the centripetal force put him *into* the turn, not causing him to bear out. With his great chestnut neck pumping up and down like an oil rig, Secretariat broke out and drew ahead. By the backstretch, he was racing to the lead. Then, in the words of William Nack, (It is too rich a phrase to pass up.) "Turcotte hit the cruise control." Secretariat took the lead on the backstretch and never gave it up. Sham rallied in vain to catch up, but (Turcotte remembered) he "had all kinds of horse left under me. So I just galloped through the lane. I never really asked him to run." Secretariat cruised home and crossed the wire ahead by 2 1/2 lengths. The official time was eventually fixed at 1:54 2/5.[2]

---

[2] This is the only controversial part of Secretariat's Triple Crown. The official race clock somehow malfunctioned, and gave the time at 1:55, a second slower than

In the interval between the Preakness and Belmont Stakes, Secretariat became a national hero. Not since Man o'War had one horse received so much attention. He appeared on the cover of *Sports Illustrated*. In that same week, he also was the cover story for both *Time* and *Newsweek*. It was virtually impossible to go anywhere and not see the chestnut horse with the blue and white silks. Secretariat was one of the bright spots in the difficult year of 1973.

> *"But going into the race, going to the paddock and that, a lot of people of people were sticking mikes in my face and saying, 'Ronnie, are you nervous? Are you nervous? And I would say, 'No, I'm not nervous.' You know, I actually was nervous. If I wasn't nervous, I wouldn't have been human."*
> — Ron Turcotte, 1997,
> remembering the 1973 Belmont Stakes

> *"I couldn't go anywhere or I couldn't live just a normal life because, by that time, I was recognizable, and everybody wanted to know about the horse or wish me luck. And the phone was constantly ringing for interviews. And one woman showed up at my house before I had breakfast. And it was just kind of wild."*
> — Penny Tweedy, 1998,
> recalling the days before the 1973 Belmont Stakes

The pressure on the Secretariat team was immense, far greater than any previous Triple Crown team. It had been *so* long since Citation; it was *such* a bad time for the country. But Turcotte, Laurin, and Mrs. Tweedy handled it well, for they knew the mettle of the horse they had. A few days before the Belmont Stakes, Turcotte and Laurin were having dinner. They had had a few drinks, and Turcotte had never been much of a drinker. But it wasn't false bravado: they both felt, justifiably, that their horse was the greatest "that had ever looked through a bridle." Over the food, Turcotte said to Laurin: "If this horse don't win, I'll hang up my tack." Laurin replied: "Ronnie, if you don't

---

Canonero II's record time two years earlier. However, the *Daily Racing Form* had Secretariat running at 1:53 2/5, faster than the record time. Two other clockers reported Secretariat's Preakness time at 1:53 2/5 and 1:53 3/5. After a hearing, the time was fixed at 1:54 2/5, faster than the official clock, still slower than the record. Secretariat has to be content with an unofficial time record in the Preakness. Were the *Daily Racing Form* time official, Secretariat would hold the Preakness record, just as he holds the records in the Kentucky Derby and Belmont Stakes, although he would have to share it with Tank's Prospect, who ran the 1985 Preakness in official time of 1:53 2/5 and Louis Quatorze, who tied that mark in the 1996 Preakness.

win this race. I'm going to put away my condition book."

About 4:00 A.M. on the day of the Belmont Stakes, writer William Nack went out to Belmont Park to see Secretariat. Things were starting to move around the backside of the track in preparation for that day's races. An hour later, a handler led Secretariat out of his stall. Someone rattled a bucket: Secretariat reared up on his hind legs, turned a circle, and clawed the air in front of him with his forelegs. Then he put all four legs on the earth and proceeded to run around his paddock, bucking and kicking at no one in particular. Nack thought Big Red was keyed up. Perhaps. Or, perhaps the rattle was the signal for him to show the world what he could do later that day and he was just impatient to proceed.

SECRETARIAT with Ron Turcotte up. © *Collection of L.S. Sutcliffe, C. Ken Grayson, owner. Used by permission.*

"He ran because he felt good and he wanted to. He was out in front and things were going well and he was just in his groove, and I think he could have kept going. He was just having a fine time."
— Penny Tweedy, 1998,
remembering Secretariat in the 1973 Belmont

The single greatest horse race of all time occurred on the hot, humid Saturday of June 9, 1973 at the 1973 Belmont Stakes at Belmont Park. Secretariat was again the favorite. Before pole time the final odds shifted dramatically. Secretariat was rated at the incredible rock-bottom odds of 1 to 10. Secretariat went into the gate at the pole position, with Sham in second. They broke cleanly enough. Secretariat stayed with the pack, but Turcotte noted earlier that day that Sham had warmed up "pretty good." Was Sham to go out early for the lead? Turcotte had to make a decision; if he dropped back too far, Secretariat might never catch up. Sham "…was a horse to be reckoned with." An opening appeared and Turcotte remembered, "I just picked up his head and let him ease through that hole in the rail there, which I had room for, and he just took off." Mrs. Tweedy recalled, "But a horse like Secretariat, you can't really place him. You can tell him if it's time to go, but you can't make him do something that he hadn't already figured out that he was going to do."

Incredibly, it turned into a match race between the two: Turcotte allowed Sham to have a little lead, but Secretariat had other ideas. He stayed close to his challenger, and it was a head in front, then a head behind down the backstretch. Secretariat had run to the three-quarter pole in 1:09 4/5, the fastest time in Belmont history. Sham and Secretariat began the far turn and Secretariat took a length lead. Then Turcotte noticed something: His horse was breathing easily. Secretariat was breathing smoothly, steadily, as smooth and steady as his stride.

Now think about that: Secretariat had run the Bay Shore, the Gotham, the Wood Memorial, the Kentucky Derby, the Preakness, all the workouts in between, and now a record 3/4 of a mile on a hot, humid day, *and he wasn't breathing heavily*. It was *nice, normal breathing with no straining*. Turcotte couldn't see the use in holding him back and cutting his stride down. The jockey figured, well, why fight him? Let him do what he wants to do. So Turcotte let him go and IT happened.

Let Chic Anderson, who was at the Belmont microphone that day, once again call the rest of the race:

"…for the turn, it's Secretariat. It looks like he's opening. The lead is increasing — make it three, three-and-a-half. He's moving into the turn. Secretariat holding onto a large lead. Sham is second and then it's a long way back for My Gallant and Twice A Prince. They're on the turn and Secretariat is BLAZING along. The first three-quarters of a mile in 1:09 4/5. Secretariat is WIDENING now. He is moving LIKE A TREMENDOUS MACHINE. SECRETARIAT BY TWELVE, Secretariat by fourteen lengths on the turn. Sham is dropping back. It looks like they'll catch him today. But My Gallant and Twice A Prince are both

coming up to him now. But Secretariat is ALL ALONE; he's out there almost a sixteenth of a mile from the rest of the horses.

(Turcotte and Secretariat were so far in front that the jockey couldn't hear any hoof beats to the rear. His curiosity got to him, and he looked back to see what was behind him. There was nothing.)

> *"...Secretariat is in a position that is impossible to catch. He's into the stretch. Secretariat leads this field by eighteen lengths. And now Twice A Prince has taken second and My Gallant has moved back into third.*

(Turcotte knew he had it won, and it was no time to make a mistake. He tightened up on the rein to keep Secretariat's mind on the race.)

> *"...They're in the stretch. Secretariat has opened a TWENTY-TWO-LENGTH LEAD. HE IS GOING TO BE THE TRIPLE CROWN WINNER..."*

In the homestretch, Turcotte uttered the most unintentionally hilarious statement in Thoroughbred racing, and perhaps, in all sports history. "Pal," Turcotte said to Secretariat, who was then some twenty-plus lengths ahead of the rest of the pack, "Just don't fall down now."

Secretariat won the Belmont by thirty-one lengths in 2:24 flat to set both a length and a time record. It had been twenty-four years, eleven months, and twenty-eight days since Eddie Arcaro had seen a blanket of white flowers drape Citation. In winning the Triple Crown, Secretariat set two official time records and an unofficial one. He broke Count Fleet's length record in the Belmont. If there is such a thing as total victory in horse racing, Secretariat had achieved it.[3]

> *"...we really witnessed the performance of a very gifted and very intelligent and joyous horse."*
> — Penny Tweedy, 1998,
> on Secretariat in the 1973 Belmont Stakes

Like Gallant Fox, Omaha, Whirlaway, Assault, and Citation before him, Secretariat went to Arlington Park in Chicago for the Arlington Invitational on June 30. Meadow Stable discussed that move; it was only three weeks after the

---

[3] Secretariat set one unofficial record in the 1973 Belmont. As Ron Turcotte pulled him up over the next 1/8-mile, Secretariat's overall time for the race and the pull-up would have been a record for a 1 5/8-mile race.

231

Belmont Stakes and there would be the trip from Belmont Park to Chicago. But Secretariat had raced almost exclusively in New York. The Kentucky Derby was the farthest-west race that had he had run, and it was time that others saw him. After a few light workouts Secretariat and Turcotte traveled to Chicago.

At Arlington Secretariat broke awkwardly from the starting gate. He slammed it as he left, but he recovered quickly and took the lead in the first quarter-mile. The track was bad, and Turcotte kept him in the middle of it. He ran the first mile of the 1 1/8-mile race in 1:35, and cruised home nine lengths ahead of the other three horses. Despite the awkward start and the bad track, nothing seemed to faze him. He finished only 1/5 of a second off the track record. Like most of his Triple Crown predecessors who ran at Arlington, he was successful. It seemed he could do nothing wrong.

He rested for a month, and Meadow Stable took him to the Saratoga races in August. He ran in the Whitney Stakes at Saratoga on August 4, 1973.

Since Gallant Fox's loss to Jim Dandy in the 1930 Travers, Saratoga had acquired the reputation of being a stronghold of horse racing upsets. Allen Jerkens, a fine trainer, had a horse called Onion ready and waiting for Secretariat in the Whitney Stakes. Onion had set a track record for 6 1/2 furlongs just four days earlier, and he was certainly a contender. But then again, he was up against Secretariat...

The Triple Crown winner and National Hero looked good until the day before the Whitney Stakes. Turcotte had worked him very well the previous week (1 1/8 mile at 1:47 4/5) without pushing him. That time would have been a track record had it been run in a race. But the day before the Whitney, Turcotte worked him again and Secretariat ran an unimpressive half-mile in 48 1/5 seconds. Perhaps Secretariat had worked *too* hard the week before.

In the Whitney Stakes, he didn't break well. He banged his head against the stall doors as he left, and Turcotte kept him back. Onion jumped to an early lead. In the backstretch, Turcotte let him go and he moved up. In the stretch, Turcotte took him to the inside and they battled Onion. But this time, the Triple Crown winner didn't have it; Onion crossed the finish line first, a full length ahead of Secretariat.

The jockey was upset, naturally. Had he pushed Secretariat too hard for too long? The explanation arrived that same evening; Secretariat had a viral infection and fever. Illness, not fatigue, was Secretariat's enemy in the Whitney Stakes.

The virus immediately canceled further plans to race Secretariat at Saratoga. The Marlboro Cup, sponsored by the cigarette company, was only six weeks off, at Belmont Park on September 15. Both of Meadow Stable's great horses, Riva Ridge and Secretariat, were entered in it. Of course, everyone hoped to see Secretariat run. But could he recuperate in time? Could Laurin get him ready for the Marlboro Cup?

The Whitney Stakes loss took some of the luster off Secretariat. No matter how understandable, he *had* lost a major race. The Marlboro Cup field was strong; besides Riva Ridge and Secretariat, Onion was entered. Key to the Mint, a horse that beat Riva Ridge for best three-year-old the year before, would also race. The 1973 Travers Stakes winner, Annihilate 'Em, was also entered, as were two powerful horses trained by Charlie Wittingham: Cougar II and Kennedy Road. It was a tough race; as tough as any in racing history.

Incredibly, there were still some doubters. In a copy of a tout sheet for the 1973 Marlboro Cup, Key to the Mint is picked to win it, with the notation, "Likes Soft Turf." Secretariat is picked second, with the laconic phrase, "Well Regarded."

The Meadow Stable crew faced hopelessly divided loyalties. Who should they cheer for; their own Riva Ridge, a horse that had won the Kentucky Derby and Belmont Stakes, or their own Secretariat?

Lucien Laurin had both Riva Ridge and Secretariat ready for the Marlboro Cup. Turcotte rode Secretariat, while Eddie Maple rode Riva Ridge. Both horses broke well, and Riva Ridge went into second place early, while again, Secretariat stayed back. After the half-mile, Turcotte took him again to the outside and he passed the other horses. By the 3/4-mile, Riva Ridge had taken over first place. Secretariat had fallen to third, but was moving steadily. With 3/16 of a mile to go, Secretariat passed his stable mate. Eddie Maple recalled, "When we turned for home, Riva was all out. I saw a big red head and body coming right at me. There was nothing I could do. Secretariat went by in about three steps. He just swallowed me."

Turcotte pushed his horse and he drew away to win the 1 1/8-mile race by 3 1/2 lengths. Moreover, Secretariat set a new world's record: 1:45 2/5. Riva Ridge finished second. Turcotte crowed, "I could have asked my horse for more, but I didn't want to knock him out. I wanted the record, and I knew we had it without trying any harder." (Secretariat avenged his loss in the Whitney Stakes; Onion finished fourth. The tout's pick, Key to the Mint, finished last.)

Meadow Stable thought strategically: it was time to try Secretariat on grass, and the Man o'War Stakes at Belmont Park on October 6 (three weeks off) was the place to do it. Laurin and Turcotte decided to concentrate on that race, and focused their efforts on training Secretariat for the turf.

But Penny Tweedy had her own idea: she wanted one of her horses, Riva Ridge or Secretariat, to run in the 1 1/2-mile Woodward Stakes at Belmont on September 29. She decided against running both of them in the same race. She considered both horses. If the track was fast, she would enter Riva Ridge and scratch Secretariat. If the track was muddy, Secretariat would run and Riva would be scratched.

It rained, and Riva Ridge was scratched. Turcotte recalled that the entry in the Woodward Stakes had thrown off the plans. They were training him for the grass in the Man o'War, and Secretariat had not been properly trained for the Woodward. Still, it was a good race. Secretariat stayed close to the lead and took over at the mile. In the stretch, Prove Out, trained by Allen Jerkens, came on strong at the end and caught Secretariat. Prove Out drew away to win by 4 1/2 lengths. The loss was inexplicable to the racing community, but Turcotte understood. "We just didn't train him at all for the Woodward."

"...after the Man o'War, I said, 'Mr. Laurin, as great as this horse is, I know a lot of people say I'm crazy. As great as this horse is on the dirt, he is at the minimum ten to fifteen lengths a better horse on the grass."
— Ron Turcotte, 1997,
recalling the 1973 Man o'War Stakes.

It's hard to believe Turcotte's statement. Grass racing is not for every horse: some do well on grass, others perform better on dirt. Secretariat would run only once in an all-grass race, but the result seems to bear out Turcotte's statement. On October 8, 1973, at the Man o'War Stakes at Belmont Park, Turcotte let him go to the lead early, in the first quarter-mile. Secretariat never let it go, and finished five lengths ahead of the pack. His time for the 1 1/2-mile race was 2:24 4/5 to set a new track record.

Secretariat's last race was on Sunday, October 28, 1973, at the Woodbine track in Toronto, Ontario, Canada. He had been invited to run in the Canadian International Championship (later renamed the Rothman's International Championship.) The track was almost all turf with one small part dirt. It was tailor-made for Secretariat. But, ironically, Turcotte was unable to ride Big Red in his only appearance on the track where his jockey career had started out. Turcotte had been suspended for five days for a riding infraction, and the suspension term coincided with the Canadian International. Eddie Maple, a fine jockey, was given perhaps the most unenviable task of any jockey in racing history; riding Secretariat in his last race.

Turcotte, present as an ABC-TV sports commentator, recalled that Maple "was very, very nervous." Who wouldn't be? Here was possibly the greatest horse of all time, in his last race. Maple had never ridden him before, and on top of that the track was a quagmire from a week of rain in Toronto. Moreover, Maple rode Riva Ridge on an off-track in the Jockey Club Gold Cup and had been beaten. So Turcotte gave some advice: "Just ride him. Just let him run on his own the first part, but when you pick up his head, he'll be taking off with you. Just hold him together so he doesn't bobble, you know, in that deep going, so he doesn't fall down...just let him gallop as long as you want, and then when you pick him up, don't worry. He'll be going all the way." Maple did just what Turcotte told him to do.

The late October afternoon in Toronto was chilly, damp, foggy, and overcast. The horses broke well enough, but Secretariat and Kennedy Road bumped into each other after about a half-mile. Maple steadied Secretariat and let the horse go. Secretariat opened up a twelve-length lead, but then cut back a bit. The films of the race show Secretariat, far in front, pounding for the wire, puffing steam from his nose. He resembled nothing so much as a fire-breathing dragon. He won by 6 1/2 lengths.

Secretariat won the Triple Crown and established two official records in the process. He set a world record and a track record. He was named best three-year-old, best dirt horse, and based upon the Man o'War Stakes, best grass horse. He was again named Horse of the Year. It was complete and total victory for Secretariat, Ron Turcotte, Lucien Laurin, Penny Tweedy, and Eddie Sweat. It is unlikely that we shall ever see such total domination of racing again.

A few days later on November 6, Secretariat appeared at Aqueduct for a "Farewell to Secretariat Day." Turcotte paraded the champion up and down the track before the spectators. Penny Tweedy thought that Secretariat looked puzzled: He looked like he wanted to run another race. Secretariat was draped with a special farewell blanket donated by the NYRA. Before the crowd Turcotte dismounted Secretariat for the last time.

> *"Oh, the worst day of my life."*
> — Penny Tweedy, 1998,
> remembering November 11, 1973

On November 11, Secretariat was flown from New York to Lexington. Claiborne Farm handlers would be waiting to take the champion to Paris, Kentucky, for his career as a sire. The mood aboard the flight was inexpressibly sad; Mrs. Tweedy could not believe how hard it was to say goodbye to him. Upon landing, the Claiborne handlers took Secretariat away to start his new life.

But a few hours earlier, at Belmont Park, there was a gentle, peaceful end to two great partnerships. While Turcotte watched, Riva Ridge and Secretariat were led into a horse van destined for the airport and the flight to Kentucky. Turcotte followed Riva Ridge and Secretariat into the van. First he said goodbye to his pal, his first Kentucky Derby winner, Riva Ridge.[4] Then he took Secretariat's halter strap and looked at him. The Triple Crown jockey kissed the Triple Crown horse on the nose, and quietly said: "Goodbye, old friend."

---

[4] In retirement, Riva Ridge occupied the stall next to Secretariat at Claiborne Farm. He died in 1985. Riva Ridge was elected to membership in the National Museum of Racing and Hall of Fame in 1998, an overdue tribute to a fine horse unfortunately overshadowed by one of the three greatest horses of all time.

235

Turcotte raced for a few more years, but on July 13, 1978, in a race at Belmont Park, his mount, Flag of Leyte Gulf, went down. Flag of Leyte Gulf had clipped heels with another horse that veered out in front of him, and Turcotte went down along with his horse. Turcotte was paralyzed from the waist down; He remains confined to a wheelchair, and in constant pain.[5]

He was elected to the National Racing Museum and Hall of Fame in 1979.

His spirit, despite the obstacles, remains indomitable: in 1989-90, he finished his high school work and got a diploma by going to a school and attending class with people thirty years younger than he. He still hunts on occasion and regularly goes into town to a local donut shop for coffee and conversation. He remains a gentleman, willing to talk and reminisce about his riding days to those who call on him. He keeps up faithfully with racing by attending an off-track betting parlor near his home, where he watches the races and places an occasional bet.

Always there is the memory of Secretariat. Turcotte recalled, "Nobody had seen the true Secretariat, because his actions changed there. His last four races, his actions changed immeasurably, you know. It was like he had put everything all together. He wasn't heavy-handed any more...He was just like a cannon shot." And, in eerie words exactly like those said of a long-ago champion, Turcotte said of Secretariat, in his full *Nouveau*-Brunswick accent: "He was the most horse."

Lucien Laurin stayed with Meadow Stable for three years after Secretariat's retirement, when he and Mrs. Tweedy parted amicably. Laurin was elected to the National Museum of Racing and Hall of Fame in 1977. During 1976-1990, he retired and un-retired several times. His last stakes-winning horse ran in 1985. He had his last victory in 1989 and his last running horse the year after. Then he retired for good in Florida. In the late 1990s his health began to fail. On June 26, 2000, at the age of eighty-eight, Lucien Laurin died at Miami's Baptist Hospital from complications following surgery for a broken hip.

Churchill Downs's President, Alex Waldrop, issued a statement: "Lucien Laurin occupies a special place in the great history of the Kentucky Derby. His name will forever be linked with the great Secretariat, who won the 1973 Derby in a record-shattering time that stands today and went on to become a true American sports legend. His work with Riva Ridge was just as remarkable, as the two horses won five of six Triple Crown races over those two years and both were enshrined in racing's Hall of Fame. Lucien Laurin will

---

[5] Tragedy also struck Secretariat's first jockey, Paul Feliciano. He was killed in an automobile accident, in May, 1994, just before the 1994 Preakness.

he deeply missed by all who love the Kentucky Derby and Thoroughbred racing."

Perfectly true and wonderfully worded, but there was more insight in Ron Turcotte's simple statement about the Hall of Fame trainer: "I can't say enough for him...He definitely doesn't get the credit he deserves for all his achievements or where he came from."

"People ask me why Secretariat was so special. First of all, he was a ham. When he'd hear a camera click or a camera rolling, he'd just pull up and look at the photographer, or he'd try to show off. I'd just let him do his thing. He knew what was going on...Secretariat loved people. He was a kind horse and a gorgeous horse. And I guess, with the Watergate scandal, people were looking for a hero. Secretariat was their hero."
— Ron Turcotte,
quoted in Jim Bolus's *Derby Magic*,
1997.

At Claiborne Farm, Secretariat's personality came out. During his racing career, he could be playful at times; writer William Nack recalled one time when Secretariat stole a reporter's notebook, and another when Big Red took a groom's rake in his mouth and started to rake the hay in his stall. But Mrs. Tweedy also remembered "...quiet times when I'd go to his stall with an apple or something. He was not a cozy horse. I mean you could easily lose a finger. But he was a character. He was playful and loved attention." In retirement, he became the most photographed Thoroughbred of all time. People stopping along the road hung over the fence surrounding Claiborne Farm just to get a snapshot of Secretariat grazing in his paddock. Thousands saw him, and he enjoyed playing the part of racing's great champion. Few people who saw Secretariat, either on the track or at Claiborne, ever forgot him.

His impact on the American people continued after his death. In the late 1990s, the United States Postal Service issued a series of stamps commemorating important subjects of the decades of the Twentieth Century. The subjects were chosen by popular vote. In 1998 the public chose Secretariat as one of the sports subjects for the 1970s stamp sheet. He was the first race horse ever honored on a postage stamp issued by the U.S. Post Office.

For many years Secretariat was like Whirlaway: a good sire, but not a great one. Then in 1986 one of his daughters, Lady's Secret, was named Horse of the Year and later elected to the National Museum of Racing and Hall of Fame. Two years later a son, Risen Star, won the 1988 Preakness and Belmont Stakes.[6] Secretariat did it all: like Man o'War, Gallant Fox, and Count Fleet,

---

[6] Risen Star won the Belmont by 14 3/4 lengths in a fittting tribute to his sire. It was enough to place fourth on the list of longest winning margins in the Belmont, behind

Secretariat sired great racehorses.

But the Greeks had a name for what came next; *nemesis,* the punishment of the hero. Now that Secretariat had indeed done it all, he would not be given a long life as were Man o'War, Gallant Fox, and Count Fleet. Secretariat's life was shortened by laminitis, a frequently fatal inflammation of the hooves. In September, 1989, Secretariat was diagnosed with it. He was treated for a month, and seemed to improve. Then, in early October, he took a turn for the worse. Further treatment was deemed hopeless, and at 11:45 A.M., October 4, 1989, Secretariat was euthanized to prevent further suffering. He is buried at Claiborne Farm, near Buckpasser, Swale, Gallant Fox, and his sire, Bold Ruler.

Many photographs were taken of Secretariat in the home stretch of the 1973 Belmont Stakes, but one is especially noteworthy. The photo was taken at rail level, and shows Secretariat in profile. Turcotte is pictured looking earnestly over his left shoulder, trying to find the rest of the pack. Secretariat is more revealed: his lips are parted. Perhaps it was due to the bit in his mouth, or the rush of air against his face and head…Or perhaps it was a grin.

Secretariat, Count Fleet, and Man o'War.

IX. THE THINKING MAN'S HORSE: SEATTLE SLEW

Triple Crown, 1977. Jockey, Jean Cruguet

Sometimes greatness comes in an unlikely package. On February 15, 1974, a filly named My Charmer gave birth to a dark brown colt at White Horse Acres at Lexington, Kentucky. The foal seemed fairly homely: the head was coarse and large, and his legs seemed longer than other newborn foals. All right, maybe the colt *did* have some good stock in him; his sire was Bold Reasoning, a grandson of Bold Ruler, Secretariat's sire, and My Charmer could trace back to Myrtle Charm, the champion two-year-old filly of 1948.[1] The wife of White Horse Acres' farm manager thought, *maybe, well maybe, this one would run in the Derby in three years' time.* But then again, who knew what would happen...?

Over the next year the dark brown colt was weaned, ran with other colts, and grew accordingly. The colt had a good disposition, but he was clumsy, like a school-age athlete too big for his age group.

On May 2, 1975, the dark brown colt, together with other colts from White Horse Acres, was evaluated for auction. The colt's head still wasn't outstanding, but he had filled out and gave the impression of strength, balance, and quickness. He looked good, and Ben Castleman, owner of White Horse Acres, decided to sell him for $15,000 or more if he could get it. The colt was auctioned off in July, 1975. Mickey and Karen Taylor, newcomers to the horse business, purchased the dark brown son of Bold Reasoning for $17,500.

Now that the Taylors had the colt, it needed a name. They sat down with

---

[1] By 1974, the bloodlines of Thoroughbreds had become highly intermingled. The dark brown colt in question not only had some of Bold Ruler in him, but also had some of Princequillo, Secretariat's maternal grandsire, in him on My Charmer's side. Also on the My Charmer side of the colt's pedigree were Alsab, Whirlaway's challenger in 1942; Jet Pilot, winner of the 1947 Kentucky Derby; and Busher, one of the great fillies of all time, who was sired by War Admiral, which in turn brings Man o'War remotely into the scene.

their partners, Dr. and Mrs. Jim Hill (a veterinarian), and they came up with a name that reflected the partnership. The Taylors came from Washington State, and Dr. Hill had grown up in south Florida in an area filled with marshy, alligator-ridden sloughs, or "slews." The quartet put together an alliterative name reflecting their respective origins, and mailed the name application off to the Jockey Club in November, 1975. In January, 1976, the Jockey Club approved the colt's name, and the dark brown colt would be forever known as Seattle Slew.

In September, 1975, even before he had been officially named Seattle Slew, the colt was taken to Andor Farm in Monkton, Maryland. He was big in size, awkward, and a notoriously big eater, almost always first to the feed tub. The colt was neither mean nor faint of heart. He loved to play with other horses, and wouldn't be bullied by or bully the others. When Paula Turner, the person assigned to break the colt, saw him for the first time, he wasn't graceful or sleek-looking by any means. His head was still large, his body was big, and his tail was absurdly short. The horse reminded her of a cartoon character named Baby Huey, giant baby duck who was simultaneously clumsy and loveable. Later, after Seattle Slew filled out and won races, the nickname changed to Hugo.

Paula Turner didn't have many horses to work with that summer of 1975, so she was able to give some extra time to Huey. She hypothesized that, due to his size, his brain needed to catch up to the rest of his body. She taught him voice commands such as "Walk" or "Whoa", then started him with a bit and saddle, and went to having him turn circles on a lunge line.

At last it was time to ride Huey. Turner got on him and started him in circles. The horse turned a few circles and then stopped dead in his tracks, refusing to budge. It was a critical moment: Paula knew that she had to make him go somehow, to understand that a human was his boss from now on. Steve Cady and Barton Silverman later wrote: "The argument lasted several minutes." Paula resorted to whacking Huey with her whip, at times, hard enough to leave welts. Finally, Paula was so tired that she "…was ready to swing, miss, and fall off." And just then the horse got the message: Huey started forward and was immediately rewarded with a pat on the neck from Paula Turner. He did everything that Paula asked him to do, but in an interesting way. He wasn't subservient or sullen, just confident. Paula remembered that she "…never really needed a stick after that."

Huey turned out to be one of the most interesting equine pupils Paula Turner had ever had: he marched though fields, he didn't walk through them. He didn't spook at dead trees, stone walls, or other things that surprise most yearlings. One evening, she called her husband, Billy Turner, who was to become Huey's trainer, and told him: "This is an unusual horse, Billy. Very determined. I can't believe how businesslike he is."

240

The breaking phase wouldn't last much longer, but before it ended, Huey, now officially Seattle Slew, was jogging more than three miles per day. It was a good, promising start. The horse was sent to Belmont Park for the next phase of his education, and the Slew had some surprises ready for everyone.

Seattle Slew's initial training has its own poignant aspect. Paula Turner had grown up in an orphanage, and she became acquainted with horses through the books written by Walter Farley; *The Black Stallion* and many of his others. In the orphanage, Paula didn't have much opportunity to ride a horse. If you wanted to ride a horse there, you had to find a broomstick or use your imagination.

Throughout her childhood, she had a recurring dream in which she was riding a big, black stallion that she had trained. "I could hear him; I could feel him with my hands if I patted him. But if I looked down to see him, it would always be the broomstick or my legs and no real horse there. But I kept having that dream over and over and over again." So it could only have been with special feeling on one day that Paula jogged the big, very dark brown stallion now named Seattle Slew back to her husband, and told him, "This is the one...This is it. This is the one you've been waiting for. This is it right here."

"He had the absolute insanity to run. You could see it in his eyes and he had a way of going, and you just knew that he was different from the rest."
— Billy Turner, Seattle Slew's trainer,
1997, on Seattle Slew

The horse was still clumsy, and his hoofs hit the track with a heavy sound. Not a few seasoned stable hands around Belmont wondered if he'd ever make it as a racer. One day in April, 1976, Billy Turner decided to try out Seattle Slew. Turner told exercise rider Mike Kennedy, "We have to get this guy started sometime. Breeze him [ride him hard] three-eighths of a mile. No big deal."

The plan was straightforward: gallop Slew for a mile and then ride him hard for the rest of the exercise. To help matters, a stable pony rode alongside Kennedy and Seattle Slew. The first mile was uneventful: Seattle Slew just galloped clumsily and lazily alongside the pony. Then Kennedy put the reins together, chirped for speed, and got the shock of his life.

"Huey just put his head in the air and opened his mouth so wide you could have thrown a baby in there. He took hold of that bit and started running away from that older horse and I thought, 'What the hell is going on here?'"

That was Kennedy's recollection a year later of the Slew's first good ride. Seattle Slew, a/k/a Baby Huey, later a/k/a Hugo, had found it. When Kennedy finally pulled up Seattle Slew, the horse turned around and started snorting and blowing hard in joy. It was a lesson to all connected with Seattle Slew: Like Count Fleet, like Citation, like Secretariat, Seattle Slew loved to run without stopping.

Billy Turner was Seattle Slew's trainer. He was thirty-six years old in 1976. He grew up around horses in southern Pennsylvania, and had been a steeplechase rider. Turner was literally a late-bloomer: he was 5'5" when he entered college, but grew another seven inches in height over the next two years. That earned him the nickname "Jockey Toolong" and spelled the end of his jockey career. He became a steeplechase trainer, and in the mid-1960s became a trainer of flat-race horses. He met his future wife Paula one summer while she was working at a racetrack where he trained horses. That meeting was propitious: Paula broke Seattle Slew to the saddle; Billy trained Seattle Slew.

Turner was meticulous and thorough in his training methods. He didn't believe in pushing Seattle Slew too quickly. Rather, he was careful, slow in preparation, bringing Seattle Slew along deliberately and not taking any unnecessary chances. Turner paid attention to every detail: for example, he wouldn't allow a hayrack in the Slew's stall. Instead, hay was simply spread on the floor of the stall for Seattle Slew to eat. A hayrack, Turner explained, was simply one more thing in a stall that a horse could mess with and be hurt by.

Turner hooked up with Slew very casually. He knew Jim Hill, and Hill sent Turner some young horses to train. One of them was Seattle Slew. After that first exercise, Turner knew what he had: he didn't push Seattle Slew for two months in order to let him to grow and become fit. But the Slew was tough and determined to run. Turner recalled, "Training this particular horse, he was different from any horse I had ever trained up to that point. He was very aggressive. All he wanted to do was get out there and do things and do a lot of it...But when we did breeze him, he was quite generous. And he always did a little bit more than we really wanted."

The Taylors and the Hills still lacked a jockey. There were plenty of them around Belmont Park: Eddie Maple (who rode Secretariat in his last race), Jorge Velasquez; Angel Cordero, or Jean Cruguet, a good French jockey who had been in the U.S. over ten years.

Seattle Slew had worked impressively at Belmont Park for several months, and still he hadn't started a race. A jockey was needed soon, but Turner and Mike Kennedy hadn't settled on one for the Slew. All the names mentioned above were discussed, but it was quickly resolved one day. Turner scheduled Eddie Maple to ride the Slew one morning at Belmont. Maple's agent appeared; Maple had another horse to ride, but he would be glad to come by a little later. The trainer turned to Jean Cruguet, who was standing nearby. Turner told Cruguet to work the Slew at three-quarters of a mile. The French immigrant had worked Seattle Slew once during the summer, so he had some experience with Turner's horse. Turner remembered that the work out was so impressive that they "...left the clockers a little bit confused, and that was that." Jean Cruguet was to ride Seattle Slew.

Jean Cruguet was born in Agen, France, on March 8, 1939. He started riding in France at a young age. He was a good athlete, but he said later, "I was pretty good in any sport, but my body forgot to grow up. I found a job riding because of my size." Cruguet spent three years in the French Army, some of it as a radioman in the agonizing War of Algerian Independence. After French Army service came a brief stint as a boxer; that didn't last too long, and Cruguet returned to riding. He came to the U.S. in 1965 and established a reputation as a good jockey. Cruguet was scheduled to ride Hoist the Flag in the 1971 Kentucky Derby, but Hoist the Flag fractured a leg in a workout before the race. Cruguet returned to France for the next two years.

His penchant for bad luck at critical times followed him across the Atlantic: in 1972, Cruguet was scheduled to ride San San in the prestigious French race, the Arc de Triomphe. Ten days prior to that race, Cruguet broke both hands in a spill. Another jockey rode San San to victory. The bad luck dogged Cruguet into Seattle Slew's career. After riding the Slew in all of his two-year-old races, (with Seattle Slew resting over the winter) Cruguet went to Florida to ride. There he suffered a shoulder separation in a spill during a race at the Calder track. Cruguet's agent kept in touch with Seattle Slew's owners and trainers, and Cruguet rode the Slew in his three-year old season as well. But it was a near thing.

Bad luck doesn't last forever; time and time again in *Down to the Wire*, we have seen how a jockey and horse fit together perfectly. Seattle Slew and Jean Cruguet were in that category. During the Slew's racing career, Steve Cady and Barton Silverman published a book on the Triple Crown winner, simply entitled, *Seattle Slew*. The book is heavily illustrated; in almost all the photos in it that show the Slew on the track, there is a curious image: Cruguet's hands are almost never seen off of the reins. No matter what Mach speed Seattle Slew is going, the French jockey is firmly in control, hunched over the Slew's withers, sighting down the horse's head and nose, hands grasping the reins. Jean Cruguet was the best jockey Bill Turner could have found for Seattle Slew.

> *"You could do anything you wanted to do with Seattle Slew. Anytime, anything. Yes, he had great speed. Yes, he had great courage, a very brave horse. He also had great stamina. But he was able to do whatever you wanted, and that's why he was the best from the start."*
> — Jean Cruguet,
> *quoted in the New York Times,*
> June 1, 1997

Now that they had the horse, the jockey, and the trainer, only one more thing was needed: a race. Most two-year-olds start in June. Not Seattle Slew; his clumsiness, coupled with Turner's careful training, kept him from running in

243

June, 1976. Turner planned for him to start at Saratoga that July, but the Slew injured a leg in his stall. The injury put everything off for a time. He didn't start until September, 1976.

On September 20, Seattle Slew with Jean Cruguet up made his racing debut. It was a minor race, a 6-furlong race for maiden horses at Belmont Park worth $5,400. All the eleven horses entered carried 122 pounds. Curiously, the Slew was the bettor's favorite, at $2.60 to 1. (In the strange way that news gets around, perhaps his reported workout times were what made the bettors favor a never-raced horse against other entrants in the race. Some great jockeys opposed Cruguet and the Slew: among the eleven jockeys in that race were Bill Shoemaker, Ron Turcotte, Pat Day, Eddie Maple, Jorge Velasquez, and Don Brumfield; all eventual Hall of Fame jockeys.) It really didn't matter who else was on the track: Cruguet bolted the Slew out of the starting gate, took the lead by the quarter-mile, and never gave it up. Cruguet remembered later, "He went by those other horses like they were just standing still." He won by five lengths and covered the distance in time of 1:10 1/5. Like Man o'War, War Admiral, Whirlaway, and Citation before him, Seattle Slew broke his maiden in his first race.

Fifteen days later he ran again at Belmont Park. Now it was a seven-furlong allowance race worth $6,600. The field wasn't as large, only eight horses, but Turcotte, Maple, Day, and Velasquez were back opposing Cruguet and the Slew. Once again Turner's horse and jockey made it look easy. They took the lead by the quarter-mile, held it for the entire race, and won by 3 1/2 lengths in time of 1:22.

The racing world was about to find out what had hit it. The one-mile Champagne Stakes has often been the critical race for two-year-olds; the victor is a contender for best two-year-old horse and an early favorite for the Kentucky Derby. Seattle Slew was entered. He was again the favorite, at odds of $1.30 to $1. The second choice in the betting, For the Moment, was ridden by Eddie Maple and carried odds of $2.00 to $1.

For the Moment had won the Cowdin and the Belmont Futurity; in most other years he would have been the favorite in the Champagne Stakes. But there against him was Seattle Slew, the dark brown colt with only two races under him. It must have jarred the owners of For the Moment. Seattle Slew came along nicely; three days prior to the Champagne Stakes he ran three furlongs in 34 1/4 seconds. The time made people notice him.

The race was never seriously in doubt. Cruguet again sent Seattle Slew to the lead, and he stayed there the entire time. For the Moment stayed with him, but tired in the stretch. Seattle Slew finished *9 3/4* lengths ahead of the Belmont Futurity winner. The purse was $82,350.

In a breathtaking twenty-six days he ran three races, won all of them, and brought home $94,350 for his owners. Turner, the Taylors, and the Hills figured that the great victory in the Champagne Stakes put Seattle Slew in line for best two-year-old horse. Besides, there was next year to think about: the Flamingo Stakes at Hialeah, the Wood Memorial, the Triple Crown races....

They decided to rest him for the winter. Their prediction was borne out: with only three races in his career, Seattle Slew was named Best Two-Year-Old for 1976.

He started racing again almost five months later at Hialeah, the scene of Citation's triumphs twenty-nine years earlier. Seattle Slew won a seven-furlong allowance race on March 9 worth $7,000. The race chart is almost an exact duplicate of where he left off: he took the lead immediately, never gave it up, and won by nine lengths. But there is a story behind the race that is not shown by the race chart. The number two horse was White Rammer, a horse that had been unbeaten before March 9. White Rammer had a style like the Slew: take an early lead and hang on to it. But this time, he met his match.

In Cady and Silverman's book, *Seattle Slew*, they write of the allowance race:

> *"It was unreal. They went the first quarter in 22 1/5 seconds, head to head, with the rider on White Rammer slapping and banging and Cruguet just sitting still. Then Huey shook loose with a half [half-mile time] in 44 flat...He was gone. At the eighth pole, he had run six furlongs in 1:08, faster than any horse in the history of Hialeah. He just galloped home from there, his ears pricked like a saddle horse out for a leisurely canter. Cruguet hadn't touched him once, yet the final time of 1:20 3/5 was less than a second short of the world record for seven furlongs."*

Twenty years later, Cruguet remembered Seattle Slew that day: "Very, very easy he went seven-eighths [of a mile.] He could have pulled the track record that day. He was unbelievable."

> *"Today was the last chance they had to beat him.*
> *He ran fast but could have run much faster,*
> *and he even improves every time."*
> — Jean Cruguet,
> quoted in *The New York Times,*
> March 27, 1977

When Hialeah became a major track in the 1930s, one of its races, the Flamingo Stakes, became a major preparatory race for the Triple Crown campaign. Today, the Florida Derby at Gulfstream Park has taken over that honor, but on March 26, 1977, the Flamingo Stakes was still the race to watch in Florida. Naturally, Seattle Slew was entered. He made it look easy; once again he took the lead at the start and never faltered. At one point he led by six lengths, but remembering Turner's strategy not to burn him out too soon,

245

Cruguet eased him up. He won by four lengths in time of 1:47 2/5. It was the third fastest time in Flamingo Stakes history.

> *"I know he come out of the gate, and again he went from the...he made the first turn, and he went to the lead, and he was just walking. I don't know, someone said he was the horse to beat, and they just kind of decided to follow me most of the time, and nobody pressed me, and it was just walking, and the five-eighths pole, I said, 'Well, see you later,' and I just clucked to him, and in a matter of seconds, he opened up ten lengths."*
> — Jean Cruguet, 1998,
> on Seattle Slew in the 1977 Wood Memorial

The last major preparatory race for the Triple Crown is often the Wood Memorial at Aqueduct. Gallant Fox, Count Fleet, and Assault all won the Wood Memorial prior to their Triple Crown victories, while Omaha and Secretariat had both been defeated in it. The Slew was entered in the Wood Memorial for his last race prior to the Kentucky Derby. He was the favorite at odds of $0.10 to $1, and the bettors were unerring in their judgments. The Slew faced seven other horses, but once again, he was in the lead for the whole race. He won by 3 1/4-lengths.

> *"He was never a relaxed horse. He was always on the fight. He was always on the go. He wouldn't just walk with his head down to the starting gate. Some horses will. He was always trying to pull the exercise rider out of the saddle and pull me out of the saddle as well. He was just very strong."*
> — Anne Scardino, 1999,
> pony rider for Seattle Slew in the 1977 Swaps Stakes.

There he was, a horse with only six races on him. (Ben Jones must have been spinning in his grave!) But those six races included the Champagne Stakes, the Flamingo Stakes, and the Wood Memorial. It was a *blitzkrieg* seldom seen before in horse racing.

Seattle Slew went to Kentucky the clear favorite for the Derby. He only worked nineteen times before the Triple Crown, a dearth of exercise in Turner's words, "...almost unheard of." So, he was still an unknown quantity to some extent. He wasn't a mean horse, but he was very strong willed and strong physically. Once, in Florida, he was on the way to a workout when the stable pony aside him started to act up and nipped his neck. Seattle Slew surprised everyone by what he did. He administered one good lesson, applied properly. He just reached out and grabbed the part-Percheron, part-Clydesdale stable pony on the side of the neck and lifted the huge horse off the ground.

He was calm in the barn, but nervous people, crowds, and noise agitated him. Still, it often seemed that, like Man o'War, he didn't get stirred up until he entered the starting gate. At the March 9 race at Hialeah, he stood in his stall, listless. Then he laid down and fell asleep.

Turner had a fit; what had suddenly happened to his horse? Had he taken ill? Turner searched out Jim Hill and told him, "We'd better take this horse's temperature, Jim. He could be sick. What if he did this an hour before the Derby?" So they checked him for a fever, and Seattle Slew's afternoon reverie was rudely interrupted.

It turned out to be nothing at all; the horse just wanted to take a nap before the race. For all his powerful stride, he seemed to run just hard enough to win impressively, but not hurt himself. To this observer, Seattle Slew looked like the Thinking Man's Horse.

On the afternoon of May 7, 1977, the day of the Kentucky Derby, excitement and tension started to build at Seattle Slew's stall. The handlers, the groom, and even the watchdog seemed restless. Not so the Thinking Man's Horse. About 3:30 P.M., two hours before post, Seattle Slew knew exactly what to do: he laid down in the stall, stretched out on his side, and went to sleep. No use worrying unnecessarily.

But ninety minutes later, things looked bad. Seattle Slew broke out in sweat, a condition called "washing out," in the paddock. He kicked the side of the stall and began to sweat profusely in an apparent case of pre-race jitters caused by the noisy Derby crowd. Mike Kennedy said to groom John Polston, "This guy is feeling very bad, John. He's not shaking, though. That'd really blow his mind."

A few minutes later, the jockeys were called for the Derby race. Cruguet saw the Slew, and began to despair. How could he win in that condition? Then Cruguet noticed Seattle Slew wasn't trembling. There was hope still. The Slew may have been nervous, but he wasn't afraid to race.

The signal came for "riders up." Turner boosted Cruguet onto Seattle Slew, and gave one last instruction: "Remember Jean, keep him busy from the quarter pole home. Keep flicking that stick, even if you're fifty in front. Remember, this is the Derby."

Seattle Slew heard the Kentucky Derby theme song, "My Old Kentucky Home," and got more stirred up. On television, Eddie Arcaro said to Howard Cosell, "Look at him, Howard. He's washed out. That's a very bad sign." Cruguet kept his horse on the backstretch, away from the other horses, away from any more agitating stimuli. They were loaded in to the gate, the Slew at the number four pole position. Almost immediately after the last horse was loaded in, the starter pushed the button and the gates slammed open. The 1977 Kentucky Derby was underway.

It was the worst Derby start of any Triple Crown Winner in history. The assistant starter in Seattle Slew's stall held onto his lead for just a split-second after the gates opened. The Slew therefore broke late and off-balance. That

247

SEATTLE SLEW with Jean Cruguet up. 1977 Kentucky Derby.
© *Collection of L.S. Sutcliffe, C.Ken Grayson, owner. Used by permission.*

caused him to start high and to the right, which nearly unseated Cruguet. By the time the jockey righted his horse, they were two or three lengths behind the pack. In an amazing display, Cruguet and the Slew went after the pack, saw an opening, and the Slew cut loose. He forced his way through the pack, bumped another horse, and by the quarter-mile mark was even with the leader, For the Moment, ridden by Angel Cordero.

Now they were out of trouble, running just one-on-one with Cordero and For the Moment. Seattle Slew was on the outside, For the Moment on the rail. Cruguet knew Cordero's game plan: take command, fight off the challengers, put pressure on the rest, and make the others quit. Cruguet tested Cordero. He tried to get the Slew into the lead, saw Cordero staying with him, and then throttled back. No use burning up energy too early.

For the Moment and Seattle Slew stayed together through the clubhouse turn and into the backstretch. The rest of the horses were back four lengths or more behind the speed duelists. At 3/4 of a mile, Cruguet eased the Slew back a bit, and held him steady down the backstretch. At the three-eighths pole,

248

Seattle Slew with Jean Cruguet up, in the Winner's Circle, 1977 Kentucky Derby.
© *Collection of L.S. Sutcliffe, C.Ken Grayson, owner. Used by permission.*

Cruguet knew it was now or never. He cut his horse loose and the black and yellow silks surged forward with plenty in reserve. Cordero stayed on the rail, not giving up, but not blocking the Slew either. At the quarter-pole, Cruguet went to the whip, the first time he had ever done that to his great horse, and Seattle Slew began to pull away. He changed leads, from a left-foot lead to a right-foot lead, and Cruguet rapped him again. The Slew's margin went to two lengths, and For the Moment began to fade. Another horse, Run Dusty Run, took second, and started to charge. Cruguet looked over his shoulder, rapped the Slew a few more times, and held steady. They crossed the finish line two lengths in front in time of 2:02 1/5. Wonderfully, as an outrider helped pull him up, Seattle Slew tugged at the bit. Now that he'd warmed up, he wanted to run some more.

A few minutes later, while Cruguet, Turner, the Taylors, and the Hills were receiving the Kentucky Derby trophy, John Polston was leading Seattle Slew away. The enormity of it hit Polston; the groom had grown up on the streets of Baltimore, and here he was, on national television, taking the Kentucky Derby winner back to the barn. Polston patted Seattle Slew and said, "Hugo, you one helluva racehorse." Then the tears came.

249

Two weeks later, at Pimlico, eight horses challenged the Slew. Only two Derby horses, Run Dusty Run, and Sir Sir, were among the eight. The Slew's pre-Preakness workouts were impressive. Cruguet was confident: "I can do anything I want," he said. A record attendance of 77,346 souls jammed Pimlico for the Preakness. Seattle Slew was the 2 to 5 favorite in the betting. This time he was calm in the paddock and alert in the gate. When the race started, he was firmly in control. He and another horse, Cormorant, immediately got into a speed duel. They stayed close throughout the clubhouse turn and the backstretch. The Slew ran the mile in the fastest time ever run in the Preakness, 1:34 4/5, and halfway through the final turn, cut loose. Another horse, Iron Constitution, caught Cormorant and moved up to challenge Cruguet and the Slew, but it was too late. Seattle Slew won by one and one-half lengths in time of 1:54 2/5, identical to Secretariat's official time four years earlier. Eddie Arcaro still wasn't overly impressed. He commented, "To be considered great, a horse has to be able to win at a mile and a half."

> *"The first one gonna try to catch me gonna die."*
> — Jean Cruguet
> on the prospects for the 1977 Belmont Stakes

The final challenge came three weeks later at Belmont.[2] Turner was concerned about the length of the Belmont Stakes, so he worked the Slew longer than the horse had ever been worked before in two one-mile exercises. As at Pimlico, Seattle Slew was relaxed. The Belmont track was muddy. The race started at 5:47 P.M., and the Slew, fifth from the post, went to the lead immediately. Cruguet kept Seattle Slew under some restraint, holding him back, not letting the Slew break free too early and burn out on the longer Belmont course. In any event, the Slew was first after a quarter-mile, and still in first by 1 1/2 lengths after the half-mile. Cruguet knew at that point that it was over. Turner, in the stands, knew it too. He looked at the toteboard and saw the fractions: a quarter-mile in 24 3/5 seconds, a half-mile in 48 2/5, six furlongs in 1:14. Turner knew the Slew couldn't be worked any slower than that. The trainer remembered, "I knew right away that the race was over because he could sprint from there and beat anything that came down the road." And still, the challengers hadn't gone after him. At the 1 1/4-mile Seattle Slew was still in first. Sanhedrin, ridden by Jorge Velasquez, made a late charge in the final turn, drawing even with Cruguet and the Slew at the top of the home stretch. Cruguet turned Seattle Slew loose, and he pulled away to a four-length lead.

---

[2] Your author vividly remembers the 1977 Belmont Stakes. He had been out late with a lady friend the previous evening and was nursing a Richter Scale 4 hangover that day. It was cool and overcast in his hometown of Colorado Springs. He turned on the TV set and wound up seeing Cruguet and Seattle Slew win the final race of the Triple Crown.

They were firmly in the lead, and Seattle Slew was breezing along, ears pricked up like Gallant Fox or Citation. He had the Triple Crown nailed down, sealed shut, and everyone watching knew it. About twenty yards from the finish, Cruguet added a little bit of himself to the Triple Crown saga: in the most unforgettable gesture of any jockey in the Triple Crown, Cruguet stood up in the irons and raised his whip high over his head in celebration of victory. It only lasted a split-second. Cruguet lowered the whip, and the Slew stormed across the finish line in triumph.

Seattle Slew was the first horse to win the Triple Crown unbeaten in any previous race: neither Gallant Fox, nor War Admiral, nor Whirly, nor Count Fleet, nor Citation, nor Secretariat, had ever accomplished that. The unbeaten state of affairs wouldn't last long, but it was well worth savoring. To date the record stands intact. Seattle Slew remains the only horse to have won the Triple Crown previously undefeated in his career.

Had Billy Turner been Ben Jones, Seattle Slew would have had some twenty career starts before the Kentucky Derby. That, of course, wasn't Turner's style. As we have seen, he believed in careful preparation and not in taking too many chances. That strategy had paid off in the Triple Crown; the Slew was one of the least-raced horses in Triple Crown history, but he had managed to escape injury and remain undefeated. Those were the plusses of Turner's strategy. But Seattle Slew was mentally exhausted. Turner planned for him to rest for two months and send him to Saratoga in August.

The Taylors and the Hills were drawn to California racing. The Swaps Stakes at Hollywood Park was not far off, and they thought that Seattle Slew should be entered in it. Turner resisted; he knew what the Triple Crown had taken out of Seattle Slew, and moreover, the Swaps Stakes required a long airplane flight to California. In Turner's opinion, the stress of the flight could add to the situation. He objected, but was overruled.

Turner's instincts were unerring. The Swaps Stakes, on July 3, 1977, was little short of a disaster. The crowd at Hollywood Park got the Slew excited. Moreover, he warmed up on the inside rail and that wound him up even more. Finally, the track surface at Hollywood Park was shallow and stinging to his feet. (The eastern tracks where the Slew had run previously were much deeper, more sandy, and easier on a horse's feet.) It was a recipe for disaster; mental and physical fatigue, excitement from the crowd, and an uncomfortable race surface.

Nevertheless, Seattle Slew broke well from the gate and ran a good quarter-mile. Then he tried to lug inwards to the rail, and started to gain ground. At the 3/4-mile pole, the third horse, Text, blocked him in. Thereafter, it was no contest: he tired and finished a miserable fourth, *sixteen* lengths behind the winner, J.O. Tobin. Cruguet remembered later, "It was a very bad feeling when you're the only horse that was never beat, and then when you make the first turn, you know you're beat already. Believe me, that's a bad feeling."

Seattle Slew had finally been defeated, and miserably so. Turner pulled the horseshoes off him for a good rest in preparation for racing in the autumn. Perhaps he would enter the Woodward Cup in September, or the Marlboro Cup or the Jockey Club Gold Cup in October. Those latter races required one preparatory race in September.

But now everything came crashing down. In August, the New York State Racing Commission suspended the Taylor/Hill team for thirty days. The regulations stated that no licensed racing veterinarian (in this case, Jim Hill) could have a financial interest in a horse (in this case, Seattle Slew) racing in New York State. The suspension ended on September 27, 1977 but it effectively put "paid" to any ideas of Seattle Slew racing in the autumn New York races. He was retired for the winter.

The relationship between Turner and the Taylors and the Hills soured after the Swaps Stakes. Turner no longer went to some of the parties the Taylors and Hills wanted him to attend. Moreover, Seattle Slew became an industry, and merchandising of his image occurred. Turner objected to that.[3] Then the Taylors and Hills wanted him to stop training for other owners and concentrate on their horses and those owned by a friend, Milton Ritzenberger. Turner didn't like that idea, either. His outspoken style no longer sat well with the Slew's owners. He started talking about a loss of control over Seattle Slew.

The announcement in December, 1977 that Turner had been fired as Seattle Slew's trainer startled the racing world. On top of it all, *another* problem confronted Seattle Slew's owners: Jean Cruguet fired his booking agent, Oliver Cutshaw. Cutshaw was popular in the racing community, and Cruguet's dismissal of him brought more unwelcome attention.

Seemingly lost in all this was the champion horse himself. He came down with a cough during the autumn, but he was shipped to Hialeah for a winter racing campaign nonetheless. More disaster struck. In January, 1978, Seattle Slew came down with a virus. His temperature soared to 102.1 degrees and in one twelve-hour period he neither ate food nor drank liquid. His bodily functions even stopped briefly. The fever broke after that dicey twelve hours, but any winter racing was out of the question.

By February 1, 1978, the "carnage" was complete: the owners had been

---

[3] The Taylors and Hills also wanted Seattle Slew to appear at a Madison Square Garden Horse Show. Turner objected to that on two grounds: first, Seattle Slew's safety couldn't be guaranteed. The horse was nervous around crowds and it can only be grimly guessed at what he would have done with all the lights, flashbulbs, and crowd noise at Madison Square Garden. Turner knew that the show-horse people would not have liked Seattle Slew taking all the attention from their horses.

suspended, the trainer fired, the jockey mired in controversy. The unbeaten horse had been beaten, had missed the major autumn races, and nearly died from illness. Just seven months earlier it seemed that nothing could go wrong for the Taylors, the Hills, Billy Turner, Jean Cruguet, and Seattle Slew. Now it seemed that nothing could go right.

The Taylors and Hills hired Douglas Peterson of Denver, Colorado, as the Slew's new trainer. Peterson was young, only twenty-six; but he had been around racing for much of his life. He had worked at tracks during summers in high school and at the age of eighteen, won a $100,000 Futurity race at Raton, New Mexico.

The Slew's first four-year-old start was at Aqueduct on May 14, 1978, in a seven-furlong allowance race. Cruguet still had the mount, and they faced five other horses. The track was sloppy, the worst that the Slew had ever run on, but it didn't bother him. He stayed second behind Gallant Bob for the first quarter-mile, and then Cruguet took him to the outside. He passed Gallant Bob in the far turn, drew away, and won by 8 1/4 lengths. His time was 1:22 4/5; excellent, in view of the fact that he had been eased up in the final stages of the race. Cruguet remembered, "He [Seattle Slew] didn't think nothing of it. He just galloped all the way."

It had been ten months since he had raced, but he returned looking like the Seattle Slew of October, 1976-June, 1977. The streak of bad luck seemed over.

The "Slew Crew's" misfortunes eased. They pointed him to the Metropolitan Handicap at Belmont Park two weeks later, followed by one race in the summer, and then the fall races he had missed the prior year. But roughly ten days after the allowance race at Aqueduct, Seattle Slew somehow bruised his right hind leg. The leg filled up slightly, and instantly the Taylors and Hills reacted. It was a minor injury, and had there been a more important race scheduled, they probably would have kept him in it. But the Slew's stud value was incredible, and there was no point in taking chances. He was off again for another three months.

Had Seattle Slew been retired in May, 1978, the verdict on him would have been mixed: a good horse, certainly, but one lightly raced who won the Triple Crown against uncertain opposition. The real tests were now to come: from August 12 to November 11, 1978, he waged the campaign that enshrined his place in racing history.

He had missed both prior racing seasons at Saratoga due to injury and fatigue. Now was his chance: he was entered in a seven-furlong allowance race worth $25,000 on August 12. Despite the long layoff — only one race in *thirteen* months — he was the betting favorite again, at odds of $0.10 to $1.00. There really wasn't much to the race: as usual, Cruguet took him out quickly and once again he grabbed the lead, never letting it go. Across the wire it was a classic Seattle Slew victory margin: six lengths. He was back all right, back with a vengeance.

It was his only Saratoga race, and Seattle Slew made the most of it. He got three weeks rest before racing in the nine-furlong Paterson Handicap at the Meadowlands track in New Jersey. He carried 128 pounds in this race, and that might have made the difference: it was eleven pounds more than his nearest competitor, and fourteen pounds more than was carried by another entrant, Dr. Patches. There were two other obstacles for Seattle Slew: First, he was shipped in the middle of the night to the Meadowlands track, which disoriented him; second, Dr. Patches was, in Cruguet's words, "...on top of the game." Dr. Patches was ridden by Angel Cordero, who rode For the Moment against the Slew in the 1977 Derby. One suspects that Cordero was out for revenge.

He got it. In the race, Cruguet took the Slew out of the gate and into first place. But Cordero kept Dr. Patches near the champion, never more than two lengths back. In the stretch Cordero sent his horse, and the two battled down to the wire. It was just too much for the Triple Crown winner: Dr. Patches won by a neck.

The loss, when viewed from history's perspective, wasn't bad at all. Seattle Slew had been through *so* much, and carried all the extra weight in the Paterson Handicap. It should have been chalked up as "just one of those things that happens."

Controversy returned. The owners felt that Cruguet no longer had the confidence in his Triple Crown horse. Moreover, the Triple Crown jockey wasn't impressed with Peterson's training. Cruguet voiced his concerns. The owners and trainer huddled; it was a unanimous decision. Just as it had been time to change trainers the year before, now it was time to change jockeys.

Up popped Angel Cordero. He lobbied for the job of riding the Slew, and was chosen. But if he thought he would have an easier time than Cruguet had, Cordero was badly mistaken.

While Seattle Slew was in repose for much of 1978, another horse/jockey combination had grabbed the headlines. (More proof that nature abhors a vacuum.) Steve Cauthen and Affirmed waged the most cliff-hanging Triple Crown campaign in history. Cauthen had been chosen "Sportsman of the Year" by *Sports Illustrated* in 1977. The truly magnificent story of Affirmed and Cauthen will be related in the next chapter, but their success created a public relations man's dream: never before had there been *back-to-back* Triple Crown winners. It was inevitable, then, that Seattle Slew and Affirmed would face each other in the autumn of 1978.

Their first encounter was in the Marlboro Cup at Belmont Park on September 16, 1978. For once, Seattle Slew was second choice in the betting, at $2.10 to $1, while Affirmed and Cauthen were favored at $0.50 to $1. But the odds makers should have followed their past practices. Cordero did what Cruguet had done so often in the past: He took Seattle Slew to the early lead and stayed with him for the duration. Affirmed and Cauthen never got closer than 2 1/2 lengths and finished second. Seattle Slew had beaten his Triple Crown successor.

The Marlboro Cup was worth $180,000 and brought the Slew's winnings to $883,470. (Affirmed's second place money of $66,000 made him the top money winner for a single season. It was what Seattle Slew could have accomplished the year before had luck been more favorable.)

In retrospect, it was scarcely a fair match. As Steve Cauthen said in 1996, "I think any time when you have great horses like that, the four-year-old has a great advantage, because it's kind of like a 25-year-old man taking on a 16-year-old." Yes, the Slew had not been racing. Yes, the Slew had just lost the Paterson Handicap. But he was, after all, a year older, a year stronger, and a year more experienced.

The Woodward Stakes at Belmont Park on September 30 was Slew's next race. It was a 1 1/4-mile race, the same distance as the Kentucky Derby. Like the Derby, every horse carried 126 pounds. The Slew's major competition was Exceller, the champion European horse of the day. Befitting Exceller's status was his jockey, Bill Shoemaker. Cordero was still on the Slew and this race was no threat to them: Cordero used the Seattle Slew style: Get a quick lead and keep it to the finish line. The Slew and Cordero finished four lengths ahead of Exceller and Shoemaker. But Exceller and Shoemaker stayed with their adversary. Only at the end of the race did Seattle Slew edge into his four-length lead. They were usually 2 or 2 1/2 lengths behind the winner. Shoemaker learned much from that defeat.

The Woodward Stakes purse was $150,000 and made the Slew the twenty-third Thoroughbred millionaire. Citation was the first; fittingly, the second Triple Crown winner since Citation was the latest one.

The victories in the Marlboro Cup and Woodward Stakes virtually required the Slew to run in the 1 1/2-mile Jockey Club Gold Cup at Belmont on October 14. And so he did, together with Exceller and Affirmed. The Slew was the odds-on favorite, at $0.60 to $1.00. Affirmed and his entered stable mate, Life's Hope, were paired at second in the betting at $2.20 to $1. Exceller was third, at $3.80 to $1. Those present thought that Affirmed was the Slew's main challenger, and he was for a while: Slew took the early lead while Affirmed was in second, followed by Life's Hope. The first quarter-mile was run in a tremendous time of 22 3/5 seconds, while they ran the half-mile in 44 1/5. Then disaster struck Cauthen and Affirmed: Affirmed's saddle slipped, and Cauthen fought hard just to stay on the horse. That gave Exceller his opening. He rocketed up, took on Seattle Slew and at one point, had a 1 1/2 length lead over him.

Shoemaker and Exceller now saw a side of Seattle Slew not made public since the 1977 Kentucky Derby. The Triple Crown champion wasn't going to let Exceller get away with the race. He dug in, came roaring back, and the two horses charged down the stretch. Neither one gave an inch; at the end, Exceller stuck a nose in front of Seattle Slew as they crossed the wire.[4]

It was an incredible race, a great race, and one not likely to be forgotten by racing fans.

There was one more race left for Seattle Slew: the Stuyvesant Handicap at Aqueduct on November 11. Both Turner and Cruguet were watching from different vantage points, but they had identical feelings. When asked their thoughts, each one replied, "I miss the horse, but not the people." (As a coda, Cruguet actually rode against the Slew on Jumping Hill.)

In the Stuyvesant Handicap Slew carried 134 pounds, the most of his career. Not that it made any difference: As always, he took the lead and never lost it. Cordero and Seattle Slew finished 3 1/4 lengths over Jumping Hill. The purse of $100,000 brought his winnings to a total of $1,208,726, fifteenth position on the list of top money-winning horses.

Nineteen days later, Seattle Slew was flown to Kentucky. Governor Julian Carroll pronounced the occasion, "Seattle Slew Day," a tribute of a type rarely awarded. And then he went into the gentle retirement, so richly earned, of a great stallion.

He had raced only seventeen times, the same number of races as Gallant Fox; less than Man o'War, Sir Barton, Omaha, War Admiral, Whirlaway, Count Fleet, Assault, Citation, and Secretariat. It was his unbeaten Triple Crown campaign and his duels with Affirmed and Exceller that cemented his place in racing history. In 1992, a panel of racing experts placed him ninth on the list of great Thoroughbreds.[5] Given all the handicaps he endured, some might say he should be ranked higher.

> *"He always was his own horse."*
> — Billy Turner
> on Seattle Slew, 1997

There was life after Seattle Slew for Paula Turner, Billy Turner, and Jean Cruguet. Cruguet raced for two more years, then he retired on July 12, 1980, to

---

[4] The "firm" of great horses that have challenged Triple Crown winners now reads: Man o'War, Seabiscuit, Alsab, Armed, Noor, and Exceller.

[5] The top ten list was: 1-Man o'War; 2-Secretariat; 3-Citation; 4-Kelso; 5-Count Fleet; 6-Sysonby; 7-Native Dancer; 8-Nashua; 9-Seattle Slew; 10-Colin. The list can be found in the special Fall, 1992, issue of *Sports Illustrated*.

become a trainer. That didn't last long: he returned to riding in 1982. The following year he was badly injured when his mount in a race stumbled, threw him, and then trampled him. He recovered from that and rode into the 1990s. On June 8, 1984 at Belmont Park, he became the first rider to win three stakes races in one day. At age fifty-three, on July 19, 1992, he even tried his hand at steeplechase at a race in Saratoga.

Cruguet retired in 1996 to become a horse trainer in Kentucky. He rode 25,165 races and won 3,215. He has a creditable 12.5% win percentage and a 38.5% money percentage. Many more famous riders do not have such a fine record.[6]

The Turners divorced in the early 1980s, and Paula settled in North Carolina as a horse trainer. Billy Turner went back to training. For some time, he had his own stable, but sold it in 1991 and became a public trainer in Saratoga. He didn't visit his great horse for fourteen years. In February, 1992, he went to Three Chimneys Farm and visited Seattle Slew for the first time since his departure in 1977. Not too much had changed in the interim: Turner said, "He looked really fit and there's no question he remembered me. He didn't treat me with any respect when I trained him, and he didn't show any respect at the farm. But he knew who I was." Then Billy Turner pronounced the true judgment on Seattle Slew's racing career: "He's a horse who loved what he was doing, the most insane horse about running that I ever saw. But that was the key to his success."

Like all of us, Billy Turner had his successes and made his mistakes. He reaped the rewards of the former and took the consequences of the latter. He is a charming individual who is eager to share his experiences with others. And he has one credential that no other trainer can claim: neither Guy Bedwell, nor Sunny Jim Fitzsimmons, nor George Conway, nor Ben Jones, nor Don Cameron, nor Max Hirsch, nor Jimmy Jones, nor Lucien Laurin — none of them before him, nor Lan Darrera after him, accomplished what Billy Turner did: He took a horse through the Triple Crown undefeated.

Seattle Slew first stood at Spendthrift Farm, where his stall neighbors were his successor Triple Crown winner, Affirmed, and the aged Nashua, winner of the 1955 Preakness and Belmont Stakes. It was as worthy a combination of racing greatness as had ever been gathered. After Spendthrift Farm fell into financial difficulties, the Slew was moved to Three Chimneys Farm, where he remained until shortly before his death in 2002.

Seattle Slew was a magnificent sire. Early in his stud career, he sired

---

[6] Jean Cruguet is friendly, outgoing, and enjoys relating his racing career. As with Steve Cauthen, John Longden, Warren Mehrtens, and Ron Turcotte, Jean Cruguet is a gentleman.

Landaluce, the champion two-year-old filly of 1982, and Swale, the winner of the 1984 Kentucky Derby and the Belmont Stakes. Both had their careers cut short: Landaluce died after her two-year-old season, and Swale died suddenly of unknown causes shortly after the Belmont Stakes. Others of his get have been more fortunate; as of March 6, 2002, Slew sired seven champions, fifty-nine group/graded stakes winners, and one hundred overall stakes winners.

His progeny's total winnings were $75,484,533. The leader is Slew o'Gold, with a total winning of $3,533,534[7]. Seattle Slew remained a sire much in demand. In 1995, he mounted seventy-one mares and got sixty-nine of them in foal. As late as 2001, a daughter, Flute, won the Kentucky Oaks.

Slew's grandchildren must be considered: one of them, Cigar, retired as the world's all-time money-winning horse in 1996, with total earnings of $9,999,815.

Spinal surgery in 2000 reduced Seattle Slew's siring somewhat, but he was still sought after. He underwent additional spinal surgery in 2002. At that time Karen and Mickey Taylor, who still owned Slew, decided it was time to separate the old racer from the mares' temptations. On April 1, 2002, Slew was moved from Three Chimneys to Hill 'n' Dale Farm near Lexington. But it was all too late; his body had worn out.

Early on the morning of May 7, 2002, with Karen and Mickey Taylor by his side, Seattle Slew died in his sleep at Hill 'n' Dale Farm. It was exactly twenty-five years to the day since he had pushed through the wall of horses at Churchill Downs to challenge For the Moment and win the Kentucky Derby. Seattle Slew is buried underneath a statue at Hill 'n' Dale.

On a cloudy day in December, 1995, I visited Three Chimneys Farm. Mike Gordon of Three Chimneys brought the Slew out of his stall for me. The Slew was bigger than he was in his racing days, but in good shape. At that time, he was ridden one mile six mornings per week. He was calm and reserved, even aloof and aristocratic, as if he understood his status as the greatest living Thoroughbred. He paid little attention as I took his picture; thousands, perhaps a million times, he had seen people raise a black and chrome box and make a clicking noise with it. He posed well and didn't carry on.

Seattle Slew did not take orders: if you told him to do something, he just wouldn't do it. Put the same thing to him as a question, and he responded. Mike Gordon of Three Chimneys told me: "He's good natured. But he's seen it all and done it all, and if you try to make him do something your way, you'll lose every time."

---

[7] Slew o'Gold was elected to membership in the National Racing Museum and Hall of Fame in 1992. He resided at Three Chimneys Farm in the stall next to his sire.

SEATTLE SLEW, December, 1995 at Three Chimneys Farm, Kentucky. *Photo by author Robert L. Shoop*

Author's note: The original photographs here and on page 249 were in color. The mane, forelock, and tail are dark in the photo on page 249, but shot through with gold in this photograph where he is twenty-two years old. Seattle Slew was aging gracefully.

Seattle Slew's stall had three windows, and as I left, the old racer was looking out one of them. There were mares at a nearby farm, and Seattle Slew was curious about them.

Perhaps one of his foals will duplicate his achievements on the turf. Or perhaps a grandchild, another Cigar, will come along. The staff at Three Chimneys agreed that Seattle Slew's influence will be felt in racing for many years to come: Mike Gordon said, "Fifty, a hundred years from now, all the great race horses will trace back to this one."

X. THE DUELISTS:
AFFIRMED AND ALYDAR

Affirmed:Triple Crown, 1978. Jockey, Steve Cauthen
Alydar: 2nd in Triple Crown Races, 1978. Jockey, Jorge Velasquez

*"If Whirlaway had the name that rolled off your tongue, and Citation
had four explosive gears and Secretariat set track records and Seattle Slew had
an undefeated record, Affirmed had unshakable grit. His saddlecloth should
have read: Refuse to Lose."*
— Rick Bozich,
Louisville *Courier-Journal*, June 3, 1997

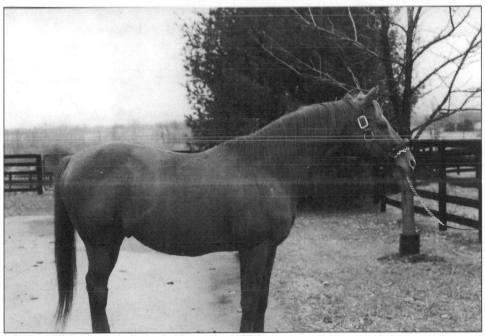

AFFIRMED at Jonabell Farm, Kentucky, 1995
Photo by author Robert L. Shoop

"You can't hardly write a book without him," Phillip Hampton of
Jonabell Farm said to me as we crossed an access road to a paddock. At its far

261

end a grazing chestnut horse raised its head.

"That's him?" I asked.

"That's him." Hampton unlatched the paddock gate.

"C'm here, bud," Hampton said, and Affirmed, the last horse to win the Triple Crown, slowly walked across the paddock. To show his independence, Affirmed stopped part way to nuzzle on some grass. Hampton clipped the lead on him and led him out. Affirmed was in good shape, frisky in the cool December morning. He looked ready for Steve Cauthen to show up with his tack and take the two of them five furlongs at Keeneland or Churchill Downs.

It was a pleasant time, and Affirmed was alternately indifferent and interested in what was going on around him. Like Seattle Slew, Affirmed has learned to pose for pictures, and I took several photos of him. When I was finished, Hampton led him back into the paddock.

Holy Bull, the 1994 Horse of the Year, was in an adjoining paddock, and I took some photos of him, too. I turned around, and there was the last Triple Crown winner peering at me through the fence. Hampton explained, "He's curious about what you're doing." Perhaps Affirmed thought all my attention should be focused on him.

Later, I realized that was a symbol of Affirmed's life: from Alydar or Seattle Slew on the race track to Holy Bull in the next door paddock, he always had to share the attention with some other horse. By all rights, this should be Affirmed's story, and his alone. But it is not solely his story, and can never be.

There are many epic contests between athletes: in baseball, think of Bob Feller pitching to Ted Williams or Joe DiMaggio; think of Warren Spahn pitching to Stan Musial; Sandy Koufax to Willie Mays or Hank Aaron. Thoroughbred Racing has its own contests: Citation-Noor; Whirlaway-Alsab; Hill Prince-Middleground; and the epic battles between Nashua and Swaps in the 1950s. But all those other rivalries pale when compared to what happened in the Spring of 1978: the duels between Affirmed and Alydar.

After World War Two, horse breeders settled in north-central Florida near Ocala and began a thriving Thoroughbred industry. Success struck quickly: Needles, winner of the 1956 Kentucky Derby and Belmont Stakes, was the first great Florida horse. Then Carry Back emerged in 1961, racing's second equine millionaire, the horse that won the 1961 Derby and Preakness. Other fine horses came from Florida, including Foolish Pleasure, the 1975 Kentucky Derby winner. But just nine weeks prior to Foolish Pleasure's Derby victory, the greatest horse to ever come out of Ocala was born at Louis and Patrice Wolfson's Harbor View Farm. On February 21, 1975, a thirteen-year-old filly named Won't Tell You foaled a chestnut colt sired by Exclusive Native. The colt was named Affirmed.

He had good bloodlines: on his sire's side was Native Dancer, "The

Grey Ghost," winner of the 1953 Preakness and Belmont Stakes. And there was racing's first TV star; Polynesian, winner of the 1945 Preakness; Shut Out, winner of the 1942 Kentucky Derby; and Equipoise, one of the great horses of all time.

That was impressive enough, but Affirmed's dam had even better blood in her: Sir Gallahad III, Gallant Fox's sire, appeared in her pedigree, and also (remotely) War Admiral, which brought Man o'War (okay, *very* remotely) into the picture.

Most of those great horses were far back in his pedigree and probably had little influence on the racing ability of the colt Affirmed. He was good looking: some have said the adult Affirmed had near-perfect conformation. But handsome is as handsome does, and it took a fine trainer and fine jockey to bring out the best in Affirmed. Harbor View Farm had a trainer who could do the job: Lazaro S. ("Laz") Barrera.

> *"...Affirmed was the horse that really made him break through into the super-trainer echelon."*
> — Steve Cauthen, 1996,
> on Laz Barrera and Affirmed

Laz Barrera was born on May 8, 1924 in Havana, Cuba. In the pre-Castro days, Cuba attracted tourists from all of North America, and a thriving horse racing industry mushroomed in response to tourist demand. Barrera grew up close to a racetrack, and as he said, "I knew that I would end up working there." That certainty took him from the tracks in Cuba to the tracks in Mexico, and finally, in 1948, he came north of the border.

Success eluded him for many years, as it had for Lucien Laurin. He brought a fine Puerto Rican horse, Tinajero, to the United States in 1971, and that brought him the attention for which he had worked so long. His real breakthrough came in 1976, when Bold Forbes, one of the horses he trained, won the Wood Memorial, the Kentucky Derby, and the Belmont Stakes. Barrera didn't have long to wait for his next winner.

He was ambitious and wanted to win. But he wasn't all ambition: Laz Barrera was remembered by Steve Cauthen as "...almost like a father figure for me, and I have nothing but good things to say about him. He was a great man and a great guy to ride for..." It would be hard to say much better about anyone.

Affirmed's first start was on May 25, 1977 in a 5 1/2-furlong race at Belmont Park. The race was for maidens only, and ten horses entered. Affirmed was rated sixth, at $14.30 to $1. Jockey Bernie Gonzalez took him right to the lead and he stayed there throughout the race. Affirmed won by 4 1/2 lengths. In the tradition of War Admiral, Whirlaway, Citation, and Seattle Slew, Affirmed broke his maiden in his first race.

Affirmed raced again in the 5 1/2 furlong Youthful Stakes at Belmont Park on June 15. The Youthful is a notable early race for two-year-olds, and Angel Cordero rode Affirmed. (A very good sign!) It was a large field (eleven horses), but this time, Affirmed's standing with the odds makers had improved somewhat: He was second in the betting at $3.40 to $1. Cordero kept Affirmed in second place for most of the race, but took him to the lead by the top of the stretch. They hung on to win by a neck. Now the Florida horse was two-for-two on the track.

The bettors' choice in the Youthful had been rated at $1.80 to $1. That horse finished fifth, but there was much familiar about Affirmed's chief competition. Before it all ended, the racing world would be treated to an immortal rivalry: the bettors' choice carried the devil's red-and-blue silks of Calumet Farm and carried the name of Alydar.

> *Question: "Unfortunately, Affirmed is forever linked with Alydar."*
> *Answer: "Well, not a bad horse to be linked with, really, because*
> *Alydar was a great horse, too.*
> *Any other year, he would have been a Triple Crown winner."*
> — Steve Cauthen, 1996

Alydar was the last great horse of "Old" Calumet Farm. Recall that Warren Wright, the guiding light of Calumet, died in 1950. His widow, Lucille Wright, carried on the tradition of Calumet's greatness. Even though Armed retired in 1950, and Citation in 1951, Calumet remained the stable to beat throughout the 1950s. Things brightened personally for Lucille Wright: sometime in 1951, Mrs. Wright traveled to Los Angeles where she met screenwriter (Admiral) Gene Markey. They fell in love and married in 1952.

Gene Markey brought a new joy to her life, and he enjoyed living at Calumet Farm. By all accounts, Gene and Lucille Markey had a wonderful life together...

Things weren't going so well for Calumet on the racetrack. Ben Jones retired from Calumet in the late 1950s (and died in 1961); Jimmy Jones left in 1964 to head the Monmouth Track in New Jersey. Jimmy's departure ended an era. Twenty-five years of racing history and cachet that included Whirlaway, Citation, Armed, Coaltown, Bewitch, and Twilight Tear left with him. In the lull Lucille Markey talked to a breeder who had reduced his stable, and she followed suit. Calumet's stable was cut from sixty horses to just twenty-five. People at Calumet urged her not to do it, but she prevailed. The decision was eventually rescinded, but the damage was done: Calumet just didn't have enough horses.

The era from 1964 to 1977 was a rather bleak one for Calumet. The farm went through several trainers. In February, 1976, Margaret Glass, who had worked for Calumet some thirty-six years, visited Lucille Markey at her winter home in Florida. When Lucille asked Margaret what could be done to restore Calumet's racing glory, Margaret Glass relayed the advice of Melvin Cinnamon, Calumet's farm manager: get a new trainer. Lucille agreed. Two months later, Calumet hired John Veitch. Veitch was only thirty, the youngest horse trainer in Calumet history, but he was the son of Hall of Fame Trainer Sylvester Veitch. John Veitch had grown up around horses. He proved to be an excellent choice.

When Veitch got to Calumet Farm, among other horses, he found a two-year-old named Alydar.[1] Alydar's sire was Raise a Native, Affirmed's grandsire, thus relating Alydar and Affirmed. Alydar's dam was Sweet Tooth, and she had fine Calumet blood in her: Bull Lea (Citation's sire); Blenheim II (Whirly's sire); and both Pensive and Ponder, winners of the 1944 and 1949 Derbies, respectively.

The stage was set; two fine horses, related to each other, one carrying the heritage of racing's greatest stable, would make racing history. The score after the Youthful stood Affirmed 1, Alydar 0. It would not stay that way for long.

Alydar ran again at Belmont on June 24 in a 5 1/2-furlong maiden race and won it by 6 3/4 lengths. His next race was the Great American Stakes at Belmont on July 6, which set up a rematch with Affirmed. Eddie Maple rode Alydar, while Angel Cordero was again on Affirmed. Based on his last race, Alydar was the prohibitive favorite: $0.80 to $1, while Affirmed was third choice in the betting, at $4.60 to $1. Affirmed took an early lead, but by the 3/8-mile mark, Alydar was in the lead by a head. It was close through much of the race, but in the stretch, Alydar and Maple pulled away to win by 3 1/2 lengths in time of 1:03 2/5. That was only a second behind the record set by his sire, Raise A Native, in 1963. *The New York Times* prophesied, "The days of wine and roses may be on their way back for Calumet Farm..."

Maybe. But Affirmed ran a good race as well, and many, many, more races lay ahead. The score was tied, one each.

Affirmed was shipped to California to race at Hollywood Park. Cordero remained in the east, so Laffit Pincay rode Affirmed in California. They raced in the six-furlong Hollywood Juvenile Championship on July 23. Affirmed was unaffected by the long trip to California and the new jockey: in the race, Pincay took the horse to the lead quickly and they never gave it up. Affirmed won by seven lengths, as the race chart notes put it, " with speed to spare."

Now the regional influence on racing showed. Affirmed had done well, but Alydar remained in the east at the core of horse racing. The Calumet horse

---

[1] The name came from one of Lucille Markey's greetings to Aly Khan: "Aly, darling..."

won the Tremont Stakes at Belmont on July 27 and then prevailed in the Sapling Stakes at Monmouth on August 13. He *was* impressive and seemed to the New York sportswriters the best two-year-old of 1977.

It was time for Saratoga and the summer races.

Laz Barrera and Harbor View Farm sent Affirmed back east to race at Saratoga. They entered Affirmed in the Sanford Stakes on August 17, but they encountered a problem. Pincay decided to stay in California, and Cordero wanted to ride another horse in the Sanford Stakes. That left Affirmed in need of a jockey. Barrera remembered a young jockey, only seventeen years old, who rode a few races for him in the past. He'd done fairly well. The young jockey was available, and history repeated itself: like John Loftus, Earl Sande, and all the other Triple Crown jockeys, Steve Cauthen happened to be in the right place at the right time.

Racing had a vacuum in 1977 in the ranks of star jockeys. Arcaro and Longden had retired in the 1960s, and Bill Hartack had also retired. Bill Shoemaker still rode well, but he was about the only true superstar around on the tracks. There were fine jockeys, even great ones: Ron Turcotte, Jean Cruguet, Eddie Maple, Angel Cordero, and Laffit Pincay. But none of them had the drawing power of an Arcaro or a Longden.

The man who filled that void was, appropriately, a native Kentuckian. Steve Cauthen was born on May 1, 1960, in Covington, Kentucky, the son of Ronald ("Tex") and Myra Cauthen. It was foreordained that Steve would spend his life around horses.

Ronald Cauthen came from Sweetwater, Texas (hence "Tex") and worked on ranches and bush tracks. At sixteen, Tex went to the Fair Grounds in New Orleans and took a job with one of the stables there.

He worked for years at first one track, then another; but horse racing was his life, and he never really left it. He met Myra Bischoff, the sister of trainer Tommy Bischoff, and the two worked the circuits: Scarborough Downs in Maine; Rockingham Park in New Hampshire, then the tracks in Chicago. They were never hugely successful, but they were people that make horse racing: going from one track to another, shoeing and training horses, and doing an honest day's work for an honest day's wage.

When Myra found herself pregnant, she continued to work for a time, then went back to her family home in Covington to have the baby. Steve arrived on May 1, 1960, a healthy, normal baby. Horse racing remained the Cauthens' life and livlihood, so Tex and Myra took Steve to their next job, back at the Fair Grounds in New Orleans. Several moves followed: a stint at farming in Oklahoma, another stint at the Fair Grounds, a brief trip to Ocala. In 1965, the Cauthens bought a place in Walton, Kentucky, about seventy miles north of Lexington.

Steve's first ride came early, at age one. His horse heritage stuck as he followed his father on the morning chores at Latonia Park in Covington. Even as a preschooler, Steve got to ride Thoroughbreds: one morning, a track official saw a Thoroughbred galloping at full speed. Atop him was the five-year-old Steve Cauthen, handling the horse like an exercise rider.

At seven Cauthen walked horses around the shed rows of Latonia, not at all scared of the large creatures behind him. At age twelve he made his decision: He wanted to be a jockey.

Behind the Cauthen house stood a barn with a low-ceilinged loft. Steve nailed a set of reins to the wall and spent hours in the loft, holding the reins, imagining he was riding in a race. Tex Cauthen showed his son the art of whipping, and Steve spent more hours in the loft, sitting on a bale of hay, transferring a stick from one hand to another and whipping the hay bale. Eventually, Steve got to the point where he whipped within an eighth of an inch, near perfection. All the practice would pay off on June 10, 1978.

At age fifteen, Cauthen got a movie projector and borrowed the race films from the nearby tracks. For the next few months he played and replayed the films over and over again, looking for jockeys' mistakes. He almost wore out the films by May 1, 1976, his sixteenth birthday. Now he was eligible for a jockey license.

Steve Cauthen's first race was at Churchill Downs on May 12, and he rode a $5000 claiming horse named King of Swat. Steve rode a creditable race, but King of Swat didn't have it: they finished tenth. Five days later, at River Downs near Cincinnati, he rode a horse named Red Pipe in the eighth race. They won it by a length and half.

He didn't stop for another seventeen years and 2793 more wins. He would be named the 1977 Sportsman of the Year by *Sports Illustrated*, and the 1977 Athlete of the Year by the Associated Press, to become the first jockey ever so honored. He was the youngest jockey in history to win the Triple Crown, and ultimately, the only jockey to win all five of the world's great Derbies. Kentucky, Epsom (U.K.), Irish, French, and Italian.

Over the next year, Steve Cauthen rapidly gained a reputation and came to Laz Barrera's attention. The truly great team of Affirmed and Steve Cauthen made its debut at Saratoga Springs, New York, in the Sanford Stakes on August 17, 1977.

Young Steve Cauthen in red and white silks. *Photo courtesy of Steve Cauthen.. Used with permission*

"...really, he was the ideal type of horse to ride because A [sic], he was very intelligent, and he was probably one of the most intelligent horses I ever rode...He used his intelligence for his betterment. He also had desire. He loved to race and loved to win... ...he was as perfect a mount as you could ever want."
— Steve Cauthen
on Affirmed, 1996.

Affirmed was the bettors' favorite in the Sanford, at odds of $1.30 to $1. The Sanford was a six-furlong race, and Affirmed broke well from the gate. He bore out around the turn and was back for most of the race. Then Cauthen got after him: under the whip, Affirmed closed, caught the leader, and won by 2 1/2 lengths.

Affirmed and Alydar were due for a rematch, and it came ten days after the Sanford in the Hopeful Stakes. Alydar was the betting favorite, at even money, and Affirmed was second choice at odds of $2.30 to $1. Cauthen kept Affirmed in second place behind Tilt Up, while Alydar held a little farther back, in fourth. In the stretch, both horses made their moves. Affirmed and Alydar moved up and the pair battled down the stretch. Affirmed edged a half-length ahead going down to the wire.

For Cauthen, the victory was sweet. He had won the Sanford and the Hopeful on Affirmed, and could expect to ride him for the foreseeable future. It was the prototype of races to come: Affirmed in the lead, Alydar coming from behind, a great duel in the stretch, and Affirmed by a slight margin. The score was now Affirmed 2, Alydar 1.

Affirmed and Alydar met again two weeks later at Belmont, in the seven-furlong Futurity on September 10. Now the racing world had spotted the rivalry between the two horses: Affirmed was a slight favorite in the betting, at $1.20 to $1, while Alydar was just behind him, at $1.50 to $1. The two great horses did it again: Affirmed let another horse, Rough Sea, take the early lead. Then, he moved into first place by the half-mile mark. Alydar challenged him, and the two dueled for the rest of the race. First it was Affirmed by a head over Alydar, then Alydar by a head, and then, at the wire, Affirmed by a nose. Both Cauthen and Eddie Maple, Alydar's jockey, praised their mounts; Cauthen said that Affirmed "...never gave up the stretch, even when he was headed." Maple responded, "My colt never quit and tried his best." Affirmed 3, Alydar 1.

The Champagne Stakes is often the race that determines the two-year-old champion. Seattle Slew won it as his third race the previous year, and with it, the title of two-year-old champion.

Rarely had two such fine two-year-olds raced at the same moment in time as Affirmed and Alydar. Affirmed won the Youthful, the Hollywood Juvenile, the Sanford, the Hopeful, and the Belmont Futurity. Alydar won the Great American, the Tremont, and the Sapling Stakes, and had been barely beaten by Affirmed in the Hopeful Stakes and Belmont Futurity. These were not normal times for racing. The Champagne, whatever its usual importance, was not the determining factor in 1977.

Alydar had a new jockey, Jorge Velasquez. Velasquez was great, an eventual Hall of Famer. The Velasquez/Alydar team proved to be as great a team as Cauthen and Affirmed. They showed it in the Champagne Stakes: Cauthen put Affirmed in the lead at the 3/4-mile mark. But two things were at work: the track was muddy, and occasionally, when Affirmed got in front, he relaxed a little bit (shades of Gallant Fox!). True to form, Affirmed, then in the lead, relaxed and slowed slightly. Velasquez took Alydar wide, so wide that Affirmed didn't see him coming. The track conditions prevented Affirmed from digging in and charging back. Alydar went on to win by 1 1/4 lengths.

Now the score was Affirmed 3, Alydar 2. The title of Best Two-Year-Old was suddenly up for grabs. The Laurel Futurity at Laurel Park in Maryland would be the clincher.

It was very nearly an exact replay of the Hopeful or Belmont Futurity. Alydar was the favorite, at $0.40 to $1, while Affirmed was at $1.40 to $1. Cauthen was ready: he wouldn't allow Alydar to storm from the rear and blow by Affirmed, as had happened in the Champagne Stakes. Affirmed was second through most of the race, and in the far turn, took over first. But this time, there was a difference: Affirmed went wide, more towards the center of the track. Velasquez had to take Alydar close to the rail, enabling Affirmed to keep his rival in view. Affirmed thundered toward the finish leading by a head, with Alydar gaining ground at every step. Affirmed triumphed by a neck at the finish. Again, it had been a duel right down to the wire.

None of Affirmed's victories were by large margins, but he *had* beaten Alydar four times out of six. The Laurel Futurity settled it: Affirmed was named Best Two-Year-Old, beating Alydar yet again.

Affirmed was retired for the season after the Laurel Futurity, but Alydar was raced one last time. On November 27, he ran in the Remsen Stakes at Aqueduct. It may have been one race too much: He finished second to a horse named Believe It.

By then, the battle lines for the coming racing year were drawn: Affirmed and Alydar were clearly the ones to beat, but there were other good horses such as Believe It, Star De Naskra, and Sensitive Prince. The year 1978 was going to be a vintage year for racing fans.

Curiously, racing's greatest rival horses had similar personalities: both were kind, easy to work with, and enjoyed people. But there were differences as well.

Affirmed was intelligent, curious, a ham when cameras appeared, and he loved people and loved attention. He was usually very relaxed and cooperative. Equine artist Richard Stone Reeves noted that the horse posed all day for him (five different times) with no problems.

He was friendly and nipped playfully at visitors. He had quick reflexes, "Like a cat, you know," Steve Cauthen recalled. If something surprised him, Affirmed immediately reacted. One day in California, an exercise rider was galloping him. Something startled Affirmed, and at full gallop, he did a U-turn and dumped the exercise rider on his head.

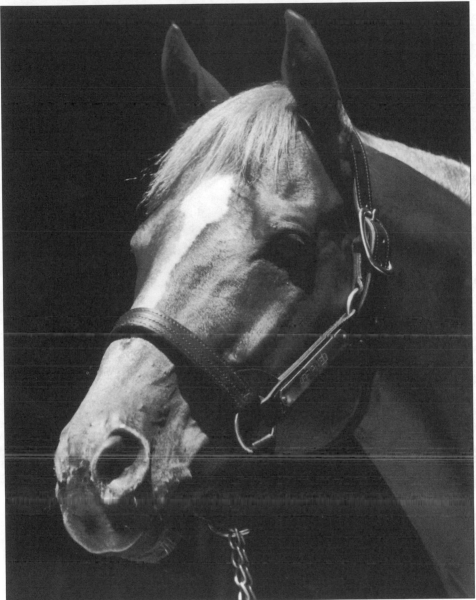

AFFIRMED. *Photo courtesy of Steve Cauthen. Used with permission.*

As for Alydar, he was Lucille Markey's idol. Margaret Glass, Lucille's longtime employee and close friend, said that Alydar added four or five years to Lucille's life. The horse loved attention, and Lucille heaped attention on the horse. By 1978, getting around Calumet was not easy for Lucille Markey. Still, she visited Alydar as often as she could. She put her face near Alydar's, and the horse nuzzled her.

271

There is a wonderful memory of Alydar and Lucille Markey. Alydar ran in the Blue Grass Stakes at Keeneland Race Track, adjacent to Calumet. Ted Bassett, President of Keeneland, sent a car to pick up Gene and Lucille Markey. The couple was elderly and their sight was poor. They were at the outside rail when the post parade for the Blue Grass started. Velasquez brought Alydar over to see the Markeys. Then Alydar did something uniquely memorable. He put his right leg out, bent his left leg, and bowed his head to the lady that loved him so much.

Two fine, good-natured, highly-talented representatives of the equine racing world would battle against each other in 1978. They were the jockeys: Cauthen, the young superstar, and Velasquez, the experienced hand. Over the course of their careers, the two became close friends as well as worthy opponents. When Cauthen was elected to the National Museum of Racing and Hall of Fame in 1994, Velasquez made a special trip to Saratoga just to attend Cauthen's induction. It all sounds too good to be true, but true it is: the two fine horses and the two fine jockeys embodied the real meaning of sportsmanship.

The Florida horse started his 1978 racing year in California and the Kentucky horse started in Florida. Ironic, yes, but there were sound reasons: Calumet Farm had participated in winter racing in Florida going back to Whirlaway's day, while Laz Barrera had established a niche in southern California.

Alydar was first to make the headlines. He won an allowance race at Hialeah on February 11 by two lengths, and followed that with a dazzling 4 1/2-length win in the Flamingo Stakes (then the premiere Florida race) on March 4. A month later he won the Florida Derby at Gulfstream Park on April 1. The New York sportswriters were down in Florida for the winter, and Alydar naturally received their attention.

Following the Florida victories, Alydar returned to Kentucky. For once, the Wood Memorial was *not* the last major prep race for the Triple Crown; that honor belonged in 1978 to the Blue Grass Stakes at Keeneland on April 27. Velasquez rode Alydar against eight other horses, and he won by thirteen lengths.

While Alydar was winning races in the Florida sun, Affirmed was splashing through California mud. The winter of 1977-78 was one of the wettest in California history. The Golden State had three years of drought preceding, but that winter set records for rainfall.[2] The rain interfered with the training of racehorses, and entire weeks passed when the Santa Anita track was so muddy

---

[2] Your author was in law school in California at that time and can personally vouch for the rainfall that winter.

that it was unsafe for a horse to use. At times Barrera simply kept Affirmed in the barn. Moreover, even on the few good days, Barrera was reluctant to exercise his champion horse. A tunnel connected the barn area to the training track, and the trainer worried that Affirmed might become agitated in the tunnel, rear up, and smash his head on the tunnel roof.

The result: Affirmed didn't start until March 8, in a 6 1/2-furlong allowance race worth $30,000 at Santa Anita. Cauthen kept him back at the start, but halfway through rushed him into the lead. They won by five lengths.

Ten days later came the San Felipe Handicap, a 1 1/16-mile, $60,000 race at Santa Anita. Affirmed and Cauthen won that one by two lengths.

The Santa Anita Derby is to California racing what the Flamingo Stakes and then later the Florida Derby are to Florida racing: the major preparatory races for the Kentucky Derby. But in 1978 there was a twist. Cauthen was suspended for a riding infraction. It was his first suspension, and it occurred before the San Felipe Handicap in a race in which Cauthen's horse had finished out of the money. Unusually, the complaint was not registered by another jockey, but by the racing stewards, who stated that "...Cauthen had 'failed to keep a straight course' in the run down the backstretch." Cauthen was suspended for five days.

Cauthen went to court and got a stay on the suspension, hoping he could still ride Affirmed in the Santa Anita Derby. The strategy backfired: the court reviewed the case and sustained the suspension. That meant Cauthen had saved the ride in the San Felipe Handicap only to miss the Santa Anita Derby. Barrera contacted both Angel Cordero and Laffit Pincay to ride Affirmed in the Santa Anita Derby, and they both met with Barrera to toss a coin. Pincay won the toss, and he got the mount on Affirmed.

Cordero's agent objected and went away with hurt feelings. Even considering Affirmed's two victories thus far, that period was difficult for Harbor View, Laz Barrera, Steve Cauthen, and Affirmed.[3]

"This horse has every chance to be like Secretariat and Sham. He does absolutely anything and everything you ask of him."
— Laffit Pincay
on Affirmed,
The New York Times, April 3, 1978.

Affirmed, under Pincay, won the Santa Anita Derby on April 2, 1978, and it helped his reputation. The race was worth $150,000 and was 1 1/8-miles in length. Pincay broke him well and took him into the lead by the half-mile mark. He drew away to win by eight lengths. Pincay, mindful of Affirmed's

---

[3] The reader will recall from the previous chapter the string of disasters that had afflicted the Seattle Slew crew. Gremlins seem to have set upon Affirmed as well.

tendency to cruise when in the lead, hit him a couple of times to keep the horse focused. "He had so much left when we hit the backstretch, I didn't want to take a chance of getting trapped by horses moving up on the outside, so I let him run a little. I started to ride him at the three-sixteenths and hit him twice at the eighth pole just to remind him we were still in a race," Pincay explained.

The win was impressive, and the California racing *cognoscenti* believed he was the favorite for the Kentucky Derby. But Alydar had won the Florida Derby just the day before the Santa Anita Derby, had the Calumet connection. He benefited from the easier access New York sportswriters had to the Florida tracks. *The New York Times* on April 3 published a telling layout. On page 3 of the sports section, the Red Smith column appeared at the top of the page. It carried the title, "A Colt Built for Two" and spoke of Alydar and Jorge Velasquez. Directly beneath the Red Smith column was the legend: "Racing: Affirmed Easy Victor."

Affirmed raced one last time in California before resuming the duel with Alydar. On April 16, Cauthen rode him in the Hollywood Derby at Hollywood Park. The race was 1 1/8 miles, and worth $250,000. Affirmed was the favorite, at $0.30 to $1.

Laz Barrera badly wanted to win this one, the last race for Affirmed before Churchill Downs. Perhaps it was the missed training caused by bad weather, perhaps victories were coming too easy. Laz told Cauthen, "I want to make sure Affirmed gets something out of this race."

The jockey complied. Cauthen took him right to the lead. Radar Ahead stayed behind him for most of the race, and then Think Snow (an incongruous name for a horse running in California) nipped Radar Ahead and challenged Affirmed.

But the race was never really in doubt. Affirmed was firmly in first, idling and relaxed, pricking his ears, and looking around at the scenery (much like Gallant Fox or Citation). Cauthen remembered, "He was just floating along." Mindful of the trainer's instructions, Cauthen smacked his horse on the butt five or six times. That got Affirmed's attention: he put his mind back on the race and bolted home two lengths ahead of Think Snow.

Now Affirmed was four for four, including the San Felipe Handicap, the Santa Anita Derby, and the Hollywood Derby. His winnings thus far: $490,000.

But the experts were still not convinced. If anything, Cauthen's use of the whip in the Hollywood Derby merely confirmed Alydar's superiority. "The big talk at the time was, 'Oh, Steve Cauthen had to really get after Affirmed, and he only won by two lengths,'" Cauthen remembered.

The experts overlooked something: like Gallant Fox before him, Affirmed needed competition. When he was too far in front he relaxed and slowed down. If Alydar had been at Hollywood Park that day, Affirmed would have responded to Alydar's challenge and the two would have resumed their duel. In Cauthen's words, Affirmed and Alydar would have been "...ten lengths clear of the field." In the Hollywood Derby, Affirmed was much the best, and the horse knew it: He was "...always two lengths in front, you know, just far enough in front where he thought he was done with the race, and yet still, you know, he was just floating along," the jockey remembered.

They challenged each other as two year olds, and Affirmed stood four to two over Alydar. Affirmed was unbeaten thus far as a three-year-old and had won nearly a half-million in purses already.

And yet...and yet...Affirmed's 1977 victories over Alydar had all been close. And, with the exception of the Santa Anita Derby, none of his 1978 California victories were impressive.

On the other hand, Alydar's two-year-old victories over Affirmed *were* impressive. Now he was a year older, and perhaps Alydar would have the extra step on Affirmed that Affirmed had had on him the year before. Alydar, too, was four-for-four, and he had captured $423,000 in purses so far, almost as much as Affirmed. Affirmed had the San Felipe, Santa Anita, and Hollywood Derbies to his credit, while Alydar boasted of victories in the Flamingo Stakes, the Florida Derby, and the Blue Grass Stakes.

Gene and Lucille Markey were both in their eighties, infirm and with failing vision. They had gone through Calumet's joys of the Fifties and its misfortunes of the Sixties. Now, at last, Calumet had first-class horses again, and one in particular. Alydar was the favorite for the 1978 Kentucky Derby at odds of 6 to 5. Affirmed was second, at 9 to 5.

> *"He is one of those horses who know exactly who they are,*
> *and the look I got seemed to say,*
> *'You are looking at a Triple Crown winner,*
> *and don't you EVER forget it!*
> *I beat that "other" horse three for three when it counted.'"*
> — A racing enthusiast,
> recalling a visit with Affirmed in the 1980s.

May 6, 1978, Churchill Downs, Louisville, Kentucky.
104th Running of the Kentucky Derby:

Eleven horses are entered. Besides Affirmed and Alydar, Believe It and Sensitive Prince are the only ones whose odds are in single digits. The other seven entrants have odds ranging from $33 to $1 to $123.70 to $1. The Churchill Downs Track is fast. All eyes are on Affirmed and Alydar.

Cauthen leads his horse onto the track for the post parade. The sound of the crowd singing "My Old Kentucky Home" stirs the blood of the Kentucky native. He turned eighteen just five days ago, and has not yet graduated from high school. After the post parade, the horses are loaded into the gate. Affirmed, second from the post, goes in easily with no hesitation. Affirmed and Cauthen wait while the remaining horses enter the giant green-painted machinery. Alydar, in tenth, is loaded into the gate next to last. At 5:41 P.M., after the last horse, Sensitive Prince, is loaded in. The starter presses the button and the gates fly open.

Affirmed breaks easily. Dr. Valeri and Raymond Earl, two of the longshots, take an early lead, but Affirmed is only a head behind them. Alydar is far back, ninth of eleven horses. The horses round the first turn, but Cauthen keeps his horse in reserve. He lets Affirmed drop into third, six lengths back. Sensitive Prince passes Raymond Earl and moves into in first. Velasquez keeps Alydar back in the pack. He knows that Alydar is like his Calumet predecessor Whirlaway: He can make one good run, and time it perfectly.

Affirmed relaxes through three-quarters of a mile. Cauthen keeps him in third, still six lengths back, but he knows that Affirmed has plenty of speed left. Alydar moves up a little bit, but not much. At the three-quarter mark, Alydar is in eighth.

Then both favorites make their move: Cauthen gets after Affirmed and he passes Sensitive Prince. Believe It had earlier caught Sensitive Prince and is in first. But the California horse is charging, now only a length behind the leader.

In the back, Velasquez has taken Alydar wide. The Calumet silks, so familiar at Churchill Downs, steadily pass horses. At the head of the stretch, Affirmed has passed Believe It and is two lengths in front. Believe it stays in second, but Alydar gains on him.

Cauthen smacks Affirmed a couple of times just to make sure that the horse keeps his mind on the race; he doesn't want a replay of last year's Champagne Stakes. Alydar passes Believe It, but Alydar's last-minute charge is a trifle *too* late and a bit *too* wide. He is in second, 1 1/2 lengths behind, as Steve Cauthen and Affirmed cross under Churchill Downs' finish line.

AFFIRMED winning the 1978 Kentucky Derby, Steve Cauthen up in the pink and black silks of Harbor View Farm. *Photo courtesy Steve Cauthen.*

May 20, 1978, Pimlico Race Track, Baltimore, Maryland.
103rd Running of the Preakness Stakes:

The Preakness Stakes field is smaller, only seven horses. Affirmed is now the favorite at $0.50 to $1. Alydar is second-choice at $1.80 to $1. The odds have switched, as have the pole positions of the horses. Alydar is in the second spot while Affirmed is loaded next to last. The horses again go into the starting gate. And again, at 5:41 P.M., the starter presses the button. The gates again fly open, and the horses break.

Track Reward, an $88.70 to $1 longshot, takes the early lead. Cauthen keeps Affirmed right with Track Reward, only a head behind the leader. In the first turn, Track Reward drifts out a little bit. Affirmed and Cauthen scoot by to take the lead. During this whole play, Alydar is once again in the back of the pack at sixth. Velasquez on Alydar is waiting.

Cauthen and Affirmed slow the pace, keeping something in reserve for Alydar's certain late charge. The pace is fairly slow for a fast track, a half-mile in 47 3/5 seconds (later, Cauthen remembers the slow time, saying, "…for those horses, that's a very slow pace.")

Affirmed stays in first throughout the half-mile, the three- quarter mile, and the stretch. No horse has yet seriously challenged him. Until now…

Alydar moves up. He has passes Indigo Star, Believe It, and Noon Time Spender. Now there is only the bright red horse, the pink-white-black silks in front of him. Alydar surges up to challenge Affirmed in the stretch. Affirmed is in front by only a head as they pass the sixteenth pole.

Now the horses and jockeys are moving almost in unison, and it will look on the film afterward much like a ballet: Cauthen, whip/Velasquez, whip; Cauthen, whip/Velasquez, whip; Cauthen, whip/Velasquez, whip; Cauthen, handride/Velasquez, handride. *Affirmed just will not let Alydar pass him.* He keeps his head in front, his right car slightly cocked towards his perennial challenger. They cross Pimlico's finish line. Affirmed wins by a neck.

> *"The race was really going to be between the two of us again…I think*
> *their theory was that this time, with a mile and a half…if they challenged us*
> *soon enough or early enough, they would just wear us down."*
> — Steve Cauthen, 1996,
> on the 1978 Belmont Stakes.

AFFIRMED with Steve Cauthen up wins the 1978 Preakness Stakes over **ALYDAR** with Jorge Velasquez up. *Photo courtesy Steve Cauthen. Used with permission.*

June 10, 1978, Belmont Park, Long Island, New York.
110th Running of the Belmont Stakes:

The Belmont Stakes field is even smaller than the Preakness, just five horses. Three good horses, Darby Creek Road, Judge Advocate, and Noon Time Spender are entered with Affirmed and Alydar. It has been true for the last year: Affirmed and Alydar are the ones to beat.

The pressure on Cauthen, Barrera, and the rest of Affirmed's crew has been immense these last three weeks since the Preakness. Twenty-five years separated Citation and Secretariat; now in a span of just five years, there is the possibility of three Triple Crown winners. And, with Seattle Slew having won the Triple Crown the year before, there is the possibility of back-to-back Triple Crowns. That has *never* happened before. It could happen today.

Cauthen handles it well, but he is only eighteen years old. He is constantly interviewed, even by Japanese media. But he is poised as well as youthful. He tries to relax, hoping just to go out and do his best. It is difficult: "The one thing I don't want to do is not win the Triple Crown because of *my* mistakes," the jockey remembers later[4].

Affirmed is again the bettors' favorite, at $0.60 to $1. The odds on him have dropped even lower since the Derby and Preakness. The odds have dropped on Alydar, too: He is at $1.10 to $1.

Affirmed draws pole position number three, smack in the middle of the five-horse race. Alydar is on his left, at pole position number two. It really doesn't matter much since the field is so small.

Instead of "*My Old Kentucky Home*," or "*Maryland, My Maryland*," Cauthen hears "*The Sidewalks of New York*." And again the horses load into the starting gate. At 5:43 P.M., two minutes later than the Derby and Preakness, the starter presses the button. The final leg of the 1978 Triple Crown begins.

Affirmed's crew knows that Alydar is not a front-running horse, so as in the Preakness, Cauthen hustles Affirmed right to the lead in order to set the pace. He eases his horse over to the left, so that Alydar cannot come by on the inside. When the challenge comes, as it surely will, Alydar must come from the outside.

Alydar and Velasquez have a different game plan. Instead of keeping Alydar back, Velasquez puts him close to Affirmed early. He won't let Affirmed get too far ahead.

Alydar stays right behind Affirmed through most of the race. The pace is very slow: the half-mile is run in fifty seconds. Cauthen *wants* this part of the race to be slow for he knows that Alydar's challenge will make the second half of the race very fast.

But then, with seven furlongs to go, over three-quarters of a mile,

---

[4] In a 1996 interview with author Robert L. Shoop.

Velasquez eases Alydar to the outside to begin the challenge. It is very far out from the wire to do that, but this is not just any Belmont. The crowd sees it, and starts to roar: this is what they came for, Affirmed and Alydar, battling for every step.

For a little while, Affirmed and Alydar eye each other: neither one wants to be the first to make a move. Affirmed is still in the lead, but only by a head. Alydar is close, almost on Affirmed. Then the deadly ballet begins again: Cauthen, whip/Velasquez, whip; Cauthen, whip/Velasquez, whip. The pace increases with every step. Cauthen lets out the reins on Affirmed. So does Velasquez on Alydar.

It has been a long five months for Affirmed: the miserable weather in California, the races at Santa Anita and Hollywood, the Kentucky Derby and the Preakness. He starts to tire, ever so imperceptibly, and Cauthen feels the distress signals from him coming through the reins. Cauthen thinks, *We're going to have to pull everything out. It's time to give it our best shot.*

A moment later, Alydar gets a nose in front of Affirmed.

Affirmed is tiring. Cauthen has used the whip on him, and it may just be that their time is over, that Affirmed has been raced just *too* much to win the Triple Crown. Velasquez and Alydar are *very* tight on Affirmed's right. There is no time to panic. There is only one thing to do.

Now, all the long-ago hours practicing in the loft in Kentucky pay off for Cauthen. If you blink while watching the film, you will miss it: Cauthen switches the whip from his right hand to his left. Cauthen does what he has *never* done before: He hits Affirmed on the left side. How will the horse react?

"He went into a gear I didn't know he had," Cauthen remembers years later.

The gear then-unknown to Cauthen is the same gear that made War Admiral and Count Fleet set Belmont Stakes records on just three good legs each. It is the same gear Assault found to wrest control of the 1947 Butler Handicap from the greatest jockey of all time and defeat Stymie by a neck.

Affirmed digs in, drives forward relentlessly, and gets his head back in front of Alydar. They stay that way down the stretch, Affirmed a head in front, Alydar never giving up, as they cross the finish line in the 1978 Belmont Stakes.

AFFIRMED/Cauthen inside, **ALYDAR**/Velasquez outside, 1978 Belmont Stakes. Note whip in Cauthen's LEFT hand. *Photo courtesy Steve Cauthen. Used with permission.*

> *"...that's the mark of a true champion...you're starting to get weary and you can still find it within yourself to pull out that [little] bit extra...when in my heart I wasn't sure that there was anything left, he found something."*
> — Steve Cauthen, 1996,

282

on Affirmed in the 1978 Belmont Stakes.

"That's the only race I ever cried over," Margaret Glass remembered.

Affirmed won the Triple Crown by margins of 1 1/2 lengths in the Kentucky Derby, a neck in the Preakness, and a head in the Belmont. Totaled, he had won all three races by less than two lengths. His winning times were simply incredible: 2:01 1/5 in the Derby, then the fifth-fastest time; 1:54 2/5 in the Preakness, equal to Secretariat's and Seattle Slew's times; 2:26 4/5 in the Belmont, then the second-fastest time in Belmont history. Affirmed and Alydar were both *that* good, and Affirmed was just that *one* bit better. The score was now Affirmed 7, Alydar 2.

But Affirmed had won the Triple Crown fair and square, and it was time to get on with racing. Affirmed took a two month rest, but Alydar, like so many other great ones, was taken to Arlington Park near Chicago to run in the Arlington Classic on July 22. He won by thirteen lengths. Then Calumet Farms took him to Saratoga: the Travers Stakes there would be the rematch between him and Affirmed. Calumet decided he needed a tune-up first: Alydar was entered in the Whitney Stakes at Saratoga on August 5. He won by ten lengths.

Affirmed's first race after the Triple Crown was the Jim Dandy Stakes on August 8. It was a rematch with Sensitive Prince, and Cauthen kept him back for most of the 1 1/8-mile race. At the head of the stretch, Sensitive Prince had a four-length lead. Then Cauthen let Affirmed go, and the Triple Crown winner surged forward. It was a cliff-hanger, but Affirmed caught Sensitive Prince to win by a half-length. His time of 1:47 4/5 broke the race record. Steve Cady put it very well in *The New York Times* account of the race: "A few yards past the finish line in today's $36,295 Jim Dandy Stakes, first-place Affirmed pricked his ears forward as if to ask his fans, 'What were you so worried about?'"

But the next day, disaster struck. At Saratoga, Cauthen's horse went down and he suffered a dislocated shoulder and broken kneecap. Now he was out for the Travers. Barrera called on Laffit Pincay and he was available. Pincay was a great jockey, to be sure; but the Cauthen accident signaled the beginning of a long dry spell for Affirmed.[5]

Ever since Jim Dandy upset Gallant Fox in the 1930 Travers Stakes, the summer races at Saratoga had the reputation as being fertile ground for racing controversy. Affirmed was the favorite, while Alydar was again second choice. At the start, Affirmed and another horse, Shake Shake Shake (ridden by Angel Cordero) took an early lead. Alydar was last in the four-horse field. After a quarter-mile, Shake Shake Shake was on the inside rail. He was close to Affirmed, and Pincay took Affirmed to the outside. There matters stayed for about half a mile; then Velasquez saw a hole and steered Alydar towards it.

---

[5] In December, 1999, Pincay broke Bill Shoemaker's record to become the winningest jockey in history. He retired in early 2003.

Pincay must have thought that Alydar would come from the outside, and he may have panicked. Pincay steered Affirmed towards the rail and shut Alydar off. Velasquez quickly pulled up Alydar; the reaction caused Alydar to bump the rail and almost threw Velasquez off. Somehow, Velasquez got Alydar back into the game and they finished second, 1 3/4 lengths behind Affirmed.

Immediately the "Inquiry" light flashed on. The stewards looked at the race film, and held that Pincay's action constituted a foul. Affirmed was disqualified and Alydar was moved into first place.

The two rivals never met again on a race track. The Travers had left a bad taste in everyone's mouth. The final score was Affirmed 7, Alydar 3, but one of the races was tainted. Still, they were memorable contests. One wonders when we shall see such competition again in horse racing.

The Travers result marked the beginning of misfortunes for both horses. It was Alydar's last race of 1978. Calumet planned to enter him in the Marlboro Cup in September, but he suffered a hairline fracture in his right foot and was out for six months.

He came back at the end of March, 1979, to win an allowance race at Hialeah. Alydar was then taken to Oaklawn Park at Hot Springs, Arkansas, to run in the Oaklawn Handicap on April 13. He finished second. Another second-place finish followed in the Carter Handicap at Aqueduct on May 5, then a sixth-place finish in the Metropolitan Handicap at Belmont on May 28.

Alydar's last win was on June 17, 1979, in the Nassau County Handicap at Belmont Park. He raced one more time, in the Suburban Handicap at Belmont on July 4, where he finished third. Calumet entered Alydar in the Brooklyn Handicap, but he suffered a hairline fracture in his right hind ankle shortly before the race. He was retired permanently.

Alydar was the first horse (and to date, *only* horse) to *place* in all three Triple Crown races.[6] There is nearly universal agreement that in almost any other racing year, he would have won the Triple Crown.

Never before had there been back-to-back Triple Crown winners, and it was inevitable that Affirmed would face Seattle Slew. The first meeting between the two of them occurred on September 16, 1978, in the Marlboro Cup at Belmont Park. Cauthen was back on Affirmed, but even with Cauthen, Affirmed was at a disadvantage; Seattle Slew was a year older, stronger, and more experienced. Recall Cauthen's comment: "I think any time you have great horses like that, the four-year-old has a great advantage, because it's kind of like a twenty-five-year-old man taking on a sixteen-year-old."

---

[6] In the interests of completeness, one horse, Mane Minister, finished third in all the Triple Crown races in 1991.

In the bettors' minds, that physical inequality wasn't apparent: Seattle Slow had raced only intermittently in 1978 with mixed success. Affirmed was the favorite, at $0.50 to $1, while the Slew was at $2.10 to $1. The entire race was between the Triple Crown winners: Angel Cordero, Seattle Slew's jockey, took his horse straight to the lead. Cauthen kept Affirmed close to the Slew, but Seattle Slew was just the best. Every time Cauthen and Affirmed tried to catch Cordero and the Slew, Seattle Slew just increased the lead. Cauthen remembered, "He was just on that day too good for us."

Still, second place always paid some money: $66,000 in this case. Affirmed had now won $901,541 during 1978. That set a new record for a single year's winnings.

Affirmed's last race of 1978 was the Jockey Club Gold Cup at Belmont on October 14. The Affirmed crew wanted their horse to be near the front during the race, so Seattle Slew couldn't get away. But it can only be said of Affirmed in this race that he was "snake-bit." The Slew jumped out quickly, as did Affirmed. For the first time, however, Affirmed got a bit rank: he wanted to pull at the bit. Then total disaster struck: Cauthen was trying to get him focused when his saddle slipped. The jockey wound up straddling his horse's withers.

That just made Affirmed run harder, and all Cauthen could do was hang on for dear life. They went through the race that way and finished fifth of out of the six horses entered. It was the only time in his racing career he finished out of the money. (Seattle Slew went on to stage a memorable duel with Exceller, the European horse entered. The Slew lost by a nose.)

It was a miserable end to a great year: eleven races, eight wins, one win which was disqualified, one second, and one unplaced finish due to circumstances beyond Affirmed's control. He had won the Triple Crown and broken the previous one-year winnings record. Yes, he accomplished all those things, but there were the challenges from Alydar and the losses to Seattle Slew. Still, he was named Horse of the Year for 1978, and he richly deserved it.

Barrera again took his horses out to California during the winter, and Cauthen went along to ride. The winter of 1978-79 was a very wet one, and all the problems of the previous winter repeated themselves.[7] Barrera simply could not get his horses in peak form early. None of them, Affirmed included, were running well.

On top of that, Steve Cauthen was having his problems. Jockeys go into slumps, like batters in baseball. Starting January 1, 1979, Cauthen suffered a 110-race losing streak, a *very* rare occurrence for a high-caliber jockey. He just wasn't getting good horses: Laz Barrera's horses weren't ready, while other trainers didn't give Cauthen many horses to ride. That put him into a spin of sorts: He lost a little confidence in his career and became confused about his

---

[7] Your author suffered through this California winter, too. It was another record-setter for rainfall.

riding.

Affirmed hadn't won a race since the Jim Dandy Stakes. He, too, was in a slump. He would climb out of it eventually, but not without some hard choices.

Affirmed's first race of 1979 was the seven-furlong Malibu Stakes on January 7 at Santa Anita. He was the favorite, but he didn't run like it: he finished third. He broke well, and ran well early, but "...when it came time to press the button and go ahead and do what we all knew he could do, he just never really fired...," Cauthen recalled.

Affirmed raced again thirteen days later in the San Fernando Stakes at Santa Anita, and again, the results were much the same. He finished second in a field of eight horses. Again, he just failed to fire.

Counting the Travers disqualification, Affirmed had now lost five consecutive races. The Travers was due to bad handling and the Jockey Club Gold Cup loss was beyond Affirmed's control, but clearly, *something* was at work. In fact, Cauthen and Affirmed were booed after the San Fernando Stakes.

The recriminations started, many of them aimed at the Triple Crown jockey. Even Laz Barrera was concerned: "There's nothing wrong with him [Affirmed]; he isn't hurting. He'll run in the Strub [Stakes]. Stevie, I'm worried about...Maybe Stevie needs a little change, to go someplace else for a while..."

Maybe it *was* time. William Steinkraus, one of America's greatest equestrians, wrote in 1990: "There will come a time when a rider must get out on his own; he can't always rely on the advice of his teacher. An excellent example of this is Steve Cauthen; if he hadn't taken the decision to move to England when the opportunity presented itself, I don't think he would have been the rider that he is today."

Shortly after the San Fernando Stakes, Steve Cauthen left California to ride in the winter meets in New York. But Robert Sangster, a successful English businessman and horse enthusiast, needed another jockey. He made Cauthen an offer, and the jockey accepted. He traveled to England that April to begin the second phase of his jockey career.

Of all the Triple Crown winners, only Count Fleet had one jockey, John Longden, for his entire racing career. The others had multiple jockeys. But typically, one jockey stood out and was clearly identified with a particular horse. So it was with Affirmed: Cauthen was "his" jockey. Just as Citation seemed slightly incomplete without Eddie Arcaro, Affirmed seemed slightly incomplete without Steve Cauthen.

Bill Shoemaker, Steve Cauthen, and John Longden. *Photo Courtesy Steve Cauthen. Used with permission.*

Laffit Pincay was forgiven for the Travers Stakes. On February 4, at Santa Anita, Pincay rode Affirmed in the Charles H. Strub Stakes. The jockey change worked; Pincay kept him back in the early part of the race, but then sent him forward in the backstretch. Affirmed took command and won by *ten* longths. His time of 2:01 for the 1 1/4-mile race set a new track record.

After that came the Santa Anita Handicap on March 4. It was a 1 1/4-mile race, and again, Affirmed made it look easy: He was in first by 3/4 of a mile and never gave it up. He won by 4 1/2 lengths in time of 1:58 4/5. It was another track record.

Could anyone stop him now? He rested two months and raced at Hollywood Park on May 20 in the Californian Stakes, a 1 1/16-mile race. That one proved just as easy as the previous two races had been: Affirmed set no track record time, but he captured first by five lengths.

Up to this point, racing's all-time money winner was Kelso, who earned $1,977,896 over nine seasons. Affirmed had earned $1,769,218. The Hollywood Gold Cup, one of California's greatest races, would be run on June 24. It was worth $275,000. Could Affirmed do it? Could Affirmed cross the $2 million mark?

Affirmed took an early lead, but was pressed throughout the race by Sirlad. For a bit, it reminded people of the previous duels with Alydar. Sirlad at times was only a neck behind the Triple Crown champion. In the stretch, Affirmed pulled away to win by 3/4 of a length.

Racing's first equine millionaire was Citation; racing's first multi-millionaire was his latest Triple Crown successor, Affirmed. Both of them set those records in the Hollywood Gold Cup.

Barrera sent Affirmed east for a two-month rest, and then ran him at Belmont Park in a non-betting exhibition race on August 29. The exhibition race was a prep race for the Woodward Stakes on September 22 and the Jockey Club Gold Cup on October 6. He beat two other horses handily. Patrice Wolfson, one of his owners, looked at him in the paddock. "He knows where he is, all right," Patrice said.

Affirmed ran the Woodward like many of his past races: he hung back, even dropping into fourth in the five-horse field, but at the 3/8 pole, Pincay sent him. He won by 2 1/2 lengths.

Finally there was the Jockey Club Gold Cup, the race where his saddle had slipped the year before. Three other horses challenged him, and he faced the 1979 Triple Crown race winners: Spectacular Bid, winner of the Kentucky Derby and Preakness, and Coastal, winner of the Belmont Stakes. Moreover, Spectacular Bid's owners were not going to let Affirmed have this one; to make things worse, they hired Bill Shoemaker to ride the Bid.

It really didn't matter much: Affirmed took the lead by the half-mile and held onto it for another mile. It was close at one point: both Coastal and the Bid took their shots at him, but he hung on to win by 3/4 of a length. Steve Cady wrote: "The golden Florida-bred chestnut colt showed once more that he almost never allows a rival to get past him once he takes the lead. If you don't believe it, just ask Spectacular Bid."

It was an appropriate valediction for one of racing's greatest horses. He had sewn up the title of Horse of the Year for 1979. Barrera and the Wolfsons entered him in the Turf Classic at Aqueduct. It was a grass race, and Barrera tried him out on the new racing surface. He didn't show the same qualities on grass that he did on dirt, and that clinched it. Affirmed was just too valuable to risk in a grass race. He was withdrawn from the Turf Classic. On October 22, 1979, Barrera announced that Affirmed had been retired from racing.

There was a goodbye party for him at Aqueduct on November 10. (Whirlaway, Citation, and Secretariat had been honored with similar days.) Affirmed was jogged up and down in front of the stands at Aqueduct. A few days later, he was flown to Spendthrift Farm in Kentucky to begin stud duty.

Pincay was asked later what impressed him most about Affirmed: "He was a fighter. I never see a horse likes to fight so much to win a race," the jockey said.

Affirmed's record stood at: 29 starts, 22 wins, 5 seconds, 1 third, 1 unplaced finish. He was the last horse to win the Triple Crown, and racing's first equine multimillionaire, with earnings of $2,393,818. Best Two-Year-Old Male Horse of 1977, Best Three-Year-Old Male Horse of 1978, Best Handicap Male Horse of 1979, Horse of the Year for 1978 and again in 1979. Of his Triple Crown predecessors, only Whirlaway boasted as many accolades. Affirmed had come, had seen, had conquered.

> *"Affirmed had that extra ounce, but whether it was ability to stay the distance, whether it was pure determination, whatever it was, he just seemed to have that extra ounce that made the difference."*
> — Racing historian Thomas Gilcoyne, 1995

Much happened after 1979 to the principals in this last of the Triple Crown sagas. Steve Cauthen went to Europe in 1979 and continued riding in England and on the continent. He stayed overseas for fourteen years. He was the champion jockey in England in 1984, the first American to win that title in seventy-one years. He won the Epsom Derby in England in 1985, the French Derby and the Irish Derby in 1989, and the Derby *Italiano* in 1991. Added to his Kentucky Derby win on Affirmed, those victories made him the only jockey to have won the world's five major derby races.

Cauthen returned to the USA for the 1992 Belmont Stakes. Over the years, he grew four more inches to 5'6", tall for a jockey. The jockey's persistent problem, keeping his weight down, was exacerbated by his added height. From 1977 to 1992, he did virtually everything a rider could do. Moreover, he had married. There was a new family to consider. It was time to come home. He ended his overseas riding contract in January, 1993, retired as a jockey, and joined Turfway Park in Florence, Kentucky, as a vice-president. He was inducted into the National Museum of Racing and Hall of Fame and Museum on August 8, 1994.

Occasionally Steve Cauthen visited Affirmed at Spendthrift Farm, at Calumet, and at Jonabell. Affirmed showed little recognition of his Triple Crown jockey: on the ground, Cauthen was just another person. Maybe if Cauthen had ridden Affirmed, it might have been different: "I think the real relationship we had was when I was on his back, and I think that my...my whatever...the vibes I sent him through the reins and through being on his back was where he knew who I really was," Cauthen said.

Steve Cauthen remains a gracious gentleman, willing to reach out to others. In 1997 Gary Stevens won the first two legs of the Triple Crown on Silver Charm. Naturally, the press contacted the last Triple Crown jockey. "It was fun being the last one to win it," Cauthen recalled. He added, "I was eighteen at the time, and it was the thrill of a lifetime. So, I hope that Silver Charm and Gary Stevens can do it next Saturday, and share the thrill of a lifetime." That says much about winning the Triple Crown, and more about Steve Cauthen.

Laz Barrera kept training. In 1986, one of his horses, Tiffany Lass, was voted champion three-year-old filly. Controversy touched him after that; he and six other trainers were barred from entering horses after one of his mounts, Endow, tested positive for a cocaine metabolite. Later tests proved inconclusive and all charges were dropped. Laz Barrera died on April 25, 1991 of pneumonia in Downey, California.

On Alydar's side of the picture, Jorge Velasquez stayed on as a jockey. By 1993, he was fourth on the all-time list of winning jockeys with 6,614 wins to his credit. He retired from riding in December, 1997.

For Alydar, the years after 1979 were good ones. He may not have had that one extra step on Affirmed on the race track, but Alydar was ahead as a sire. Alydar became one of the great sires of all time, and his greatest offspring was Alysheba, who won the 1987 Kentucky Derby and Preakness.[8] Alysheba retired as the all-time leading money-winning horse, beating Affirmed's record. During the 1980s, Alydar's siring services were in great demand. In addition to Alysheba, Alydar sired Strike the Gold, winner of the 1991 Kentucky Derby, as well as championship horses such as Easy Goer, winner of the 1989 Belmont Stakes, and Althea, Turkoman, and Criminal Type.

Alydar died on November 14, 1990. The previous day he had somehow broken his leg in his stall. After thirty-six hours of desperate treatment, he was put down. Alydar is buried at the Calumet Farm Cemetery near Whirlaway and Citation.[9]

Steve Cauthen said of Alydar, "He was, you know, a truly great horse, too."

---

[8] As of March 20, 1995, Alydar's offspring had won the total of $51,143,508 in purses. He sired 708 foals, of which 496 were starters and 348 were winners. Alysheba alone accounted for $6,679,242 of the total.

[9] Alydar's death coincided with the end of the old Calumet. Overleveraged when the financial boom of the 1980s ended, Calumet eventually went bankrupt and was sold at auction in early 1992. Henryk de Kwiatkowski purchased Calumet Farm at the resulting auction and has kept it open. In 1990-92, there were many theories floating around the Bluegrass Country that Alydar's broken leg was somehow engineered to result in his death and thus enable Calumet to collect on his insurance. Ann Hagedorn Auerbach's 1994 book, *Wild Ride*, details Calumet's financial condition in the 1980s and relates some of the "conspiracy" theories surrounding Alydar's demise. However, we will never know the truth as to what happened to Alydar on November 13, 1990, and it is best to resist any speculation as to same. We should let him rest.

290

"These people go to the sales and they buy Mr. Prospector,
Seattle Slew babies that look great. But they can never look inside
and see the heart and mind, and he has both.
He has that desire to win, and he gave every ounce he had."
— Steve Cauthen on Affirmed,
ESPN *Sportszone*, May 3, 1998.

Affirmed remains the victor in this last Triple Crown story of the Twentieth Century. Some critics have linked him with Sir Barton, Omaha, and Citation as a failure at stud. Even more so than Citation, this is not true. He was an excellent sire, in demand up to the last few months of his life: through January 11, 2001, the day before he died, he sired 423 race-winning horses with seventy-seven stakes winners included for purses totaling $40,759, 855. His best foal was Flawlessly, champion grass mare in 1992 and again in 1993.

Affirmed's influence was felt internationally. He sired Irish champion Trusted Partner, Canadian champion Peteski, Irish/English champion Zoman, Canadian champion horses Charlie Barley and One From Heaven, French champions Affidavit and Bint Pasha, Italian champions Tibullo and Medi Flash, and another Irish champion, Easy to Copy. In 1998, vindication of Affirmed's siring appeared in print: *Sports Illustrated* wrote of him: "Affirmed has not sired any great Thoroughbreds, but a great many good ones, including [at that time] sixty-four stakes winners."

Affirmed stood at stud first at Spendthrift Farm, but when Spendthrift went bankrupt, he was placed at Calumet. Fittingly, he resided in a stall next to Alydar. In August, 1991 he moved to Jonabell Farm, where he lived out his life. In the autumn of 2000 he injured an ankle. An operation was technically successful, but he developed additional problems, aggravated by his advancing age. By January, 2001, it was clear the last Triple Crown winner of the Twentieth Century would not last much longer. On January 12, 2001, Affirmed was euthanized. He was buried at Jonabell Farm with a set of pink and black silks from Harbor View Farm.

"This horse knew he was good all the way through, till the end.
He knew he was in trouble, but he didn't give us any.
He had that kind of smarts. He was as much a champion in his
days of despair as he was in his days of glory."
— Jimmy Bell of Jonabell Farm
on Affirmed's last days.

Affirmed was a stellar horse, trained by a great trainer, and ridden by a great jockey. But there will always be a bit of irony, even tragedy, surrounding him. For Affirmed is unique in the Triple Crown saga: He is the only Triple

Crown winner who is forever stalked by the memory of the horse he beat.

Steve Cauthen (left) and Eddie Arcaro with their Triple Crown silks. Harbor View Farm pink, white and black; Calumet Farm red and blue. *Photo courtesy Steve Cauthen. Used with permission.*

POSTSCRIPT

As I write this, it is the 25th year since Steve Cauthen switched the whip from his right hand to his left in the 1978 Belmont Stakes. Twenty-five years have passed since Affirmed dug back in and won the Triple Crown by a head.

Since I started writing this book, Affirmed, Seattle Slew, Eddie Arcaro, Warren Mehrtens, Lucien Laurin, Jimmy Jones and, most recently, John Longden have passed away. Also, since I started this book, eight horses have won two legs of the Triple Crown: Tabasco Cat, Thunder Gulch, Silver Charm, Real Quiet, Charismatic, Point Given, War Emblem and Funny Cide. Wonderful horses, all of them; great horses, some of them. But none passed racing's greatest challenge.

Skeptics say, given the nature of modern racing (its expense, the breeding, the emphasis on early speed and a quick return on investment), that today's thoroughbreds are fragile and more likely to burn out early. These same skeptics avow that there will never be another Triple Crown horse, and that the fraternity of Sir Barton, Gallant Fox, Omaha, War Admiral, Whirlaway, Count Fleet, Assault, Citation, Secretariat, Seattle Slew, and Affirmed is forever closed to new members. At least, that is what some say.

Yet, similar prognostications were ventured during the twenty-five years between the day Eddie Arcaro guided Citation to victory and the day that Ron Turcotte noticed Secretariat wasn't straining, just breathing regularly and evenly on the backstretch of Belmont Park. So there is nothing new about the current skeptics; we've heard their pronouncements before.

Someday there will be another horse that, guided by a fine jockey, wins the three great races at Churchill Downs, Pimlico, and Belmont Park. Will the horse be an unknown, like Sir Barton? An obscurity that rose to triumph, like Assault? A favorite, like Gallant Fox, Omaha, War Admiral, Whirlaway, Count Fleet, Citation, Secretariat, or Seattle Slew? Will we be treated to another trio of great duels such as Affirmed and Alydar showed us? Or, wonder of wonders, could the exclusive men's club of Triple Crown winners be forced to accommodate a filly?

The answers to those questions are unknowable. What I DO know

295

is that Thoroughbreds will be born in Kentucky, Virginia, California, Florida, and elsewhere; that people will hear the magnificent thundering rhythm of racers rounding the far turn, and thrill to their rippling muscles and shining coats. The joy and disappointment of fans betting on their horses will endure. The hope of seeing a Triple Crown winner will arise again on every first Saturday of May in Louisville.

Yes, there will be another Triple Crown winner. But when it will happen, with which horse, which jockey, which trainer, which stable...

That is the mystery and the romance, complete and eternal, of horse racing.

Robert L. Shoop
Colorado Springs, Colorado
February 3, 2003

AFTERWORD: *SEABISCUIT,* FUNNY CIDE, AND THE TRIPLE CROWN

Laura Hillenbrand's *Seabiscuit* has been a godsend for Thoroughbred racing. Thousands, perhaps millions, have read the quintessential rags-to-riches horse racing story. *Seabiscuit* has created its own industry; older books on the horse are being reprinted. A childrens' book has been released on the Seabiscuit/War Admiral match race, with the assertion that it is the story of the greatest horse race of all time. Public Broadcasting has released a documentary and Hollywood has released a feature film based on Hillenbrand's work.

More importantly, *Seabiscuit* foaled a resurgence of popular interest in Thoroughbred racing.

Along with all that, the 2003 racing season gave us Funny Cide, a gelding, owned by a team of schoolmates in upstate New York, trained by a journeyman trainer who spent years in obscurity, and ridden by a jockey who had once been the leading jockey of his day but had suffered through injuries and a prolonged slump. Funny Cide won the Kentucky Derby against twelve-to-one odds, and breezed down to the wire to win by 9½ lengths in the Preakness Stakes. My publisher, aware that Funny Cide trained at Belmont and had never been beaten on the Belmont track, called me and told me to go to work on another chapter for *Down to the Wire.* For a few glorious weeks, it seemed that we would be treated to an incredible, magnificent convergence: a rags-to-riches horse racing story for the start of the Twenty-first Century. It looked like a contemporary Seabiscuit would garner the laurels as the first Triple Crown winner in twenty-five years.

Of course, that didn't happen, but the *Seabiscuit* story and Funny Cide's failure to win the Triple Crown simply point out just *how* special are the Triple Crown Champions. Funny Cide was touted as the Triple Crown possibility that racing so badly needs; Seabiscuit carries the mantel of the rags-to-riches runner that beat a Triple Crown winner. Both Funny Cide and Seabiscuit, must be matched to the Triple Crown. And neither of them won that most difficult of racing challenges.

So remember the Triple Crown Champions: Sir Barton, whose only real conqueror was the greatest racehorse of the Twentieth Century; Gallant Fox, whose triumphs set the path for his successors; Omaha, who still is beloved by the racing community in his namesake city; War Admiral, who exploded from the starting gate and dared his challengers to catch him; Whirlaway, whose very presence on the race track caused excitement, win or lose; Count Fleet, who was only vanquished by death; Assault, who overcame so much and always tried so hard; Citation, who stretched frictionlessly around a track to victory; the National Hero, Secretariat who set records in each Triple Crown race; Seattle Slew, who was the epitome of courage; and Affirmed, who fought harder and enjoyed it more than any other race horse. Those are the Triple Crown Champions.

Yes, one day another champion will emerge from the impenetrable mists of future races to join them. But let us remember these eleven great horses with a tear of joy for their lives and a tear of sadness for their passage.

R.L.S.
Colorado Springs, Colorado
June 25, 2003

298

ABOUT THE AUTHOR:

Robert L. Shoop is a long-time resident of Colorado Springs, Colorado. He received his BA from The Colorado College and his Juris Doctor from the Santa Clara University School of Law. He has practiced law in Colorado Springs from 1986 to the present.

He is an adjunct professor and lead faculty member for the Business Administration Department at Regis University in Colorado Springs and an instructor at DeVry University, Colorado Springs. He has also taught at Pikes Peak Community College, Webster University, Denver Technical College, and the Denver Paralegal Institute/Denver Career College. A life-long sports fan, he became interested in horse racing in 1991. He was the racing history columnist for *The Texas Horse Racing Weekly* in 1999 and is the author of *The Forgotten Champion: Middleground*, a monograph commissioned by King Ranch, Inc. He is married to the former Toni Lynn Finley, whose great grandfather, John H. Finley, was the racing commissioner for the state of New Hampshire in the 1940s.

APPENDICES

APPENDIX I
THE TRIPLE CROWN CHAMPIONS

Year	Horse	Jockey	Trainer	Owner
1919	Sir Barton	John Loftus	Guy Bedwell	J.K.L. Ross
1930	Gallant Fox	Earl Sande	Jim Fitzsimmons	Belair Stud
1935	Omaha	William Saunders	Jim Fitzsimmons	Belair Stud
1937	War Admiral	Chas. Kurtsinger	George Conway	Glen Riddle Farm
1941	Whirlaway	Eddie Arcaro	Ben Jones	Calumet Farm
1943	Count Fleet	John Longden	Don Cameron	Mrs. John Hertz
1946	Assault	Warren Mehrtens	Max Hirsch	King Ranch
1948	Citation	Eddie Arcaro	Jimmy Jones	Calumet Farm
1973	Secretariat	Ron Turcotte	Lucien Laurin	Meadow Stable
1977	Seattle Slew	Jean Cruguet	Billy Turner	Karen Taylor
1978	Affirmed	Steve Cauthen	Laz Barrera	Harbor View Farm

APPENDIX II:
WINNING TIMES
OF THE TRIPLE CROWN WINNERS

Year	Horse	Kentucky Derby	Preakness	Belmont Stakes
1919	Sir Barton	2:09 4/5	1:53 (1)	2:17 2/5 (2)
1930	Gallant Fox	2:07 3/5	2:00 3/5	2:31 3/5
1935	Omaha	2:05 1:58 2/5	2:30 3/5	
1937	War Admiral	2:03 1/3	1:58 2/5	2:28 3/5
1941	Whirlaway	2:01 2/5	1:58 2/5	2:31
1943	Count Fleet	2:04 1:57 2/5	2:28 1/5	
1946	Assault	2:06 3/5	2:01 2/5	2:30 4/5
1948	Citation	2:05 2/5	2:02 2/5	2:28 1/5
1973	Secretariat	1:59 2/5	1:54 2/5	2:24
1977	Seattle Slew	2:02 1/5	1:54 2/5	2:29 3/5
1978	Affirmed	2:01 1/5	1:54 2/5	2:26 4/5

(1) 1919 Preakness was 1 1/8 miles; Preaknesses since 1925 have been run at 1 3/16 miles.
(2) 1919 Belmont Stakes was run *clockwise* and at 1 3/8 miles; Belmont Stakes since 1926 have been run at 1 ½ miles. The Belmont Stakes has been run in a counter-clockwise direction beginning in 1921.

APPENDIX III:
WINNING LENGTHS
OF THE TRIPLE CROWN WINNERS

Year	Horse	Kentucky Derby	Preakness	Belmont Stakes.
1919	Sir Barton	5 lengths	4 lengths (3)	5 lengths (4)
1930	Gallant Fox	2 lengths	3/4 length	3 lengths
1935	Omaha	1 ½ lengths	6 lengths	1 ½ length
1937	War Admiral	1 3/4 lengths	head	3 lengths
1941	Whirlaway	8 lengths	5 ½ lengths	2 ½ lengths
1943	Count Fleet	3 lengths	8 lengths	25 lengths
1946	Assault	8 lengths	neck	3 lengths
1948	Citation	3 ½ lengths	5 ½ lengths	8 lengths
1973	Secretariat	2 ½ lengths	2 ½ lengths	31 lengths
1977	Seattle Slew	1 3/4 lengths	1 ½ lengths	4 lengths
1978	Affirmed	1 ½ lengths	neck	head

(3) 1919 Preakness was 1 1/8 miles. Preaknesses since 1925 have been run at 1 3/16 miles.

(4) 1919 Belmont Stakes was run clockwise and at 1 3/8 miles; post-1926 Belmont Stakes have been run at a distance of 1 ½ miles. The Belmont Stakes has been run in a clockwise direction beginning in 1921.

APPENDIX IV:
THE TRIPLE CROWN RACETRACKS

A. Churchill Downs (Kentucky Derby)
> Location: Louisville, Kentucky
> Seating Capacity: 48,500 (additional standing room in infield)
> First race: May 17, 1875
> Race distance: 1 1/4 miles (Kentucky Derby since 1896)
> Track shape: one mile oval
> Race date: first Saturday in May

B. Pimlico (Preakness Stakes)
> Location: Baltimore, Maryland
> Seating Capacity: 17,722 (additional standing room in infield)
> First race: October 25, 1870
> Race distance: 1 3/16 miles (Preakness since 1925)
> Track shape: one mile oval
> Race date: third Saturday in May

C. Belmont Park (Belmont Stakes)
> Location: Elmont, Long Island, New York
> Seating Capacity: 32,491 (additional standing room in infield)
> First race: May 4, 1905
> Race distance: 1 ½ miles (Belmont Stakes since 1926)
> Track shape: 1 ½ mile oval
> Race date: third Saturday after Preakness

APPENDIX V:
RACEHORSES, JOCKEYS, AND TRAINERS OF THIS BOOK ELECTED TO THE NATIONAL MUSEUM OF RACING AND HALL OF FAME

HORSE	Year Elected
Man o'War	1957
Sir Barton	1957
Gallant Fox	1957
Omaha	1965
War Admiral	1958
Whirlaway	1959
Count Fleet	1961
Assault	1964
Citation	1959
Secretariat	1974
Seattle Slew	1981
Affirmed	1980
Alydar	1989

JOCKEY (horse)	Year Elected
Eddie Arcaro (Whirlaway, Citation, also Assault)	1958
Steve Cauthen (Affirmed)	1994
Clarence Kummer (Man o'War, also Sir Barton)	1972
Charles Kurtsinger (War Admiral, also Omaha)	1967
John Loftus (Sir Barton, Man o'War)	1959
John Longden (Count Fleet, also Whirlaway)	1958
Earl Sande (Gallant Fox, also Sir Barton & Man o'War)	1955
Ron Turcotte (Secretariat)	1979
Jorge Velasquez (Alydar)	1990

TRAINER (horse)	Year Elected
Laz Barrera (Affirmed)	1979
Guy Bedwell (Sir Barton)	1971
Louis Feustel (Man o'War)	1964
"Sunny Jim" Fitzsimmons(Gallant Fox, Omaha)	1958
Max Hirsch (Assault)	1959
Ben Jones (Whirlaway, also Citation)	1958
Jimmy Jones (Citation, also Whirlaway)	1959
Lucien Laurin (Secretariat)	1977

It should be noted that the jockeys and trainers listed above were elected for their whole careers, not just the horse(s) noted in this book.

Further, at Pimlico Racetrack there was the "Jockeys' Hall of Fame." This is an inactive program, and no new jockeys have been named to membership since 1986. The National Museum of Racing and Hall of Fame in Saratoga Springs has taken the lead role in paying tribute to racing greats. However, the following jockeys listed above are also members of the "Jockeys' Hall of Fame": Eddie Arcaro, John Loftus, John Longden, Earl Sande, and Jorge Velasquez.

APPENDIX VI:

TABULATED RACING RECORDS OF THE TRIPLE CROWN HORSES

Note: Winnings are expressed in then-year dollars, not adjusted for inflation.

Win Percentage is computed by dividing the number of first place finishes by the number of starts.

Money percentage is computed by dividing the total number of 1st place finishes, 2nd place finishes, and 3rd place finishes by the number of starts.

A. Man o'War (did not win Triple Crown)

Year	Age	Starts	1sts	2nds	3rds	Unpl.	Winnings
1919	2	10	9	1	0	0	$ 83,325
1920	3	11	11	0	0	0	$166,140
Totals:		21	20	1	0	0	$249,465

Win Percentage: 95   Money Percentage: 100

B. Sir Barton

Year	Age	Starts	1sts	2nds	3rds	Unpl.	Winnings
1918	2	6	0	1	0	5	$ 4,113
1919	3	13	8	3	2	0	$ 88,250
1920	4	12	5	2	3	2	$ 24,194
Totals:		31	13	6	5	7	$116,857

Win Percentage: 42   Money Percentage: 77

C. Gallant Fox

Year	Age	Starts	1sts	2nds	3rds	Unpl.	Winnings
1929	2	7	2	2	2	1	$ 19,890
1930	3	10	9	1	0	0	$308,275
Totals:		17	11	3	2	1	$328,165

Win Percentage: 65   Money Percentage: 94

D. Omaha

Year	Age	Starts	1sts	2nds	3rds	Unpl.	Winnings
1934	2	9	1	4	0	4	$3,850
1935	3	9	6	1	2	0	$142,255
1936	4	4	2	2	0	0	$8,650*
Totals:		22	9	7	2	4	$154,755

* American equivalent of winnings in England

Win Percentage: 41   Money Percentage: 82

E. War Admiral

Year	Age	Starts	1sts	2nds	3rds	Unpl.	Winnings
1936	2	6	3	2	1	0	$ 14,800
1937	3	8	8	0	0	0	$166,500
1938	4	11	9	1	0	1	$ 90,840
1939	5	1	1	0	0	0	$ 1,100
Totals:		26	21	3	1	1	$273,240

Win Percentage: 81   Money Percentage: 96

F. Whirlaway

Year	Age	Starts	1sts	2nds	3rds	Unpl.	Winnings
1940	2	16	7	2	4	3	$77,275
1941	3	20	13	5	2	0	$272,386
1942	4	22	12	8	2	0	$211,250
1943	5	2	0	0	1	1	$250
Totals:		60	32	15	9	4	$561,161

Win Percentage: 53   Money Percentage: 93

G. Count Fleet

Year	Age	Starts	1sts	2nds	3rds	Unpl.	Winnings
1942	2	15	10	4	1	0	$76,245
1943	3	6	6	0	0	0	$174,055
Totals:		21	16	4	1	0	$250,300

Win Percentage: 76   Money Percentage: 100

H. Assault

Year	Age	Starts	1sts	2nds	3rds	Unpl.	Winnings
1945	2	9	2	2	1	4	$17,250
1946	3	15	8	2	3	2	$424,195
1947	4	7	5	1	1	0	$181,925
1948	5	2	1	0	0	1	$3,250
1949	6	6	1	1	1	3	$45,900
1950	7	3	1	0	1	1	$2,950
Totals:		42	18	6	7	11	$675,470

Win Percentage: 43   Money Percentage: 74

I. Citation

Year	Age	Starts	1sts	2nds	3rds	Unpl.	Winnings
1947	2	9	8	1	0	0	$155,680
1948	3	20	19	1	0	0	$709,470
1949	4	DID NOT RACE					$-0-
1950	5	9	2	7	0	0	$73,480
1951	6	7	3	1	2	1	$147,130
Totals:		45	32	10	2	1	$1,085,760

Win Percentage: 71   Money Percentage: 98

J. Secretariat

Year	Age	Starts	1sts	2nds	3rds	Unpl.	Winnings
1972	2	9	7	1	0	1	$456,404
1973	3	12	9	2	1	0	$860,404
Totals:		21	16	3	1	1	$1,316,808

Win Percentage: 76   Money Percentage: 95

L. Seattle Slew

Year	Age	Starts	1sts	2nds	3rds	Unpl.	Winnings
1976	2	3	3	0	0	0	$94,350
1977	3	7	6	0	0	1	$641,370
1979	4	7	5	2	0	0	$473,006
Totals:		17	14	2	0	1	$1,208,726

Win Percentage: 82   Money Percentage: 94

M. Affirmed

Year	Age	Starts	1sts	2nds	3rds	Unpl.	Winnings
1977	2	9	7	2	0	0	$343,477
1978	3	11	8	2	0	1	$901,541
1979	4	9	7	1	1	0	$1,148,500
Totals:		29	22	5	1	1	$2,393,818

Win Percentage: 76   Money Percentage: 97

N. Alydar (did not win Triple Crown)

Year	Age	Starts	1sts	2nds	3rds	Unpl.	Winnings
1977	2	10	5	4	0	1	$285,026
1978	3	10	7	3	0	0	$565,071
1979	4	6	2	2	1	1	$107,098
Totals:		26	14	9	1	2	$957,195

Win Percentage: 54   Money Percentage: 92

APPENDIX VII:
TRIPLE CROWN RACE WINNERS
SIRED BY TRIPLE CROWN CHAMPIONS

A. Man o'War:

American Flag, 1925 Belmont Stakes
Crusader, 1926 Belmont Stakes
Clyde Van Dusen, 1929 Kentucky Derby
War Admiral, 1937 *Triple Crown*

B. Gallant Fox:

Omaha, 1935 *Triple Crown*
Granville, 1936 Belmont Stakes

C. Count Fleet:

Count Turf, 1951 Kentucky Derby
Counterpoint, 1951 Belmont Stakes
One Count, 1952 Belmont Stakes

D. Citation:

Fabius, 1956 Preakness

E. Secretariat:

Risen Star, 1988 Preakness & Belmont Stakes

F. Seattle Slew:

Swale, 1984 Kentucky Derby & Belmont
Stakes
A.P. Indy, 1992 Belmont Stakes

G. Alydar:

Alysheba, 1987 Kentucky Derby & Preakness
Easy Goer, 1989 Belmont Stakes
Strike the Gold, 1991 Kentucky Derby

APPENDIX VIII:
RANKINGS OF THE TRIPLE CROWN WINNERS

A. COMPARATIVE TABLE

Horse	Starts	1sts	2nds	3rds	Win %	$ %
Man o'War (no Triple Crown)	21	20	1	0	95	100
Sir Barton	31	13	6	5	42	77
Gallant Fox	17	11	3	2	65	94
Omaha	22*	9*	7*	2	41	82
War Admiral	26	21	3	1	81	96
Whirlaway	60	32	15	9	53	93
Count Fleet	21	16	4	1	76	100
Assault	42	18	6	7	43	74
Citation	45	32	10	2	71	98
Secretariat	21	16	3	1	76	95
Seattle Slew	17	14	2	0	82	94
Affirmed	29	22	5	1	76	97
Alydar (no Triple Crown)	26	14	9**	1	54	92

*includes the races in England in 1936.

**includes the three second-place finishes in the Triple Crown.

B. HORSES RANKED BY WIN PERCENTAGE

Rank	Horse	Win Percentage
1	Man o'War	95
2	Seattle Slew	82
3	War Admiral	81
4/5/6 (tie)	Count Fleet/Secretariat/Affirmed	76
7	Citation	71
8	Gallant Fox	65
9	Alydar	54
10	Whirlaway	53
11	Assault	43
12	Sir Barton	42
13	Omaha	41

C. HORSES RANKED BY MONEY PERCENTAGE

Rank	Horse	Money Percentage
1/2 (tie)	Man o'War/Count Fleet	100
3	Citation	98
4	Affirmed	97
5	War Admiral	96
6	Secretariat	95
7/8 (tie)	Gallant Fox/Seattle Slew	94
9	Whirlaway	93
10	Alydar	92
11	Omaha	82
12	Sir Barton	77
13	Assault	74

APPENDIX IX:
THE *BLOOD-HORSE* RANKINGS

In February, 1999, the racing publication *The Blood-Horse* published its list of the top one hundred horses of the Twentieth Century. The rankings as they relate to the horses in this book are:

Rank #	Horse
1	Man o'War
2	Secretariat
3	Citation
5	Count Fleet
9	Seattle Slew
12	Affirmed
13	War Admiral
26	Whirlaway
27	Alydar
28	Gallant Fox
33	Assault
49	Sir Barton
61	Omaha

A 1992 *Sports Illustrated* list of the top ten thoroughbreds of the Twentieth Century had Man o'War–1; Secretariat–2; Citation–3; Count Fleet–5; Seattle Slew–9. The remaining Triple Crown Champions did not make the *Sports Illustrated* list.

BIBLIOGRAPHY
& CHAPTER SOURCES

I. BIBLIOGRAPHY

PRINTED SOURCES:

Eddie Arcaro, *I Ride to Win!*, (Greenberg: 1951.)

Ann Hagedorn Auerbach, *Wild Ride* (Henry Holt: 1994.)

Pete Axthelm, *The Kid,* (Viking Press: 1978.)

B.K. Beckwith, *The Longden Legend*, (A.S. Barnes & Co.: 1973.)

The Blood-Horse, Thoroughbred Champions: Top 100 Racehorses of the 20th Century, (The Blood-Horse, Inc.:1999.)

Jim Bolus, *Kentucky Derby Stories,* (Pelican Publishing Co.:1993.)

____, *Remembering the Derby*, (Pelican Publishing Co.: 1994.)

____, *Derby Fever*, (Pelican Publishing Co.: 1995.)

____, *Derby Magic*, (Pelican Publishing Co.: 1997.)

Edward L. Bowen, *The Jockey Club's Illustrated History of Thoroughbred Racing in America*, (Little, Brown: 1994.)

Jimmy Breslin, *Sunny Jim: The Life of America's Most Beloved Horseman, James Fitzsimmons,* (Doubleday & Co.: 1962.)

Fred C. Broadhead, *Here Comes Whirlaway!* (Sunflower University Press: 1995.)

Steve Cady & Barton Silverman, *Seattle Slew,* (Penguin pap. ed.: 1977.)

Churchill Downs, Inc., *One Hundred Twenty-Third Kentucky Derby* Media Guide, 1997.

Page Cooper and Roger L. Treat, *Man o' War*, (Julian Messner, Inc.: 1950.)

Marvin Drager, *The Most Glorious Crown* (Winchester Press: 1976.)

Trent Frayne, *Northern Dancer & Friends* (Funk & Wagnalls,: 1969.)

Bill Heller with Ron Turcotte, *The Will to Win: Ron Turcotte's Ride to Glory,* (Fifth House Publishing: 1992.)

John Hervey, *American Race Horses, 1936,-1937,-1938,-1940,-1941, -1942, & -1943* (Sagamore Press: 1937, 1938, 1939, 1940, 1941, 1942, 1943, & 1944, respectively.)

Laura Hillenbrand, *Seabiscuit: An American Legend,* (Random House: 2001.)

Joe Hirsch and Gene Plowden, *In the Winner's Circle: The Jones Boys of Calumet Farm*, (Mason & Lipscomb Publishers: 1974.)

Kent Hollingsworth, ed., *The Great Ones*, (The Blood-Horse: 1970.)

Robert F. Kelley, *Racing in America, 1937-1959.*

Maryland Jockey Club, *Media Guide '95, Laurel and Pimlico*, 1995.

Julian May, *The Triple Crown*, (Creative Education Childrens Press:1976.)

Mordaunt Milner, *The Godolphin Arabian: The Story of the Matchem Line*, (J.A Allen & Co., Ltd.:1990.)

William Nack, *Secretariat: The Making of A Champion,* (DaCapo reprint of *Big Red of Meadow Stable*, 1975.)

New York Racing Association, *NYRA Media Guide, 1994*. (New York Racing Assoc.: 1994.)

Joe Palmer, *American Race Horses, 1946,-1947,-1948, -1949, -1950, & -1951.* (Sagamore Press: 1947, 1948, 1949, 1950, 1951, & 1952, respectively. Palmer continued this series after Hervey's death.)

Grantland Rice, *The Tumult and the Shouting*, (A.S. Barnes & Co.: 1954.)

J.K.M. Ross, *Boots and Saddles: The Story of the Fabulous Ross Stable in the Golden Days of Racing*, (E.P. Dutton: 1956.)

Red Smith, *To Absent Friends,* (Atheneum: 1982.)

M.A. Stoneridge, *Great Horses of Our Time* (Doubleday & Co.: 1972.)

Bert Clark Thayer, *Whirlaway: The Life and Times of A Great Racer*, (Abercrombie & Fitch:1966 reprint of 1946 ed.)

Thoroughbred Record, Triple Crown Edition, April 20, 1977.

Suzanne Wilding & Anthony Del Balso, *The Triple Crown Winners*, 2d.ed., (Parents' Magazine Press:1978.)

Raymond G. Woolfe, Jr., *Secretariat*, (pub. by author: 1998 ed.)

VIDEOTAPES: Jim McKay, "Jewels of the Triple Crown," ABC Sports videotape, 1988; ESPN, "The Life and Times of Secretariat: An American Racing Legend," 1990; Decade Productions, Inc., "The Run for the Roses: The History of the Kentucky Derby," 1994; Historic Thoroughbred Collection, Inc., "Thoroughbred Heroes," 1991; Harris Video Library, "Hearts of Courage," n.d. (The ABC Sports videotape, "Jewels of the Triple Crown," is an excellent introduction to the Triple Crown story.)

II. CHAPTER SOURCES

Abbreviations & Short Titles used:

ARH 19XX	*American Race Horses & year* (both Hervey & Palmer books)
BH	*The Blood-Horse* Magazine
General Sources	McKay Tape; Drager, May, Wilding & Del Balso books on
Triple Crown.	
GHOOT	*Great Horses of Our Time* by M.A. Stoneridge.
KDM	Kentucky Derby Museum.
KL	Keeneland Library
KRA	King Ranch Archives
LC-J	Louisville *Courier-Journal*
McKay tape	Jim McKay, "Jewels of the Triple Crown," ABC Sports videotape, 1988.
Media Guides	Kentucky Derby, Laurel & Pimlico, NYRA Media Guides listed above.
NMR:	National Museum of Racing and Hall of Fame
NYT:	*New York Times*
RIA:	*Racing in America, 1937-1959* by Robert F. Kelley.
SI:	Sports Illustrated
Sun:	Baltimore *Sun*
TGO	*The Great Ones,* Kent Hollingsworth, ed.
Top 10	*Thoroughbred Champions: Top 100 Racehorses of the 20th Century*, by *The Blood-Horse*.
TT	*The Thoroughbred Times*

NOTE: BIBLIOGRAPHIC INFORMATION FOR SOURCES LISTED IN THE BIBLIOGRAPHY AND REFERENCED IN CHAPTER SECTIONS BELOW IS NOT REPEATED.

A. KENTUCKY DERBY

Opening Quote from "Recalling Conn," in Red Smith's *To Absent Friends*.

General sources, plus: Steven A.Channing, *Kentucky: A Bicentennial History*, (W.W. Norton & Co.: 1977); "The Derby's Founding Father, Colonel Clark," and "Col. Matt Winn: Mr. Derby," in Bolus, *Kentucky Derby Stories,* pp. 47-61; Laura Hillenbrand, "The Derby," *American Heritage,* June 1999, pp. 98-107; *Time* cover story, 5/10/37, pp. 59-60; J.M. Fenster, "Nation of Gamblers," *American Heritage*, September, 1994, pp. 34-51; Peter Chew, *The Kentucky Derby: The First 100 Years,* (Houghton Mifflin & Co.:1974;) Joe Hirsch and Jim Bolus, *Kentucky Derby: The Chance of A Lifetime,* (McGraw-Hill: 1988;) Bob Gorham, ed. *Churchill Downs, 100th Kentucky Derby,* (Churchill Downs, Inc.:1974;) Julian Bedford, *The World Atlas of Horse Racing,* (Mallard Press: 1989;) and the single most important source on America's greatest horse race, *Down the Stretch: The Story of Colonel Matt J. Winn* as told to Frank G. Menke, (Smith & Durrell, Inc.: 1945.) Also helpful is Decade Productions', "The Run for the Roses: The History of the Kentucky Derby," a 1994 videotape.

B. PREAKNESS

General sources, plus: Robert J. Bruegger, *Maryland: A Middle Temperament*, (Johns Hopkins University Press: 1988); and Maryland Jockey Club, *Media Guide '95, Laurel and Pimlico*, 1995; Bedford, *World Atlas of Horse Racing;* Ron Hale posting on Derby List, 2/11/97.

C. BELMONT STAKES

General sources, plus New York Racing Association, *NYRA Media Guide, 1994;* "75th Anniversary of Belmont Park," supplement to *Newsday*, 6/1/80; Bedford, *World Atlas of Horse Racing*.

D. ORIGIN "TRIPLE CROWN"

General sources, plus: *B-H*, 6/14/30, pp. 733-734; Joe Challmes, "Origin of the 'Triple Crown,'" *Turf and Sport Digest*, May/June 1982, vol. 59, #3, pp. 8-9, 36; Jim Bolus, "1930 was a landmark Derby and Gallant Fox was the Hero," *Louisville Times,* 5/3/80, p. A8; Edward Hotaling, "When Racing Colors Included Black," *NYT*, 6/2/96, p. 23; Steve Kweskin, "The Elusive Triple Crown of Racing," *Western Horseman*, September, 1976, pp. 6-8; "'Triple Crown' A Term Coined by Hatton in '30s," n.d. item in Tom Gilcoyne files–appears to be from *Daily Racing Form*, 6/10/78; *2002 ESPN Information Please Sports Almanac*, p.785.

E. MAN O'WAR

<u>On Feustel:</u> Wayne Capps, "The Place Where Louis Dwelled," *The Thoroughbred Record*, July, 1970, pp. 670-671 & 678; clippings from KL and NMR files.

<u>On Kummer:</u> plaque sheet, NMR; *NYT*, 4/5/30, p. 16; 12/19/30, p. 36; clippings, KL and NMR files.

<u>On Man o'War:</u> (The literature on Man o'War is large and continues to increase.) "Man o'War"sections in *TGO, Top 100*, and *GHOOT,* and Page Cooper and Roger L. Treat, *Man o' War*, are the best biographies. Short articles include: Peter Chew, "The 'Mostest Hoss,'" *American Heritage,* vol. XXII, #3, October, 1971, pp.24-29, & 90-95; Mel R. Allen, "As Near a Living Flame As Horses Ever Get," *Old Farmers Almanac, 1997*, pp. 176-184; Harry Disston, "Personality," *Sports History*, May, 1988, pp. 8, 58-62; Maryjean Wall, "The Mostest Hoss That Ever Was," *SPUR,* October, 1997, pp. 48-53, and the same author's article on Man o'War in the Lexington *Herald-Leader*, 7/27/97; E.R. Stuart, "The Day Man o'War Lost," *SPUR*, July/August 1994, pp. 92-95; Chapter 41 in William H.P. Robertson's *The History of Thoroughbred Racing in America,"* (1964;) William Robertson, "Man o'War: De Mostest Hoss Dat Ever Was," *The Sports Book*, Min S. Yee, ed., (1975;) and Joe Estes'"Man o'War," in *ARH 1949.* Fictional treatments of Man o'War include Walter Farley's *Man o'War* (1962, Bullseye pap. ed., 1990), and Marguerite Henry's *King of the Wind* (1948, Aladdin pap. ed., 1991,) which has a chapter on the Man o'War-Sir Barton match race.

<u>Newspaper/Magazine Articles:</u> *Sun*: 5/29/20. *NYT:* 6/7/19, p. 10; 6/10/19, p. 16; 6/22/19, p. 21; 6/24/19, p. 10; 7/6/19, p. 18; 8/3/19, p. 19; 8/14/19, p. 17; 8/24/19, p. 20; 8/31/19, p. 18; 9/14/19, sect. 9, p.1; 5/19/20, p. 13;5/30/20, p. 19; 6/13/20, sect. 8, p. 1; 6/23/20, p. 18; 7/11/20, p. 17; 8/8/20, p. 19; 8/22/20, p. 16; 9/5/20, p. 15; 9/12/20, p. 19, 9/19/20, p. 19; 10/13/20, p. 1;11/2/47, sect.5, p. 1.

<u>Race Charts/Notes:</u> from *American Racing Manuals*, *1919, 1920*, Media Guides, and race charts reprinted in Cooper & Treat, *Man o'War.*

F. SIR BARTON

<u>On J.K.L. Ross:</u> J.K.M. Ross, *Boots and Saddles: The Story of the Fabulous Ross Stable in the Golden Days of Racing* is a memoir by Ross's son and is essential to Sir Barton's story. Also: *NYT*, 7/27/51, p. 19; "Retrospect," *B-H*, 2/28/87, p. 1547.

<u>On Bedwell:</u> plaque sheet, NMR; *NYT*, 1/2/52, p. 25; Tom Pappas, "A Hard Guy With Horses," *American TURF Monthly*, January, 1987; clippings in NMR files, also Ross, *Boots and Saddles*.

<u>On Cal Shilling:</u> *NYT,* 1/13/50, p. 23, also Ross, *Boots and Saddles.*

<u>On Loftus:</u> plaque sheet, NMR; *B-H*, 3/29/76, pp. 1356-1357; *NYT,* 3/24/76, p. 42; Red

316

Smith column, *The Louisville Times*, ca. 12/7/60 (found in KDM files); "'Big Red' Had Excuse for Only Loss, "*LC-J*, 3/8/53; "Record Forum," n.d., clipping in KDM files; also Ross, *Boots and Saddles*.

On Sir Barton: General Sources, plus: "Sir Barton" in *TGO* and *Top 100*; "Greener Pastures for Sir Barton," in Bolus, *Remembering the Derby*, pp. 41-50; J.A. Estes, "The Story of Sir Barton," *B-H*, 11/20/37, p. 702-706; Floyd Allen, "Sir Barton: Triple Glory," in *The Backstretch*, July, 1989; chart from "A Century of Champions," *B-H*, 12/24/73, pp.5306-5307; Naomi K. Chesky, "Sir Barton of Equine Royalty, " Casper, Wyoming *Star-Tribune*, 4/25/93, p. E1; also Ross, *Boots and Saddles*.

Newspaper/Magazine Articles: *New York American*, May 13, 1927, p.1. *LC-J*: 5/10/19, p. 9. 5/11/19, p. 1. *Sun*: 5/15/19, p. 26. *NYT*: 7/7/18, p.4;8/2/18, p. 8; 8/4/18, p. 5; 8/15/18, p. 12; 9/1/18, sect. 2, p. 3; 9/15/18, p. 4; 5/11/19, p. 21; 5/15/19; 5/25/19, p. 19; 6/12/19, p. 13; 7/11/19, p. 8; 9/12/19, p. 15; 9/14/19, sect. 9, p. 1; 9/25/19, p. 11; 9/28/19, sect. 10, p. 5; 10/5/19, sect. 10, p. 4; 11/6/19, p. 11; 11/8/19, p. 17; 11/12/19, p. 14; 4/20/20, p. 11; 4/25/20, p. 21; 4/28/20, p. 13; 5/1/20, p. 21; 5/5/20, p. 13; 8/3/20, p. 10; 8/29/20, p. 17; 10/13/20, p. 1; 10/24/20, p. 3; 11/6/20, p. 18; 11/11/20, p. 14, and 11/13/37, p. 16.

Race Charts/Notes: from *American Racing Manuals, 1918, 1919, 1920*, Media Guides, & Ross, *Boots and Saddles*.

Sir Barton's last years: Gene Smith, "The Seventeenth Largest Army," *American Heritage*, December, 1992; Albert D. Manchester, "Descendant of the Remount," *Western Horseman*, October, 1986, pp. 60-62;Colonel E.J. Purfield, "Thirty Years of Remount Service," *Western Horseman*, August, 1949, pp. 8-9,50-54;Franklin Reynolds, "Remount Service, R.I.P.," *Western Horseman*, June, 1950, pp. 18-19, 36-37; D. Todd Gresham, "Remount," *Western Horseman*, May-June, 1946, pp. 10-11, 50-52; Peg Layton, "Hobby Horse Breeder," *Western Horseman*, January, 1971 (on Gordon Turner;) clippings from files of Wyoming Pioneer Memorial Museum; clippings from files of Fort Robinson, Nebraska Museum.

G. GALLANT FOX

Author's Interview: Tom Gilcoyne, 2/15/95 (who also supplied his original program of the 1930 Travers Stakes for my review.)
The opening quote is from "Gentleman from Sheepshead Bay," by James Roach in David F. Woods, ed., *The Fireside Book of Horse Racing* (Simon & Schuster: 1963), p.250; the final quote is from Neil Newman, *Famous Horses of the American Turf; Vol. 1: 1930* (1931.) The Jimmy Breslin quotes regarding Gallant Fox's "laziness" and Gallant Fox /Earl Sande in the 1930 Kentucky Derby are from his book, *Sunny Jim*, (1962,) pp. 197 and 203-204, respectively.
On Claiborne Farm/Belair Stud: Edward L. Bowen, "Claiborne Farm," in *SPUR*, Jan./Feb 1995, p. 48; Karen Kopp: " Belair: The Years of the Fox,", *The Horseman's Journal*, Feb., 1984; Dan Farley, "Two Crowns for Woodward," *B-H*.

<u>On Sunny Jim Fitzsimmons:</u> Jimmy Breslin, *Sunny Jim: The Life of America's Most beloved Horseman, James Fitzsimmons*; "The Happiest Life," in Bolus, *Derby Fever,* pp. 233-245; Julie R. Howell, "Sunny Jim," *B-H,* June 2, 1975, p. 2126; "James Edward Fitzsimmons," in *The Thoroughbred Record,* March 19, 1966; "Gentleman from Sheepshead Bay," by Roach in Woods, ed., *The Fireside Book of Horse Racing*; *NYT,* 3/12/66, p. 1; and Arthur Daley, "Mr. Fitz," in *NYT,* 3/14/66, p. 44.

<u>On Sande:</u> the versions of "A Handy Guy Like Sande" are from Damon Runyon, *Poems for Men,* (Permabooks pap. ed.:1946), pp. 137-142; plaque sheet, NMR; "The Handy Man" by Gene Smith, *American Heritage,* September, 1996, pp.110-111; "Handy Sande" by Quentin Reynolds, *Collier's,* July 17, 1935, p. 17;*NYT:* 4/4/30, p. 3;5/12/30, p. 18; 8/21/68, p. 45; "Memories of A Master," by Sam Renick, *B-H,* 3/16/91, p. 1496; "The Handy Guy," by Horace Wade, *The Backstretch,* July, 1986, pp. 60-65; "Maybe There'll Be Another..." by Horace Wade, *Turf and Sport Digest,* April, 1965.

<u>On Gallant Fox:</u> General Sources, plus: William Woodward, *Gallant Fox: A Memoir* (pvtly printed, 1931;) "Gallant Fox" in *TGO* and *Top 100*; Eva Jolene Boyd,"Like Sire, Like Son," *SPUR,* May/June 1996; "The 1930 Derby Was a Landmark and Gallant Fox Was the Hero," in Bolus, *Derby Magic,* pp. 119-130; John Hervey, "1930: Gallant Fox Dates an Epoch," in *Racing in America, 1922-36,* (pvtly printed, 1937). Debra Ginsburg's, "Jim Dandy," *The Backstretch,* July/August 2000, pp. 144-151, is a look at the upset winner of the 1930 Travers Stakes.

<u>Newspaper/Magazine Articles:</u> *LC-J:* 5/18/30, p. 1. *Sun:*5/9/30, p1; 5/10/30, p. 10. *NYT:* 6/25/29, p. 26; 6/30/29, p. 7;7/30/29, p. 13; 8/4/29, sect. 4, p. 1; 9/15/29, sect. 11, p. 1; 9/29/29, sect. 11, p. 1; 4/27/30, sect. 11, p. 1; 5/10/30, p. 12; 5/18/30, p. 1;6/8/30, sect. 11, p.1; 6/29/30, sect. 10, p.1;7/6/30, sect. 10, p. 8; 8/16/30, p. 10; 8/17/30, sect. 10, p. 1; 8/31/30, sect. 10, p. 1; 9/7/30, sect. 11, p. 1; 9/18/30; 10/2/30, p. 20; 10/7/30, p. 32; 10/12/30, sect. 10, p. 1; 10/28/30, p. 31; 11/16/54, p. 38.

<u>Race Charts/Notes:</u> from *American Racing Manuals, 1929, 1930,* Media Guides, and race charts which appear in Woodward, *Gallant Fox: A Memoir.*

H. OMAHA

<u>Interviews:</u> author's interview with Morton Porter, 10/23/02; Jim Bolus with Willie Saunders,3/29/75, & 3/8/77 (in KDM files.)

<u>On Saunders:</u> Bolus-Saunders interviews; *B-H,* 8/9/86, p. 5736; various clippings in KDM, KL, & NMR files; Jefferson County, Kentucky, court file, #68755, *Commonwealth vs. Schaeffer & Saunders*, 1935.
<u>On Omaha</u>: General Sources, plus: "Omaha" in *TGO* and *Top 100*; "Omaha Abroad" in *ARH 1936;* Eva Jolene Boyd,"Like Sire, Like Son," *SPUR,* May/June 1996; *RIA:* "1935: Omaha and Discovery"*;* clippings in AK-Sar-Ben race track files; Morton Porter letter to Jim Bolus, 8/12/83 (in KDM files;) "The Ultimate Odyssey," by Morton Porter (pvt. monograph, n.d.;) Morton Porter interview; Bolus-Saunders interviews; "A 'Savage'

Racehorse Named Omaha," in Bolus, *Derby Magic,* pp. 131-144; Mark Aveyard, "Aksarben [*sic*] items to be auctioned," *Thoroughbred Times Today,* March 3, 1997; assorted clippings in KDM and KL files.

Newspaper/Magazine Articles: *B-H*: 5/2/59, p. 853. *LC-J,* 5/5/35, p. 1. *Sun*: 5/12/35, p. 1. *NYT*: 4/22/35, p.23;4/23/35, p. 30; 4/27/35, 14; 4/28/35, sect. 5, p.1; 5/2/35, p. 26; 5/3/35, p. 27; 5/4/35, p. 6; 5/5/35, sect.5,p.1; 5/6/35, p. 25; 5/7/35, p. 31; 5/11/35, p. 13; 5/12/35, sect.5, p.1; 5/12/35, p. 23; 5/25/35, p. 10; 5/26/35, sect.5, p.1;6/8/35, p. 21; 6/9/35, sect.5, p.1; *NYT Magazine*, "Fleet Omaha: The Biography of a Horse," sect. 7, p.8; 6/23/35, sect.5, p.1; 6/11/35, p. 27; 6/30/35, sect. 5, p. 1; 7/16/35, p. 16; 7/17/35, p. 26; 7/21/35, sect. 5, p. 1; 12/7/35, p. 25; 12/14/35, p. 22; 12/25/35, p. 33; 1/1/36, p. 38; 1/3/36, p. 15; 1/9/36, p. 28; 1/16/36, p. 28; 5/10/36, sect. 5, p. 9; 5/31/36, sect 5, p. 1; 6/18/36, p. 32; 6/19/36;6/20/36, p. 14; 6/15/37, p. 31; 9/4/37, p. 11; 9/14/37, p. 30; 9/16/37, p. 32;4/26/59, p.6S ; *TT*, April 24, 1992, p. 10, & May 20, 2000, p. 58; "43 Years After His Death, Omahans Love Omaha," *Omaha World-Herald*, July 14, 2002.

Race Charts/Notes: from *American Racing Manuals, 1934 & 1935* & Media Guides.

I. WAR ADMIRAL

Author's Interview: Tom Gilcoyne, 2/16/95;

On George Conway: *NYT,* 6/21/39, p. 23; clippings in NMR files; also *ARH* 1939, p. 12.

On Kurtsinger: plaque sheet, NMR; Quentin Reynolds, "A Man and A Horse," *Collier's,* 5/14/38, pp. 22, 70-71; copies of clippings, KDM, KL, & NMR files; *NYT*, 9/25/46, p. 27.

On War Admiral: General Sources, plus: "War Admiral" in *TGO* and *Top 100*; "Man o'War Flotilla" in *ARH, 1936;* "Horse of the Year" in *ARH 1937;* "War Admiral," in *ARH 1938; RIA*:"War Admiral and the Triple Crown: 1937," pp. 3-6 and "War Admiral and Seabiscuit Finally Meet:1938," pp. 15-18; Jane B. Jewett, "Fleet Was The Admiral," *B-H,* 4/23/83, p. 2888; Jay Hovdey, "Four-star Admiral," *SPUR,* September/October 1989; Quentin Reynolds, "A Man and A Horse," *Collier's,* 5/14/38, pp. 22, 70-71."Seabiscuit" sections in *GHOOT* and *Top 100*, and Laura Hillenbrand's *Seabiscuit: An American Legend,* are accounts of War Admiral's most famous adversary. Hillenbrand's "Four Good Legs Between Us," in *American Heritage*, July/August 1998, is an earlier, shorter version of that work. Mordaunt Milner's *The Godolphin Arabian: The Story of the Matchem Line*, pp. 120-123, has an account of the famous match race. Also, Red Smith's "A Horse You Had To Like" and "Death of the Iceman," in *To Absent Friends*, contain important information on the War Admiral-Seabiscuit match race.

Newspaper/Magazine Articles: *B-H*: 11/7/59, p. 1116. *Sun*: 5/16/37, sports, p.2;11/2/38, p.1.*NYT*: 4/26/36, sect. 5, p. 9; 5/22/36, p. 30; 6/7/36, sect. 5, p. 8; 7/2/36, p. 16; 9/20/39, p. 59;10/11/36, sect. 5, p. 36;4/15/37, p. 29; 4/25/37, sect. 5, p. 9; 5/9/37, sect. 5, p. 1; 5/16/37, sect. 5, p. 1; 6/6/37, sect. 5, p. 1; 10/27/37, p. 26; 10/31/37, sect. 5, p. 1; 11/4/37;

2/20/38, sect. 5, p. 1; 3/6/38, sect. 5, p. 1; 6/7/38, p. 27; 6/30/38, p. 27; 7/31/38, sect. 5, p. 1; 8/28/38, sect. 5, p. 1; 8/21/38, sect. 5, p. 1; 10/2/38, sect. 5, p. 1; 11/1/38, p. 28; 11/2/38, p. 29; 11/13/38, sect. 5, p. 1; 2/19/39, p. 32; 6/7/39, p. 32; 10/31/59, p. 18L; various clippings, KDM, KL, and NMR files.

Race Charts/Notes: from *American Racing Manuals, 1936, 1937, 1938, 1939* & Media Guides.

J. WHIRLAWAY

Author's Interviews: Tom Gilcoyne, 2/15/95; Margaret Glass, 12/26/96; Jimmy Jones, 2/18/97; John Longden, 2/9/94.
Opening/closing quote is from McKay tape, © ABC Sports; used with permission of ABC Sports.

On Calumet Farm: Ann Hagedorn Auerbach, *Wild Ride*; "Calumet Farm: One of a Kind," in Bolus, *Derby Fever,* pp.195-205; Margaret Glass, "The Calumet Story," (pvt. monograph: 1982.)

On Ben Jones: Joe Hirsch and Gene Plowden, *In the Winner's Circle: The Jones Boys of Calumet Farm*; Jimmy Jones interview; "Plain Ben; The Greatest of All Derby Trainers," in Bolus, *Kentucky Derby Stories,* pp. 131-135; plaque sheet, NMR; Jim Bolus, "Two Fellows From Missouri," *The Thoroughbred Record*, May, 1990, pp. 84-89; *NYT* , 7/14/61, p. 19; clippings from NMR files.

On Arcaro: Eddie Arcaro, *I Ride to Win!*; W.C. Heinz, "The Smallest Titan of Them All," in *Once They Heard the Cheers* (Doubleday & Co.:1979;) plaque sheet, NMR; Kent Hollingsworth,"What's Going On Here," *B-H*, 3/8/86, pp. 1805, 1823-1826 and "Five With Style," *B-H*, 4/25/70, pp. 1230-1231; clippings from NMR files. Also, Arcaro's comments on Whirlaway in Joseph Durso, "Triple Crown: Five Voices From the Saddle," *NYT,* 6/1/97, p. 25; Eddie Arcaro, "The Art of Race Riding," *SI,* 6/17/57, pp. 14-17, 37-38; and Stanley Frank, "A Visit With Eddie Arcaro," *Saturday Evening Post*, 6/28/58, pp. 26-27, 125-126.

On Whirlaway: General Sources, plus: "When Mr. Longtail Feasted on Racing,",by Jim Bolus, *SI,* November 4, 1991, pp. 6-8, expanded into "That Temperamental Mr. Longtail," in Bolus, *Derby Fever,* pp.207-215. Fred C. Broadhead's *Here Comes Whirlaway!* is a recent look at Mr. Longtail, while Bert Clark Thayer's *Whirlaway: The Life and Times of A Great Racer* is an older look at the champion, long on photographs. Also: sections on Whirlaway in *TGO, Top 100, GHOOT,* and *ARH, 1940, -1941, & - 1942; RIA*: "Whirlaway, Ben Jones, and Calumet," pp. 55-60; Anita Brenner, "Whirlaway: Problem Horse," *NYT Magazine*, 8/10/41, pp. 12-13,20 and interviews with Tom Gilcoyne, Jimmy Jones, and John Longden. "Alsab" in *Top 100* is useful for Whirly's most famous adversary. Mordaunt Milner's, *The Godolphin Arabian: The Story of the Matchem Line*, has comments re. Whirly. Red Smith's "The Swiftest Halfwit," in *To Absent Friends*, has the Eddie Arcaro-Johnny Gilbert colloquy in the 1941 Preakness, as well as Ben Jones' lament, "he's making a halfwit out of me."

Newspaper/Magazine Articles: *B-H*: 4/11/53, p. 830. *Time*: 5/12/41, p. 58; 11/9/42, p. 92;7/12/43, .p. 48. *Newsweek* : 5/12/41, p. 52; 5/19/41, p. 58; 6/16/41, p. 54; 8/4/41, p. 40;9/1/41, p. 40; 9/22/41, p. 47; 12/22/41, p. 54; 7/27/42, pp. 67-68. *LC-J*: 5/4/41, p. 1. *Sun*:5/11/41, p. 1; 10/29/42, p. 18. *Wall Street Journal*: "Calumet Farm Hits the Finish Line Out of Money,", 3/26/92, p. B4. *NYT*: 7/3/40, p. 24; 7/21/40, sect. 5, p. 7; 7/28/40, sect.5, p. 1; 8/4/40, sect. 5, p.1;8/11/40, sect. 5.,p.1; 8/25/40, sect. 5, p. 1; 9/1/40, sect. 5, p.1; 9/25/40, p.37; 9/29/40, sect. 5, p. 1; 10/9/40, p. 37; 10/20/40, p. S11; 11/3/40, sect. 5, p. 11; 11/15/40, p. 31; 2/9/41, sect. 5, p. 1; 2/19/41, p. 29; 3/23/41, sect. 5, p. 1; 3/29/41, p. 12; 4/12/41, p. 22; 4/25/41, p. 27; 4/30/41, p. 26; 4/27/41, sect. 5, p. 9; 5/3/41, p. 11; 5/4/41, sect. 5, p. 1; 5/11/41, sect. 5, p. 1; 5/21/41, p. 31; 6/7/41, p. 14; 6/8/41, sect. 5, p. 1; 6/22/41, sect. 5, p. 1; 7/16/41, p. 24; 7/27/41, sect. 5, p. 1; 8/7/41, p. 24; 8/17/41, sect. 5, p. 1; 8/24/41, sect 5, p. 1; 9/14/41, sect. 5, p. 1; 9/21/41, sect. 5, p. 1; 9/28/41, sect. 5, p. 1; 4/10/42, p. 26; 4/16/42, p. 28; 4/26/42, sect. 5, p. 1; 5/7/42, sect. 5, p. 1; 5/31/42, sect. 5, p. 1; 6/14/42, sect. 5, p. 1; 6/23/42, p. 5; 6/28/42, p. 3; 7/5/42, sect. 5, p. 1; 7/16/42, p. 24; 8/2/42; 8/30/42, sect. 5, p. 1; 9/13/42, sect. 5, p. 1; 9/20/42, p. 4; 9/27/42, p. 4; 10/4/42, sect. 5, p. 1; 10/11/42, sect. 5, p. 1; 10/25/42, sect. 5, p. 3; 10/29/42, p. 28; 11/4/42; 11/12/42, p. 32; 12/13/42, p. 2; 6/23/43, p. 27; 6/27/42, sect. 5, p.1; 6/29/43, p. 23; 1/4/48, sect. 5, p. 1; 7/14/50, p. 24; 4/8/53, p. 39; 8/16/59, sect 5, p. 1.

Race Charts/Notes: from *American Racing Manuals, 1940, 1941, 1942, 1943* & Media Guides.

K. COUNT FLEET

Author's Interview: John Longden, 2/9/94
Opening quote by Longden from McKay tape; final quote from Longden in "The Best I Ever Rode," *SI*, Special Edition, autumn, 1992, pp. 8-9.The quote from Mike Barry is from Bolus, *Kentucky Derby Stories*, p. 22.

On Longden: plaque sheet, NMR; Longden interview; B.K. Beckwith *The Longden Legend* ; "This was Longden," in Trent Frayne, *Northern Dancer & Friends*; Jack G. Jones, "Unique Double," *Thoroughbred Times,* 5/17/69, p. 1132-1133; Robert Hebert, "Ten Years Later," *B-H*, 3/15/76; Maryjean Wall, "Longden Pining for Roar of the Track," *Lexington Herald*, 3/9/93; George Dougherty, "He Simply Won't Quit," *Sports Review*, August, 1965, pp. 14-17.Also, Longden's comments on Count Fleet in Joseph Durso, "Triple Crown: Five Voices From the Saddle," *NYT,* 6/1/97, p. 25; Reg Lansberry interview with John Longden, *TT*, 4/27/02, pp. 20-22; and *B-H.com*, February 15, 2003.

On Count Fleet: General Sources, plus: chapter 8 in *The Racing Memoirs of John Hertz* (pvtly.printed, 1954); *RIA*:"The Year of Count Fleet:1943;", pp. 77-80; Dan Mearns, "The Strong and The Fleet," *B-H*, 4/24/82, pp. 2840-2849; "Count Fleet," in *TGO, Top 100, GHOOT,* and in *ARH, 1942, & -1943*; Edward L. Bowen, "Triple Crown History: Count Fleet," *B-H* Internet edition, 4/15/97; assorted clippings in KDM & KL files.

Newspaper/Magazine Articles: *B-H:* 12/10/73, p. 5086. *LC-J:* 5/2/43, p. 1. *Sun*: 5/9/43, sports sect., p. 1. *NYT:* 6/2/42, p. 29; 6/16/42, p. 16; 6/20/42, p. 19; 7/5/42, p. 4; 7/16/42, p. 24; 7/23/42, p. 24; 8/16/42, sect. 5, p. 1; 9/16/42, p. 33; 9/25/42, p. 28; 10/4/42, sect. 5, p. 1; 10/11/42, sect. 5, p. 1; 10/21/42, p. 29; 11/1/42, sect. 5, p. 8; 11/11/42, p. 33; 1/16/43, p. 18; 4/14/43; 4/16/43, p. 28; 4/18/43, sect. 5, p. 1; 4/19/43, p. 26; 4/25/43, sect. 3, p. 4; 5/1/43, p. 19; 5/2/43, sects. 3&5, p. 1; 5/8/43, p. 12; 5/9/43, sect 5, p.1; 5/11/43, p. 25; 5/23/43, sect. 3, p. 1; *NYT Magazine,* Sunday, 5/30/43, sect 6, p. 11; 6/5/43, p. 29; 6/6/43, sects. 3&5, p. 1; 12/18/43, p. 18; 7/23/44, sect. 5, p. 1; 12/4/73, p. 58; 12/6/73; Red Smith, "When Jimmy Wrote to End Writing," 12/7/73, p. 51.

Race Charts/Notes from *American Racing Manuals, 1942, 1943* & Media Guides.

L. ASSAULT

Author's Interviews: Bill Boland, 3/19/97; Tom Gilcoyne, 2/16/95; Warren Mehrtens, 5/10/96; and Monte Moncrief, DVM, 8/6/96.
Opening quote is from Eva Jolene Boyd, "All-out Assault," *SPUR*, May/June 1992, p. 73.

On King Ranch: Tom Lea, *The King Ranch* (Little, Brown & Co.,2 vols,: 1957;) *Time* cover story on King Ranch, 12/15/47; Jane Clements Monday & Betty Bailey Colley, *Voices From the Wild Horse Desert* (University of Texas Press: 1997;) Robert Moorman Denhardt, *The King Ranch Quarter Horses* (University of Oklahoma Press: 1970;) Cindi Myers, "King Ranch: Texas Giant," *Historic Traveler*, January, 1996, pp. 26-37; and Skip Hollandsworth, "When We Were Kings," *Texas Monthly*, August, 1998, pp. 112-117, 140-144.

On Max Hirsch: plaque sheet, NMR; obituary in *B-H*, April 12, 1969, pp. 1144-1145; Red Smith, "Max Hirsch,"in *To Absent Friends*, (1982;) numerous clippings in KDM, KL, and NMR files.

On Mehrtens: Mehrtens interview; Richard Tijerina, "Texas' Triple Crown Connection," in the *Corpus Christi Caller-Times*, May 3, 1996; James Michael, "King Ranch celebrates Assault's Triple Crown: Jockey Mehrtens remembers key to victories," *Kingsville, TX, Records*, May 5, 1996; p.6a; newspaper item re. Mehrtens' death, *The Gazette*, Colorado Springs, Colo., 1/1/98, p. SP2; notes on Mehrtens from NMR files.

On Assault: General Sources, plus: Eddie Arcaro, *I Ride to Win!*, (1951) describes Arcaro's "epiphany" towards Assault; "Assault," in *TGO, Top 100,* and in *ARH 1946, -1947 &-1949;* "Assault: The Little Horse with the Heart of a Giant," in Bolus, *Derby Magic,* pp. 59-68; Richard Tijerina, "Texas' Triple Crown Connection," in the *Corpus Christi Caller-Times*, May 3, 1996; Eva Jolene Boyd, "All-out Assault," *SPUR*, May/June 1992, pp. 68-73; *RIA:*"Assault's Triple Crown: 1946," pp. 107-112; Edward L. Bowen, "The Heart of Assault," *B-H*, 4/25/81, pp. 2402-2411; and Don Webb, "Assault Won the Crown Despite 4-F Feet," *Western Horseman,* September, 1964, p. 29. Vol. 2 of Tom Lea's *The King Ranch* contains material on Assault in pp. 663-665, as does

Monday & Collier's *Voices From the Wild Horse Desert*, pp. 74-77."Stymie" in *GHOOT,* "Armed" in *TGO,* and the sections on Armed, Gallorette, and Stymie in *ARH 1947* and *Top 100* are all good accounts of Assault's prominent opponents. The Max Hirsch quote on the proposed Armed-Assault-Stymie match race is from Grantland Rice, *The Tumult and the Shouting*, pp. 274-275. Finally, clippings from KDM, KL, and especially KRA files and author's notes from King Ranch celebration of the 50th Anniversary of Assault's Kentucky Derby victory, May 4, 1996. The KRA files contain a letter dated March 12, 1974 from Monte Moncrief, D.V.M., to racing writer Jim Bolus describing the nature of Assault's youthful hoof injury and stating that Dr. Moncrief put down Assault. Also useful is the author's *The Forgotten Champion: Middleground*, monograph commissioned by King Ranch, Inc., 1999.

Newspaper/Magazine Articles: *Time*, 5/13/46, p. 62. *Newsweek*: 5/13/46, p. 83; 5/20/46, p. 89. *B-H*, 9/13/71, p. 3255. *LC-J:* 5/5/46, p. 1. *Sun*:5/5/46, sports sect., p. 1; 5/12/46, p. 1. *NYT:* 6/5/45, p. 15; 6/13/45, p. 27; 6/24/45, sect. 5, p. 3; 7/13/45, p. 7; 7/19/45, p. 18; 8/7/45, p. 18; 9/6/45, p. 20; 9/13/45, p. 19; 10/9/45, p. 18; 4/10/46, p. 10; 4/21/46, sect. 5, p.1; 5/1/46, p. 35; 5/3/46, p. 18; 5/4/46, p. 19; 5/5/46, sect. 5, p.1; 5/6/46, p. 26; 5/11/46, p. 20;5/12/46, sect. 5, p. 1; 5/13/46, pp. 29 & 31; 6/1/46, pp. 17 & 19; 6/2/46, sects. 3&5, p. 1; 6/16/46, sect. 5, p. 1; 7/28/46, sect. 5, p. 1; 9/8/46, sect. 5, p. 1; 9/15/46, p. 11; 9/26/46, p. 37;10/20/46, sect. 5, p. 1; 10/27/46, sect. 5, p. 1; 11/10/46, sect. 5, p.1; 1/7/47, p. 36; 5/4/47, sect. 5, p. 1; 5/10/47, p. 17; 5/31/47, p. 10; 6/22/47, sect. 5, p. 1; 7/13/47, sect. 5, p. 1; 7/20/47, sect. 5, p. 1; 9/28/47, sect. 5, p. 1; 2/15/48, sect. 5, p.1; 2/22/48, sect. 5, p.1; 2/23/48, p. 22; 6/25/49; 7/3/49, sect. 5, p. 1; 8/14/49, sect. 5, p. 1; 9/11/49, sect. 5, p. 1; 10/16/49, sect. 5, p.1; 10/18/49, p. 40; 12/10/50, sect. 5, p.1; 5/27/64, p. 27; 9/2/71, p. 45.

Race Charts/Notes from *American Racing Manuals, 1945, 1946, 1947, 1948, 1949, 1950* & Media Guides.

M. CITATION

Author's Interviews: Tom Gilcoyne, 2/16/95; Margaret Glass, 12/26/96; Jimmy Jones, 2/18/97.

The "call" of 1948 Kentucky Derby, © WHAS Radio, is reproduced here with permission of WHAS Radio, Louisville, KY.
Opening quote is from Gilcoyne interview; closing quote by Arcaro is from the McKay tape.

On Jimmy Jones: Joe Hirsch and Gene Plowden, *In the Winner's Circle: The Jones Boys of Calumet Farm*; Jimmy Jones interview; Jim Bolus, "Two Fellows From Missouri," *The Thoroughbred Record*, May, 1990,

On Arcaro: sources listed for Arcaro in Whirlaway notes, plus: "Man on A Horse," *Time*, May 17, 1948, pp. 78-87; *NYT*, 11/15/97, p. A24; "He Knew A Horse," *SPUR*, January/February 1998, p. 64; David Schmitz, 'The Master,", *B-H Internet Edition*,

11/20/97; William Nack, "The Headiest Horseman," *SI*, 11/24/97, p. 21; "Fast Eddie," *People*, 12/1/97. Also, Arcaro's comments on Citation in Joseph Durso, "Triple Crown: Five Voices From the Saddle," *NYT*, 6/1/97, p. 25.

On Citation: "Citation," in *TGO, Top 100, GHOOT*, and *ARH*, *1947, -1948, -1950, -1951;* "Citation:1945-1970;" *B-H*, 8/15/70, pp. 2622-2624; John Chandler, "Calumet's Citation: Last to Capture the Triple Crown," *B-H*, 6/4/73, pp. 1945 & 1948; Leon Rasmussen, "Lest We Forget," *The Thoroughbred Record,*, 6/2/56, p. 13; various clippings in KDM, KL, and NMR files; and Hirsch and Plowden, *In the Winner's Circle: The Jones Boys of Calumet Farm* which has an excellent narrative of Citation's career. Also see Edward L. Bowen, "1998: The Milestone for Citation, Secretariat, Affirmed," *The Backstretch*, March/April 1998, pp. 40-46. B.K. Beckwith, *The Longden Legend*, has Longden's comments on the Citation-Noor rivalry and "Noor,"in *Top 100* is a good look at Citation's rival. Also helpful is Ann Hagedorn Auerbach's *Wild Ride*, which relates the rise, retreat, re-rise and calamitous fall of Calumet Farm. The Tom Gilcoyne, Margaret Glass, and Jimmy Jones interviews were invaluable. The 1991 videotape, "Thoroughbred Heroes," by Historic Thoroughbred Collection, Inc., has a clip of Citation's last race.

Newspaper/Magazine Articles: *Time:* 5/10/48, p.61; 6/7/48, p. 44; 6/21/48, p. 51; 1/23/50, p. 45; 3/13/50, p. 66; 6/12/50, p. 76. *Newsweek:* 1/12/48, p. 70; 4/26/48, p. 81; 5/10/48, pp. 73-74; 5/24/48, p. 88; 6/21/48, p. 83; 9/6/48, p. 71; 10/11/48, pp. 80-81; 10/25/48, p. 90; 11/8/48, p. 82; 1/8/51, pp. 68 & 70; 1/23/50, p. 72; 6/12/50, p. 82; 3/13/50, p. 68; 3/6/50, pp. 72-73; 7/23/51, pp. 78-79; 7/30/51, p. 45. *LC-J:* 5/2/48, p. 1. *Sun:* 10/29/48, p. 21; 10/30/48, p. 14. *NYT:* 4/23/47;5/4/47, p. 3;5/22/47, p. 39; 10/1/47, p. 41; 10-5-47, sect. 5, p. 1; 11/9/47, p. 10S; 2/3/48, p. 33; 2/12/48, p. 34; 2/19/48, p. 32; 2/29/48, sect. 5, p. 1; 4/13/48, p. 35; 4/18/48, sect. 5, p. 1; 4/28/48, p. 36; 5/2/48, sect. 5, p. 1; 5/16/48, sect. 5, p. 1; 5/30/48, sect. 5, p. 1; 6/12/48, p. 13; 6/13/48, sect. 5, p. 1; 7/6/48, p. 30; 8/22/48, sect. 5, p. 1; 8/28/48, sect. 5, p. 1; 9/30/48, p. 37; 10/3/48, sect. 5, p. 1; 10/17/48, sect. 5, p. 1; 10/30/48, p. 19; 12/4/48, p. 18; 12/12/48, sect. 5, p. 1;1/12/50, p. 37; 1/27/50, p. 31; 2/2/50, sect. 5, p. 2; 2/26/50, sect. 5, p. 1; 3/5/50, sect. 5, p.1; 5/18/50, p. 43; 6/4/50, p. 15; 6/18/50, p. 15; 6/25/50, p. 15; 4/19/51, p. 45; 4/27/51, p. 30; 5/12/51, p. 17; 5/31/51, p. 36; 6/15/51, p. 31; 7/5/51, p. 53; 7/15/51, sect. 5, p. 1.

Race Charts/Notes: from *American Racing Manuals*, *1947, 1948, 1950, 1951* & Media Guides.

N. SECRETARIAT

Author's Interviews: Penny Chenery, 2/27/98; Tom Gilcoyne, 2/16/95; Ron Turcotte, 2/27/97.
The call of the 1973 Belmont Stakes, © CBS Sports, is reproduced here with the permission of CBS Sports.

On Meadow Stable: Chenery interview; William Nack, *Secretariat: The Making of A Champion*; Carol Atwater, "Secretariat," *Equus*, December, 1993, pp. 26-35.

On Laurin: plaque sheet, NMR; Nack, *Secretariat; LC-J*, 6/27/00, *NYT*, 6/27/00, p. A23; clippings from NMR files.

On Turcotte: plaque sheet, NMR, Turcotte interview; Bill Heller with Ron Turcotte, *The Will to Win: Ron Turcotte's Ride to Glory*; Ron Turcotte, "Secretariat and Me," special advertising section in *SI*, 5/3/93; "Horses Run for Turcotte," in Frayne's *Northern Dancer & Friends*; Gerald Strine, "Still Ride in Triumph Over Mischance," *B-H*, 9/20/86, p. 6804-6809; Neil Milbert, "Riding the Big Red Express," *TT Online edition*, 4/25/98; and Nack, *Secretariat*. Also, Turcotte's comments on Secretariat in Joseph Durso, "Triple Crown: Five Voices From the Saddle," *NYT,* 6/1/97, p. 25; author's interview with Warren Mehrtens, 5/10/96.

On Secretariat: (As with Man o'War, the literature on Secretariat is large and also continues to increase.) General Sources, plus: Chenery interview; Gilcoyne interview; Turcotte interview; "Eddie Sweat: One Man's Love for Secretariat, " in Bolus, *Derby Fever,* pp. 29-41; Also Nack, *Secretariat* and the same author's "Pure Heart," *SI*, 6/4/90, pp. 78-91; reprinted in *SI,* 10/24/94, pp. 76-88; Raymond G. Woolfe, Jr., *Secretariat*; "Secretariat, " in *Top 100*; "Secretariat: Triple Crown Winner," *Western Horseman*, 8/73, pp. 20-21 & 146-151; Carol Atwater, "Secretariat," *Equus*, December, 1993, pp. 26-35; David Schmitz, "End of An Era," *B-H Internet Edition*, 10/24/98; and Eddie Sweat, "Red, Sweat, and Tears," *B-H Internet Edition*, 4/27/98; clippings from KDM, KL, and NMR files; and Edward L. Bowen, "1998: The Milestone for Citation, Secretariat, Affirmed," *The Backstretch*, March/April 1998, pp. 40-46. The ESPN videotape, "The Life and Times of Secretariat: An American Racing Legend," (1990,) is a very good look at the great racer. The Nack quote, "Secretariat exploded..." is from his book, *Secretariat*, pp. 111-112, and the comment about the 1973 Preakness, "Turcotte hit the cruise control," is from Nack, "Pure Heart."

Newspaper/Magazine Articles: *Time:* 6/11/73, pp.85-89 (Cover story;) 6/18/73. *Newsweek:* 6/11/73, pp. 62-69 (Cover story;) 6/18/73, p. 95. *SI:* 11/27/72, p. 91; 3/26/73, pp. 23-24; 4/20/73, pp. 16-19; 5/14/73, pp. 18-21; 5/18/73, pp. 24-27; 6/11/73, pp. 34- 37 (Cover story;)6/18/73, pp. 14-19. *LC-J:* 5/6/73, sect. C, p. 1. *Sun:*5/20/73, p. 1. *NYT:* 7/5/72, p. 49; 7/16/72; 8/1/72, p. 43; 8/17/72, p. 45; 8/27/72, p. 6; 9/17/72, sect. 5, p. 1; 10/15/72, sect. 5, p. 1; 10/29/72, sect. 5, p. 1, 11/19/72, sect. 5, p. 1; 3/18/73, sect. 5, p. 1; 4/8/73, sect. 5, p. 1; 4/22/73, sect. 5, p. 1; 5/6/73, sect. 5, p. 1; 5/19/73, sect. 5, p. 1; 5/20/73, sect. 5, p. 1; 5/21/73, p. 33; 6/10/73, sect. 5, p. 1; 7/1/73, sect. 5, p. 1; Red Smith, "Secretariat, Potatoes, and Things," 7/2/73, p. 33; 8/5/73, sect. 5, p. 1; 9/16/73, sect. 5,.p.1; 9/30/73, sect. 5, p. 1; 10/9/73, p. 5510/10/73, p. 56; 10/29/73, p. 49.

Race Charts/Notes: from *American Racing Manuals, 1972, 1973,* Media Guides, and Raymond G. Woolfe, Jr., *Secretariat,* (1998 ed.)

O. SEATTLE SLEW

Author's Interviews: Jean Cruguet, 2/16/98; Tom Gilcoyne, 2/16/95;Anne Scardino, 1/14/99; Bill Turner,8/20/97; Paula Turner, 5/13/97.

On Bill/Paula Turner: Bill Turner and Paula Turner interviews; Steve Cady and Barton Silverman, *Seattle Slew;* clippings in KDM, KL, and NMR files.

On Cruguet: Cruguet interview; NYRA Media Guide; Cady & Silverman, *Seattle Slew;* clippings in KDM, KL, and NMR files. Also, Cruguet's comments on Seattle Slew in Joseph Durso, "Triple Crown: Five Voices From the Saddle," *NYT,* 6/1/97, p. 25.

On Seattle Slew: McKay Tape, Wilding & Del Balso, *The Triple Crown Winners*, plus: Cady & Silverman, *Seattle Slew*; "Seattle Slew Was a Special Racehorse," in Bolus, *Derby Magic*, pp. 213-220; "Seattle Slew" in *Top 100*; Charles P. Pierce, 'The Stud," *Esquire*, August, 2001, pp. 46-49; Kimberly S. Herbert, "Remembering 1977 Triple Crown Winner Seattle Slew," *B-H Archives*, orig. printed 4/30/94; Three Chimneys Farm, "Stallions, 1995," Three Chimneys Farm promotional brochure, 1995; Steve Kweskin, "Seattle Slew: Triple Crown Winner," *Western Horseman*, August, 1977; Larry Adler, "Chapter 12: Seattle Slew and His Lucky Crew," *Famous Horses in America,* (1979;) Billy Reed, " A great one for a Slew of Reasons," *TT*, 4/27/02, pp. 17-19; numerous clippings in KDM, KL, and NMR files.

Newspaper/Magazine Articles: *SI:* 10/25/76, pp. 90-92; 4/4/77, pp. 36-39; 5/2/77, pp. 89-90; 5/9/77, pp. 34-39; 5/16/77, pp. 18-23 (Cover story;) 5/30/77, pp. 20-21; 6/13/77, pp. 41-51; 6/20/77, pp. 16-21 (Cover story;) 7/11/77, pp. 54-55; 8/21/78, pp. 24-25; 9/25/78, pp. 22-23; 10/23/78, pp. 88 & 93. *Time:* 4/28/97, p. 27; 5/20/02. *Newsweek:* 5/20/02, p. 10. *B-H Internet edition:* 2/22/02; 4/5/02; 5/7/02; 7/.26/02. *TT:* 3/16/02, p. 55; 5/18/02, pp. 1, 20-23. *LC-J:* 5/8/77, special Kentucky Derby section; *Sun*:5/22/77, sect. N, p. 1; *NYT:* 9/21/76, p. 9; 10/6/76, p. 30; 10/17/76, sect. 5, p. 1; 3/10/77, p. 44; 3/27/77, sect. 5, p. 1; 4/24/77, sect. 5, p. 1; 5/8/77, sect. 5, p. 1; 5/22/77, sect. 5, p. 1; 6/12/77, p. 1; 6/13/77, p. 39; 7/4/77, p. 1; 5/15/78, p. C3; 11/12/78, sect. 5, p. 1.*The Gazette-Telegraph*, Colorado Springs, Colo.: 8/13/78, p. 8-C; 9/6/78, p. 2-C; 9/17/78, p. 12-F; 10/1/78, p. 5-C;10/15/78, p. 5-C; 5/8/02, Sports, p. 1. *Rocky Mountain News*, Denver, Colo.5/8/02, p. 6C. William H. Rudy: "A Clash of Crowns," *B-H*, 9/25/78, pp. 4364-4367.

Race Charts/Notes: from *American Racing Manuals, 1976, 1977, 1978* & Media Guides.

P. AFFIRMED & ALYDAR

Author's Interviews: Steve Cauthen, 5/17/96; Tom Gilcoyne, 2/16/95, Margaret Glass, 12/26/96; Anne Scardino, 1/14/99.
The quote re. Affirmed, "he is one of those horses," is courtesy of Sarah McCarthy, DVM, e-mail of 1/27/97; the quote from Jimmy Bell of Jonabell Farm re. Affirmed's last days is from *TT:* "Triple Crown hero Affirmed Euthanized," 1/20/01, p. 1. The Cauthen quote re. Gary Stevens and Silver Charm is from Cauthen's comments on Affirmed in Joseph Durso, "Triple Crown: Five Voices From the Saddle," *NYT,* 6/1/97, p. 25.

On Barrera: plaque sheet, NMR; clippings, KDM, KL, and NMR files.

On Cauthen: Cauthen interview; Pete Axthelm, *The Kid;* Cauthen's comments on Affirmed in Joseph Durso, "Triple Crown: Five Voices From the Saddle," *NYT,* 6/1/97, p. 25; Guy Wathen, "Steve Cauthen," in *Great Horsemen of the World* (Trafalgar Square Publishing: 1990,) pp. 60-66. The William Steinkraus quote on Cauthen is found in Wathen, p. 163. Also: Eddie Arcaro, "An Old-Time Jockey Rates a Young One," *NYT,* 6/11/78, sports, p. 2; Jim Bolus and Billy Reed, "The Walton Wonder Boy wins on the Wonderful Affirmed," *LC-J,* 5/7/78, p. 2; *SI:* 12/19/77 (Cover story;) and 6/19/97, p. 15. *Time:* 5/29/78, (cover story) pp. 56-59 and 5/13/96, p. 39; clippings from KDM, KL, and NMR files.

On Affirmed: McKay tape, plus: Cauthen interview, "Affirmed and Alydar, Racing's Greatest Rivalry," in Bolus, *Kentucky Derby Stories,* pp. 153-157; "Diary of A Derby Winner," in Bolus, *Remembering the Derby,* pp. 197-217; Sections on "Affirmed" in *Top 100* and in Richard Stone Reeves with Jim Bolus, *Royal Blood: Fifty Years of Classic Thoroughbreds* (The Blood-Horse Inc.:1994;) Edward L. Bowen, "1998: The Milestone for Citation, Secretariat, Affirmed," *The Backstretch,* March/April 1998, pp. 40-46; Eva Jolene Boyd, "Always Affirmed," *SPUR,* May & June 1998, pp. 54-59; ___, "Affirmed," *Kentucky Sports World,* February, 1980, pp. 76-77; Rick Bozich, "Affirmed Still Looks Like a Champ," *LC-J,* 6/3/97; ___, "Affirmed still looks good 20 years after Triple Crown," *ESPN Sportszone,* 5/3/98; clippings in KDM, KL, and NMR files.

On Alydar: Margaret Glass interview, also her monograph, "The Calumet Story;" Ann Hagedorn Auerbach, *Wild Ride;* "Alydar" in *Top 100;* clippings in KDM, KL, and NMR files.

Newspaper/Magazine Articles: *B-H Internet Edition:* "Triple Crown Winner Affirmed Euthanized," 1/12/01. *TT:* "Triple Crown hero Affirmed Euthanized," 1/20/01, p. 1. *Time:* 5/29/78, (cover story) pp. 56-59; and 6/19/78, p. 88. *Newsweek:* 5/8/78, pp. 117-119; 5/15/78, p. 55; 6/12/78, p. 74; 6/19/78, pp. 88-91. *SI:* 9/5/77, pp. 85 87; 10/24/77, pp. 76-77; 3/6/78, pp. 52-54; 4/10/78, pp. 24-25; 3/13/78, pp. 20-23; 3/27/78, pp. 80-82; 5/8/78, pp. 28-29;5/15/78 (Cover story) pp. 18-23; 5/29/78, pp. 20-21; 6/19/78 (Cover story) pp. 16-19; 8/14/78, pp. 53- 54; 8/28/78, pp. 20-21; 10/23/78, pp. 88-93; 7/2/79, pp. 53-54; 1/29/79, pp. 38 40; 10/1/79, pp. 59-61; 10/15/79, pp. 32-33; 10/29/79, pp. 38 41; 6/8/98, p. 12. *NYT:* Affirmed only races and Affirmed/Alydar races: 5/25/77, p. A24; 6/16/77, p. D19; 7/7/77, p. D12; 8/18/77, p. B21; 8/28/77, sect 5, p. 9; 9/11/77, sect. 5, p. 1; 10/16/77, sect. 5, p. 1; 10/5, p. 13; 3/9/78, p. D14; 4/3/78, p.C6; 4/17/78, p. C11; 5/5/78, p. A19; 5/5/78, p. B1; 5/6/78, p. 17; 5/7/78, sect. 5, p. 1; 5/29/78, p. A26; Red Smith, "The Preakness: What They Say," 5/20/78, p. 16; 5/21/78, sect. 5, p. 1; 6/9/78, p. A22; 6/10/78, p. 13; 6/11/78, sect. 5, p. 1; 1/21/79, p. 105; 3/5/79, p. C8; 5/21/79, p. C7; 6/25/79, p. C2; 8/30/79, p. C18; 9/23/79, p. S-3; 10/7/79, sect. 5, p. 1; 10/23/79, p. B15; 10/24/79, p. A25; 11/11/79, p. S-3; Alydar only races: 6/25/77, p. 14; 7/28/77, D16; 8/14/77, sect. 5, p. 1; 11/27/77, sect 5, p.1; 3/5/78, sect 5, p. 1; 4/2/78, sect. 5, p.1; 4/28/78, p. A19; 7/23/79, sect. 5, p. 9; 4/1/79, sect. 5, p. 11; 4/14/79, p. 26; 5/6/79, sect 5, p. 11; 5/29/79, p. B5; 6/18/79, p. C6; 7/5/79, p. B11; 7/22/79, sect. 5, p. 1; Steve Cady, "Saying Goodbye to Alydar," 7/25/79, p. A17; Robert Daniel Fierro, "Alydar's Rainbow," 7/28/79, p. 17. *Gazette-Telegraph,* Colorado Springs, Colo.:8/6/78, p. 4-C;

8/20/78, p. S-9; 9/17/78, p. 12-F;10/15/78, p. 5-C. William H. Rudy: "A Clash of Crowns," *B-H*, 9/25/78, pp. 4364-4367.

Race Charts/Notes: from *American Racing Manuals, 1977, 1978, 1979* & Media Guides.

INDEX

Note: Race horse *names* italicized. Triple Crown Champions **boldfaced**.

Note: *denotes Hall of Fame

A

Aaron, Hank, 262
ABC Sports, 207, 234
Adams, John*, 156
Affidavit, 291
Affirmed*, v, vii*, 6, 10, 13, 23 n. 15, 30,
  49 n. 12, 66, 111, 193, 254, 255, 257,
  261-93, *261*, 267, 269, *277, 279,* 295
    birth of, 262
    bloodlines, 262, 275
    burial place, 291
    career summary, 285, **289**
    conformation, 262
    death of, 291
    foul in Travers Stakes, 283-84
    injuries, 291
    personality, 262, 270-72
    photographs, *261, 271, 277, 279*
    progeny, 291
    races
        in maiden race, 263
        in allowance race (Santa Anita,
            1978), 273
        in Belmont Stakes, 10, 280-81
        in Belmont Futurity, 269
        in Californian Stakes, 287
        in Champagne Stakes, 269-72
        in Charles H. Strub Stakes, 287
        in exhibition race, Belmont, 288
        in Great American Stakes, 275
        in Hollywood Derby, 274, 275
        in Hollywood Gold Cup, 287-88
        in Hollywood Juvenile
            Championship, 265, 269
        in Hopeful Stakes, 268, 269
        in Jim Dandy Stakes, 283
        in Jockey Club Gold Cup, 255,
            285, 287, 288
        in Kentucky Derby, 23 n. 15, 275-
            77, *277*
        in Laurel Futurity, 269-70
        in Malibu Stakes, 286
        in Marlboro Cup, 254-55, 284
        in Preakness Stakes, 278, *279*
        in San Felipe Handicap, 273
        in San Fernando Stakes, 286
        in Sanford Stakes, 267-68
        in Santa Anita Derby, 273-74,
            275
        in Santa Anita Handicap, 287
        in Travers Stakes, 283-84
        re: Turf Classic, 288
        in Woodward Stakes, 288
        in Youthful Stakes, 263-64, 265
    racing record
        as two-year-old, 264-72
        as three-year-old, 272-79
        as four-year-old, 286-89
    retirement, 49 n. 12, 288
    silks, buried with, 291
    siring record, 291
    winnings, 255, 285, 288
African-Americans
    Harbut, Will, 17, 30, 106
    Lewis, Oliver, 2
    Murphy, Isaac*, 2, 69 n. 2, 207
Agua Caliente Track (Mexico), 126
Air Lift, 164
A.J. Joyner Handicap, 124, 125
AK-Sar-Ben Racetrack, 92, 93, 113 n. 18
Alamo Downs, 182
Alcibiades, 67
A Lark, 209
Allen Z., 80
*Alsab**, 139-41, 239 n. 1, 256 n. 4, 262
Althea, 290
*Alydar**, v*, 23 n. 15, 30, 49 n. 12, 66,
    193, **261-293**, 264-65, 268,-270, 278,
    279, 282, 290
        bloodlines, 265
        burial place, 290
        career summary, 284
        death of, 290
        fouled in Travers Stakes, 283-84
        personality, 270-71, 272
        injuries, 284, 290
        naming, 265 n. 1
        photographs, *279, 282*
        progeny, 290n 8
        races
            in allowance race (Hialeah,
                1978), 272
            in Arlington Classic, 283
            in Belmont Futurity, 269, 280-
                81
            in Blue Grass Stakes, 272

re: Brooklyn Handicap, 284
in Carter Handicap, 284
in Champagne Stakes, 269
in Flamingo Stakes, 273
in Florida Derby, 124, 273,
274
in Great American Stakes, 265
269
in Hopeful Stakes, 269
in Kentucky Derby, 275-77
in Laurel Futurity, 269-70
in Metropolitan Handicap, 284
in Nassau County Handicap, 284
in Oaklawn Handicap, 284
in Preakness Stakes, 278, *279*
in Remsen Stakes, 270
in Sapling Stakes, 266, 269
in Suburban Handicap, 284
in Travers Stakes, 283-84
in Tremont Stakes, 265, 269
in Whitney Stakes, 283
in Youthful Stakes, 264
retirement, 49 n. 12, 290
siring record, 289-91, 290n 8
Aly Khan, 265 n. 1
Alysheba*, 30, 290
Amberoid, 218
Ambrose, Eddie, 20, 25, 27 (*see* Jockeys)
American Derby, 19, 91, 133, 199
American Handicap, 209
American Flag, 30, 95
American Merchant (vessel), 91
American Race Horses: 1877 (book), 104,
178 n. 10, 189
American Triple Crown, 10
Anderson, Chic, 230
Andor Farm, 240
Angle Light, 223, 225
Annapolis, 7
Annapolis Subscription Plate, 6
Annihilate 'Em, 233
Anti-gambling laws (*see also* betting), 4
passed in New York, 4, 11
bookmaking banned in Lexington, 4
Appomattox, 1
Aqueduct, 11, 18, 25, 56, 60, 62, 70, *78,*
80, 81, 86, 88, 99, 106, 131, 136, 152,
167, 174, 178, 181, 181, 218, 224, 235,
246, 253, 256, 270, 284, 288, 295
Aquitania (vessel), 90
Arab Oil Embargo, 215
Arcadia Purse, 124
Arcaro, Eddie*, *vii*, 82 n. 2, 83, 89, *121,*
125 131, 131 n. 9, 134, 135, 136, *137,*
139, 143, 144, 145, 164, 168, 169,
172, 173, 175, 175 n. 7, 178, 179, 182-
83, 193 n.5, 195, *196, 197,* 198, 200,

204-05, **206**, 210, 212, *213*, 220, 231,
266, 286, *293*, 295
birth of, 125
broadcast commentator, 258, 250
career highlights, 193, 206
career summary, 125, 206
death of, 207
early days, 125-26
Hall of Fame, 206
photographs, *125, 142, 196,* 197,
213, 293
president, Jockey Guild, 206
product promotions, 206
suspensions, 131, 138, 140, 193 n.5,
193
Arc de Triomphe, 243
Argonaut Handicap, 209
Aristides, 2, 3, *12*
Arlington Classic, 66, 70, 88, 103, 131,
132, 135, 174, 199, 283
Arlington Downs, 176 n. 9
Arlington Futurity, 120, 190
Arlington Invitational, 231
Arlington Park, 70, 88, 119, 120, 131,
138, 190, 199, 208, 231, 283
Arlington Special Event Purse, 131
Armageddon, 67
Armed*, 11, 116, 166, 179, 179, 189,
192, 199, 210, 256 n.4, 264, 275
Army Remount Service, 51
Ascot Gold Cup (G.B.), 2, 76, 90, 96
Askmenow, 154, 154 n. 4
Assault*, 6, 10, 13, 15, 16 n. 9, 21 n. 12,
34 n. 1, 49 n. 12, 66, 128 n. 8, 144,
161, **163-85**, *164, 170, 171, 172,* 190,
193, 199, 225, 246, 281
appearance, 167
birth of, 163-64
bloodlines, 16 n. 9, 164
burial of, 184
career summary, 165, 176, 180, 185
death of, 184
eating habits, 176
hoof, deformed, right front, *165,*
173, 177
illnesses, 174, 181
injuries, 164-65, 174, 176, 180,
181, 184
nicknames, 165
photographs, *164, 165, 170, 171,*
172, 177, 172
personality, 176-77, 178, 183-184
progeny, 189
races
in Arlington Classic, 174
in Babylon Handicap, 167
in Belmont Stakes, 13, 173

in Brooklyn Handicap, 178, 181
in Butler Handicap, 166, 178,
  281
in Cowdin Stakes, 167
in Discovery Handicap, 174
in Dixie Handicap, 177
in Dwyer Stakes, 173-74
in East View Stakes, 167
in Edgemere Handicap, 181
in Experimental Free
  Handicap No.1, 167
in first races, 167
in Flash Stakes, 167
in Gallant Fox Handicap, 174
in Glengarry Purse, 181, 181 n. 11
in Gowanus Purse, 167
in Grey Lag Handicap, 177, 181-
  82
at Hialeah 5th Race, 180
in Hyde Park Purse, 183
in International Gold Cup, 179
in Jersey Handicap, 174
in Kentucky Derby, 128 n. 8,
  168, *170*, *171*
in Kentucky Derby Trial, 168
in Manhattan Handicap, 174
in Massachusetts Handicap, 181
in match race against *Armed*, 180
in Pimlico Special, 175, 177
in Preakness Stakes, 170-172, *172*,
  177
in Roamer Handicap, 174
in Suburban Handicap, 177
in Westchester Handicap, 175
in Westwood Purse, 183
in Widener Handicap, 180-81
in Wood Memorial Stakes, 168
racing record
  as two-year old, 167-76
  as three-year-old, 167-76
  as four-year-old, 176-80
  as five-year-old, 180-83
  as six-year-old, 181
retirement, 49 n. 12, 181, 183-84
siring record, 181-82, 182 n. 12, 189
temperament, 165, 176
tests sterile, 181, 182 n. 12
winnings, 167, 174, 176-78, 182,
  183, 185
Associated Press, 83, 133, 135, 202, 267
asterisk, naming convention, 34, 34 n. 1
Atkinson, Ted*, 156-57, 157, 168, 173,
  198-99
Attention, 120, 132, 135, 136, 142
Audley Farm, 50
Auerbach, Ann Hagedorn, 290 n 9

B

"Baby Huey", 240
Babylon Handicap, 167
Baird, R.L., 200
Baker, Frank, 71
Balladier, 81
Baltimore Fire, 8
Baltimore Evening Sun (newspaper), 23,
  67
Baltimore Sun (newspaper), 7 n. 6, 40,
  201, 227
Bannerette, 70
Barry, Mike, 156
Barrera, Lazaro "Laz"*, 262, 263, 266,
  272, 273, 280, 283, 286, 288, 289-90
    birth of, 263
    career summary, 289
    death of, 290
    early years, 263
Bassett, Ted, 272
Battleship*, 30
Bay Meadows, 209
Bay Shore Stakes, 224
Beasley, Pat, 90, 91
Dedwell, H. Guy*, **34-37**, *39*, 45, 49,
  50, 51, 54, 268
    birth of, 35
    death of, 50
    early years, 35-36
    elected to Hall of Fame, 50
    photograph, *43*
    trainer's license suspended, 50
    unusual methods, 36
Belair Handicap, 45
Belair Stud, 56, 72, 74, 80, 82, 88, 149
Believe It, 270, 275, 278
Bell, Jimmy, 291
Belmont, August, 10, 13, 15-16
Belmont family, 15
Belmont Futurity, 21, 25, 36, 56, 81, 99,
  122, 153, 221, 244, 269
Belmont Futurity Trial, 122, 190, 244
Belmont Park, 3, 9 n 7, 10, 11, 14, 15,
  19, 21, 42, 73, 86, 99, 111, 121, 130,
  152, 154, 159, 167, 179, 197, 210,
  218, 224, 240, 242, 244, 263, 274, 280,
  284, 288, 295
Belmont Purse, 204
Belmont Stakes, *v, vii,* 3, **10-12**, 15, 16,
  24, 30, 33, 41, 49, 56, 57, 69, 76, 86,
  97, 103, 103 n. 15, 134, 135-136, 136,
  139, 155, 158-59, 158 n. 7, 158 n. 8
  172-73, 176, 220, 229-31, 231 n. 3,
  250-51, 262, 265, 280-81, *282*, 283, 289

same day running as Preakness
Stakes, 11 n. 8
Ben Ali, 3
Better Self, 197, 198-99
betting
banned in New York, 4, 11
outlawed in Louisville, 5
pari-mutuel, 5
Bewitch*, 189, 190, 197, 203, 209, 210, 264
Big Burn, 218
"Big Red", 17, 20, 30
Billy Kelly, 37, 38, 43, 44, 49, 68
Bint Pasha, 291
Bischoff, Myra, 266
Bischoff, Tommy, 266
black-eyed Susans, 9
Black Stallion, The (book), 241
Blazes, 28
Blenheim II, 34, 34 n. 1, 55, 116, 116 n. 2, 188, 265
Blind, Eddie, 152
Blood Horse, The (magazine), 14, 31 n 22, 44, 89, 116 n. 2, 210 *(interactive edition),*
blood poisoning, 37, 37 n. 5
Bluegrass Fair, 56
Blue Grass Stakes, 124, 194, 194, 220, 224, 272
Blue Pair, 125
Blue Swords, 156, 157
Bobsleigh, 90
Boland, Bill, 166, 181 n. 11, 183
Bold, 206
Bold Forbes, 263
Bold Gallant, 202, 204
Bold Reasoning, 239
Bold Ruler*, v; 55, 57, 206, 210, 216, 220, 238, 239, 239 n. 1
Bold Venture, 163, 166, 181
Bolero, 207-08
Bolingbroke, 140-41
Bolster, 45
Bolus, Jim, 237
bookmaking, 4
Boots and Saddles (book), 33, 39, 46 n. 10
Bossuet, 156
Bottle Cap, 100
bounce-back, 42
Boussac, Marcel, 144
Bovard, 197, 198
Bowie, Oden, 7
Boxthorn, 84, 85
Bozich, Rick, 261
Brann, W.L., 136

Brannan Brothers Stable, 57
Brannon, 85
Breckenridge Stakes, 8 n 6, 9
Breeder's Cup, 13
Breeder's Futurity, 122
Breslin, Jimmy, 59, 68, 93 n. 10
Bridal Flower, 175-76
Brightwaters Purse, 99
Brooklyn, New York, 56
Brooklyn Dodgers, 166
Brooklyn Handicap, 14, 18, 87, 136, 178, 181, 284
Brooks, Steve*, 190, 203-04, 205-06, 207, 209, 210
Brumfield, Don*, 244
Brushup, 95
Buckingham Purse, 199
Buckpasser*, 55, 238
Buick (General Motors), 206
Bull Lea, 116, 188, 190, 192, 198, 265
Burgoo King, 5
Burke, J.H., 60
Burns, Robert (quoted), 38
Busher*, 111, 161, 204, 239 n. 1
Busy K., 106
Butler Handicap, 137, 166, 281
But Why Not, 205-06
buzzer, electric, 217

C

Cable, 173
Cady, Steve, 240, 243, 245, 283, 288
Calder Track, 193 n. 4
Californian Stakes, 287
Calumet Baking Powder Company, 83, 115
Calumet Farm, 47 n. 11, 52, 55, 82 n. 2, 83, 115-127, 116 n. 2, 117, 122, 123, 125, 130, 135, 144-45, 166, 169, 179, 187, 189, 189 n 1, 96, 191, 200, 201, 202, 205, 208, 217, 264, 265, 271, 272, 276, 283, 284, 289, 291
silks, red-and-blue, 264, 276, 293
sold in bankruptcy, 145, 290 n 9
Calvert Purse, 100
Cameron, Don, 148, 150, 268
Canada, 27
Calgary, Alberta, 82
Saint-Paul de Joliet, Quebec, 217
Taber, Alberta, 148
Toronto, Ontario
Windsor, Ontario, 28, 47
Canadian International Championship, 234
Canadian National Railway, 35
Canadian Navy, Royal, 35, 47, 49

Canadians
  Laurin, Lucien*, 217 (*see* at name)
  Ross, J.K.L. (*see* at name)
  Turcotte, Camille (*see* at name)
  Turcotte, Ron* (*see* at name)
  Turcotte, Rudy (*see* at name)
Canonero II, 227 n. 2
Capote, Truman, 97
Captain Alcock, 20
carnations, white, 11, 199, 231
Carroll, Julian, 256
Carry Back, 210, 262
Carry Over, 82
Carter Handicap, 136, 284
Cartier's, 215
Caruso, 61
Caruso, Enrico, 47 n. 11
Cassidy, Mars, 19, 21
Castleman, Ben, 239
Cauthen, Myra, 266
Cauthen, Ronald "Tex", 266, 267
Cauthen, Steve*, 63, 254, 255, 262, 263,
  266-86, *277, 279,* 280 n. 4, *282, 284, 287,*
  293, 295
    birth of, 266-68
    career summary, 267, 289-91
    early years, 266-67, 270
    first race, 267
    Hall of Fame, 272, 289
    injuries, 283
    jockey record, 267
    losing streak, 285-86
    personality, 289
    photographs, *268, 277, 279, 282,*
      293
    races in England, 287, 289
    retires as jockey, 288
    suspension, 273
    wins five great International
      Derbies, 267
Cavalry, U.S., 56
Celt Purse, 136
Century Handicap, 209
Chaffee, Earl, 71
Challedon,135
Challenge Purse, 202
Champagne Charlie, 224
Champagne Stakes, 81, 221-22, 255, 269
Charismatic, 295
Charlie Barley, 291
Chenery, C.T., 215-16, 223 (death of)
Cherbourg, France, 56
Chesapeake Stakes, 100, 195
Chicago, 80
Chicago Heights Purse, 120
chrysanthemums, 201

Churchill Downs, **1-5,** 9 n. 7, 36, 40, 47,
  60, 67, 84, 101, 125, 126, 135, 156,
  169, 172, 195, 210, 224, 246, 258,
  262, 266, 267, 274, 275-77
    groom statue, 9 n. 7
    twin spires built, 3
Church Hill Purse, 104
Chutney, 204
Cicada, 216
Cigar, 10, 30, 204, 258, 259
Cincinnati Limited, 85
Cinnamon, Melvin, 265
Citation, 10, 11, 15, 31, 31 n 22,
  34 n. 1, 35, 47 n. 12, 66, 89, 104, 115,
  116, 117 n. 3, 144, 147, 161,
  178 n. 10, 179, 183, **187-205,** 195 n. 6,
  196, 197, 197 n. 7, 215, 223, 240, 241,
  244, 245, 256 n. 5, 261, 262, 264, 274,
  280, 286, 287, 288, 290, 291, 295
    birth of, 188
    bloodlines, 116, 188
    burial place, 212
    career summary, 187, 197, 209
    D-bit, 195
    death of, 212
    naming, 188
    injuries, 199, 203
    personality, 187-88
    photographs, *196, 197*
    progeny, 212
    races
      in American Derby, 199, 200
      in American Handicap, 209
      in Argonaut Handicap, 209
      in Belmont Futurity, 191
      in Belmont Futurity Trial, 190-
        191
      in Belmont Gold Cup, 201
      in Belmont Purse, 204
      in Belmont Stakes, 10, 198-99,
        198 n. 8
      in Buckingham Purse, 199
      in Century Handicap, 209
      in Challenge Purse, 202
      in Chesapeake Stakes, 195
      in Chesapeake Trial, 194
      in Elementary Stakes, 190
      in Everglades Stakes, 192
      in Flamingo Stakes, 192
      in Forty-Niners Handicap, 208
      in Golden Gate Handicap, 205-
        06, 208
      in Golden Gate Mile Handicap,
        207, 208
      in Ground Hog Purse, 191
      in Havre de Grace (1st start),

189
   in Hollywood Gold Cup, 209
   in Hollywood Premier
     Handicap, 209
   in Jockey Club Gold Cup, 200-
     01
   in Kentucky Derby, 195, *196,
     197*
   in Kentucky Derby Trial, 195
   in La Sorpesa Handicap, 204
   in Perry Point Purse, 189
   at Pimlico (May 3, 1947), 189
   in Pimlico Futurity, 197
   in Pimlico Special, 201-02
   in Preakness Stakes, 197,
     197 n. 7
   in San Antonio Handicap, 205
   in San Juan Capistrano
     Handicap, 207
   in Santa Anita Handicap, 205-
     06
   in Sealeggy Purse, 190
   in Seminole Purse, 192
   in Stars and Stripes Handicap,
     199
   in Surprise Purse, 207
   in Sysonby Mile, 200
   in Tanforan Handicap, 202
   in Uncle Tom's Cabin Purse,
     209
   in Veterans Hospital Day Purse,
     209
   in Washington Park Futurity,
     190
  racing record
    as two-year-old, 189-91
    as three-year-old, 191-92, 293
    as four-year-old, 203
    as five-year-old, 203-08
    as six-year-old, 209
  retirement, 49 n. 12, 209-20, 274
  rivalry with Noor, 203, **204-09**
  siring record, 212
  temperament, 187-88
  winnings, 191, 197 n. 7, 199, 200-
    03, 207, **208, 210**
Civil War, *see also* wars, 9, 215
Claiborne Farm, 55, 56, 74, 80, 91, 235,
  235 n. 4
Clark Handicap, 135
Clark, Merriwether, 1
Clark, Meriwether Lewis, Jr., 1
  suicide, 3
Clark, William, 1
Clay, Nancy, 56
Cleveland, Grover, 57
Cleveland Indians, 131

Climax Handicap, 45
Clyde, Thomas, 9
Clyde Van Dusen, 23, 30, 95
Coaltown*, 116, 189, 190, 193, 195,
  196, 199, 203, 209, 210, 264
Coastal, 288
cocaine, 34, 289
Coconut Grove Purse, 123
Cold Shoulder, 86, 87
Colin*, 22, 22 n. 13, 256 n. 5
Collier's (magazine), 97, 98
Congress
  adjourns for race, 1797. 9
  issues MCJ Charter, 7
  declares war on Germany, 15
Considine, Bob, 4
Constancy, 21, 44
Conway, George, 22 n. 14, 25, 28, 96,
  100, 103, 104, 106, 107, 111, 112,
  268
  death of, 112
  early years, 100
Cordero, Angel*, 242, 248-49, 254, 255,
  256, 264, 265, 266, 273, 283, 285
Cormorant, 250
Corum, Bill, 4
Cosell, Howard, 247
Cougar II, 233
Counterpoint, 159
Count Fleet*, 7 n. 5, 9, 10, 11, 15, 24,
  41, 46, 49 n. 12, 50, 65, 90 n. 6, 104,
  115, 120, 129, **147-61**, *160,* 168, 168,
  184, 187, 193, 195, 199, 205, 206,
  225, 231, 241, 246, 256 n. 5, 280, 281,
  286, 295
  appearance, 151
  blinkers, 152
  bloodlines, 147, 148 n. 2
  career summary, 147, 152, 168
  death of, 160
  injuries, 156, 158, 159
  personality, 151-52
  photographs, *160, 203*
  progeny, 159-60, 184
  races
    in Army and Navy Purse, 153
    in Belmont Stakes, 129, 158-67
    in Champagne Stakes, 154
    in East View Stakes, 153
    in Jockey Club Experimental
     Free Handicap No. 1,
     155 n. 5
    in Kentucky Derby, 156-65
    in Mars Purse, 153
    in Morello Purse, 153-54
    in Pimlico Futurity, 154
    in Preakness Stakes, 7 n. 5, 157

in St. James Purse, 155
in Thunderclap Purse, 154
in Wakefield Stakes, 153
in Walden Stakes, 155
in Washington Park Futurity, 153
in Widener Stakes, 152
in Willow Springs Purse, 153
in Withers Stakes, 41, 155
in Wood Memorial Stakes, 155, 156, 225
    racing record, 147, 160
        as two-year-old, 152- 55
        as three-year-old, 155-59
    retirement, 159-60
    silks, bright yellow, 157
    siring record, 159-60
Count Turf, 159, 159 n. 10
Count Speed, 167, 167 n. 3
Court Scandal, 100
Coventry, 29
Cowdin Stakes, 167, 255
Crack Brigade, 66, 67
Craig, Arthur, 135
Craig, Andy, 140
Criminal Type, 290
Cruguet, Jean, 239, 242, 244, *248*, 250, 252, 254, 256, 257, 266
    birth of, 243
    career summary, 257
    early years, 243
    injuries, 243, 257
    jockey record, 257
    personality, 257 n. 6
    photographs, *248, 250*
    retirement, 257
    steeplechase (Saratoga), 257
Crusader, 30, 95, 96
Crystal Ford, 42
Cubbage, Brenda, *12*
Cudgel, 43, 44
Cunard White Star Line, 90
Cutshaw, Oliver, 252

D

Daily Racing Form (periodical), 13, 17, 75, 81, 85, 98, 188, 218, 227 n. 2
Damask, 27
Dangerfield, Elizabeth, 29
Danger Point, 106
Dapper Dan, 220
Darby Creek Road, 280
Dark Jungle, 169
David Harum, 24
Day, Pat*, 244

Declaration if Independence, 6
Delaware Park, 220
Delegate, 192
Delormier Park (Montreal), 217
Democratic National Committee, 85
Dempsey, Jack, 129
Depression, the Great, 81, 87, 89, 100, 106, 112, 123, 131, 148, 216
Derby *Italiano,* 267, 289
Derby Magic (book), 237
Derby Trial, 83
Dern, John, 165
Desert Light, 66
Desoronto, 158, 158 n. 7
Devil Diver,* 135, 194
Dike, 218
DiMaggio, Joe, 131, 145, 207, 262
Dinner Party Stakes, 7
Discovery,* 87
Discovery Handicap, 174
Dixiana, 169
Dixie Handicap, 135, 136, 177
Dodson, Doug, 166, 169, 171, 172, 190-91, 197-98
Dooley, James E., 140
Dominion Handicap, 46
Donelson, A.J., 6, 8
Donnacona, 24, 28
Donerail, 4 n. 1, 4
Doublrab, 136
Douglas (Wyo.) Junior Chamber of Commerce, 52
Desert Light, 70
Drager, Marvin, 93, 108 n. 17, 116 n. 2
Dr. Clark, 21
Dr. Patches, 254
Dr. Valeri, 276
Drone, 218
Dudley, Bruce, 84
Duke of Hamilton, 7, 7 n. 4
Dunboyne, 37
Duncannon, 6
Dunne, Dominick, 97
du Pont, William, 164, 169
Dustwhirl, 116, 116 n. 2
Dwyer Stakes, 16, 25, 28-29, 42, 43, 66, 70, 88, 97, 102, 103, 106, 131

E

Eads, Wendell, 123, 124-25, 130, 132, 134, 135, 139, 142
Eastern Shore Stakes, 99
Easter Stockings, 50
Easy Goer,* 290
Easy To Copy, 291

East View Stakes, 153
Effendi, 8
Egan, Bill, 163
embalming of racehorses, 31, 31 n. 21
Empire City Track (Yonkers), 61, 137, 153, 167
Endow, 289, 290
England, 2
English Grand National Steeplechase, 30
English reform laws, 7 n. 4
English Triple Crown, 10, 34, 92
Epsom Derby (G.B.), 2, 10, 13, 116, 267, 289
Epsom Oaks, 2
Epson Track (Houston), 176 n. 9
Equipoise*, 263
Equipoise Mile, 143
ESPN *Sportszone*, 291
Esposa, 107, 108
Esposito's Tavern, 9 n. 7
Eternal, 37, 38, 40
Evening, 96
Everglades Stakes, 192
Exceller*, 255, 285
Exclusive Native, 262
Exterminator*, 5, 33, 43, 46, 159 n. 11
Experimental Free Handicap, 155, 167

F

Fabius, 212, 212 n. 11
Fair Play*, 16, 16 n. 9
Fairy Hill, 99, 100
Fairy Manhurst, 158, 158 n. 7
Fairymant, 133, 134
Famous Horses of the American Turf (book), 76
Faraway, 198-99
Faraway Farm, 15, 29, 30, **32**, 55, 95, 102, 111, 189
Farley, James, 85
Farley, Walter, 241
Fator, Laverne*, 70
Faultless, 189, 192, 197 n. 7
Feliciano, Paul, 218, 236 n. 5
Feller, Bob, 131, 262
Fervent, 197 n. 7
Feustel, Louis*, 16, **22-29**, 45, 96
    birth of, 16
    death of, 29
Field, Bryan, 4, 16, 69, 71, 72, 73, 87, 107, 110, 134, 136, 142, 153
Finley, John H., 299
Firethorn, 86, 87
First Landing, 216
Fitzsimmons, Sunny Jim*, 59
    (*see* Fitzsimmons, James Edward)
Fitzsimmons, James Edward*, 55, 56,

62, 64, 68, 74, 78, 80, 82, 108, 117, 149, 166, 210,
    arthritis, spinal, 57
    birth of, 56
    career accomplishments, 57
    childhood, 57
    death of, 57
    early career, 57
    nickname "Sunny Jim", 57
    photographs, *58, 78, 210*
    retirement, 57,
    training history, 61
Five Crown (*see* V Crown)
Flag of Leyte Gulf, 236
Flambino, 80
Flaming Page, 92
Flamingo Stakes, 124, 192, 223, 245, 272, 273
Flaming Top, 92
Flares, 76
Flaring Top, 92
Flash Stakes, 61
Flawlessly, 291
Florida Derby, 124, 245, 272
flowers
    black-eyed susans, 9
    chrysanthemums, 201
    daisies dyed, 9
    roses, 5
    white carnations, 11, 15, 199, 231
Flute, 258
Flying Ebony, 64
Flying Fox, 107
Flying Scot, 102
Foolish Pleasure, 262
Foreground, 50
Fort Erie Track (Canada), 46
For the Moment, 244, 248, 258
Fort Pierce Purse, 115
Fort Robinson, 51
Forty-Niners Handicap, 208
Francis, the talking mule, 4 n. 2, 53
Frayne, Trent, 154 n. 4, 158 n. 7
Free America, 190, 200
French and Indian War, 6
French Derby, 267, 289
Frisius, 72, 73
Funny Cide, 7 n. 5, 157 n. 6, 295, 297

G

Gallant Bob, 253
Gallant Fox*, *v*, 6, 10, 13, 14, 18, 34 n. 1, 38, 46 n. 10, 49 n. 12, **55-77**, *59*, 80, 84, 85, 87, 93 n. 10, 101 n. 13, 104, 115, 133, 149, 172, 174, 193, 223, 225, 238, 246, 261, 263, 274, 283, 295, 297

appearance, 56, 59
birth of, 56
blinkers, 60
bloodlines, 79
burial place, 238
career summary, 74
death of, 76
doping allegations, 60 n. 1
eyes, 63
illness, 74
personality, 58, 59, 60, 61, 74
photograph, 59
progeny, 76, 76 n. 3, 79
races
    in Arlington Classic, 70
    in Belmont Futurity, 61
    in Belmont Futurity Trial
        Purse, 61
    in Belmont Stakes, 10, 69-70
    in Dwyer Stakes, 70
    in first start, 60
    in Flash Stakes, 61
    in Jockey Club Gold Cup, 72,
        73-74
    in Junior Champion Stakes, 62
    in Kentucky Derby, 64, 66, 67-
        69, 72
    in Lawrence Realization, 72, 73
    in Preakness Stakes, 67, 172
    in Saratoga Cup, 72
    in Saratoga Stakes, 77
    in Travers Stakes, 71-72, 76,
        283
    in Tremont Stakes, 60-61, 65
    in United States Hotel Stakes,
        61
    in Wood Memorial Stakes, 62,
        66, 225
racing records
    as two-year-old, 60-62
    as three-year-old, 66-72
retirement, 49 n. 12, 74-75
scratched, Kentucky Jockey Club
    Stakes, 62
siring record, 76-77, 76 n. 3
temperament, 58, 59, 60, 61
winnings, 70, 73, 74, 76
Gallant Fox Handicap, 81, 174, 181,
    197 n. 7, 269
Gallant Fox: A Memoir (book), 14
Gallant Knight, 70
Gallorette*, 166, 175, 178
gambling laws, 4, 11
Garcia, Pastel, 182, 183
Garden State Park, 139, 222
Garden State Stakes, 222

Gentry, Howard, 217
George Smith, 17
Gilbert, Johnny, 129, 141, 206
Gilcoyne, Tom, 119, 168, 187, 289
Gilman, Manuel, 226
Glass, Margaret, 117, 187, 264-65, 271,
    283
Glengarry Purse, 181
Glen Riddle Farm, 16, 22, 25, 96, 97,
    103, 111, 116
Glisson, Gordon, 207
Gnome, 47
Gold Brook, 66, 67, 71
Gold Cup (see Belmont Gold Cup,
    trophies)
Golden Broom, 19, 22
Golden Gate Fields, 205, 207
Golden Gate Handicap, 205-06, 208
Golden Gate Mile Handicap, 207
Gold Shower, 153, 157
Gonzalez, Bernie, 263
Good Gamble, 88
Goode, John M., 17
Gordon, Mike, 258, 259
Gorman, Dave, 181
Gotham Stakes, 224
Governor Bowie Handicap, 142
Gowanus Purse, 167
Graham, Elizabeth Arden, 29
Graham, Frank, 4
Grand Union Hotel Stakes, 21, 71, 121
Granville*, 81, 76 n. 3
Gravesend Park, 3, 8, 96
Grayson, Dr. Cary, 47 n. 11
Grayson, C. Ken, 39, 42, 48, 59, 65, 78,
    84, 86, 96, 97, 110, 116, 119, 121,
    128, 129, 137, 145, 160, 196, 197,
    211, 213, 229, 248, 248
Great American Stakes, 99
Great Depression, 81, 87, 91, 100, 107,
    123, 148, 216
Great Ones, The (book), 205 n. 10
Great Thoroughbreds List, 1972, 256
Greenwood Raceway (Toronto), 219
Greentree Farm, 125, 135, 135, 136,
    138, 175 n. 7, 181, 194
Grey Ghost, 262
Grey Lag*, 166
Grey Lag Handicap, 177
Ground Hog Purse, 191
Guerin, Eric*, 168, 173, 198
Gulfstream Park, 124, 193 n. 4, 207, 245,
    272

H

Haas, Leon, 136, 140
Haggin, James Ben Ali, 3
Halifax, Lord, 30
Hall of Fame (*see* National Museum of Racing), 123 n. 7
Hamburg Place, 34, 35, 53, 111
Hamilton, Duke of, 7, 7 n. 4
Hampden, 169, *170*, *172*, 173, 181
Hampton, Phillip, 261-62
Hancock, Richard Johnson, 55
Hancock, Arthur B., 55, 80, 218
"*A Handy Guy Like Sande*" *(poem)*, 62-63, 68-69
Hanford, Ira, 166
Harbor View Farm, 262, 263, 266, 273, 277, 291, 293 (silks)
Harbut, Will, 15, 30, *32*, 102
Hartack, Bill*, 63, 207, 266
Hash, 130
Haseltine, Herbert, 31
Hastings, 16
Hatton, Charles, 13
Havre de Grace, 31, 45, 50, 99, 100, 189, 199, 194
Hawthorne Gold Cup, 74
Hayward, Billy, 7
Head Play, 97
Heather Purse, 109
Hefty, 194
Henry of Navarre Stakes, 130, 198
Hertz, John, 123 n. 7, 147, 150
Hertz, Mrs. John, 148 n. 2, *151*
Hertz Rent-A-Car Company, 147
Hervey, John, 93, 98, 104, 140
Hialeah, 105, 111, 124, 180, 191, 193, 203, 245, 255, 263, 272, 284
Hibiscus Stakes, 220
Hidalgo, 92
High Foot, 67
High Gun, 166
Hi-Jack, 61
Hildreth, Sam, 18
Hillenbrand, Laura, 105 n.16, 113, 307
Hill Gail, 116, 117, 206
Hill 'n' Dale Farm, 258
*Hill Prince**, 206, 216, 262
Hill, James, Dr. & Mrs., 240, 242, 244
    suspension, 252
    conflict of interest, 252
Hip Hip Hooray Purse, 43
Hirsch, Max*, 21, 21 n. 12, 24, 164, 166, 172, 173, 174, 178, 179, 268
    early days, 166
    jockey career, 166
    trainer career, 166-
History of Thoroughbred Racing, The

(book), 20
Hitler, Adolph, 167
Hoist the Flag, 243
Hollingsworth, Kent, 93
Hollywood Derby, 220, 274, 275, 281
Hollywood Gold Cup, 183, 209, 287-88
Hollywood Juvenile Championship, 265
Hollywood Park, 150, 183, 209, 210, 251, 265, 274, 287
*Holy Bull**, 262
Holy Grail (of racing), 210 (*see* Triple Crown)
Hoodwink, 27
Hoop Jr., 169, 194
Hopeful Stakes, 19, 21, 36, 56, 121-22, 221, 268
Hophead, Great, 39
Howard, Charles S., 108, 108 n. 17, 109, 204
Hudson Stakes, 20
"Hugo" (*see Seattle Slew*, nicknames), 240, 241
Hugo K. Asher, 149
Huntley, Gordon, 219
Husing, Ted, 4
Hyde Park Stakes, 120
Hydroplane II, 34 n. 1, 188
Hylton, Dr. Joseph Roy, 51
Hypnos, 192

I

"Iceman, The", 109, 123
    (*see* Woolf, George*)
Igual, 163
Impecunious, 222
Imperatrice, 216
imported horse annotation convention, 34 n. 1
Independence Day, 137, 153
Indigo Star, 278
Information Please Sports Almanac, 14
influenza epidemic, 37 n. 5
International Gold Cup, 179
I Ride to Win! (book), 130, 144
Irish Derby, 267, 289
Iron Constitution, 250
Isaacson, J.J., 93
Isinglass, 34
isinglass, 138
Islam Prince, 168
Itabo, 130-31
Italian Derby (Italy), 267, 289
    (*see* Derby *Italiano*)

J

Jackson, Andrew, 6
Jack Stuart, 17
Jamaica Jockey Club, 49
Jamaica Race Track, 18, 25, 66, 82, 154, 155, 167, 168, 177, 204
James, Basil, 124, 132, 133
Jay Ray, 218
Jeffords, Mrs. Walter, 21, 27, 173
Jerkens, Allen*, 232, 234
Jerome Park, 2, 10
Jersey Handicap, 174
Jet Pilot, 239 n. 1
Jewel Dorsett, 102
Jim Dandy, 71, 72, 133, 232, 283
Jim Dandy Stakes, 283, 286
Jockeys (*see also* jockey name)
    Adams, John*, 156
    Ambrose, Eddie, 22, 25, 27
    Arcaro, Eddie*, *vii*, (*see also* at name), 63, 87, 88, 89, 117, *121*, 125-26, 131, 131 n. 9, 134, *142*, 139, 140, 143, 144, 169, 172, 173, 175 n. 7, 178, 182-83, 193, 193 n.5, 195, *196, 197*, 198, 200, 204, 205, **206**, 207, 210, 212, *213*, 220, 231, 258, 266, 286, 287, *293*
    Atkinson, Ted*, 156-57, 157, 168, 173, 198-99
    Baird, R.L., 200
    Baker, Frank, 71
    Beasley, Pat, 90, 91
    Boland, Bill, 166, 183
    Brann, W.L., 136
    Brooks, Steve*, 190, 203-04, 205, 206, 207, 209, 210
    Brumfield, Don*, 244
    Burke, J.H., 60
    Cauthen, Steve*, *vii*, 63, 254, 255, 261, 262, 263, **266-68**, 273, *277, 279*, 280 n. 4, *282*, 284, 285-86, *293*, 295
    Cordero, Angel*, 242, 248-249, 254, 255, 261, 264, 265, 266, 273, 283, 285, *287*, 289-90, *293*
    Craig, Arthur, 135
    Craig, Andy, 135, 140
    Cruguet, Jean, 239, 242, 243, 244-63, *248*, 254, 257, 266
    Day, Pat*, 244
    Dodson, Doug, 166, 176, 177, 172, 190-91, 197-98, 204, 198
    Eads, Wendall, 123, 124-25, 130,

132, 134, 135, 139, 140, 142
Fator, Laverne*, 70
Feliciano, Paul, 218, 236 n. 5
Gilbert, Johnny, 129, 141, 206
Glisson, Gordon, 207
Gonzalez, Bernie, 263
Gorman, Dave, 181
Guerin, Eric*, 168, 198
Haas, Leon, 136, 140
Hanford, Ira, 166
Hartack, Bill*, 63, 207, 220, 266
Hayward, Billy, 7
James, Basil, 124, 132, 133
Keogh, Frank G., 47, 47 n. 11
Knapp, Willie*, 19, 20
Kummer, Clarence*, 15, 16, 23-25, 26, 29, 44, 45 n. 9, 47, 193
    (*see* at name)
Kurtsinger, Charles*, *vii*, 81, *96*, 96-100, 98 n. 12, 99, 100, 101-02, 105, 111, 109, 149, 193, 207
    death of, 118
    racing record, 118
    retirement, 118
Lewis, Oliver, 2
Loftus, John*, *vii*, 18, 21, 25-27, 29, 37, *39*, 43, 44, 45, 46 n. 10, 48, 50, 206, 266 (*see* at name)
Longden, John*, *vii*, 63, 89, 97, 106, 120, 123 n. 7, 133, 136, *137*, 138, 140, 143, 147, 147 n. 1, 148 n. 3, 149-50, *149*, 150, *151*, 156, 157, 157, *160*, 160-61, 167 n. 3, 168, 173, 183, 193, *202*, 204, 205, 207, 208, 220, 266, 286, *287*, 295 (*see* at name)
Maiben, John, 62
Maple, Eddie, *vii*, 233, 234, 242, 244, 265, 266, 269
McAuliffe, Dan, 61
McCreary, Conn*, 1, 156, 157, 173, 179
Mehrtens, Warren, *vii*, 89, 138, 163, 166-67, *170, 171, 172*, 172-74, 173 n. 6, 176-77, 180, 184, 190, 196, 197-99, 220, 295
Murphy, Isaac*, 2, 73, 207
Peters, Maurice, 107
Pierson, Newbold L., 200
Pincay, Laffit, Jr.*, 227, 265, 266, 273, 274, 283, 283 n. 5, 284, 287
Pollard, Red, 109
Renick, Sam, 69
Robertson, Alfred*, 132, 133, 143
Sande, Earl*, *vii*, 26-27, 29, 36, 43, 46, 46 n. 10, 47, 50, 51, 62-64,

65, 66-70, 75-76, 97, 148, 193, 207, 276 (*see* at name)

Saunders, Willie, *vii,* 79, 80, 82, *84,* 85, *86,* 87-89, 197-98, 204 (*see* at name)

Shilling, Carroll "Cal"*, 37, 37 n. 6, 50

Schuette, Herman, 70

Schuttinger, Andy, 27, 46

Shellhammer, Alfred, 132

Shoemaker, Bill "Willie"*, 63, 125-26, 149, 161, 207, 220, 244, 255, 266, 283 n. 5, *287,* 288

Snider, Al, 189, 191, 192, 194, 210

Stevens, Gary*, 289-90

Stout, Jimmy*, 167

Turcotte, Ron*, *v, vii,* 89, 148, 193, 215, 218, 221-23, 225, 228, *229,* 231 n. 3, 234, 235, **236,** 237, 244, 266, 295

Turcotte, Rudy, 223

Vedder, R.L., 124, 134

Velasquez, Jorge*, 242, 244, 250, 261, 269, 272, 274, 276, 278, *279,* 280, 281, *282,* 284, 289-90

Venezia, Mike, 224

Westrope, John*, 103, 140-41, 190

Woolf, George*, 97, 101, 109, 123, 136, 138, 138, 140-41, 143, 153, 155, 156-57, 158

Workman, Raymond "Sonny"*, 74, 75, 77

Wright, Wayne, 88, 88 n. 4, 106, 107, 112, 158

Jockey Club Gold Cup, 27, 27 n. 17, 66, 73-74, 81, 97, 108, 133, 140, 200, 234, 285, 288

Jockey Club Experimental Free Handicap, 155 n. 5, 167 n. 2

"Jockey Toolong", 242

John P. Grier, 25-26, 102, 106

Johnstown*, 57, 128, 168, 169 n. 4

Jonabell Farm, 261, 289, 291

Jones, Ben*, 117, 117 n. 3,118, *121,* 125, 126, *129,* 130, 131, 133, 138, 140, 142, 166, 188, 189, 194, *196, 210,* 264
    birth of, 117
    cuts *Whirlaway's* blinker, 127-28
    death of, 122
    early years, 117
    nickname, 117
    photographs, *121, 129, 196, 210*
    retirement, 274
    training record, 117-18

Jones, Bobby, 129

Jones, H.A. "Jimmy"*, 47 n. 11, 52,

117 n. 3, 118, 179, 188, 191, 191, 194, *196, 197,* 198, 200, 201, 202, 204, 205, 208, 209, 209, 210, *210,* 264, 295
    career summary, 210
    death of, 210
    Hall of Fame, 209
    Monmouth Track director, 264
    photographs, *196, 197, 210*
    retirement, 210

J.O. Tobin, 251

Judge Advocate, 280

Jumping Hill, 256

Junior Champion Stakes, 61, 62, 81

K

Keene Memorial Stakes, 17

Keeneland, Kentucky, 124

Keeneland Race Track, 122, 224, 262, 272

Kelly, Joseph B., 201

Kelso*, 10, 144, 147, 159, 159 n. 11, 161, 178 n. 10, 193, 256 n. 5, 279, 287

Kempton Park (U.K.), 90

Kenilworth Park, 28, 47

Kennedy, Mike, 241, 242, 247

Kennedy Road, 233, 234

Kentucky
    Commonwealth of, 1
    Louisville, 1

Kentucky Derby, *v, vii,* 1, 2, 3, 12, 22-23, 23 n. 15, 28, 30, 38, *39,* 49, 57, 60, 64, 67, 81, 83, 85, 97, 100-101, 117, 125, 128 n. 8, 131, 137, 147, 149, 155, 168, *170, 171,* 176, 220, 224, 226-27, 243, 244, *248, 249,* 262, 267, 273, 275-77, 281, 283, 288, 289, 297

Kentucky Derby Media Guide (periodical), 14

Kentucky Derby Trial, 168

Kentucky Horse Park, 34, 113, 132

Kentucky Jockey Club Stakes, 62

Kentucky Oaks, 50, 258

Keogh, Frank G., 47, 47 n. 11

Kempton Park (G.B.), 94

Key to the Mint, 233

King of Swat, 267

King Ranch, 163, 165, 166-67, 168, 170, 175 n. 8, 176, 178, 180, 206
    silks, tan and white, 168, 174

King's Plate, 217

Kiss Me Kate, 159, 184

Kleberg, Robert J., 163, 166, 173, 179

Knapp, Willie*, 19, 20

Knight of Ellerslie, 55

Knockdown, 168, 169

Koufax, Sandy, 262

Ksar, 73

Kummer, Clarence*, 15, 16, 19, 23-25, 26, 29, 44, 45, 45 n. 9, 47
    injury, 26
    jockey record, 29
    death of, 29
Kurtsinger, Charles*, *vii*, 81, *96*, **96-100**, 98 n. 12, 99, 100, 101-02, 105, 109, 111, 112, 113, 118, 149, 193, 207
    birth of, 97
    career history, 101, 112
    death of, 113
    injury, 112-13
    photograph, *100*
    retirement, 112
Kwiatkowski, Henryk de, 290 n. 9

L

Lady's Secret, 237
Lady Sterling, 34, 53
Landaluce, 257
La Sorpesa Handicap, 204
Latonia Race Park, 16, 125, 266
Latonia Championship, 74
Latonia Park, 19, 125, 266 (*see* Latonia Race Park)
Laurel Futurity, 222, 269-70
Laurel/Pimlico Media Guide, 76
Laurel Track, 43, 220, 222
Laurin, Lucien*, *v*, 217, 220, 224, 225, 228, 232, 235, 263, 268, 295
    birth of, 217
    death of, 236
    early years, 217
    Hall of Fame, 246
    jockey career, 217-28
        banned as jockey, 217
        ban lifted, 218
        buzzer incident, 217
    retirement, 236
    Waldrop, Alex, tribute, 236
Lawrence Realization, 10, 73, 81, 97, 103, 133-34, 158
Lawrin, 117, 126
laws
    betting, 5, 14
    English Reform (animal rights), 8
Lets Dance, 177
Lewis and Clark Expedition, 1
Lewis, Oliver, 2
Lexington track, 2
Library of Congress, 6
Life's Hope, 255
Limbus, 70
Lincoln Fields, 119
Linda's Chief, 222

Loftus, Frank, 22
Loftus, John*, *vii*, 16, 17, 18, 21, 22, 23, 26, 29, 37, *39*, 43, 44, 45, 47, 48, 50, 193, 206, 266
    birth of, 16
    career summary, 17, 50
    death of, 50
    early years, 16-17
    election to Hall of Fame, 50
    photograph, *39*
    suspensions, 23, 47, 50
    technical advisor, film, 50
London, England, 96
Longden, John*, *vii*, 63, 89, 97, 106, 120, 123 n. 7, 127, 133, 136, *137*, 138, 143, 147 n. 1, 148 n. 3, *149*, 150, *151*, 152-153, 156, 157, 158, *160*, 161, 167 n. 3, 168, 183, 193, 202, 204, 205, 207, 220, 266, 286, *287*, 295
    birth of, 148
    in Canada, 149
    career summary, 166
    death of, 161
    early career, 149
    early years, 148-49
    jockey record, 161
    photographs, *137*, *149*, *152*, *160*, *287*
    trainer, 161
Lone Star Flag, 173
Lookover Stallion Station, 92
Lord Boswell, 166, 168, 169, 171, 172, *172*, 177, 173, 181
Lord Derby, 188
Lord Halifax, 30
Lord Kitchener, 133
Lorillard, George P., 8
Louis, Joe, 131, 143
Louisiana Handicap, 142
Louisville Jockey Club and Driving Park Association, 2
Louisville Courier-Journal (newspaper), 37, 38, 67, 84, 261
Louis Quatorze, 227 n. 2
Lucky Debonair, 159, 220
Lucullite, 44

M

Mackenson, Agatha, 89
Madden, John E., 33, 34, 35, 40, 53
Madden, Preston, 52
Mad Hatter, 44, 46
Madison Square Garden Horse Show, 252 n. 3

Mad Play, 64
Mahout, 173
Mahubah, 16 n. 9
Maiben, John, 62
Maine Chance Farm, 50, 168
*Majestic Prince**, 161, 210
Major Treat, 22, 25
Malibu Stakes, 286
Man and a Horse, A (article, Collier's), 97, 98
Mane Minister, 284 n. 6
Manhattan Handicap, 140
*Man o'War**, 11, **15-32,** 31 n 22, *32*, 45, 46 n. 10, 47, 48, *48*, 49 n. 12, 50, 68, 74, 79, 85, 98, 98 n. 11, 101 n. 13, 103, 106, 108, 124, 132, 144, 147, 187, 193, 198, 215, 221, 223, 239 n. 1 244, 256 n. 4, 256 n. 5, 263
   birth of, 15
   bloodlines, 16
   colic, 25, 30-31
   career winnings, 112
   death of, 30-31
   drinks from trophy cup, 28
   eating habits, 22
   embalmed, 31, 31 n. 21
   final resting place, 31, 132
   hoof chewing, 22
   injuries, 28
   illnesses, 33-34
   personality, 16, 22
   photographs, *35, 48*
   progeny, 22 n. 14, 30, 79, 95, 102, 108, 148 n. 2, 239 n. 1
   races
      in American Derby, 22
      in Belmont Futurity, 21
      in Belmont Stakes, 10, 24, 28
      in Dwyer Stakes, 25-26
      in debut race, 17
      in Grand Union Hotel Stakes, 21
      in Hopeful Stakes, 21
      in Hudson Stakes, 18
      in Jockey Club Gold Cup, 27, 28
      in Keene Memorial Stakes, 17
      at Kenilworth Park, 28
      re:Kentucky Derby, 22-23
      in Lawrence Realization, 27
      in match race with Sir Barton, 28, 29 n. 20
      in Miller Stakes, 26, 47
      in Potomac Handicap, 28
      in Preakness Stakes, 25
      in Sanford Stakes, 19-20, 23
      in Stuyvesant Handicap, 25
      in Travers Stakes, 27, 143
      in Tremont Stakes, 18
      in United States Hotel Stakes, 18
      in Withers Stakes, 24, 28
      in Youthful Stakes, 18
   racing record
      as two-year-old, 17-21
      as three-year-old, 21-28
   retirement, 29-30, 49 n. 12
   sabotage, 29
   Sir Barton match race, 28, 29 n. 20, 47
   siring record, 30
   statue, 30, 31
   threats, 22
   winnings, 21-22, 28, 45, 107
Man o'War Stakes, 233
Mantle, Mickey, 166
Maple, Eddie, *vii*, 233,234, 242, 244, 265, 266, 269
Marathon Handicap, 45
Marlboro Cup, 232, 233, 255, 284
Marguerite, 56
Marguerite Stakes, 81
Market Wise, 134, 136
Markey, Gene (Admiral), 264, 272, 275
Markey, Lucille (*see also* Wright, Lucille), 264, 265 n. 1, 271, 272, 275
Mars Purse, 153
Maryland Handicap, 46 n. 10
Maryland Horseman's Association, 50
Maryland Jockey Club, 6, 8, 182, 239
   fire destroys grandstand, 8
   fire destroys records, 8
   issued charter, 6
   archive location, 6
   moves to Baltimore, 6
   Pimlico, 8
"*Maryland, My Maryland*", 280
Mary Phema, 148
Masda, 16 n. 9
Masked General, 104
"Master, The" (see Arcaro, Eddie*), 193
Massachusetts Handicap, 106, 138
Matthews, Sandra, 58
Maya, 70
Mayo Clinic, 51
Mays, Willie, 166, 262
McCaffrey, T.H., 126
McAuliffe, Dan, 61
McCarthy, Clem, 4, 195
McClelland, J.W., 37
McCreary, Conn*, 1, 3, 156-57, 173, 179
McKay, Jim, 115, 146
McMeekin, Sam H., 37, 38 n. 7, 44

Meadowlands, 254
Meadow Skipper, 31 n. 21
Meadow Stable, *v*, 215, 225, 231, 232
Medi Flash, 291
Mehrtens, Warren, *vii*, 89, 138, 163,
  166-72, 168, *171*, *171*, *172*, 173 n. 6,
  172-74, 176-77, 180, 184, 190, 196,
  197-99, 220, 295
    ashes from cremation, 185
    birth of, 166
    death of, 184
    dental work, 176
    early years, 166
    photographs, *170*, *171*, *172*
    racing steward, 184, 220
Melodist, 149
Menow, 106
Menton, Paul, 67
Merchants and Citizens' Handicap, 47,
  77
Mesa County fairgrounds, 40
Metropolitan Handicap, 11, 14, 18, 253,
  264, 284
Miami Springs Purse, 124
Miche, 204, 205
Middleground, 163, 166, 176, 182,
  182 n. 13, 183, 262
"Mighty Atom, The", 99
Miller Stakes, 26, 47
Milner, Mordaunt, 118
Milkmaid, 40, 43, 44, 45
Minisi Tribe, 7
Mioland, 135
Mister Ed, the talking horse, 53
"Mr. Longtail", 119, 141
MJC, 8 (*see* Maryland Jockey Club)
Moncrief, Dr. Monte, 182, 182 n. 12,
  183
Monmouth Park, 2, 210, 264, 276
Montague, 8
Moreland, George, 16, 17
Morello Purse, 153-54
Morgan, Bert, 171
Mori, Gene, 202
Morris Park, 8, 11, 11 n. 8
Morris Ranch, 166
Most Glorious Crown, The (book), 93, 108,
  116 n. 2
Mount Brilliant Farm, 29
"Mr. Fitz", 61
"Mr. Longtail", 115
Mr. Prospector, 291
Mucho Gusto, 110
Murphy, Isaac*, 69 n. 2, 207
Museum of Racing, 179, 193
    (see at National Museum…)

Musial, Stan, 262
Muybridge, Edward, 29 n. 20
My Charmer, 239, 239 n. 1
My Gallant, 231-32
"My Old Kentucky Home", 247, 276,
  280
Myrtle Charm, 239
Myrtlewood Purse, 122

N

Nack, William, 207, 221, 227, 229, 237
Napoleon (quoted), 194
Narragansett Futurity, 99
Narragansett Park, 109, 110, 133, 139,
  217
Narragansett Special (Purse), 133, 139
*Nashua**, 10, 57, 144, 193, 206, 210,
  256 n. 5, 257, 262
Nashville track, 2
Nassau County Handicap, 284
Natchez, 166, 173, 200
National Museum of Racing and Hall of
  Fame, *vii*, 37 n. 6, 55, 76 n. 3, 108,
  123 n. 7, 127, 143, 157, 161, 173 n. 6,
  179, 177, 194, 204, 206, 210, 212,
  235 n. 4, 237, 258, 258 n. 7, 272, 289
National Stallion Stakes, 103
*Native Dancer**, 210, 256 n. 5, 262
Natural Bridge, 41
necropsy, 224
Nedayr Purse, 120
*Needles**, 159, 159 n. 10, 262
Nellie Flag, 82, 82 n. 2, 84, 85, 126
Newman, Neil, 76
Newmarket, England, 91
New Moon, 157
New Orleans, 2
New Orleans Fair Grounds, 142, 266
Newport, Rhode Island, 61
Newsweek (magazine), 228
New York, 4
New York Giants, 166
New York Handicap, 140
New York Mets, 125
New York Racing Association, 225, 235
New York State Off-Track Betting, 206
New York State Racing Commission, 252
New York Times (newspaper), 14, 17, 18,
  22, 24, 25, 26, 31, 41, 50, 51, 69, 72,
  73, 85, 87, 99, 100, 101, 102, 104,
  107, 136, 139, 141, 153, 158, 158 n. 7,
  158 n. 8, 176, 177, 191, 201, 206, 243,
  245, 265, 273, 274, 283
New York Yankees, 166, 189 n 1
Nijinsky II, 92, 92 n. 8

Noon Time Spender, 278, 280
Noor*, 34 n. 1, 161, 166, 183, 183 n. 14, 193, 203, **204-09**, 205, 205, 207, 208, 209, 256 n. 4, 262
Northern Dancer*, 210
Northway, Dr. J. K., 164, 165, 183
Nursery Farm, 15
Nursery Stud, 15
NYRA, 226, 235 (*see* New York Racing Association)

O

Oaklawn Handicap, 284
Oaklawn Park, 284
Oak Park Purse, 120
Obash, 141
Occupation, 153-54, 155
"Old Bones" (see Exterminator*)*, 33, 46
Old Hilltop, 7, 108
Old Rosebud, 4, 5, 128, 168, 169 n. 4,
Omaha*, *v*, 10, 18, 49 n. 12, 57, 65, 76, **79-94**, *84*, *86*, 97, 105, 149, 198
204, 212, 225, 246, 291, 295, 297
    appearance, 79
    bloodlines, 79, 80
    birth of, 80
    burial location, 96, 118
    career summary, 98
    death of, 92, 113 n. 18
    in English racing, 90-91
    final resting place, 118
    injuries, 88, 91
    personality, 80, 80 n. 1, 92, 98
    photographs, *84*, *86*
    progeny, 96
    races
        in Arlington Classic, 88
        in Ascot Gold Cup (G.B.), 90-91
        in Belmont Futurity, 81
        in Belmont Stakes, 10, 86-87
        in Brooklyn Handicap, 87, 88
        in Champagne Stakes, 81
        in debut/maiden race, 80
        in Dwyer Stakes, 88
        in Hopeful Stakes, 81
        in Junior Champion Stakes, 81
        in Kentucky Derby, 84-85
        in Preakness Stakes, 85
        in Preakness Trial, 85
        in Princess of Wales Stakes (G.B.), 91
        in Queen's Plate Race (G.B.), 90
        in Sanford Stakes, 85
        in Saratoga Special, 85
        in South Shore Purse, 82, 88

        in United States Hotel Stakes, 85
        in Victor Wild Stakes (G.B.), 90
        in Withers Stakes, 86, 87, 88
        in Wood Memorial Stakes, 87, 88, 225
    racing record
        as two-year-old, 80-81
        as three-year-old, 82-88
        in England, 90-91, 93
    retirement, 49 n. 12, 91
    siring record, 91-92, 92 n. 9
    size, unusual, 85
    temperament, 80, 80 n. 1, 81
    winnings, 79, 87, 88
Omaha Gold Cup, 98
Omaha, Nebraska, 97
Omaha Stock Show, 97
One Count, 159, 206
One From Heaven, 291
Onion, 232-33
On Trust, 208
osselet, 203
Our Boots, 123

P

Paige, Satchel, 45
Palmer, Joe H., 165, 176, 178 n. 10, 179, 179, 189, 209
Papa Redbird, 200
Parker, Dan, 4
Pari-mutuel betting, 5
Paris, Kentucky, 59, 80, 91
"Paris-Mutuel", 2
Paterson Handicap, 254, 255
Paul Jones, 23 n. 15, 28, 31 n. 15
Pavot, 169, 194
Payson, Mrs. Joan, 125
Pearl Harbor, 188
Pelletier, Tony, 142
Penn Station, 109
Pensive, 159, 159 n. 10, 265
Perfect Barham, 168
Perry Point Purse, 189
Peters, Maurice, 107
Peterson, Douglas, 253
Peteski, 291
Pettingill, C.J., 19, 19 n. 11, 22
Phar Lap, 149, 161
Philadelphia Handicap, 45
Phipps, Mrs. Henry Carnegie, 82
Phipps, Ogden, 216
Phipps, Mrs. Ogden, 149
Phoenix Handicap, 135
Pictor, 136
Pierson, Newbold L., 200

Pimlico, 3, 67, 81, 99, 102, 108-09, 122, 210, 210, 220, 227, 278
    geometry, unusual, 102
    named, 7 n. 3
    weathervane, 9, 9 n. 7
Pimlico Dream, A (poem), 24 n. 16
Pimlico Futurity, 99, 122, 155
Pimlico Special, 104, 108, 141, 175 n. 7, 182, 201
Pincay, Laffit, Jr.*, 227, 265, 266, 273, 283, 283 n. 5, 284, 287, 300
Plain Ben Jones, 117 (*see* Jones, Ben*)
Plat Eye, 84
Plucky Liege, 56
Point Given, 10, 295
Pollard, Red, 109
Polston, John, 247, 249
Polynesian, 263
Pompoon, 99, 100-102, 103, 172
Ponder, 159, 159 n. 10, 204, 205, 206, 265
Porter, Grove, 92, 93
Porter, Morton, 92, 93, 113
Porter, The, 43, 44, 46
post parade, 11
Potomac Handicap, 28, 47
Preakness, 7, 7 n. 4, 288
Preakness Stakes, *v*, vii, **6-10**, 16, 24, 39, 47, 55, 60, 67, 81, 97, 101-02, 102 n. 14, 104, 129, 155, 157, 157-58, 170, *172*, 197 n. 7, 227, 227 n. 2, 278, *279*, 280, 283, 288, 297
    Congress adjourns to watch, 7
    at Gravesend Park, 8, 9
    at Morris Park, 9
    lost years, 8-9
    same day running as Belmont Stakes, 11 n. 8
Preakness Trial, 83
Prevaricator, 92
Price, Charles, 3
Princequillo, 216, 239 n. 1
Princess of Wakes Stakes, 91
Prove Out, 234
Psychic Bid, 84, 85
punji stakes, 165 n. 1
Purchase, 36, 42

Q

Quashed, 90, 91
Quebec, 218
Quebec, Canada, 217
Queens County Handicap, 106
Queens County Jockey Club, 87
Queen's Plate, 90

Questionnaire, 69, 72, 73
Quickly, 147, 148 n. 2
Quill, 217-18

R

rabbit, 37
race, first filming of, 32 n. 20
races
    A.J. Joyner Handicap, 124, 125
    American Derby, 19, 87, 199
    American Handicap, 209
    Arcadia Purse, 124
    Arc de Triomphe (France), 243
    Arlington Classic, 66, 70, 75, 88, 132, 174, 199
    Arlington Futurity, 190
    Arlington Handicap, 139
    Arlington Invitational, 231
    Arlington Special Event Purse, 131
    Army and Navy Purse, 153
    Annapolis Subscription Plate, 7
    Ascot Gold Cup (G.B.), 2, 81, 90
    Babylon Handicap, 167
    Bay Shore Stakes, 224
    Belair Handicap, 45
    Belmont Futurity, 24, 25, 36, 56, 99, 121, 154, 221-22, 244, 269
    Belmont Futurity Trial Purse, 61, 190-91, 244
    Belmont Gold Cup, 201
    Belmont Purse, 204
    Belmont Stakes, 7, **10-12**, 16, 18, 27, 30, 49, 56, 57, 62, 69-70, 81, 97, 102-03, 130-31, 139, 155, 172-73, 174, 198, 229-31, 250-51, 262, 280-81, *282*, 288, 289, 290
    Blue Grass Stakes, 124, 194, 220, 224, 272, 275
    Buckingham Purse, 199
    Breckenridge Stakes, 7 n. 6
    Breeders Cup, 10
    Breeders Futurity, 122
    Brightwaters Purse, 99
    Brooklyn Handicap, 14, 18, 20, 87, 136, 178, 181, 284
    Butler Handicap, 137, 166, 178, 281
    Californian Stakes, 287
    Calvert Purse, 100
    Canadian International Championship, 234
    Carter Handicap, 284
    Century Handicap, 209
    Challenge Purse, 202
    Champagne Stakes, 81, 139, 222, 244, 269

Charles H. Strub Stakes, 287
Chesapeake Stakes, 100, 195
Chesapeake Trial, 194
Chicago Heights Purse, 120
Church Hill Purse, 104
Clark Handicap, 135
Climax Handicap, 45
Coconut Grove Purse, 123
Cowdin Stakes, 167, 244
Derby *Italiano*, 267, 289
Dinner Party Stakes, 2, 7
Discovery Handicap, 174
Dixie Handicap, 9, 135, 177
Dominion Handicap, 51
Dwyer Stakes, 16, 19, 25, 42, 43,
   66, 70, 81, 97, 102, 131, 174
Eastern Shore Stakes, 99
East View Stakes, 153
Edgemere Handicap, 181
Elementary Stakes, 190
Empire Gold Cup, 179
Epsom Derby (G.B.), 2, 11, 13, 289
   120, 267, 289
Epsom Oaks (G.B.), 2
Equipoise Mile, 143
Everglades Stakes, 192
Experimental Free Handicap
   No.1, 167
Flamingo Stakes, 124, 192, 223,
   245, 246, 272, 273, 275
Flash Stakes, 61, 167
Florida Derby, 124, 245, 272, 275
Fort Pierce Purse, 115
Forty-Niners Handicap, 208
French Derby (France), 267, 289
Gallant Fox Handicap, 81, 174, 181,
   197 n. 7
Garden State Stakes, 222
Glengarry Purse, 181
Golden Gate Handicap, 205-06, 208
Golden Gate Mile Handicap, 207
Gotham Stakes, 224
Governor Bowie Handicap, 142
Gowanus Purse, 167
Grand Union Hotel Stakes, 23, 71,
   121
Great American Stakes, 99, 265, 269
Ground Hog Purse, 191
Havre de Grace Handicap, 43
Hawthorne Gold Cup, 74
Heather Purse, 109
Henry of Navarre Stakes, 130, 198
Hibiscus Stakes, 220
Hip Hip Hooray Purse, 47
Hollywood Derby, 220, 274, 275
Hollywood Gold Cup, 183, 209, 287-88
Hollywood Juvenile Championship,
   265, 269
Hollywood Premier Handicap, 209
Hopeful Stakes, 19, 23, 36, 81, 121
   -22, 221, 262, 269
Hudson Stakes, 20, 23
Hyde Park Stakes, 120
International Gold Cup, 179
Irish Derby, 267, 289
Italian Derby (Italy), 267, 289 (*see*
   Derby *Italiano*)
Jersey Handicap, 174
Jim Dandy Stakes, 283, 286
Jockey Club Gold Cup, 27, 27 n. 17,
   66, 77, 81, 97, 108, 133, 200,
   234, 285, 286, 288
Jockey Club Experimental Free
   Handicap, 155 n. 5
Junior Champion Stakes, 61-62, 81
Keene Memorial Stakes, 17, 20
Kentucky Derby, **1-5**, 2, 3, 4, 7, 17,
   18, 19, 30, 33, 38, 49, 56, 57, 62,
   64, 67-69, 81, 83, 85, 97, 100, 117,
   125, 128 n. 8, 131, 139, 147, 149,
   155, *170*, *171*, 176, 204, 224, 226-
   27, 244, 247-49, *248*, *249*, 263,
   267, 275-77, 281, 288, 289, 290,
   297
Kentucky Derby Trial, 125, 168
Kentucky Jockey Club Stakes, 62
Kentucky Oaks, 17, 50, 258
La Sorpesa Handicap, 204
Latonia Championship, 74
Laurel Futurity, 222, 269-70
Lawrence Realization, 10, 27, 66,
   73, 91, 97, 103, 133-34
Malibu Stakes, 286
Manhattan Handicap, 140, 174
Man o'War Stakes, 233
Marathon Handicap, 45
Marlboro Cup, 232-33, 255, 284
Marguerite Stakes, 81
Mars Purse, 153
Maryland Handicap, 43, 46 n. 10
Massachusetts Handicap, 111
Merchants and Citizens'
   Handicap, 51, 72
Metropolitan Handicap, 12, 14, 18,
   253, 284
Miami Springs Purse, 124
Miller Stakes, 26
Morello Purse, 153-54
Myrtlewood Purse, 122
Narragansett Futurity, 99
Narragansett Special, 133, 139
Nassau County Handicap, 284
National Stallion Stakes, 99
Nedayr Purse120

Oaklawn Handicap, 284
Oak Park Purse, 120
Omaha Gold Cup, 93
Paterson Handicap, 253, 255
Perry Point Purse, 189
Philadelphia Handicap, 45
Phoenix Handicap, 135
Pimlico Autumn Handicap, 44
Pimlico Fall Serial Weight-for-Age
   Race No. 2, 44
Pimlico Fall Serial Weight-for-Age
   Race No. 3, 44
Pimlico Futurity, 99, 122, 155
Pimlico Special, 104, 108, 109, 141,
   175 n. 7, 181, 178, 201
Preakness Stakes, 7, **6-10,** 16, 17,
   19, 33, 49, 56, 57, 67, 97, 101-
   02, 102 n. 14, 129, 155, 157, 170,
   *172,*178, 197 n. 7, 227, 227 n. 2,
   250, 262, 263, 278, *279,* 280, 281
   288, 290, 297
Princess of Wales Stakes, 91
Queens County Handicap, 106
Queen's Plate, 90
Raton Futurity, 264
Remsen Stakes, 270
Rennert Handicap, 46
Rhode Island Handicap, 110
Richard Johnson Handicap, 99
Riggs Handicap, 142
Roamer Handicap, 174
Rothman's International
   Championship, 234
San Antonio Handicap, 205
San Felipe Handicap, 273, 274, 275
San Fernando Stakes, 286
Sanford Stakes, 21, 23, 81, 220-21,
   266, 267, 268, 269
San Juan Capistrano Handicap, 89,
   207
Santa Anita Derby, 273, 274-75
Santa Anita Handicap, 134, 205-06,
   287
Santa Margarita Handicap, 89
Sapling Stakes, 266, 269
Saranac Handicap, 132, 133
Saratoga Cup, 66, 72, 107
Saratoga Handicap, 46, 46 n. 10, 107
Saratoga Special, 81, 120
Saratoga Stakes, 77
Seminole Purse, 192
Sesquicentennial Handicap, 135
Silver Springs Purse, 124, 125
South Shore Purse, 82, 87
Special Event Purse, 131-32
Stars and Stripes Handicap, 199

St. James Purse, 155
St. Leger Stakes (G.B), 2, 13, 17
Strub Stakes (see Charles H. Strub
   Stakes), 286
Stuyvesant Handicap, 25, 256
Suburban Handicap, 14, 17, 19,
   110, 111, 136, 284
"Summertime Derby", 71, 143
   (*see also* Travers Stakes)
Surprise Purse, 207
Swaps Stakes, 246, 251
Sysonby Mile, 200
Tanforan Handicap, 202
Thunderclap Purse, 154
Travers Stakes, 17, 27, 71-72, 73,
   92, 103, 112, 133, 143, 232, 283,
   284, 286, 287
Tremont Stakes, 20, 35, 60, 265, 269
Trenton Handicap, 139
Turf Classic, 288
2,000 Guineas Race (G.B.), 13
Uncle Tom's Cabin Purse, 209
United States Hotel Stakes, 21, 61,
   80, 120
Veterans Hospital Day Purse, 209
Victor Wild Stakes (G.B.), 90
Wakefield Stakes, 153
Walden Stakes, 122, 155
Washington Handicap, 104, 141
Washington Park Futurity, 153, 190
Westchester Handicap, 182
Westwood Purse, 183
Whitney Stakes, 107, 283
Widener Handicap, 105, 111, 180-
   81
Wilson Stakes, 111
Withers Stakes, 10, 17, 20, 24, 40,
   41, 49, 86, 102, 155, 158, 172
Wood Memorial Stakes, 10, 62, 66,
   75, 82, 97, 155, 156, 168, 172,
   223, 224, 246, 263, 272
Woodward Stakes, 233, 255, 288
Youthful Stakes, 20, 23, 263, 265,
   269
Race King, 11
racetracks
   Agua Caliente Track (Mexico), 126
   AK-Sar-Ben Racetrack, 92, 93
   Aqueduct, 12, 14, 20, 181, 218,
      224, 235, 253, 256, 270, 284, 288
   Alamo Downs, 176 n. 9
   Arlington Downs, 176 n. 9
   Arlington Park, 70, 88, 119, 120,
      132, 138, 190, 199, 208, 231, 283
   Bay Meadows, 209
   Belmont Park, 3, 12, 14, 19, 23,

103, 111, 154, 159, 167, 179, 197, 210, 218, 224, 244, 269, 274, 284, 285, 288, 295, 297

Calder Track, 193 n. 4, 243

Churchill Downs, **1-5**, 36, 40, 66, 72, 84, 101, 125, 126, 135, 156, 169, 172, 195, 210, 224, 246, 258, 262, 266, 267, 274, 275-77, 295

Delaware Park, 220

Delormier Park (Montreal), 217

Empire City Track (Yonkers), 61, 137, 153, 167

Epson Track (Houston), 176 n. 9

Fort Erie Track(Canada), 46

Garden State Park, 139, 222

Golden Gate Fields, 205, 207

Gravesend Park, 3, 96

Greenwood Raceway (Toronto), 219

Gulfstream Park, 124, 193 n. 4, 207, 245, 272

Havre de Grace, 98, 99, 189, 194

Hialeah Track, 105, 110, 123, 124, 180, 191, 192, 203

Hollywood Park, 183, 209, 210, 251, 265, 274

Jamaica Race Track, 20, 25, 26, 66, 87, 154, 155, 177

Jerome Park, 2, 12

Keeneland Race Track, 122, 124, 135, 224, 262, 272

Kempton Park (G.B.), 94, 95

Kenilworth Park (Ontario), 31, 52

Latonia Race Park, 16, 17, 74, 125, 266

Laurel Track, 43, 99, 104, 141, 220, 222, 269

Lexington, 2

Lincoln Fields, 119

Meadowlands, 254

Monmouth Park, 2, 210, 264

Morris Park, 8, 12, 14

Narragansett Park, 110, 133, 217

Nashville, 2

New Orleans, 2

New Orleans Fair Grounds, 142, 266

Oaklawn Park, 284

Pimlico Racetrack, 3, 8, 99, 122, 133, 136, 210, 220, 250, 295

River Downs, 267

Rockingham Park, 266

Santa Anita Park, 29, 134, 202, 283

Saratoga, 2, 3, 20, 23, 25, 26, 51, 103, 111, 220, 232, 267, 276, 283

Scarborough Downs, 266

Sheepshead Bay, 3, 56, 57

Suffolk Downs, 106, 138

Tanforan, 82, 202

Tropical Park, 123, 124

Turfway Park, 289

Washington Park, 133, 153, 179, 199

Woodbine Racetrack (Toronto), 219, 234

Woodlawn, 1

Racing Associations
    Woodlawn Racing Ass'n, 10
    Westchester Racing Ass'n, 15

Radar Ahead, 274

radio, 4, 89

Raise a Native, 265

Rancocas Stable, 64

Ransom, Sam, 152

Raymond Earl, 276

Real Quiet, 295

Reconstruction, the, 2

Red Pipe, 267

Reeves, Richard Stone, 270

*Regret**, 4, 4 n. 2

Rehabilitate, 220

*Reigh Count**, 89, 89 n. 6, 147, 150, 155, 159, 159 n. 10

Remsen Stakes, 270

Renick, Sam, 65

Rennert Handicap, 46

Retrieve, 17

Revolutionary War, 6

Reynolds, Quentin, 97, 98

Rhode Island Handicap, 110

Rhymer, 140

Rice, Grantland, 4, 98 n. 11, 123, 147, 179

Richard Johnson Handicap, 99

Rico Monte, 166, 174, 177, 178

Riddle, Samuel D., **15-32**, 45, 74, 95, 101 n. 13, 103, 105, 107-09, 108 n. 17, 111, 124, 133, 198

Riggs Handicap, 142

Rippey, 169

Risen Star, 212, 237 n. 6

Ritzenberger, Milton, 252

*Riva Ridge**, v, 210, 218, 220, 223, 232, 233, 234, 235 n. 4

River Downs, 267

Riverland, 142

Roach, James, 176, 177, 201

Roamer Handicap, 174

Robert Morris, 130

Robertson, Alfred*, 132, 133, 134, 143

Robertson, William H. P., 20

Rockingham Park, 266

Rock Sand, 16

Roman In, 207

Roman Soldier, 85
Roosevelt, Franklin Delano, 89
Rosemont, 86, 87
roses, 5 (*see* flowers)
Ross, J.K.L., 26, 34, 39, 42, 45,
    46 n. 10, 49, 59, 64, 215
        death of, 54
        Triple Crown Cup, 215
Ross, J.K.M., 33, 37, 38, 39, 51
Rothman's International Championship,
    234
Rough Sea, 269
Rowe, Jim, 25
Royal Canadian Navy, 39, 47, 49
Rudie, 106
*Ruffian**, 11
Run Dusty Run, 249, 250
Run for the Roses
        origin (*see* Corum, Bill), 5
        Burgoo King, 5
Running "W", 168
Runyon, Damon, 4, 62, 68-69
Ruth, Babe, 129
*Ruthless**, 11

S

Sabath, Albert, 139
Saggy, 194
Sailor, 37
Sailor Beware, 81
Salmagundi, 198
Saint Francis Hospital, 210
San Antonio Handicap, 205
Sande, Earl*, *vii*, 26, 29, 36, 37, 42, 44,
    46, 46 n. 10, 47, 50, 51, 55, **62-65**, 65
    66, 69, 75-76, 80, 97, 148, 207, 220,
    266
        birth of, 63
        as breeder, 75
        death of, 76
        death of wife, 68
        early years, 63-63
        early career, 63
        financial problems, 75
        injuries, 68
        personality, 69
        photograph, *69*
        as trainer, 68
San Felipe Handicap, 273, 275
San Fernando Stakes, 286
Sanford, Milton H., 7
Sanford Stakes, 21, 22, 23, 55, 220-21, 266
Sangster, Robert, 286
Sanhedrin, 250
San Juan Capistrano Handicap, 89, 207

San San, 243
Santa Anita Derby, 273-74, 275
Santa Anita Park, 29, 202, 209, 273, 283,
    286
Santa Margarita Handicap, 89
Saranac Handicap, 132, 133
Saratoga, 2, 7, 26, 36, 40, 51, 61, 71,
    80, 99, 103, 125, 147, 167, 218, 220,
    232, 244, 266, 268, 283, 295
Saratoga Cup, 66, 77, 107
Saratoga Handicap, 46, 46 n. 10, 107
"Saratoga mud", 71
Saratoga Sales, 188
Saratoga Special, 81, 120
Saratoga Springs, *vii*, 267
Saunders, Willie "Smokey", *vii*, 79, 80,
    82, *84*, 85, *86*, 87, 88-89, 197-98, 204
        accessory to murder, 88-89, 89 n. 5
        birth of, 82
        career summary, 89
        death of, 89
        early career, 82
        nickname "Smokey", 82
        retirement, 89
Scarborough Downs, 266
Scardino, Anne, 246
Sceneshifter, 103
Schaeffer, Walter, 89, 89 n. 5
Schuette, Herman, 70
Schuttinger, Andy, 27, 46
Schwartz, M.L., 163, 166
*Seabiscuit**, 95, 105, 105 n. 16, 106,
    108, 108 n. 17, *110*, 112, 135, 137,
    138, 141, 159 n. 11, 204, 256 n.4, 297
Seabiscuit: An American Legend (book),
    105 n.16, 108 n. 17
Seagram's, 206
Sea Mint, 27
*Seattle Slew**, *v*, *vii*, 10, 11, 15, 30,
    49 n. 12, 51, 55, 66, 104, 111, **239-
    259**, *248*, *249*, 256 n. 5, *259*, 262, 263,
    267, 269, 280, 283, 284, 285, 291,
    295, 298
        birth of, 239
        bloodlines, 239, 239 n. 1
        burial place, 258
        career summary, 250
        death of, 258
        illnesses, 252
        injuries, 244, 253, 258
        naming of, 240
        nicknames, 240
        personality, 242, 244, 247, 268-258,
        270
        photographs, *248*, *249*, *259*
        progeny, 257-58

races
    in allowance race (Aqueduct,
      1978), 253
    in allowance race (Saratoga,
      1978), 253
    in allowance race (Belmont),
      244
    in maiden race (Belmont),
      244
    in Champagne Stakes, 244
    in Flamingo Stakes, 245
    in Hialeah allowance race, 245-
      46
    in Jockey Club Gold Cup, 255
    in Kentucky Derby, 247-49,
      248, 249
    in Marlboro Cup, 254-57, 285
    re: Metropolitan Handicap, 253
    in Patterson Handicap, 254
    in Preakness Stakes, 250, 283
    in Stuyvesant Handicap, 256
    in Swaps Stakes, 246, 251
    in Wood Memorial Stakes, 246
    in Woodward Stakes, 255
racing record
    as two-year-old, 244-45
    as three-year-old, 245-53
    as four-year-old, 253
retirement, 49 n. 12, 256, *259*
siring record, 257-58
temperament, 239, 240-251, 242,
    246-47, 258
washing out, 247
winnings, 244, 255, 256
Seattle Slew (book), 243, 245
Secretariat*, *v*, 6, 10, 15, 31, 31 n 22,
    35, 49 n. 12, 55, 66, 57 98, 104,
    113 n. 19, 115, 127, 129, 147, 166,
    187, 193, 210, **215-238**, 227 n. 2, *229*,
    231 n. 3, 235 n. 4, 238, 239 n. 1, 242,
    246, 256 n. 5, 280, 283, 288, 295, 298
    abscess, 225
    appetite, 226
    birth of, 215, 217
    bloodlines, 57, 216-17, 239 n. 1
    breeding rights, syndication of, 223
    burial, 238
    career summary, 235
    death of, 238
    debut at Saratoga, 229
    first race, 218
    heart, size of, 224
    illnesses, 225, 232
      abscess, 225
      laminitis, 238
      virus, 232
    naming of, 217

necropsy, 224
personality, 218, 223-24, 229, 239-
    40
photographs, *229*
postage stamp honoring, 237
progeny, 238
races
    in Arlington Invitational, 231-
      32
    in Bay Shore Stakes, 224
    in Belmont Futurity, 221
    in Belmont Stakes, 129, 229-
      31, 231 n. 3
    in Canadian International
      Championship, 234-35
    in Champagne Stakes, 221, 222
    in debut race (Saratoga, July
      31, 1972), 220
    in Garden State Stakes, 222
    in Hopeful Stakes, 221
    in Kentucky Derby, 226-27
    in Laurel Futurity, 222
    in Man o'War Stakes, 233-34
    in Marlboro Cup, 232, 233
    in Preakness Stakes, 227,
      227 n. 2, 283
    in Sanford Stakes, 220-21
    in Whitney Stakes, 232
    in Woodward Stakes, 233-34
racing record
    as two-year-old, 220-23
    as three-year-old, 225-35
retirement, 49 n. 12, 235-38,
    235 n. 4
silks, 237
siring record, 237-38, 237 n. 6
temperament, 223-24, 229
timing controversy, 1973 Preakness
    Stakes, 227 n. 2
Seminole Purse, 192
Sensitive Prince, 270, 275, 283
Sesquicentennial Handicap, 135
Shake Shake Shake, 283
Sham, 225, 227, 230
Sheepshead Bay, 3, 56, 57
Shelhammer, Alfred, 134
Shilling, Carroll "Cal"*, 37, 37 n. 6, 50
Shoemaker, Bill*, 63, 125-26, 149, 161,
    207, 220, 244, 255, 266, 283 n. 5, *287*,
    288
Shoop, Robert L., 259, 280 n. 4, 299,
    299
Shut Out, 194, 262-63
"Sidewalks of New York, The", 280
silks, 10
Silver Charm, 289-90, 295
Silverling, 192

Silverman, Barton, 240, 243, 245
Silver Spoon*, 212
Silver Springs Purse, 124, 125
Sir Barton*, *v*, 5, 10, 13, 14, 16, 24, 26,
  31, **33-53**, *39, 42, 53*, 64, 65, 81, 83,
  96, 111, 193, 212, 290, 295, 297
  birth of, 34
  blood poisoning, 36
  colic, 57
  career summary, 44
  death of, 52
  final resting place, 52, *53*
  "The Great Hophead", 34
  hooves, sore, 34
  nickname, 39
  personality, 34, 34 n. 2, 34 n. 35
  photograph, *43, 46, 53*
  progeny, 50
  races
    in Allowance Race, 43
    in Belair Handicap, 45
    in Belmont Futurity, 40
    in Belmont Stakes, 10, 40-41
    in Climax Handicap, 45
    in Dominion Handicap, 46
    in Dwyer Stakes, 42, 43
    in Havre de Grace Handicap,
      43
    in Hip Hip Hooray Purse, 48
    in Hopeful Stakes, 36
    in Kentucky Derby, 38-39, *39*
    in Man o'War match race, 52
    in Marathon Handicap, 45
    in Maryland Handicap, 43
    in match race with Man o'War,
      28, 47, 47 n. 11
    in Merchants and Citizens'
      Handicap, 47
    in Philadelphia Handicap, 45
    in Pimlico Autumn Handicap,
      44
    in Pimlico Fall Serial Weight-
      for-Age Race No. 2, 44
    in Pimlico Fall Serial Weight-
      for-Age Race No. 3, 44
    in Potomac Handicap, 43
    in Preakness Stakes, 39
    in Rennert Handicap, 46
    in Saratoga Handicap, 46,
      46 n. 10
    in Tremont Stakes, 35
    in Withers Stakes, 40, 45
    in Wood Memorial Stakes, 40
  racing record
    as two-year-old, 35-38, 39 n. 4
    as three-year-old, 38-39, 44
    as four-year-old, 45
  retirement, 49, 49 n. 12, 50
  soft hooves, 43
  siring record, 50
  statue, 52, *53*
  winnings, 44
Sir Beverly, 87
Sir Gallahad III, 34, 34 n. 1, 55, 56, 263
Sirlad, 288
Sir Lamorak, 80
Sir Michael, 217
Sir Oracle, 105
Sir Sir, 250
Slew o'Gold*, 258, 258 n. 7
Slide Rule, 156, 157
Sliwinski, Evelyn, 88
Smith, Gene, 63, 75
Smith, George, 19
Smith, Red, 4, 34, 123, 129, 274
Smith, Tom*, 108
Snark, 106
Snider, Al, 189, 191, 192, 194, 210
Snider, Duke, 166
Snowflake, 67
Somethingroyal, *v*, 216, 220
Sonny Joe, 99
South Dakota, 92
South Shore Purse, 82, 87
South Shore Racetrack, 87
Sparrow, C. Edward, 23, 40
S.P.C.A., 180
Spectacular Bid*, 288, 289, 291
Spendthrift Farm, 55, 257, 288, 289
Spinach, 72
splint, 124
Sports Illustrated (magazine), 31, 144,
  207, 228, 254, 256 n. 5, 267, 291
Sports Illustrated Top Ten List, 256 n. 5
Spy Song, 169, 171, 200
Star De Naskra, 270
Star Pilot, 180
Stars and Stripes Handicap, 199
Star Shoot, 34, 41, 53
Steinkraus, William, 286
Stepfather, 208
Step Nicely, 222
Stevens, Gary*, 289-90
St. James Purse, 155
St. Leger Stakes (G.B.), 2, 13, 17
Stoner Creek Farm, 147, 152, 159, 160
Stoneridge, M.A., 14
Stop the Music, 222
Stout, Jimmy*, 167
"Streetcar Derby", 156, (*see* Kentucky
  Derby)
Strike the Gold, 290

Strub Stakes, 286
Stubbs, 105
Stuyvesant Handicap, 256
*Stymie**, 166, 174, 175 n. 7, 176, 177-179, 179, 199, 209, 281
Suburban Handicap, 14, 18, 19, 110, 111, 136, 284
Suffolk Downs, 106, 138
"Summertime Derby", *see* Travers Stakes
*Sun Beau**, 135
Sun Falcon, 72
"Sunny Jim" (*see* Fitzsimmons, James E.)
Sunny Jim: The Life of Ameica's Most Beloved Horseman (book), 93 n. 10
Surprise Purse, 207
Survivor, 7, 7 n. 5, 9, 158
Sutcliffe, L. S., photographs from collection of, *35, 39, 42, 48, 59, 65, 69, 78, 84, 86, 96, 97, 110, 116, 123, 128, 129, 134, 229, 248, 249*
Swale, 55, 238, 257-58
*Swaps**, 161, 210, 262
Swaps Stakes, 246, 251
Sweat, Eddie, 225-26, 235
Sweep On, 41
Sweet Tooth, 265
Swiftest Halfwit, The (book), 129
Swinfield, 67, 69
Swing and Sway, 136, 138
Sysonby, 11, 14, 256 n. 5
Sysonby Mile, 200, 201

T

Tabasco Cat, 295
Taber, Alberta (Canada), 148
Taj Akbar, 91
Taj Mahal, 15
Tanforan, 82, 202
Tanforan Handicap, 202
Tank's Prospect, 227 n. 2
Tarn, Hazel, 150
Taylor, Mickey & Karen, 239, 258
Teddy, 56
Tetrarchal, 71
Texas-bred horses, 176
Texas Horse Racing Hall of Fame, 184 n. 15
Text, 251
The Porter, 43, 44, 46
The Rhymer, 140-41
Think Snow, 274
Thomas, W.H., 2
Thompson, Toots, 34
"*Thoroughbred Heroes" (videotape)*, 210
Thoroughbred Racing Association, 49,

215
Thorson, 83
Three Chimneys Farm, 257, 258, 259
Thunderclap Purse, 154
Thunder Gulch, 295
Tibullo, 291
Tiffany Company, 9, 13
Tiffany Lass, 290
Tilt Up, 268-69
Time (magazine), 228
*Tim Tam**, 210
Tinajero, 263
Tip-Toe, 158
Titanic, RMS (vessel), 148 n. 3
Today, 83
Tola Rose, 138
Tom Rolfe, 220
Top Radio, 99
Touch Gold, 10
tracks, racing. *See* racetracks
Track Reward, 278
Travers Stakes, 27, 71-72, 73, 103, 112, 133, 232, 283, 284
Tremont Stakes, 20, 35, 60
Trenton Handicap, 139
Triple Crown, 7, 281, 283, 295
    first use, 9, 17
    Maryland's Triple Crown (1796), 8 n. 6
    origin, **13-14**
    prevented in 1832, 71
    same-day running (1870), 11 n. 8
    summary, 210
trophies
    Annapolis Subscription Plate, 6
    Belmont Silver Tray, 15
    Cartier gold cup, 215
    Tiffany Bowl, 11, 15
    Woodlawn Vase, 9
Tropical Park, 123, 124
Trusted Partner, 291
Turbine, 175-76
Turcotte, Camille, 219
Turcotte, Ron**, *v*, *vii*, 94, 148, 193, 215, 218-20, 221-22, 225, 228, *229*, 231 n. 3, 235, **236**, 237, 244, 266, 295
    early days, 219
    Forward by, i
    Hall of Fame, 236
    jockey record (Canada), 220
    jockey record (U.S.), 220-47
    paralyzed, 236
    personality, 236
    photograph, *229*
    suspension, 234
Turcotte, Rudy, 223
Turf Classic, 288

Turfway Park, 289
Turkoman, 290
Turner, Billy, *vii*, 240, 241, 244, 256, 257
    career summary, 257
    early years, 242
    fired by Hills, 252-53
    personality, 257
    steeplechase jockey, 242
    trainer, 240, 242-46, 257, 268
Turner, Gordon, 52
Turner, Paula, 240, 242, 257
Twain, Mark, 185
Tweedy, Penny, 216, 217, 223, 225, 226, 228, 229, 231, 233, 235, 237
*Twenty Grand**, 81, 97
2,000 Guineas Race (U.K.), 13
Twice A Prince, 231-32
*Twilight Tear**, 264
Two Lea, 205-06

U

Uncle Tom's Cabin Purse, 209
United States Hotel Stakes, 21, 61, 80, 120
United States Post Office, 237
University of Chicago, 56
Upset, 19, 22, 24, 25, 29
U.S. Army, 134
U.S. Army Quartermaster Corps, 51
U.S. Army Remount Service, 51
U.S. Cavalry, 51
U.S. Coast Guard, 188

V

Vanderbilt, Alfred Gwynne, 109, 217
Vedder, R.L., 124, 134
V Crown, 44
Veitch, John, 265
Veitch, Sylvester*, 265
Velasquez, Jorge*, 242, 244, 250, 269, 274, 276, 278, *279*, 280, 281, *282*, 284, 289-90
Venezia, Mike, 224
Veterans Hospital Day Purse, 209
Vicaress, 83
Victory Gallop, 13
Victor Wild Stakes (G.B.), 90
Vietnam, 165
Victory Gallop, 10
Vincentive, 156, 157
Vito, 29
Volcanic, 200
Vulcan's Forge, 197, 198

W

Wakefield Stakes, 153
Walden Stakes, 123, 155
Walden, Wyndham, 166
Waldrup, Alex, 236
*War Admiral**, *v*, 6, 10, 11, 15, 22 n. 14, 23, 30, 31, 49 n. 12, 55, 65, 81, **95-114**, *96, 97*, 103 n. 15, 132, 149, 159, 161, 172, 193, 198, 239 n. 1, 244, 263, 280, 281, 291, 295, 297
    birth of, 95
    bloodlines, 99
    career summary, 95, 112
    death of, 113-14, 113 n. 19
    declared dead, 113 n. 19
    final resting place, 119, 132
    illnesses, 99, 100-101, 111
    injuries, 103
    loss to *Seabiscuit*, 117
    nickname, 95
    personality, 98, 98 n. 11, 98 n. 12, 103 n. 15
    photographs, *96, 97, 110*
    progeny, 111, 204, 239 n. 1
    races
        in maiden race, 98
        in Belmont Stakes, 10
        in Brightwaters Purse, 99
        in Calvert Purse, 100
        in Chesapeake Stakes, 104
        in Church Hill Purse, 104
        in Eastern Shore Stakes, 103
        in Fort Pierce Purse, 111
        in Great American Stakes, 99
        in Heather Purse, 105
        in Jockey Club Gold Cup, 112
        in Kentucky Derby, 101, 149
        in Massachusetts Handicap, 106
        in Seabiscuit match race, 106, 108, 108 n. 17, 109, *110*
        in National Stallion Stakes, 99
        in Pimlico Special, 104, 109, *110*
        in Preakness Stakes, 101-02
        in Queens County Handicap, 106
        in Rhode Island Handicap, 110
        in Richard Johnson Handicap, 99-100
        in Saratoga Cup, 107
        in Saratoga Handicap, 107
        in Washington Handicap, 104
        in Whitney Stakes, 107
        in Widener Handicap, 105, 115
        in Wilson Stakes, 107
    racing record

as two-year-old, 98-100
as three-year-old, 100-105, 111
as four-year old, 105-111
retirement, 49 n. 12, 143
siring record, 111
size, 110
temperament, 102 n. 13, 103 n. 15, 107
winnings, 100, 104, 105, 107, 108, 112
War Admiral Purse, 143
War Cloud, 17
War Emblem, 295
War Knight, 153
War Minstrel, 106
War Relic, 31, 132, 133
wars
Civil War, 1, 8, 9, 215
French and Indian War, 6
Revolutionary War, 6
Vietnam War, 215
War of Algerian Independence, 243
World War One, 17, 35
World War Two, 76, 93, 134, 138, 147, 151, 153, 167, 188, 262
wartime ban, Florida racing, 155
Washington, George, 6
Washington Handicap, 104, 141
Washington Park, 133, 143, 153, 179, 199
Washington Park Futurity, 153
Watergate scandal, 215, 237
Waterloo, Battle of, 172
weathervane (Pimlico), 10
web barrier, 19, 22
Webster, Reginald, 217-18
Wellesley, Arthur, 172
Wellington, Dule of, 172
Westchester Handicap, 182
Westchester Racing Association, 11
Westrope, John*, 99, 140-41, 190
Westwood Purse, 183
Wheatley Stable, 82, 113, 149
Whichone, 61, 69, 71, 72, 73
Whirlaway*, 6, 10, 13, 17, 49 n. 12, 55, 65, 80, 104, **115-146**, *116*, *119*, *128*, *129*, *145*, 147, 161, 168, 169 n. 4, 172, 181, 193, 198, 209, 239 n. 1, 262, 263, 264, 272, 276, 288, 289, 290, 295, 297
blinkers, 127
bloodlines, 120
burial place, 143
career summary, 143
death of, 125, 144
injuries, 121, 124, 132, 138, 142
multiple jockeys, 132, 143
nickname, 118

personality, 118, 119 n. 5, 123
photographs, *116*, *119*, *128*, *129*, *145*
progeny, 144
races
in A.J. Joyner Handicap, 124, 125
in *Alsab* challenge race, 139
in American Derby, 133
in Arcadia Purse, 124
in Arlington Classic, 132, 135
in Arlington Futurity, 120
in Arlington Handicap, 138
in Arlington Special Event Purse, 131
in Belmont Futurity, 122
in Belmont Futurity Trial, 122
in Belmont Stakes, 10, 130-31
in Blue Grass Stakes, 124
in Breeders' Futurity, 127
in Brooklyn Handicap, 136-37
in Butler Handicap, 137-38
in Carter Handicap, 136
in Celt Purse, 136
in Chicago Heights Purse, 120
in Clark Handicap, 135
in Coconut Grove Purse, 123
in Dixie Handicap, 135
in Dwyer Stakes, 131
in Equipoise Mile, 143
re: Flamingo Stakes, 124
in Governor Bowie Handicap, 142
in Grand Union Hotel Stakes, 121
in Henry of Navarre Stakes, 130, 198
in Hopeful Stakes, 121
in Hyde Park Stakes, 120
in Jockey Club Gold Cup, 134, 140-41
in Kentucky Derby, 127-30, *128*, *129*
in Kentucky Derby Trial, 125
in Lawrence Realization, 134
in Louisiana Handicap, 142
in first race, 119
in Manhattan Handicap, 140
in Massachusetts Handicap, 138
in Miami Springs Purse, 124
in Myrtlewood Purse, 122
in Narragansett Special, 133, 139
in Nedayr Purse, 120
in New York Handicap, 141
in Oak Park Purse, 120
in Phoenix Handicap, 135

in Pimlico Futurity, 122
in Pimlico Special, 141
in Preakness Stakes, 129-32
in Riggs Handicap, 142
in Santa Anita Handicap, 134
in Saranac Handicap, 132
in Saratoga Special, 120-121
in Sesquicentennial Handicap, 135
in Silver Springs Purse, 124
in Special Event Purse, 131
in Suburban Handicap, 136
in Travers Stakes, 133, 143
in Trenton Handicap, 139
in United States Hotel Stakes, 120
in Walden Stakes, 123
in War Admiral Purse, 143
in Washington Handicap, 141
racing record
as two-year-old, 119-23
as three-year-old, 123, 124-34
as four-year-old, 139-42
retirement, 49 n. 12
siring record, 143
tail, 122
temperament, 118, 119 n. 5, 123
winnings, 123, 131, 134, 135, 136, 137, 138, 139, 141-42
Whispering Wind, 219
white carnations, 11, 199, 231
Whitehill, L.T., 82
White Horse Acres, 239
White Rammer, 245
Whitney, Harry Payne, 19, 25, 27
Whitney Stakes, 107, 232, 283
Whopper, 84
Widener Handicap, 105, 111, 180-81
Widener, George, 179
Widener, Joseph, 62
Wildair, 25, 28, 45, 46
Wild Ride (book), 290n 8
Williams, Bert, 82 n. 2
Williams, Ted, 131, 145, 161, 262
Willow Springs Purse, 153
Wilshire Stable, 71
Wilson Stakes, 107
Wilson, Woodrow, 47 n. 11
Windfield Farms Stable, 219
Windfields, 178
Winn, Matt, 1, 2, 3, 4, 5, 47, 68, 156
Withers Stakes, 11, 20, 24, 40, 41, 45, 49, 69, 86, 102, 155, 158, 172
Wittingham, Charles*, 233
Won't Tell You, 262
Woodbine Racetrack (new), 219, 234

Woodbine Racetrack (old), 219
Wood Memorial Stakes, 44, 62, 66, 81, 82, 83, 87, 97, 149, 155, 156, 168, 223, 224-25, 226, 246, 272
Woodlawn Racing Association, 9
Woodlawn track, 1
Woodlawn Vase, 9
Woodward Stakes, 233, 255, 288
Woodward, William, 14, 55, 56, 58, 61, 64, 68, 73-74, 80, 85, 87, 91, 92, 101 n. 13, 149
Woodward, Mrs. William, 91
Woolf, George*, 102, 109, 123, 136, 138, 140, 143, 153, 155, 156-57
Woolford Farms, 117, 126
Wolfson, Louis & Patrice, 262-63, 288
Workman, Raymond "Sonny"*, 69, 70, 71, 73, 77
World Series, 5
World War Two, 81, 93, 135, 167, 188, 262
Worth, 4, 37 n. 1
wreaths, 5
Wright brothers, 11
Wright, Warren, 82 n. 2, 83, 119, 123, 124, 138, 140, 179, 188, 189, 197 n. 7, 203, 205, 206, 209, 264
death of, 209, 274
Wright, Lucille, 87, 209, 264
Wright, Mrs. Warren (Lucille), 82 n. 2, 209, 210, 264
Wright, Wayne, 87, 88, 88 n. 4, 106, 107, 112, 119, 157, 158
Wright, William, 115
"W", Running, 168

X
Xenofol, 70

Y
Yankee Chance, 130
Yarn, 72, 73
Yellow Cab, 143, 157
Yellow Hand, 25
Youthful Stakes, 20, 263, 265

Z
*Zev**, 64, 72, 77
Zoman, 291